ALSO BY FRED ALAN WOLF

The Eagle's Quest
Parallel Universes
The Body Quantum
Star* Wave
Taking the Quantum Leap
Space-Time and Beyond: The New Edition
(with Bob Toben)

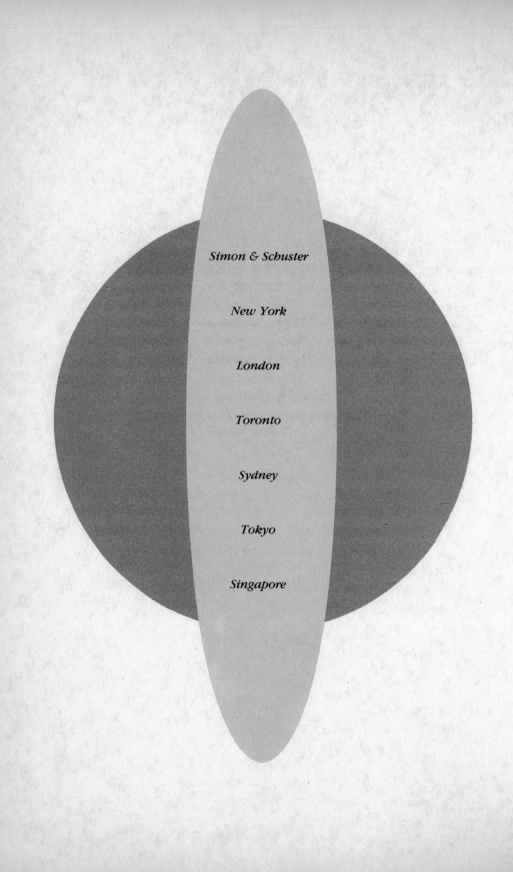

Simon & Schuster

New York

London

Toronto

Sydney

Tokyo

Singapore

THE

Dreaming

UNIVERSE

A MIND-EXPANDING JOURNEY INTO THE REALM WHERE PSYCHE AND PHYSICS MEET

Fred Alan Wolf, Ph.D.

A TOUCHSTONE BOOK
Published by Simon & Schuster
New York   London   Toronto   Sydney   Tokyo   Singapore

TOUCHSTONE
Rockefeller Center
1230 Avenue of the Americas
New York, NY 10020

Copyright © 1994 by Wolf Productions

First Touchstone Edition 1995
TOUCHSTONE and colophon are registered trademarks of Simon & Schuster Inc.

Designed by Liney Li
Manufactured in the United States of America

1   2   3   4   5   6   7   8   9   10

Library of Congress Cataloging-in-Publication Data

Wolf, Fred Alan.
The dreaming universe: a mind-expanding journey into the realm
where psyche and physics meet/Fred Alan Wolf.
p.   cm.
Includes bibliographical references and index.
1. Dreams.   I. Title.
BF1078.W55   1994
93-46912
CIP
ISBN 0-671-74946-3
ISBN 0-684-80159-0 (Pbk)
154.6'3—dc20

ACKNOWLEDGMENTS

———

As usual, this book involved quite a bit of traveling and meeting new and old friends, who were very helpful. In the United States, I would like to thank Dr. Michael Grosso, Prof. J. Allan Hobson, Dr. Stanley Krippner, Dr. Benjamin Libet, Dr. Kenneth Ring, Dr. Peter M. Rojcewicz, Catherine Shainberg, Saul-Paul Sirag, and Dr. Montague Ullman for their participation in allowing me to quote them from our conversations and share their novel ideas with you in the body of the book. I would also like to thank Ms. Kitty Farmer for continued support of my work and Dr. Jayne Gackenbach for helpful suggestions.

I would also like to thank Wim Coleman and Pat Perrin for permission to quote from their delightful book, *The Jamais Vu Papers,* and Dr. Jeffrey Mishlove for helpful discussions about ancient dream healing techniques.

In Australia, I would like to thank the Institute for Aboriginal Studies in Canberra for making my research into "dreamtime" as pleasant as it was. I would also like to thank Sherrill and James Sellman for hospitality and arranging my lectures in Melbourne, Billy Marshall-Stoneking of Balmain for his helpful insights into the Pintupi peoples of Central Australia, Lorraine Maffi Williams of Byron Bay for providing me with a special insight into Australian Aboriginal culture, Vicki Henricks, Graeme Wilson, and Wayne Armitage from the 7 Mile Beach Rd. house, particularly Graeme for his insights into "dreaming," Nigel

Roberts for his poetry and his hospitality, Neal Murray for an interesting drive "outback," and Jane Murray from Canberra for her hospitality.

In St. Petersburg and Moscow I would like to thank Professor Sergei Cherkosov for arranging my lectures at the University of St. Petersburg, Jana Janu for arranging my lectures in Moscow, Tanya Belyavskaya and Sasha Poroshin for their friendship, and Aleksey Kovalev for his insights into Russian art and architecture while I lived in St. Petersburg.

I would also like to thank Sarah Pinckney and Bob Asahina for editing the manuscript.

CONTENTS

———

217

CHAPTER 14. GETTING TO THE BIG DREAM

233

CHAPTER 15. THE PHYSICS OF THE IMAGINAL REALM

242

CHAPTER 16. TRANSPERSONAL DREAMING AND DEATH

261

CHAPTER 17. OVERLAPS OF THE IMAGINAL AND THE REAL: DREAMS IN ART, MYTH, AND REALITY

284

CHAPTER 18. THE SPIRIT OF MATTER

$\mathscr{I}$NTRODUCTION:
WE DREAM TO CREATE A SELF

———

Imagine, if you will, a realm in which there is no height, width, depth, or time. . . . Imagine an entity who lives in this realm—an entity called Llixgrijb. Imagine that poor Llixgrijb is trapped by some sort of extradimensional cave-in. . . . There's no escape. But Llixgrijb . . . cannot die. Its consciousness will continue, all alone and completely paralyzed for eternity—or whatever the equivalent of eternity is in such a realm. How would you deal with this situation? . . . You'd create worlds in your mind, worlds within yourself. . . . Llixgrijb created a universe.

—Wim Coleman and Pat Perrin
The Jamais Vu Papers [1]

For as long as Western cultures can remember, there has been a deep fascination with dreams. They have been taken to have the power of divination, or seeing into the future; they have also been used for reawakening memories of the past and even of past lives. Many cultures believe that during a dream the soul leaves the body and journeys to other worlds, possibly visiting another universe called the *imaginal realm.*[2]

Dreams seem to break free of space and time limitations. Indeed, the Bible reminds us of the prophetic dreams of Joseph. And, of course, there are dreams that are said to give creative powers to the dreamer. The dreams of the poet/philosopher William Blake demonstrate the prophetic and creative power of a dream.

According to Australian Aboriginal legends, the universe came into existence a long time ago, arising from an unknowable realm as the dream of a Great Spirit. This Spirit is still dreaming and will continue to dream until the end of time. For, as this legend has it, time and space also appeared in the dream, and all things, all material objects, all living creatures and plants are nothing but images of this dream that the Great Spirit infused with life and enabled all images to share in the dream. In brief, we are nothing but dreams capable of dreaming. We are the dreamer and the dream at the same time.

Are dreams more than they seem, perhaps pointing to a deeper meaning of life and a more profound insight into the nature of the universe? If so, what could that insight be? Perhaps the Aboriginal legend points to that deeper significance. Is life nothing but a dream? It certainly seems to be a lot more than that. What about the everyday world of matter and energy that we all experience around us? Is it also nothing but a dream?

It may seem like a long distance from these meandering questions and legend to the present time and our Western way of thinking and observing the universe we see around us and, in particular, to a study of consciousness and modern dream science. Yet, it is precisely this journey that I will attempt to make in this book as we begin to see that dreaming is vital to our survival as a species and a necessary "learning laboratory" wherein the self and the universe evolve. In brief, matter evolves through dreams.

Evolution and Dreams

This book will follow two tracks through time and evolution. We move backward through time as we begin to see how the brain develops and that dreams are a necessary aspect of evolution, leading to an individual's ability to develop self-awareness: a self-concept. This concept of self is, however, ever changing, ever growing. As we move backward through time we also move deeper and deeper into a theory of dreaming that is founded on neurobiology, physiology, and, at its deepest point, quantum physics.

The trip through evolution takes us to the fetus itself with a growing, developing brain capable of REM (Rapid Eye Movement suggesting that dreaming is taking place) sleep, which in turn leads to further brain development and the capacity to respond to stimuli.

From this point we move forward through time and see that dreaming becomes the laboratory of consciousness evolution. We see this in various forms: Australian dreamtime legends; telepathic dreams; lucid dreams; studies of the relationship of dreams to the body; "big dream" experiences, including transpersonal dreams; overlaps of dreaming into waking life as evidenced in art, architecture, and political systems; and the relationship of dreams to quantum physics.

What Is Dreaming?

Of course, there is the fundamental question "What do I mean by dreaming?" Do I refer to the action of visual presentations that occur during our nocturnal visits to the Land of Nod? Perhaps I am talking about lucid dreams—dreams in which the dreamer is aware in the dream that she or he is dreaming. Do I really mean that all matter dreams? Matter seems to be rather inert and lifeless. Perhaps this is a metaphor only. What about animals, do they dream? Do plants dream? How about rocks or the ocean? Do I mean that the whole planet dreams? Did the universe really "dream" itself into existence; indeed, is it still dreaming, or was it all just a big bang? Or am I referring to the world of our imaginations, our daydreams? Or perhaps I refer to the world of spirits and apparitions, UFO phenomena, and the like. The answer involves all of the above, as I hope to show in this book. In other words, dreaming is a necessary part of consciousness that enables the individual to develop a higher self-awareness.

To show how all of the above factors enter into this will require an understanding of just what we do know about dreams that occur during sleep and of what I mean by dreams occurring while we are awake. Dreams while awake? Isn't that a contradiction of terms? All these questions and considerations I hope to answer.

I wish to make a first caution to the reader at this stage. As a science writer, I am often in conflict. How much do I report as "straight" science, hopefully clearly written, and how much do I, as a philosopher and metaphysician, step beyond those well-trodden tracks into the land of speculation? Where is the dividing line between fact and fantasy?

I admit that I don't fully know. I can only speculate. Certainly some facts are evident. The neurophysiology of the dreaming brain has been studied extensively. We know a lot about our nerves. But we know little about our lack or surplus of "nerve." We understand that which we can grasp objectively but little about our own subjective experiences. In the sentence "I see," we know what must be true objectively about the verb but little about the subject, that precious "I" we all feel somehow inside of ourselves.

Thus our journey into the world of dreaming matter is at the same time a journey into the "I," eventually culminating in the explanation of my theory, which I call "the dreaming universe." To present this theory, we will need to look at a fairly wide range of phenomena, including:

The Early Science of Dreams

Dreams were studied scientifically by Sigmund Freud, Carl Jung, and others. To the world of science Freud brought terminology such as *ego* and *id,* and this led him to a structure of consciousness. Freud called the subject the *ego.* Are the ego and the Self the same thing? Is this ego inside our heads? Or is the ego or "the I" (originally Freud called the ego in German *das Ich,* translated as "the I") somewhere else? If elsewhere, how should we refer to it and where should we look for it?

Jung provided a new insight into the order of the mind that he called *synchronicity* in which events seemingly not connected by any mechanical or deterministic means played a significant role in the psyche. Because Jung's vision of synchronicity did not fit into a mechanical box, it was often dismissed as mysticism. As we will see later, in chapter 10, this "mysticism" is well-founded in quantum physics and plays a role in dreams and reality.

The Mechanics of Consciousness and Dreaming

The means by which images and memories are generated in the brain and the mechanics of consciousness, particularly the work of Benjamin Libet, strongly suggest that the brain functions projectively in space and time.

The study of the dreaming brain, including biological and physiological data and theories of Jonathan Winson, J. Allan Hobson, Sir

Francis Crick and Graeme Mitchison, Montague Ullman, and others, strongly suggests that the brain operates holographically as an image-maker, and mechanically as a neural network while awake and while dreaming. Later developments show that fetuses and infants dream to develop the self.

Mythological and Social Significance
of the Dream Realm

The mythological, sociological, and artistic import of dreams, including a closer look at the Australian Aboriginal theory of the universe and some elements of Jungian theory and quantum theory, show that dreams affect waking consciousness far more than we believed earlier.

The earliest theories and experiments concerning the brain, consciousness, and dreams prior to the REM revolutionary period, supported the idea that dreams were physiologically based. And yet many people, to this day, think that dreams are messages from the gods coming from another realm, perhaps a parallel universe.

Australian Aborigines claim to have "memory" of the realm of the "dreaming spirit" dating back nearly 150,000 years.[3] They see "reality" in two aspects: a primary universe far more extensive than the secondary physical world and the physical universe, which arose as the dream. They call this primary world "dreamtime," which in their view contains all of the past, present, and future. From this realm the world of mind, matter, and energy continually arises as a dream, not only long ago but even today, suggesting that the universe or God is dreaming all of what we experience into existence and that this dream overlaps into what we experience as reality.

What does modern science know about the realm of the dream? Certainly, it is a "space" and "time" that, in much the same way that Rod Serling put it in his television series, "The Twilight Zone," is the realm of the imagination. And yet *imagination* is not really the correct word to describe this "somewhere."

Is this realm real? Does it exist? Henri Corbin, the noted scholar of Islam and European author, coined the term *the imaginal realm* to describe it. In his view, this realm is ontologically real, and as the

Australian Aborigines and my research into the nature of shamanism[4] and dreams suggest, it may just be more real than the reality we perceive. It is, however, a reality that usually exists beyond our normal waking perception, although it does appear to us in the form of lucid dreams, prophetic dreams, and other related phenomena such as near-death experience (NDE) and possibly UFO abductions.[5]

Perhaps we are standing at a frontier in evolution—the discovery of the existence of the "Great Dreamer" and the Imaginal Realm of the Great Dream itself—that is being revealed to us individually and collectively as our own dreams.

We will look into the double aspects of this legend through our Western, scientifically trained eyes: the subjective aspect of the dream, the identity of the Self or "Big Dreamer," and the objective aspect of the dream, the realm from which the dream arises and appears as the universe.

To begin with, I will assume that dreams do come from somewhere. What that somewhere is and whether it can be found to exist in the brain and nervous system of sleeping subjects must be looked at carefully, and this we will do. Let me take it as an axiom for the moment that whatever this somewhere is, it is a "space" and a "time" that we, using our ordinary language, find great difficulty in expressing. Why? Because it is so strongly connected to the subject of the dream.

The Relationship of Dreams to Species Survival and Dream Telepathy

This will include the highly original work of several dreamworkers, including Montague Ullman, Stanley Krippner, Catherine Shainberg, and others, as well as a close look at the psychological data. Here we shall see that the apparent division of self and object, so important in grasping meaning in one's life, arises as a process. That process is really the focus of this book. The basic hypothesis, as in the above legend and the quotation at the head of the chapter, is that we dream to create a self/nonself split and that dreams are the first state of consciousness in matter in which this division occurs. Consequently, matter evolves into distinct conscious life-forms through dreaming, and as the dreaming goes on through ages of time, conscious species continue to evolve, ever differentiating themselves from their environments. The relationship of species survival and dream telepathy is examined in this light. It is a remnant of a universal connectivity that exists in all matter.

Self/nonself differentiation is the mark of sentience. Thus, dreaming is a necessary first evolutionary step for sentience to appear. Without dreams, no distinction between sentient and nonsentient behavior is even possible. Thus, the material universe dreams to become aware of itself. From this it follows that we, being composed of matter, dream to become aware of ourselves.

Self-Awareness in Dreams and Waking Life

What dreams? This question lies at the heart of the so-called mind-body problem. This will take us into concepts such as the "dream-body" by Arnold Mindell and the lucid and "witness" dream studies of Jayne Gackenbach and many others.

Recently, there has been a great deal of interest in *lucid dreams*. [6] These are quite different from ordinary dreams in content and experience. They are distinguished by the awareness that one is dreaming while the dream progresses and the vivid details one can remember after the dream. One also feels in control of the events of the dreaming entity.

I use this expression *entity* because in my own lucid dreams the dreaming entity feels different from my normal waking persona in several ways, although at the same time I know it is "I." The most striking difference is the awareness of being split into two conscious minds: the sleeping person at home in bed, and the person experiencing the dream and knowing all along that he or she is in bed at home. Upon awakening from a lucid dream one has immediate recall of the dream.

Recently, I have interviewed people who not only have lucid dreams but are also apparently capable of waking up night after night in a parallel world where they have a continuous life in a different body. (I myself have had this experience, as well as the experience of ordinary lucid dreams unrelated to other lucid dreams.) I have pre-viously written about lucid dreams as part of my study of the relation-ship of physics to consciousness.[7]

Aware of self in lucid dreams? What does that mean? What is self-awareness? We all seemingly know what it means to be aware of oneself. But this simple, everyday experience is yet to be understood, either scientifically or, for that matter, in terms of spiritual disciplines. It seems that if you talk to a representative of one or another different schools of thinking, you get various answers.

The simple meaning of self-awareness is the ability to distinguish self from not-self, and to do this, I claim here, one must dream.[8] In other words, dreaming is the process required to form the most basic distinction that exists in the universe: I and it, subject and object. How does that happen? How can such a distinction arise?

Getting into the Big Dream

The "big-dream" experience includes all imaginal-realm phenomena such as UFO experiences and near-death experiences. We will also see how the big dream overlaps into the little dream in the world of art and politics, including a close personal look at how dreams have influenced the recent change in the political system of Russia.

In my book *The Eagle's Quest,*[9] I described how the imaginal realm might be the source of big dreams. I also studied how shamans alter consciousness in order to heal and transform matter. In that book I had at times attempted to provide new metaphors for under-standing states of consciousness in terms of my academic training in physics. I also suggested that a possible explanation of shamanic states of consciousness could be incorporated into the existence of a "middle" or imaginal realm that projected itself into our lives as thoughts, feelings, and even as body illness. Here we will examine the big dream as evidence of imaginal realm intrusion into daily life.

An example of this is seen when we look at how dreams influenced the work of Wolfgang Pauli, one of the greatest and possibly the most intelligent physicists who ever lived. Recent publications about Pauli, who died in 1958, indicate that he was working toward a theory of the overlap of quantum physics and psychology and that this overlap was revealed to him by dream images.

Where Is Your I-Ness Your Highness?

Finally, even if we eventually discover where and how consciousness operates and what constitutes the difference between dreaming and waking life, we are still faced with the mystery of ourselves. The "self," if you will, is evidently present in each of us, and yet we simply do not know where "he or she" is to be found. Based on the holographic model and based on some new concepts from quantum physics dealing with self-referring automata, some new light will be shed on the mystery of why we won't find ourselves inside our skins.

The problem of the location of the self has been with us for a long time. It is called the mind-body problem. It would seem that science has been attempting to solve this problem via a number of separate disciplines, including metaphysics, philosophy, religion, neuroscience, computer science, psychology, and physics. Each has reached an important part of the answer, but none has fully synthesized all the implications of conscious awareness, specifically the role of self-awareness. I hope the ideas presented here will add some light.

Perhaps only today is it possible to formulate a solution that encompasses all these disciplines because of the remarkable discoveries of quantum physics. I am not demeaning any of the aforementioned disciplines. Indeed, each of those fields has provided essential clues to my hypothesis. But for the most part none of these disciplines have seriously taken quantum physics into account in their attempts to answer the mind-body problem.[10]

I believe that quantum physics provides the necessary link between these studies and dreaming. Let's see how I arrived at the hypothesis. The overlaps occur in the field of dreams.

Although quantum physics will play an important role in this book, I will save my discussion of it for chapter 10, after we have looked at a brief history of dream research; dream psychology as proposed by Sigmund Freud, Carl Jung, and others; and the latest dream research. Yet, I want to give you a hint, just a tiny one, of what's coming.

Quantum physics is considered today to be the most powerful, rigorous, and fruitful science ever devised by the human mind. It enables us to understand the world in terms of extremely tiny units of matter and energy and their effects. It has made possible a wide range of technological inventions, including the modern computer and the laser. But impressive as new inventions are, the implications of quantum physics are even more striking. They imply that observation disturbs and alters matter. If there is an observer active in your dreams, what role does she or he play in them?

Assuming that all of the above facts, theories, and speculations are correct, we are led to the rather strange conclusion that not only do our brains operate holographically but, based on quantum physics and David Bohm's concept of implicate order,[11] so does the world of matter and energy. What is new to this position is the idea of the subject also being distributed holographically throughout the universe and arising from it in much the same way that matter and energy are distributed and arise—as if awakening from a dream.

I should also caution the reader a second time that the choices of what to write about in the vast field of dream research were my own. Consequently, I may have omitted some recent major dream research or only briefly mentioned what possibly deserved more attention. I apologize up front about this. It couldn't be helped; the book would have been much too long. I didn't choose to research only those scientists and theoreticians who agree with me about the relationship of dreams to physics. In fact, most of the people you will read about were not in total agreement with me, although there were certainly quite a few sympathies and lots of encouragement.

A Dream of My Own

Let me begin with a dream of my own. Although it reveals certain intimate details of my life and to some extent my very personal feelings at that time, it will be instructive in pointing out what a dream can mean and how it illustrates a number of the points I mentioned above.

A little while ago, I dreamt of my former wife, Jocelyn (not her real name). Although we are now divorced and have lived apart for several years, at the time the dream had a special message for me. In fact, it was this dream that in a sense capstoned this book and made me realize just what it was I was searching for in my conceptualization of *The Dreaming Universe*.

In the dream, Jocelyn was appealing to me, saying that she wanted to be taken care of, that I hadn't been considering her needs in my endeavors to find my way through this often bewildering experience we call life.

I woke up in the middle of the night and was clearly upset. I had thought I had settled all this in our divorce and was surprised that the dream had such an impact on me.

Upon awakening, I wondered what the dream meant. I recalled my thinking at the time of the divorce. When we had decided to divorce, I felt that I no longer wanted to be responsible for her and that I no longer wanted to be her sole support. I had felt, in a very real sense, betrayed by her because she seemed to need more than I was able to provide. Of course, marriage is a tough row to hoe for all partners. My thoughts about my marriage were my own interpretations of my life with my former wife. And of course, there are always two sides to every story. I certainly wasn't the victim in all of this by any means. But why did I feel this way upon arousing myself from the dream?

Then it dawned on me. The dream was mine. Any of the characters in the dream were actors, characters that somehow "popped" into my dreaming brain from somewhere, but wherever that was, it was distinctly for my benefit or for my information. I needed to learn something from the story of the dream. But what could "Jocelyn" be for me now?

I then realized that "she" was I. She was, in Jungian terms, a representative of my anima, my feminine side. In her telling me that she wasn't being taken care of, I was telling myself that I wasn't taking care of my feminine needs, my self.

But what does it mean to take care of one's feminine needs if one is a man? Now in mythic terms, the feminine side of a man's body is the left side. Then it dawned on me. I had awakened wheezing. I have some tendency to be asthmatic, and the dream was pointing out to me that my health was in danger. I had been sleeping on my left side, and I realized that that side was congested. At the time, I had also been recovering from Graves' disease, a malady that affects the thyroid gland, well-known at the time because then-president Bush had also been stricken with it.

But were these symptoms mine? The planet is going through a left-side healing at this very moment. The goddess image, the feminization, the caring image of the "great mother," is dominant. Were my left-side needs symptoms of my illness or of the planet's illness? Did my little dream have big-dream significance? I think it did.

Although I was recovering, I was still living my life as most of us who tend to be in apparent good health do, as if I would live forever without ever suffering any form of serious illness. My disease and my lungs were giving me another message, but I wasn't listening. Hence the dream.

Isn't this a familiar story to all of us? Do we go on as if we always will, with little or no consideration of our personal futures or the future of the planet? Do we go on unconsciously minding our own business? Or have we become aware of our connections to each other? Do our dreams reflect our species as well as our individual lives?

Then I recalled my dreams over the last month. I realized that for the last few months I had been dreaming of Jocelyn and children repeatedly. But it wasn't until this dream that it all dawned on me and made sense. I wasn't taking care of myself. Furthermore, I felt betrayed by Jocelyn, the real Jocelyn, because she was no longer looking after me. My child-self still wanted its mother-image, and the dream-Jocelyn was no longer willing to serve in that capacity.

Thus, in a flash I knew what I wasn't willing to face earlier. My own mortality. The warning signals were there. Some part of me was signaling me in the only way it knew how—by invoking from some deeper realm of my self pictures from my physical life. These pictures evoked the feelings associated with memories of dealing with something that was inescapable: my own survival, my own battle with death.

Much later, I realized that the dreams I had been experiencing were literally messages appearing in visual form that somehow produced feelings and emotions. But where did these messages come from? In fact, what is a dream? And why do we have them? Is there a deeper meaning to dreams, something that deals not only with our past but also with our future? Do dreams tell us about the course of action we need to follow, and that if we ignore it, it is to our peril?

Perhaps my dreams during a stressful period of my life were trans-personal. In other words, are my own life, illnesses, stresses, and reflections about the meaning of all this very much connected to our life "out there," yours and mine?

Now that you have read the opening act, shall we dance into the dream? Are you ready to find out who you really are? Do you need some proof? Well, turn the page, Llixgrijb, and wake up.

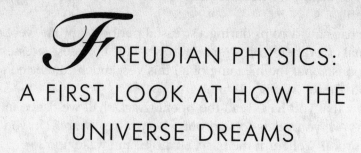 FREUDIAN PHYSICS: A FIRST LOOK AT HOW THE UNIVERSE DREAMS

Much Madness is divinest Sense—
To a discerning Eye—
Much Sense—the starkest Madness—
'Tis the Majority
In this, as All, prevail—
Assent—and you are sane—
Demur—you're straightway dangerous—
And handled with a Chain.

—*Emily Dickinson*

The dream is the small hidden door in the deepest and most intimate sanctum of the soul, which opens into that primeval cosmic night that was soul long before there was a conscious ego and will be soul far beyond what a conscious ego could ever reach.

—*Carl Gustav Jung*

I wish to concentrate here and in the next chapter on the models of the psyche and how they pertain to the dream research of just two men: Sigmund Freud in this chapter and Carl Jung in the next. This doesn't mean that other early workers in the fields of dream research and psychoanalysis are of lesser importance; simply, these two are in my mind the earliest groundbreakers to come up with what may be, although I am sure unbeknownst to both of them, a quantum-physical basis for the psyche. It is from this basis, which I will begin to elucidate in this chapter, that my own thinking about dreams, particularly the concept of the dreaming universe, arose.

Although much has been written about Sigmund Freud, including an excellent summary and history of Freud's earlier work and later developments and a good discussion of Freud's interpretation of dreams by Jonathan Winson,[1] in this chapter I want to concentrate on several elements of Freud's thinking that bear on the question of the dreaming universe. I will not even attempt to describe the intricacies of psychoanalysis. Nor will I attempt to validate or disprove Freud's models of the psyche. Winson and others[2] have already done this quite adequately, and I refer the reader to these other books.

Instead I wish to look at how the physics of Freud's time influenced his thinking. Later in this book I will examine how some of the basic constructions of Freud's model could also be used in constructing a quantum-physical model of the connection between the brain and the psyche and how concepts from quantum physics are metaphors for Freud's theoretical constructions. It is this metaphorical connection that I will pursue in both Freud's ideas and Jung's and then show how they connect with the model of the dreaming universe.

I hadn't actually fully realized the metaphorical connection until very recently, although not too long ago when I was given the opportunity to present the ideas of "quantum psychology—my attempt to use quantum-physical metaphors in modeling the psyche" to a class of psych majors at a local university, I began to see how quantum metaphors could be applied to Freudian psychology. As I was gathering my thoughts for my course, I suddenly realized that the language of classical physics provided metaphors for Freud and that these metaphors are still used in psychological analysis today.

Not least of these tools was the cause-and-effect machine so prevalent in the mechanical age. Although it was quite clear that human beings often performed irrational acts, the hope was that even these "insanities" had causes, and once these causative factors were isolated a "cure" would be possible. The game of psychology became a search. This search could only be undertaken in the spirit of mechanics— through analyses of data.

The very notion that there is a psyche that can be divided into parts consisting of an unconscious and a conscious mind is a structural analysis and owes its existence to the prevalent mechanical worldview of Freud's time. Thus to understand Sigmund Freud, who is considered by nearly all psychologists and psychiatrists as the "father of psychoanalysis," we really need to see clearly Freud's theories in terms of the physics of his time and ours.

With the coming of the "age of reason" and the mechanical picture of the universe, consciousness gradually began to be identified as a rational, logical, mechanical process. In other words, it was felt that underlying all psychic functioning there had to be a mechanical reason—a causative factor determining behavior.

In past years, this had been rekindled in the form of B. F. Skinner's *Behaviorism,* which surprisingly deviates considerably in many respects from Freudian thought. Even today, we are still attempting to use mechanical models to depict how the brain functions. For example, the modern computer with its inputs, outputs, and central processing has influenced much of psychology and brain neurophysiology; if not the modeling that psychologists and physiologists use, then certainly the metaphors that guide researchers in their search for scientific evidence.

Freud, not unlike those who came after him, saw the human brain in mechanical terms, perhaps somewhat like a steam engine. Consequently he made use of thermodynamic nomenclature. Freud was also aware of the neurobiology of his time. He viewed the brain as a complex neuro-network in which neurons built up electrical charge and, as a result, required discharging. Freud envisioned that dreams occurred during discharge.

Freud gave the dream two purposes: fulfillment of repressed unconscious desires, which were largely sexual or aggressive in nature, and the allowance of the ego—the censor of all those repressed wishes—to sleep. Lately, Winson and Hobson have disputed Freud's "censor in dreams" theory. Be this as it may, it is still useful to see Freud's theories, particularly some of Freud's conceptual framework, in terms of physics.

Freud broke the mind into parts. The main division was between what he called the conscious and the unconscious mind. The unconscious was the repository of unfulfilled and often consciously unacceptable desires. According to his model, when we have a thought in our waking minds that we feel we cannot fulfill, it reverberates in the brain, building up neuronal charge.

During sleep the ego allows repressed wishes and unacceptable thoughts to combine and stage a play in symbolic form in order to discharge the built-up electrical energy. The reason for the symbolic content was to disguise the unacceptable and unfulfilled desires so that the dreamer would remain asleep and undisturbed. Of course, the disguise does not always work, as we all know. Often dreams wake us up.

In the later chapters of this book, I will explore the possibility that dreams are vital and primary and that they will occur even if an individual does not sleep. They then take the form of altered awareness in the waking state and, in a physically disturbed brain, appear as schizophrenic episodes.

Freud's Theory of Dreams

Although dreams had been investigated for thousands of years, probably the first researcher to analyze dreams "scientifically" was Sigmund Freud, who published his seminal work, *The Interpretation of Dreams,* in 1900. Previous to (and during) his work most medical people felt that dreams were hallucinations and were therefore essentially useless, a statement that even today has some basis in scientific views. However, against the tide of the scientific (i.e., psychiatric and psychological) thinking of his time, Freud was attempting to provide a science of dreams and of psychic functioning in general.

By the early twentieth century, dreams began to lose their mythic quality as messages having revelatory powers from the gods. Although the literature of the midnineteenth century reflected the mysterious qualities of dreams as exemplified in the works of Edgar Allan Poe and William Wordsworth, by the end of the century dream literature in popular journals began to decrease, although it increased steadily in professional journals. However, popular literature still reflected a strong interest in paranormal and metaphysical concerns.

In his work, Freud attempted to base a study of dreams squarely on the shoulders of science. In *The Interpretation of Dreams,* Freud cited over two hundred references demonstrating scientific interest in dreams prior to 1900. He concluded from these studies that although they had a "quantity of interesting materials," they brought little to the study of the essential nature of dreams. Freud stated the essential nature of dreams in his preface: "[I wish] to give an account of the interpretation of dreams . . . [and to establish] their theoretical value as a paradigm."[3]

Where the ancients saw dreams as arising from external sources (gods) or, as Aristotle did, from sensory imprints, Freud believed that dreams arose from the postulated unconscious mind. As I mentioned above, previous to (and during) Freud's work most medical people felt that dreams were merely hallucinations and therefore useless as a subject of scientific study. In contrast to this, in Freud's model of dreams, the dream was an expression from the unconscious that had become repressed during early childhood after the child expressed wishes that remained unfulfilled. Wishes were therefore strongly reflected in dreams and represented yearnings that appeared during four critical stages of growth: the oral, anal, phallic, and genital stages.

Repressed wishes constituted the structure of the unconscious mind, according to Freud. In a typical psychoanalysis of a patient, Freud would ask the dreamer to say whatever came to mind in connection with each element of a dream.[4] By considering the words chosen by the dreamer, Freud hoped to help the dreamer identify these repressed wishes. The theory was that the wishes would no longer have a grip on the inappropriate behavior of the subject after their identification. Once these wishes were known, the person would then be able to alter his or her behavior and live a richer life.

What would cause the dream awareness of a repressed wish? Repressed impulses would arise during sleep, appearing as a result of the day's activity or recent experiences, triggering a movement in the unconscious that sought release. These recent experiences would appear to resemble material constituting the repressed wish.

Today we have many jokes and cartoons emphasizing this Freudian theory. The typical cartoon or "humorous" film shows a man taking a second look at a woman who passes by simply because she has large breasts. Freud might have suggested that this person had repressed wishes in regard to the breast stemming from early childhood when the mother refused to let the child suckle.

Freud also put particular emphasis on sexual strivings during dreams. American television advertising of products ranging from automobiles to washing machines emphasizes the Freudian model of repressed sexual wishes. Practically no product is sold today on television without a particularly sexy woman displaying her wares. Long, sleek cars often have bikinied starlets draped over their hoods. Freud might say that the car is a disguised symbol of the penis, and the sexy girl draping over its hood represents the unfulfilled wish of the male watching the ad to have the girl draped over his "manly hood." Consequently, symbols of this repression in dreams would reflect the outward appearance of the sexual organs. Long pointed objects would be the penis. Round, concave objects would be the vagina.

If asked why dreams appear as imagery instead of words, Freud would probably reply that imagery portrays symbols and these symbols are the only representations that the dreamer would accept. Again, this is the notion that a censor exists inside of each of us refusing to let us see the truth. Freud believed that imagery was an ancient language. I would take this a step further to mean that Freud also believed that ancient prehumans dreamed before they were able to speak words. Perhaps early prehumans dreamed before they were fully conscious and that imagery was the first language. Assuming that the unconscious is as old as the brain, it would follow that if the unconscious is the seat of repressed wishes, these wishes would have to be turned into pictures.

Thus images were disguised representations of the forbidden desires of the person. Freud would then say that such a disguise was necessary in order that the dreamer not awaken, thus placing sleep as the primary state of "consciousness" that is vital to human life. Dreams thus must occur as a result of repressed wishes, and they must be disguised in meaning so that they do not awaken the dreamer.

Although I will only touch on this very briefly here and expound on it in chapter 14, we know today that intent or, in Freud's terms, wishes do modify and alter the physical world. This is certainly obvious to most of us while we are awake. But in dreams? Does intent have any role while we are asleep in our beds? I would like to suggest that it does, and that intent can alter not only the dream world in which the dreaming entity finds itself, but also the physical world of the body. Thus dreams are affected by intent; however, that intent may lie in an entirely different realm from simple personal wishes and instead reach out to the entire universe.

What Is a Theory of Psychology?

We might ask if Freud's theories are really scientific. In a very real sense no theory of psychology is scientific because the object under scrutiny is actually not an object at all. It is the psyche itself, and no one has ever seen a psyche or measured its spatial extent or the timings of its mechanisms, assuming that it has mechanisms.

That psychoanalysis may have failed to be a scientific theory and is unprovable by refutation or testing is of a somewhat lesser concern to me. All theories when they first appear are somewhat unyielding in this regard. In fact in every scientific theory there is always a core of untestability or disprovability. Even Newton's theory of mechanical action has such a core. (Try to define mass without using the concept of force, and you will see what I mean.)

For example, in quantum physics today, we live with quantum theory. At its core lies a bizarre and untestable concept involving invisible waves (called quantum wave functions) that reflect what is possible. Yet these waves are so strange to our thinking that they cannot even be accurately imagined. Furthermore they often occupy dimensions beyond the usual three dimensions we are used to.

Be this as it may, nearly every field of scientific inquiry attempts to build on physics to make its edifices, if not by direct appliance of the actual concepts, such as energy or force field, then by some form of analogy. Undoubtedly, the reason other fields look toward physics is the belief that this science is the most powerful, rigorous, and fruitful of all. The hope is to make all sciences as rigorous as physics. Being a product of his times, Freud, like many scientists outside of physics, used the physics of his day to make a model. To understand what Freud was thinking about in this regard—and I think it is essential to grasp this because his thinking in several important ways still guides the modern dream researcher on his path—I wish to look at several of Freud's concepts, earlier and then later.

Why should we consider these concepts? Looking ahead, I wonder about the future of physics. Will it continue to search for the most fundamental objects, fleeting wisps of strings or particles folded up in hidden dimensions, or will it attempt to deal with the searcher for these objects, the subject? I believe that subjective physics is on the way in and that it will be an emerging branch of physics in the years to come. The notion of the dreaming universe is my attempt to provide some clues to how this research will be done. I am a product of my time, and it affects and conditions my thinking.

Thus, let me paint a picture of Freud's time and the physics that was known and accepted during it.

The Time of Freud

Freud was born during the heyday of classical physics. Everything under the sun was a Newtonian machine. Thus modelers of science were in one way or another attempting to construct a mechanical theory based on the models of the earlier "scientific revolution." It went along something like this: Newton, in 1687, nearly two hundred years before the birth of Freud, building upon the ideas of Galileo, Descartes, and Kepler, "figured out" that the universe was behaviorally a machine. Objects existed in ever-extending space and throughout all eternal time.

Before Newton, objects interacted with each other through *contact forces* that arose whenever objects actually touched. Think of a game of billiards and you see contact forces in operation whenever two balls collide. What if objects weren't in contact? Then, accordingly, there could be no forces acting, and the objects would be unaffected by each other, or so people thought.

When Newton came along and explained how the moon and the earth moved and mutually affected each other, he had to envision "gravity," which to those who even contemplated it was both magical and disturbing. Gravity was not a contact force.

But no mind (pun intended). Gravity was an action-at-a-distance force and that was what counted. Instead of a contact force between bodies, gravity was a *force field* in space, and the objects felt forces that were caused by their contact with the gravitational field.

In 1860, nearly two hundred years after the dawn of the "age of reason," James Clerk Maxwell would tie together electricity and magnetism using the force-field concept. Actions-at-a-distance would be accepted as invisible forces that existed "out there" influencing matter. By picturing the action-at-a-distance force field as radial lines, parallel lines, or whatever, depending on the physical-material boundaries that encompassed it, some researchers started to think of consciousness as force fields within the brain.

Erich Fromm in *Greatness and Limitations of Freud's Thought*[5] describes the milieu of bourgeois materialism in Germany as presented by men like Vogt, Moleschott, and Buechner. For example, in 1855, Buechner in his book *Kraft und Stoss,* "Force and Matter," made a case for the nonexistence of force without the presence of matter and vice versa; there can be no matter without the presence of force.

A year later, Sigmund Freud was born in Victorian Austria, at a time when psychology was still in its infancy and psychoanalysis didn't even exist. Just think what that would be like. Mental illness still meant a malfunction in one of the four humors discovered by the famed physician of ancient Greece, Galen. These were choler, causing anger; blood, causing cheerfulness; phlegm, causing calmness; and bile, causing sadness.[6]

For example, if one was sluggish and lacked vitality in those days, one would say the phlegm was acting badly. Today we might say one has a bad cold. *Sanguine* referred to the color of the blood. Blood that was very red meant a high degree of energy, while low or dark-colored blood meant a lack of optimism. Today we would give the patient oxygen or iron-enriched foods or supplements to redden the blood. Choler was found in the bile secreted by the liver and examined in the feces. Melancholy was also found in the bile and was a serious condition if that fluid was black. It is no wonder that the French attribute much to the health of their livers!

One might imagine the thrill of Freud's discovery that the human mind could be understood and even mapped using the tools of that day's science: Newtonian-Maxwellian physics. What tools? Physical-contact forces, no. But invisible force fields? Yes. The idea was that there were psychic forces, invisible urges, influencing us in much the same manner that invisible electromagnetic forces and action-at-a-distance gravitational forces influence matter.

Freud's passion was passion. He wanted to understand human emotion. Since during the Freudian period—from about 1890 to 1930—little was known about hormones, much energy was spent on the study of one phenomenon near and dear to human consciousness: sex. Although many in the medical profession disagreed with Freud's overzealous interest in sex as a causative factor in mental illness, Freud believed that sex was *the* connection between the physiological and the psychical body. In a later chapter we will examine the role of dreams in this connection when we look at the work of Arnold Mindell and his concept of the dreambody.

Sexual arousal was then, as it is today, an obvious fact of human existence that clearly lacked an obvious cause. Why one person or, for that matter, an inert object could appear sexual to one person and not to another was and is a mystery. What is the cause of sexual arousal? The human penis erection or vaginal lubrication (an action of physiological matter) *must* be due to an invisible psychical force in mechanical terms.

Coupled with this mechanical cause-and-effect view was the influence of the bourgeois and authoritarian-patriarchal world in which Freud lived. Women were regarded as physiologically and psychically inferior to men. Fromm points out that after hearing the ideas of John Stuart Mill (whom Freud greatly admired) that women and men were truly equal, Freud wrote in a letter, "on this point Mill is simply crazy."[7] *Crazy* for Freud meant "unthinkable." In his view the world consisted of two classes of humans. In Freud's mind, one class was biologically, anatomically, and psychically considerably inferior to the other class.

In the remarkable film *The French Lieutenant's Woman,* the heroine is thought to be "suffering from acute melancholia" as diagnosed by the physicians of her Victorian time. The oppressed role of women was not even considered a problem. Her physician wouldn't even begin to think of such things. Yet as the film unfolds, we see the cause. She is a creative artist. She is intelligent, something that no one thought was possible in those times (with the exception of rare women such as the queen of England and Ireland), and she cannot release her creative impulses.

Men fare not much better either. Rules upon rules govern what is allowable and what is not. Upper classes must be upper-crusted. Working classes are doomed. Men are condemned if they marry beneath their dignities. Woman are totally dependent upon men for their lives and fortunes.

Today I am reminded of the recent popular view of consciousness as a split-brain model. The left half-brain is logical, linear, capable of forming words, etc. In a sense it is what Freud would call masculine and superior. The right half-brain is alogical, holistic, nonlinear, and spatial, the ideal "nonthinking" feminine and inferior side of the brain, as it would be thought of in a masculinized Freudian mechanical world.

Although it will become clearer as we go along, I am not attempting to salvage a Freudian theory of sex, men and women. What I am interested in presenting are Freud's structural components of the psyche. Also notice that what had been evolving during Freud's time was the continuous metaphorical movement from the objective field of physics into the subjective field of the psyche.

We who think at all about the nature of reality are products of our times. We do the best we can to model our experiences. Don't blame Freud for being a pessimist or a male supremacist. The times were pessimistic, women were not considered to be "worth" much, and Freud's mind, being part of the dreaming universe's mind, if you will allow me to make a metaphorical quantum jump, was reflective of that time.

The Instinct Life-Death Field of the Unconscious

Freud's discovery of the unconscious is considered to be his greatest insight into human consciousness. To Freud the unconscious provided a rationale, a reason for the conflict between thinking and being. What we *think* is not necessarily what we do. We possess "unconscious thoughts," deeper causative factors or independent variables that are the true causes for our behavior. These true causes are never our conscious thoughts, which are nothing but rationalizations of the unconscious thoughts. These "true" thoughts are repressed conscious thoughts, initially pushed and then held down below the level of conscious existence, or preexisting in some manner as unconscious memories.

In Freud's model of the unconscious there were two basic drives or instincts, which he labeled erotic and aggressive.[8] By 1923 he had replaced these with the life and death drives. These drives were in turn attributable to the "compulsion to repeat," about which I shall speak later when I talk about habits and repeated patterns. The erotic was associated with the *life* drive, and the aggressive was associated with the *death* drive.

In discussing these instincts Freud referred to the metabolic processes of living substances synthesizing simple molecules into complex materials and the reverse, breaking complex materials down into simple molecules. He said:

> [These] special physiological processes . . . would be associated with each of the two classes of instincts; both kinds of instinct would be active in every particle of living substance, though in unequal proportions. . . . It appears that, as a result of the

combination of unicellular organisms into multicellular forms of life, the death instinct of the single cell can successfully be neutralized and the destructive impulses be diverted on to the external world through the instrumentality of . . . the muscular apparatus; and the death instinct would thus seem to express itself—though probably only in part—as an instinct of destruction directed against the external world and other organisms.[9]

This is indeed a powerful insight into the nature of human suffering. It also indicates a means by which human consciousness is reflected in the physical world. Later I will tie this into the imaginal realm and its relation to dreams. Briefly, this projection mechanism is closely tied to how dreams occur—through the projection mechanism of the living brain. We will see in a later chapter neurological evidence for the projection mechanism. If Freud's theory is true, it means that all living organisms project their own deaths onto the outside world. If this is true, it is no wonder that the prevailing view of the world as hostile occurs. It is also understandable that this way of projection is fundamentally an illusion. Every other thing out there is out to "get-cha." But as I said earlier, let's carry this model further.

For example, we have recently passed out of the threat of global nuclear destruction. Yet if you remember this period of our history, it had its "charms," Star Wars not being the least among them. Even the revelation that the Soviet Union was incapable of hitting Nevada on a good day with a land-launched nuclear missile did not deter the United States from a continued development of the means of "mutually assured destruction" (MAD). Look at the rationale: it was a fact that we had created the means for the total nuclear destruction of all living creatures. As we built more and more nuclear "games," we felt more and more compelled to keep building. We had rationalized this fascination with death by insisting that those outside of "us" are out to get us. "They" are the enemy.

But we seemingly made it through that critical period of humanity's growth. We projected the life instinct out onto the world as well. It is not hopeless by any means. It is important to realize that both drives are projectable if one of them is, since, both drives have, in Freudian terms, a common origin, the instinct field within the unconscious.

The drive to preserve life, such as the willingness of peoples to disarm, to aid each other without promise of return, the desire to love, etc., is a life-preserving projection arising from this drive in every "particle of living matter."

But what is it that feels this compulsion to be driven by these drives? In Freud's time the terms one might imagine applying would come from classical electromagnetism. Thus there would be something in the brain capable of picking up electrical charge. In other words a construction within the unconscious that is capable of being "charged."

The Ego and I

This construction is the *ego* in the Freudian model. Now in these very mechanical terms we are looking at a metaphor appropriate to this time to describe the subjective life and death instincts, as if they were opposite polar charges of an electrical field, and the ego as if it were an electrical ball inside the brain shuffling back and forth in the field. As the ball ego moves, it picks up electrical charge, either positive or negative. Consequently, depending on its charge, it is shuttled one way or the other.

The ego is capable of changing and, in this model, acquiring charge, and as a result of its acquiring, feeling the presence of the two opposite polar charges, the positive-life charge and the negative-death charge. Thus the ego is driven willy-nilly between the two depending on how much and what kind of charge it picks up. If it becomes positively charged, it is more attracted to the negative-death charge. This pulls it back from life into balance between life and death. If it acquires too much death charge, it is pulled in the other direction by the life charge—again balancing out the blind instincts that pull on it seemingly willy-nilly.

Following Freud's model further, these drives or, better, our response to these drives would be felt by us as emotions. By becoming emotionally "charged" we are more susceptible to the presence of the fundamental life and death charges within our unconscious. Thus emotional feelings are at this most fundamental level of experience the play of our unconscious selves with life and death. Our sexual energy, our libido, is then the movement of these charges through these buffeting experiences of the unconscious field lines.

In this sense *sex* is the field within the unconscious produced by the poles of life and death instinct. The *petite mort* or "little death" has been used to express the feeling of sexual climax. Sexuality contains both life and death poles in its expression.

Summarizing Freud

The ego corresponds to the sense of "I" we all experience. The *id* (more about the id in chapter 10) corresponds to the world of experience hidden as it were from the awareness of the ego. From the id, the world we experience "out there" arises. The mechanism for this is called projection, consisting of sensation, perception, and conception. Repression results from a vigilant self-observation process. All of these older ideas will appear again, but not as we see them here. The problem is how does the self arise? How does the ego-id separation occur? And how is it that dreams are the ground from which the world and its observer arise? We are just beginning to see this.

Freud is to the study of the structure of the psyche the equivalent of Isaac Newton in his study of the structure of the physical world. The question of the subject-object distinction could not be addressed in his time, simply because we had no idea how self-reference could be a physical process. This will come up later as we find it a naturally occurring concept in the many worlds interpretation of quantum physics.

In the next chapter we will look at the first attempts to blur the distinction between object and subject in the psychological studies of Jung. As Freud may be compared to Newton, we will compare Jung to Niels Bohr, the father/mother figure of quantum physics. Jung will introduce us to the idea of synchronicity—a necessary order of the universe that transcends causality and leads to a new understanding of the relationship of subject and object. Jung's synchronicity is the web that unites the dreamer and the dream, the self and the universe.

𝒥UNGIAN PHYSICS: SYNCHRONICITY—EVIDENCE OF THE UNIVERSE'S DREAM

————

Slowly, Llixgrijb thought about it. It thought of a concept called place, and it set about creating one . . . then another . . . then connecting them together . . . Llixgrijb created a universe in which everything was connected to everything else.

—Wim Coleman and Pat Perrin
The Jamais Vu Papers[1]

Any science that scientists do not understand.

—Alfred Adler, defining mysticism[2]

From an inner center the psyche seems to move outward, in the sense of an extraversion, into the physical world.

—Wolfgang Pauli[3]

Just as Freud offered science a structure of the psyche based on mechanism, Jung went further and indicated that this structure had to include meaningful relationships other than those that are time-ordered and cause-effect related. In a way Freud was hinting at this when he modeled the id as "timeless." Jung called these other kinds of relationships synchronistic. Jungian relationships are the first "scientific" attempts to establish a physics of meaning and an understanding of the self and the psyche. In this regard Jung gave dreams a far greater importance than Freud.

In this chapter I wish to deal with not only Jung's ideas concerning dreams, but also his model of the human psyche. Now why should I concern you with the Jungian model of the psyche? I wish ultimately to make a connection between the psyche and the physical. I am attempting to build a model here that shows that dreams are in a very real sense a part of matter itself—that the universe itself actually dreams. Now this appears to be a tall tale indeed. What could I possibly mean by dreams being a part of matter?

The ultimate mystery facing us is how matter becomes conscious. Simply put, if we argue that we are made of matter, then how does that matter seemingly produce or create images and thoughts? Or even put more crudely, how does meat dream? Is there some vital characteristic in matter that, if somehow revealed, would show how matter is already conscious and just waiting for the right environment to reveal its consciousness to us, as us? What is this characteristic?

To see an answer to this we need to understand what the psyche is and how it operates. I hope to show in this chapter that the Jungian concept of the psyche can be related to the laws of quantum physics —something that Jung himself believed was possible but difficult to achieve. I want to build on both Jung's and Freud's models.

An important part of my consideration here is the role of what Jung calls synchronicity—the ascendance of meaning from events that cannot be linked by any causal mechanism. It is in this concept that the richest ore in regard to making a quantum-physical connection between mind and matter is to be found. This connection will ultimately tie the dreams of the night to the dreams of the day—the imaginal realm about which I shall explain in a later chapter. Synchronicity is a clue that there is a "big dreamer," and we are part of its dream.

When we compare Carl Jung to Freud, we see that Jung offered an alternative view of dreams and of psychology. In 1907 he visited Freud in Vienna, and the two struck up a friendship that unraveled a few years later. Jung felt that Freud's fascination with psychic energy as being entirely sexual in nature was unfounded. He also thought that Freud's interpretation of dreams was too restrictive.

Jung's Theories of Dreams

Jung believed that Freud put too much emphasis on the erotic elements of dreams. He also believed that wish fulfillment was far too small a reason to underlie or be the cause of all dreams. Jung believed that dreams were not just suppressions of unaccepted desires but were necessary in a creative sense. Dreams actually produced new information for the conscious mind. Jung also felt that the symbols of dreams were not just made up to hide information, but were a form of universal language that he called archetypes. They were, in modern terms, the solutions of equations describing a new reality given in symbolic terms, much as the solutions of mathematical equations today, although written in symbolic form, represent our ideas about physical reality.

In a nutshell, while Freud believed that sleep was the cause and dreams were the necessary consequence allowing sleep to persist, Jung believed that dreams were primary and sleep was a sufficient alteration of consciousness to allow dreams to take place.

Carl Gustav Jung was born in Switzerland in 1875. From the time of his early youth until his death in 1961, he was deeply concerned with the spiritual or mystical side of the human psyche. Thus areas of research such as symbolism, parapsychology, modern physics, and religions—particularly Christianity—played a significant role in his psychological theories. He would be as concerned with the meaning of a number as with its value. In this sense he was much like the ancient Cabalists and Pythagoreans.

Jung saw that there had to be an interplay between the unconscious and the conscious that went on incessantly. The two were aspects of the one mind. In contrast, Freud felt that the material of the unconscious was "under battle" with the conscious mind and that it was always attempting to push its unpleasant contents back into the murky id.

Both agreed that our unconscious minds spoke to us through dreams. Jung believed that dreams were a natural and important part of our whole being. The dream used images that told us about ourselves. But what could a dream tell us that we didn't already know? It would speak to us about those things in our lives that we were ignoring or suppressing, or simply not making full use of. Dreams were not dangerous or crazy, and they were not necessarily wish-fulfilling. Nor were dreams couched in a hidden language; instead they were actual messages from ourselves to ourselves. While Freud believed that dreams were ultimately meant to conceal something, Jung believed they were meant to reveal something.

Jung felt that dreams dealt with origins, points where new ideas were created, and were not causes that explained our behavior in the past. Instead dreams were to be used to tell us something about our behavior in the future.

But how would Jung explain the apparent strangeness and sometimes unfamiliar images of dreams? It is here where Jung seems to go beyond the edge of science. Jung postulates the existence of a universal unconscious out of which certain images appear that have a commonality to all people. Now it is not the image itself that is important, but it is a tendency of the image—a kernel that underlies the image —that is in common to all people. Jung calls this kernel an archetype. Consequently, if we ignore some important part of ourselves, our dreams could produce visual images that reflect this archetype. The actual image might be different in different societies, but the meaning of the archetype would be the same to all societies. Later I will attempt to tie the archetype to the wave function of quantum physics, which reflects tendencies of events to occur in physical space and time and indicates that archetypes are signs of a higher level of self-reference.

This then leads to a search for the meaning of an image rather than a consideration of the image as hiding something from ourselves. Why are there dream images? It seems that we dream in images and not in words because images are a basic or perhaps primitive way of dealing with the outside world. I would also suggest that images are strongly connected with our feelings, and as we shall see in a later chapter, feelings create emotions, and emotions are vital to having any memory at all. In other words, we do not remember anything that we have no feelings about.

Now in order to consider what feelings are, let us look at how Jung dealt with them. To do this we first need to consider some important theoretical structures in Jung's model of the psyche. There are several terms differing from Freud's.

Jungian Individuation: Self From Nonself

First, an important concept in Jung's model was the process of *individuation*. This was a personal development wherein a connection between the center of psyche—that aspect which contains both the conscious and unconscious parts of the mind—and the ego, the central part of consciousness, occurs. He would say that the ego connects with the *self*.[4]

Secondly, Jung's major concepts included the attitudes. Attitudes were characterizations of behavior. He labeled them *introversion* and *extroversion*. An introvert was withdrawn, focusing on inward concerns. An extrovert was outgoing, focusing on the external world. While no one has a pure attitudinal behavior—sometimes you feel like a nut, sometimes you don't—each of us has tendencies that favor one attitude over another.

Introversion and extroversion are complementary. While engaging the world introvertedly a person deals with his own thoughts. The extrovert, on the other hand, deals with the thoughts and experiences of others. The introvert relies on her own thoughts. The extrovert depends on the outer world's thoughts. Jung dealt with these processes in terms of the *libido,* which he defined as an *energic* process —the flow of energy.

Thirdly, Jung dealt with the functions. Jung's functions are thinking, feeling, sensing, and intuiting. Each of these has a rather special meaning related to our ordinary usage of these words but different in specificity. For example, to tell a person he is incapable of thinking or that thinking is an inferior function for him would, I imagine, result in my being punched in the nose, particularly if that person had a strong superior sensing function.

These functions can be looked at as psychic dimensions or better as psychic *operators*. Remarkably they resemble quantum-mechanical operators representing observables in the physical world (see footnote 10 in chapter 10). Thinking and feeling are complementary in the same sense that position and momentum are complementary observable qualities of the physical world.[5]

In a similar manner, a person who uses her thinking function "most of the time" in dealing with the events of her life will find herself concerned with truth, impersonal objective judgments, logical criteria application to situations, abstract reasoning, and consistent argument. She will undoubtedly be a good planner.

On the other hand, if she uses her feeling function "most of the time," she will deal with events using subjective personal judgments. Truth will be relative and not absolute—she will feel "this is right," not think that it should be right. Emotional considerations will outweigh any logical reasons—good, bad, or otherwise. She will prefer strong emotional experience to bland intellectual experience.

In brief, thinkers use words and feelers use emotions to get their points across.

According to Jung, a person cannot have equally well-developed thinking and feeling. One will outweigh the other. One will be inferior. I remember being shocked when Dr. Marie-Louise von Franz (the well-known psychologist and author, a protégé of Jung's) told me that her feeling function was "inferior."

Thus thinking and feeling are operators used to evaluate choices and make decisions. A person cannot evaluate an event while being highly emotional and highly rational at the same time. In hindsight it would be possible, but while that event was being experienced, she would find herself using one operator at the clear expense of the other.

Whereas thinking and feeling are evaluatory functions—that is, one assigns value to what is thought or felt—sensing and intuiting are valueless. Sensation refers to a focus on direct experience, concrete facts, experimental evidence rather than theories, and that which can be seen, felt, tasted, touched, or heard.[6] "Sensationists" want direct tangible experiences rather than analysis. They deal with "coming to one's senses."

Sensation types deal well with immediate situations and handle crises and emergencies with relative ease. You want a sensation-type medical orderly to handle your wounded body on a battlefield. In an automobile accident, sensation types would be "cool" enough to know just what to do. They work well with tools and materials.

Complementary to sensationists are intuitives. These people deal with time in a nonlinear manner. They process information based upon past, present, and possible future experiences. The future is more important to intuitive types than either the past or present. An intuitive type could be making love and weaving a story, out loud, about extraterrestrial life, cosmic insight, and the comparison of human ejaculation to the creation of the universe as a spontaneous emission of matter out of a time-reversed black hole.

Often strongly developed intuitives add relevances and meanings to their sense experiences so quickly that people around them feel their breaths being taken away. Such people usually come off as rather intense beings. They are able to see the wholeness of the universal picture using unconventional leaps and bounds of imagination coupled with facts. They work well with ideas but suffer from little sense of practicality.

It is not possible to experience the world intuitively and sensationally at the same time. These functions are as equally complementary as thinking and feeling. However, it is possible to have both intuition and thinking or feeling superior. In other words, a person could be equally developed and functioning as an intuitive thinker or an intuitive feeler.

Or perhaps the person would have feeling and sensation as her superior functions. She would have a difficult time with mathematics, but she would be a good dancer. An intuitive-feeling superiority would make a good sales manager who lacked planning skills but got along well with many different kinds of people. She would make a good personal-development consultant or cheerleader.

Jung presented this functional typology graphically as shown in Figure 1. Here we see a person with a well-developed intuition and a somewhat developed feeling function. His thinking function is inferior (unconscious), and his sensation function is deeply unconscious. This person would appear to be walking around with his head in the clouds seeing little of the outside world. He would be concerned with how his behavior was affecting others, whether he had done well in the past, and how this would create or change the future of his relationship with certain people.

Next in Figure 2, we find a more balanced individual. He would make a good theoretical scientist but would probably be incapable of understanding why his remarks about birth control for males should strike up such animosity among the members of the local men's club.

On the other hand, the person shown in Figure 3 would make the ideal experimental scientist. He would deal pretty much with the here and now. He would enjoy puzzle-solving, and mathematics, which does not require leaps of imagination to solve, would be his forte. If he were a speaker or writer, his works would show high organizational skills. Facts would make sense and theories would be regarded skeptically.

The person shown in Figure 4, I would probably find very appealing, being a thinking-intuitive type myself.

Jung's Concept of Energy-Libido

Jung's concept of libido differs from Freud's in essential details. Where Freud felt that libido was primarily sexual energy, Jung took it to be

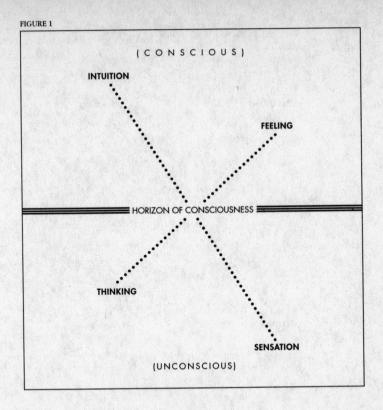

FIGURE 1

(C O N S C I O U S)

INTUITION

FEELING

HORIZON OF CONSCIOUSNESS

THINKING

SENSATION

(UNCONSCIOUS)

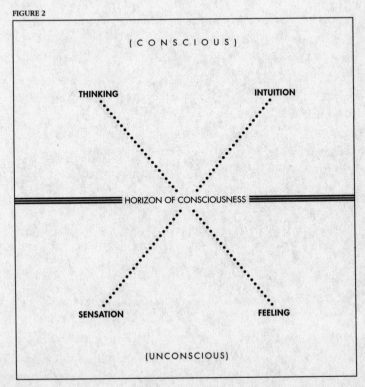

FIGURE 2

(C O N S C I O U S)

THINKING

INTUITION

HORIZON OF CONSCIOUSNESS

SENSATION

FEELING

(UNCONSCIOUS)

FIGURE 3

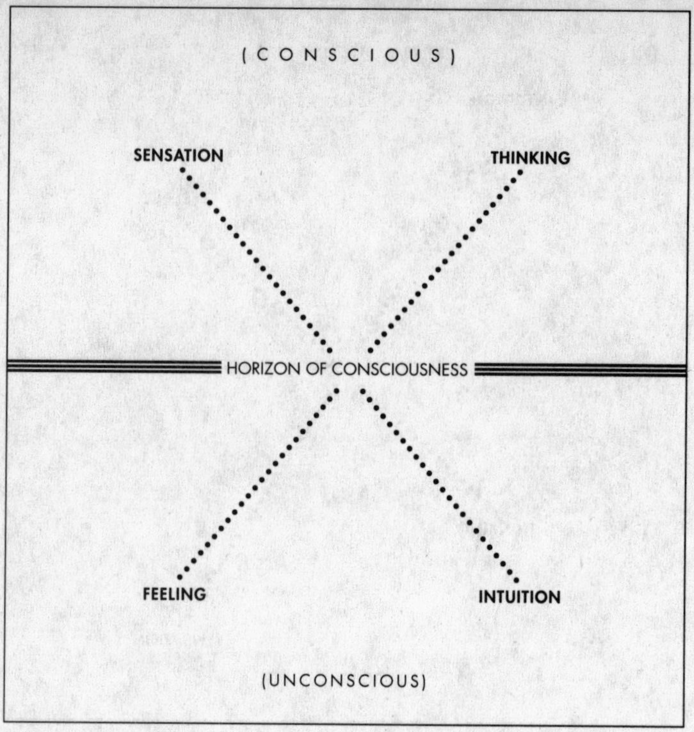

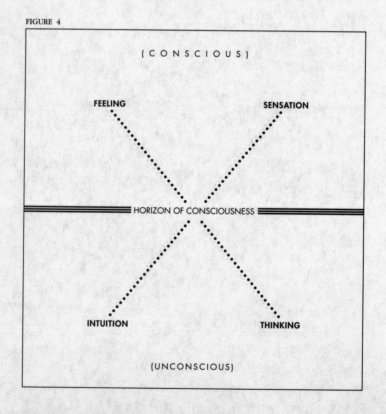

(C O N S C I O U S)

SENSATION THINKING

HORIZON OF CONSCIOUSNESS

FEELING INTUITION

(UNCONSCIOUS)

FIGURE 4

(C O N S C I O U S)

FEELING SENSATION

HORIZON OF CONSCIOUSNESS

INTUITION THINKING

(UNCONSCIOUS)

energy—the same kind of energy that is discussed in physics.[7] He believed that the concept of psychic energy is as justified in science as that of physical energy with as many quantitative measurements and different forms as are to be found in physics.

But he felt that fitting psychic energy into the framework of physical energy was not interesting because it was too vague a conjecture. Paradoxically, I suspect, he was in favor of making such a connection. His reluctance to do so may have arisen from the belief that a quantitative or numerical evaluation of this form of energy was too difficult to accomplish. Instead he reasoned that the energic concept was useful because it allowed the possibility of estimating quantities or comparing them without resorting to numerical measure.[8]

At this point, I would like to take a little side journey into the concept of energy. At the end of this jaunt, I will explain why. In discussing energy I would like to point out that there isn't a physicist alive who knows what energy actually *is*. The best that we have come up with is a concept described in terms of work or force multiplied by the distance over which that force is applied. Thus a force of ten pounds applied through a distance of five feet uses or releases an energy of fifty foot-pounds. No one has ever seen or sensed energy, in spite of the fact that we use this term as if it were quite tangible.[9]

Through mathematics and further developments in the new physics, especially Einsteinian relativity, we have modified this concept, making it abstract and nonsensible. We do not sense energy. We witness its consequences whenever a physical system undergoes transformation.

When physics recognized the generality of energy, making it more abstract, it became a more powerful concept. *Work* and *force,* terms more useful during the Freudian period, were becoming passé as the new physics period began to assert itself in consciousness. With the notion of force, however, there was an immediate sense of causality and a grounding of logical positivism. Things *were* (i.e., existed) if they worked. Mechanics was clear and not abstract. You pushed here, and it popped out there. Cause led to effect. Time present, past, and future were separated.

With the energy concept our thinking necessarily became more abstract and more timeless. There is no causality in energy. Things just transform from one form of energy to another. There is no reason why the falling egg ends up as goo on the floor energically.[10] The energy of the egg is the same either way.[11] When we trace the egg throughout its history, we can see that its sequences of transformations from solid to goo maintain the same energy. We say that the energy was conserved.

Jung was concerned with the equivalence principle of energy. It can be stated as a direct result of the law of energy conservation. When a system undergoes an energy change, either a loss or gain of energy, there must be another system also undergoing either a consequent gain or loss of energy. Thus an equivalent amount of energy is transferred from one system to another.

Jung recognized this in his investigations of the treatment of neuroses. He wrote:

> Even if its application is not always conscious, you nevertheless apply it instinctively or by feeling. For instance, when a conscious value, say a transference, decreases or actually disappears, you immediately look for the substitute formation, expecting to see an equivalent value spring up somewhere else.[12]

If the substitute formation does not occur, it will seem that the libido has disappeared. In an amusing story by Nobel prize-winning physicist Richard Feynman,[13] "Dennis the Menace" has been given twenty-eight indestructible blocks by his mother. At the beginning of the day his mother puts him in a room with the blocks and leaves. At the day's end she returns and finds him with only twenty-six blocks. Careful investigation, by her looking outside the open window of the room, discloses two blocks partially hidden in the bushes. Another day she returns and is shocked to find thirty blocks! But the mystery is soon cleared up when it is discovered that Bruce, the boy next door, had visited, leaving behind two of his blocks. Returning Bruce's blocks, carefully instructing Bruce's mother not to let him visit, and closing the window, Dennis's mother leaves again in the morning. When she returns, she finds Dennis with only twenty-five blocks. However, there is a box in the room, a toy box, and she goes to open the box. But Dennis puts up a huge fuss, "No! Don't open the box," he screams. Being clever, she knows that a block weighs three ounces. She also knows that the weight of the box when empty was sixteen ounces. So she weighs the box, finds it weighs twenty-five ounces, and applies the conservation-of-blocks formula:

$$(\text{number of blocks seen}) +$$
$$(\text{weight of the box} - 16 \text{ ounces})/3 \text{ ounces} = 28.$$
$$(25 \text{ blocks}) + (25 - 16)/3 = (25) + (9)/3 = 28.$$

The next day a new surprise awaits her. She notices that the dirty water in the bathtub is changing its level. The child is throwing blocks into the water, and because it is so dirty, she cannot see them. But she can find out how many blocks are in the water by adding another term to her formula. Since the original height of the water was six inches, and since each block raises the water level one-quarter of an inch, she writes:

(number of blocks seen) + (weight of the box − 16 ounces)/3 ounces + (height of water − 6 inches)/one-fourth inch = 28.

With each added complexity propounded by Dennis her world becomes more bewildering. After a while there will be a whole series of different terms appearing in her conservation-of-blocks formula. With the magical child-imagination of Dennis at work, perhaps he will discover how to "destroy" or annihilate a block. But his mother will persist looking carefully for sawdust in the corner or soot on the ceiling.

Each time she determines that a block that is not seen is hidden somewhere or transformed. The blocks are an analogy of the concept of energy. Energy is a useful concept only if it is conserved, i.e., if we can somehow account for it when it is not obvious. In physics, however, there are no blocks to begin with. All we have are formulas indicating how energy takes form but not what it is.

Now let me tell you why I have made this "energy" diversion. Briefly, energy is a fundamental or primitive concept. I would call it an archetype. Just like an archetype that appears in dreams, the picture of energy we have is quite different depending on how we in our societies have come to use it. I would also suggest that the concept of energy arises as part of the collective unconscious. It is universal and capable of taking many forms. The search for the energy of a system in the "out there" physical world is analogous to the search for the meaning of a dream in Jungian terms, in the "in here" of our dreaming world.

It is for this reason that Jung may be right in assuming that energy is a universal concept applicable to psychic functioning as well as the physical universe. Jung then describes how energy has two attributes, *intensity* and *extensity*. Extensity of energy is not transferable from one structure to another without changing the structure; intensity of energy is. By extensity, Jung is referring to the quality of the energy. In other words, he is pointing out that there is "something" that travels from one place to another when an energy transformation occurs.

For example, a ball that is hit straight up carries with it energy continually undergoing transformation. It has kinetic energy and gravitational potential energy. The quantity of kinetic energy is continually transferring into potential energy as the ball rises. Thus at the top of its trajectory, the ball is momentarily at rest, i.e., with no kinetic energy, but with full potential energy. The evaluation of its quantities of energy is intensive but the qualities of kinetic and potential are extensive. The ball cannot transfer its kinetic quality into potential quality without changing its form by breaking up, for example, into parts.

Similarly there is a psychic extensive factor that is not transferable.[14] Jung's concept of extensity and intensity are forerunners of David Bohm's concept of implicate and explicate order, about which I shall have more to say later. They are also forerunners of the conceptual division of the world into objects and actions of objects: subjects and verbs. They comprise a complementarity, a dual way of dealing with experience. They are hints of the division between mind and matter, physical and psychical, words and images.

Jung, Synchronicity, and How He Was Influenced by the Early "New Physics"

Carl Jung created and developed a theory of psychology that went beyond Sigmund Freud's work in one essential way: he recognized that order can exist in the human psyche in a noncausal manner. This means that humans experience some situations that cannot be related in a normal cause-and-effect temporal order, i.e., in the usual manner that we often use when we ask when faced with troubles or sudden benefits, "What did I do to deserve this?"

This new form of order has been called by Jung *synchronicity*. As the question of deserving implies, whenever an event occurs, no matter how normal or abnormal that event seems to be, our Western way of thinking about the world and the role we play in it (often regarded by materialists as the role of a victim) is to find a reason for the event. We believe that nature is not capricious, that human beings do things as a result of "influences," forces, as Freud might have put it, that are the earlier causes for things as they are—the effects of those causes. This assumption of temporal order, or causation as the fundamental or only ordering principle allowed in the universe, is the basis of mechanics. It is the result of our traditional way of thinking brought to us by the early Greeks.

Quantum physics has introduced another form of order. This order cannot be seen as a temporal or cause-and-effect form of order. Instead it arises as a meaningful pattern that can be experienced, usually in hindsight but sometimes instantaneously, wherein several events not necessarily happening at the same time nor even at the same place are correlated. This correlation is not just a functional dependence of one or more events on another event or set of events. It is not a teleological connection either (as the tree is hidden in the acorn). We cannot look at some of these events in the pattern and conclude that they were the causes of the other events in the pattern.

Yet there is a clear and quite meaningful evident connection between the events. This "meaningfulness" of seemingly unrelated events I call *quantum synchronicity,* and I'll have more to say about this in chapter 10.

At the time that Jung introduced synchronicity, Western mechanical thinking was (and is today) strongly prevalent. Thus to introduce any concept of order outside of temporal causation was sacrilege and usually met with ridicule and disdain. If there was no reason for an event, it didn't occur—it was an illusion or hallucination.

Jung was dogged by this doctrinaire attitude and as a result was not able to come up with a consistent—out-on-a-limb—definition of his own concept. He was always placating the mechanicians of academe. This kowtow was only relieved in Jung's yin-yang study of the *I Ching.* Apparently he lacked the personal courage to see his greatest insight develop fruit,[15] a fact he mentioned himself in his now classic paper "Synchronicity: An Acausal Connecting Principle."[16]

Jung was fascinated by the "new physics," that is, the physics that was new to him at the time. His first ideas about synchronicity occurred during the 1920s. This was the heyday of the "new physics" and the beginnings of the "new order" of the quantum principle of acausal connections. He was influenced by physicists Niels Bohr and Wolfgang Pauli.

FIGURE 5

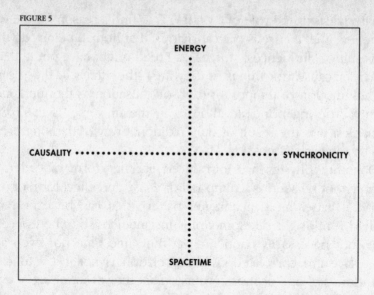

Bohr first conceived of the "new order" in his model of the atom. Bohr pointed out that electrons within the atom could make "quantum jumps" from one location (orbit) to another without any prior cause. In fact, later, after Bohr had received much notoriety for his early quantum-jumping atomic model, he had a coat of arms made up that had the yin-yang symbol embedded on it as its mandalalike center.

Wolfgang Pauli was a bright young physicist at this time, and in a later chapter I'll have more to say about how Jung influenced him through Pauli's own dreams. He contributed a brand-new idea to physics that has become vital to our understanding of atomic structure and the abilities of atoms to interact with each other and form molecular structures. This is called the *Pauli exclusion principle* (PEP).[17]

In 1952, Pauli assisted Jung with his conception of synchronicity. If we draw a cross on a paper with the vertical line representing the "connection" from one end, labeled indestructible energy, to the other end, tabbed the space-time continuum, and the horizontal line representing the "connection" from the left end, marked causality, to the right end, entitled synchronicity, we will have the schema shown in Figure 5, satisfying on the one hand the postulates of the new physics and on the other hand those of psychology.

These concepts are seen to be in opposition to each other, energy opposing space-time just as causality opposes synchronicity. Now energy and space-time are ways to describe the "out there" experience. They are convenient frameworks in which we are entitled to see the connection between events. Events that have the same energy cannot be described with certainty within space-time. Events that are seen to occur within space-time cannot be seen to be energy-conserving necessarily. The reason for this lies in the principle of uncertainty or indeterminism as put forward by Werner Heisenberg.

To the extent that we know the energy of a sequence of events, we do not know their coordinates within space-time. That is, we cannot say where and when they occur. To the extent that we know where and when events occur, we cannot say with what energy these events take place. So much is said by the uncertainty principle.

Thus space-time and energy are complementary descriptors of events, and in a similar manner synchronicity and causality are complementary to each other. They deal, just as energy and space-time do, with events. These events are marked by their psychic component as well as their physical component. Here is the crux of the matter: our Western consciousness has taken as meaningful only those events that are labeled causal. By losing track of or dismissing this other dimension of meaningfulness, we actually become unconscious of much of the universe. This is an important idea in our grasping the notion that the universe dreams. We first must begin to see that dreaming and waking are not as separated as they appear to our logical minds. Remarkably, we carry out this separation in perfect logic.

Surprisingly, this causal meaningfulness, as eighteenth-century philosopher David Hume pointed out more than two hundred years ago, is something that we cannot see. It is implied in the events that we do see. For example, we do not see a football follow a parabolic trajectory as it flies from the hand of the quarterback into the arms of the wide receiver. We sense the skill of the thrower. We take as given that the ball that leaves the quarterback's hand is the same ball that is caught by the wide receiver. We know that it is because what goes up must come down. Newton said so and so it is.

When the ball is caught, we infer it is the same as the one that was thrown. A clever magician fools us with this implication, time and time again, by just switching one ball for another. It is our inference of causality that makes for a good magic show.

Thus we map the events of our lives onto the left side of Figure 5 —the causal side. Even if we do not know the reason for a particular set of events, we imply that a reason exists. In the early version of quantum physics a similar situation existed. Through the uncertainty principle spelled out in 1927 we recognized that it was impossible to know both the space-time coordinates and the energy-momentum (momentum is the mass times the velocity) of an object as it existed.

By 1935 with the classic paper of Einstein, Podolsky, and Rosen known as the EPR paradox[18] (EPR being the initials of the authors), things had changed. This paradox showed that events happening elsewhere could have meaningful acausal consequences for events happening here and now. These latter events would resemble the distant events in some essential manner—a kind of psychic connection—even though the elsewhere and here-now events could not be connected in any causal way. In one of my earlier books,[19] I described this paradox in great detail. Thus these events would be mappable on the right-hand side of the cross.

Now there is an essential difference between the two sides of the cross and a vital connection between them that I wish to make that concerns the model of the dreaming universe. The left-hand side corresponds to what we would call memory—the linking up of events that are not occurring now with events that are. This process necessarily takes us out of the here-now and into our heads—our intellects, so to speak.

The right-hand side is *felt*. It is not thought about. It cannot be experienced this way. It is a feeling that gives rise to knowing without thinking. It is a recognition that things are as they are. It is a realization of a deep connection that can immediately be broken by logical dictate. It is affective and emotional rather than intellectual. To the extent that we say left-hand-side events become deathlike as a result of analysis, right-hand-side events become alive as a result of experience—coming to our senses. Learning a new thing creates this feeling. Falling in love does, too. And most important for us here, it is the synchronous right-hand side that plays a role in the visual information that we experience in dreams.

I will suggest here that dreams deal with synchronous events and are consequently experienced without words or thoughts.[20] When we awaken from the dream, the synchronicity appears to us. We remember the pictures and then we put them into words; we tie our experience of synchronicity to our logical way of putting events together. We, so to speak, write our scripts, tell our stories, and attempt to "make sense" of the dream. But I ask us to consider, are we thinking when we are dreaming? I will look into various theories about this later.

The process of making the dream into a narrative is of course an intellectual one. Intellect attempts to rule our waking life, but at its own disservice; it creates the loss of the sense of magic that arises through synchronicity.

Experiencing Synchronicity

It is in Jung's concept of synchronicity that we come close to the theme of this book. Before I make the connection, let me first tell you about my own experience with synchronicity. In 1979, I was given the opportunity to present the ideas of quantum physics to a large group of Jungian analysts at the annual meeting known as the Panarion Conference. I hadn't known then that Jung was quite into the new physics and had spent a good deal of his time with Wolfgang Pauli. He felt in his later years that physics and psychology had to have a common basis. This was due to the subjective element contained within both Einstein's ideas of relativity and, according to quantum physics, the necessity of the observer's presence in all physical experience.

According to relativity, the experience of time and space was dependent on the observer's frame of reference. Two observers moving relative to each other could never exactly agree on the time and space intervals separating two distinct events. If, for example, one observer saw and experienced the two events as occurring at the same place in space but separated by a time interval of three seconds, a second observer, moving with respect to the first at eight-tenths the speed of light (which is admittedly beyond our present human capacity but nevertheless possible in theory), would experience the two events separated by a space interval of four light-seconds (the distance covered by light in four seconds) and, amazing as it may seem, by a time interval of five seconds—two seconds longer than the first observer.

The period of time of one second is not important. If we replace the second by a minute, year, or even century, the difference would be in terms of minutes, years, or centuries. Thus, e.g., three years seen by observer one would be seen as five years by observer two.

According to my view of quantum physics, every act of observation by a human observer of an event is an act of recording the event. This record takes place simultaneously in the mind of the observer and physically as "out there." This "out there" experience is not out there until it is a recorded experience "in here." This is sometimes referred to as the "collapse of the wave function."

During the Panarion Conference I met with Dr. Marie-Louise von Franz, whom I mentioned briefly before. She is the author of several books on Jung's concept of depth psychology and physics.[21] She gave me an insight into the difference between the studies of physics and psychology. This insight bears directly on Jung's concept of synchronicity, the physicist's creed of mapmaking the physical universe, and the nature of time.

We physicists are following the time-honored Greek tradition of *reason* and reason beyond reason in all that we do. We, through the ideas of Einstein especially, have learned to map the physical universe. That is, we have taken the dynamic experience of time—that of living experience—and made it into a spatial and nontemporal experience. We have spatialized time.

Indeed the space-time diagram is such a map. It shows the where and *when* of experiences as if they were all where-experiences. We have successfully reduced the rhythm of dance to choreography and lost our rhythm in the process. We have explained the universe and not realized that by doing so we are only expressing it as a map laid out on a plane (indeed that is what it means to ex-plain anything).

Quantum physics is like the archetypal trickster. It laughs at us, peregrinates, and hooplas as it shows that no map contains it. Every act of observation is a surprise. Nothing is as it seems. Prediction is a statistical affair.

But the quantum trickster has even more surprises up her sleeve. She, through physicists Albert Einstein and later John S. Bell,[22] has shown that the map can sing! It shows us that there is a meaning to acausality. She has said, "If you insist on a rational universe, I will give you a rational way of understanding the nonrationality of it."

During the past few years, particularly since I became greatly interested in the subject of the relationship of physics and consciousness, synchronicity has passed my door many times. Just before completing my second book dealing with physics and consciousness,[23] I had a remarkable experience one evening during the writing. I had just completed a section concerning the Cabala and the nature of projective language. Toward the end of the day I was writing about how written music, like the projective-analogue use of the Hebrew letters, is also used as projective language. The musical notes scored on the musical staff cause the music to be heard in the mind by the composer. As happens often to writers, I suddenly realized a good example of this—Ludwig van Beethoven and his composing of the Ninth Symphony while he was stone-deaf. Thus I wrote words to that effect.

That evening, after returning from a neighborhood Christmas party, I was struck with the sudden fancy to read a paper having apparently nothing to do with what I had just written. Now it is not a synchronicity that this paper was written by Fred Hoyle, the noted astronomer, and that my first name is Fred. After all there are many Freds in the universe. Maybe we all like each other enough to read each other's papers and books. The paper was part of a preprint series on astrophysics and relativity,[24] and I hadn't read it previously.

I had settled in my bed for a quick read just before dozing off, as was my custom. Astonishingly, Hoyle had written about, of all things, the parallel-universe theory in quantum mechanics—a subject that, as you can see from my previous writings, is very dear to my heart. Briefly, he was describing how he had found it difficult to comprehend quantum physics once he had comprehended it! In other words he realized as I hoped to have shown in my previous books that quantum physics contains an essential mystery. That mystery is that no one knows how, from the multitude of possible and probable events predicted by the quantum probability function, any single event actually occurs! That is how the collapse of the quantum wave function actually occurs.

I was struck by Hoyle's writings on three accounts. First, I hadn't expected that he would be writing about this from the title of the paper. Second, I hadn't realized that he had, according to his own writing, dropped from physics in 1938 to study astronomy because of this incomprehension. Finally, I was impressed by the apparent synchronicity that Hoyle's writings were somehow paralleling what I had written just that day. Namely that according to the Cabala, there is one mystery that has never been resolved: How it is that anything at all exists!

But that was not enough for me even to include this description here. It was what I had read next that struck me uncannily. Now such events as I am describing to you happen often enough to me. My life is not a linear causal affair. With my midlife career change and my realization as a writer, I had begun to work in a highly nonlinear manner. For example, I might write chapter nine first and then jump to chapter two followed by a rewrite of chapter six, etc. I jump around and by doing so maximize my probability of realizing synchronistic events. So much so that I hardly even notice them anymore.

Now comes the punch line. Hoyle had come to the conclusion that the future determines which choice occurs in the present. Somewhere out there in time yet to be lies the reason and cause of the events that take place now. Again I was excited. I had come to a similar conclusion in the book I was writing. In order for a reality to be created, a quantum wave had to travel out to the future, and a feedback from the hoped-for future event had to return in time to the present. This mixture of waves was responsible for the way things are now.[25]

I then began to read the next paragraph, which was seemingly out of context with the rest of Hoyle's writings. It concerned Handel's *Messiah,* which Hoyle confessed to always admiring. He then quoted the passage:

> Behold, I tell you a mystery: we shall not all sleep, but we shall
> all be changed, in a moment, in the twinkling of an eye, at the
> last trumpet. The trumpet shall sound . . .[26]

He then related that last trumpet to the collapse of the wave function, which creates reality now. He next related the story of how Beethoven wrote the Ninth when he was deaf! He asked how Beethoven could even write music at that time. He concluded that Beethoven was being guided by a particular component of the cosmic signals from the future.

After reading this I was blown away. Not only was Fred Hoyle writing about Fred Wolf's interest, he was advancing my own thesis by using as an example the same Beethoven analogy. Furthermore, the chapter that I was writing concerned that very subject. Music was an analogical code. The notes on the paper were able to be heard by the composer as projections of themselves.

Now my logical mind could dismiss all this as acausal nonsense. And there is no sense for it to be comprehended with. There is no cause-effect reason for these events to conspire as they did. The example of Beethoven links to the present writing of that same example.

Thus with hindsight we see that the future was the cause of the present. The cause-effect mind can accept this in some manner. After all, Hoyle wrote the example before I did. But I didn't know that! I hadn't read it. As a further synchronicity the example confirms Hoyle's and my thesis. Namely that for an event to occur now, a confirmation "handshake" across time must take place. Thus there is the further synchronicity of the Beethoven example serving the cause of the theory being put forward by the two Freds, who are in turn writing their theories across time in different parts of the world and at very different times—unknown to each other.

What Are We to Make of Synchronicity in Relation to Dreams?

If we assume that dreaming and waking awareness are a continuum, one blending into the other, then it is synchronicity that reflects aspects of the dream in waking life.

To draw this conclusion, I need to consider carefully synchronicity in the light of quantum physics. I already mentioned that in quantum physics it is possible to have two events that are not casually linked influence each other. Earlier I mentioned the EPR paradox and how it indicated that two (or more) events that are physically unconnected could be meaningfully connected simply by their observation.

There is nothing special about the EPR paradox in that it is not just some add-on to the theory of quantum physics. Rather it is an essential element of it. The key idea of it is the wave function. This appears or can be imagined to be a field that exists in space connecting one object to another. This field however cannot be imagined to be a physical field such as a gravitational field or an electromagnetic field. It is a field of possibility.

Suppose we have two objects. Suppose that these objects have interacted at some time and now they are far apart. According to quantum physics, neither object has a definite position in space. Instead, each object has only a probable location, and that probability depends on the quantum wave function. This function provides a map of the possibilities of locating each object. It keeps track of the possible locations of both objects simultaneously. The objects are not independent of each other even though they may be far apart, and if one of the objects is suddenly located or observed, the other object will also be observed. An observation changes the wave function map and thereby changes both objects instantly. This is as close to a synchronicity that physics can come—the instantaneous correlation of two separate objects via the action of observation of one of them.

The dream is also a map of possibility. In the dream state the observer is not localized to one region of the brain. The observer is distributed throughout the brain and is picking up information from several memory locations simultaneously. The quantum wave in the brain is dependent on all of the possible locations of the observer so that memory recall in one location is instantly correlated with other locations, giving rise to surprising and meaningful overlaps of what are usually separated memories.

Thus the dream takes on a bizarre quality as images that, normally kept apart, are blended. The dreamer has entered the unconscious mind, and there is synchronicity going on all over the place.

*E*ARLY PSYCHOLOGICAL AND PHYSIOLOGICAL DREAM RESEARCH

An independent reality in the ordinary sense can be ascribed neither to the phenomena nor to the agencies of observation.

—*Niels Bohr*
Atomic Theory and the Description of Nature[1]

Having just looked at the theories of Freud and Jung, we now need to consider the early psychological and physiological research outside Freud and Jung. The above quote from the work of Niels Bohr, although pertinent to the description of atomic phenomena, should be noted in examining both the present and earlier psychological and physiological theories of dream research.

How should dreams be investigated? In many ways dreams are like atomic phenomena—they are not independent of the observer. When we look at atomic events, we ascribe an order to them after the fact. We never actually observe an atom or a subatomic phenomenon. Our machines only record tracks and electronic blips that tell us that something happened. But the interpretation is ours and is highly dependent on the theory we are using. Not only this, but the observer of these events must prepare his experiment in a certain way to gain knowledge of this fleeting world. Because of the complementary nature of physical reality, no experiment ever gives us a complete picture of the microworld.

In a similar way we must regard dreams as if they were atomic phenomena. Theories and interpretations of dreams depend on how they are investigated, and there are outstanding differences in both theories and interpretations. I will later point out how Freud and Jung differed. And we must keep in mind that a dream is a personal subjective sequence of events that we only learn about from dream reports that, like the tracks of subatomic events, are after the facts. Thus the dream and the dreamer can really never be separated. When we look at Jungian archetypes, this will become especially apparent.

The Prophetic Power of Dreams

Let us now get a brief historical perspective on dream theories. Probably the earliest notion of dreams was that they were messages from the gods. Such descriptions can be found in early records of Egyptian and Sumerian cultures. They can also be found in the writings of the Bible, especially the Old Testament, Grecian plays, historical accounts of Herodotus and Artemidorus in the later Roman period of the second century A.D., and the stories of the Greek poet Homer.

The common thread found in these accounts was the idea that dreams came from somewhere else: they were not the product of the human brain that dreamt them. Of course, we need to keep in mind that little was known about the brain during these periods, and considering the work of Julian Jaynes,[2] even human consciousness was very different from our own.

Julian Jaynes in his book *The Origin of Consciousness in the Breakdown of the Bicameral Mind* theorizes that early humans had no real consciousness and that they walked around in an automaton state of trance consciousness akin to some form of a dream state.[3] The idea that humans were in trance states akin to our recognized mental disease called schizophrenia further posits that when this trance state was broken, humans went through an evolution of consciousness.

Carl Sagan in his book *Dragons of Eden* considers seriously that there is a connection between dreams and evolution. He quotes Aeschylus, who once wrote in *Prometheus Bound:*

At first senseless as beasts I gave man sense, possessed them of mind. In the beginning, seeing, they saw amiss, and hearing, heard not, but like phantoms huddled in dreams, the perplexed story of their days confounded.[4]

Sagan points out that Aeschylus is perhaps telling us that early prehumans lived their waking lives in a state of consciousness akin to what we would call dreams.

What did these dreams tell of? According to ancient views, they spoke of the future, and they had healing power. When they spoke of the future, they gave accounts that suggested that the fate of humanity was determined—a theme we find evident in the role of mythos in culture.

There are many such accounts of the gods speaking to men and women through their dreams. Egyptian scrolls record the dreams of the pharaohs; in the Bible we have the prophetic dreams of Joseph and the story of Jacob's night battle with an angel. Even David is visited after he takes Bathsheba as a bride. There are historical accounts of Hannibal's response to his dreams, and we also have records of the dreams of Sophocles and Socrates.

The Healing Power of the Gods in Dreams

Most significant in this regard were the dream temples of Aesculapius. Today we find on the Greek island of Kos the Aesculapieion, a relic to those early days when people went to be healed by sleeping and dreaming in the temples. There, patients with various forms of illness were treated following the methods of Aesculapius. These temples were referred to as hospitals.

Who was Aesculapius? A man or a god? Aesculapius, whose actual name is somewhat obscure, is believed to have been a man by some researchers.[5] Homer referred to him as a historical personality, a mortal man who was a poet, philosopher, a man of kindness and compassion who tended to the sick.

Yet other Greek writings say that he was "the most humane of gods"[6] This admixture of god and man reminds one of the accounts of Jesus, and for that matter, during the reign of early Christianity, the cult of Aesculapius was a major competitor as a world religion.

Why this admixture? Because the technique for cure seemed to work according to historical accounts. For example there was the case of Hermo of Pasos who sought help for blindness and was cured by the gods but refused to pay for his treatment and was then struck blind again by Aesculapius, who later healed him when he paid up. In another story a lame man was cured by Aesculapius by his driving a cart and a horse over the lame man's legs! In another story, a mute girl regains her voice when she sees temple snakes approach her and she screams out for her parents. A "barren" woman dreamt in her temple sleep that a snake settled in her stomach, and she was later able to bear five children.

The technique for healing can be reconstructed by reading these early accounts. First a patient would come to the temple and be greeted by the priest-physician at the gates. There the patient would relate a brief history of the ailment, and he or she would be screened for admission. Probably the patient would then undergo a washing of the body in a sacred spring. This was for both cleanliness and purification of spirit. After this, he or she would make an offering to the gods and would then spend some time in prayer and sacred-song chanting. During the day attention would be paid to diet and exercise. But at night the "real" work would commence when the patient would recline on a couch within the temple and sleep and dream.

Dream healing was considered by ancient physicians to be the highest form and best therapy for the treatment of illness. Aristides in his work *Oratorio* wrote:

When the priest-physician came, ready to help with his own light, the dreams of the patient were revealed to him. Hearing them [the priest] yielded to the god because in his priestly wisdom he recognized the True Physician prescribing.[7]

One might reflect on this in light of the work of Arnold Mindell.[8] Mindell believes that the body contains the dream and that ailments of the body will be reflected in dream content. We will look at Mindell's work more fully in a later chapter. Perhaps this accounting by Aristides says something similar. The priest yields to the patient's account as a message from the god. In our worldview this message comes from the body and would be called "body wisdom."

Aristotle on Dreams

However, it is with the beginnings of the early Greek period of rationality that we find the roots of modern dream research, and it is

Aristotle who broke the spell of the gods.[9] Aristotle lived around 340 B.C. and rejected the notion that dreams came from the gods or for that matter from any external agency. He wrote: "It may be concluded that dreams are not sent by God. . . . Nor are they designed [to reveal the future]."[10]

Aristotle believed that dreams were the objects of sensory perceptions that remained with humans even when asleep and these perceptions were no longer present. He called them residual impressions and said that their unusual qualities came from three sources: (1) the lack of exercise of any form of reason or logic during dreams, (2) the residual impressions that remain with us and impact dreams just because of this lack of reason or logic, and (3) the ability of dreams therefore to be uncontrolled and capable of breaking up into other forms like eddies forming in a river.

In a later chapter we shall follow up on Aristotle's observations concerning the lack of logic and rationality in dreams. As I will point out, there is a good reason for this. Dreams represent an action in the brain that precludes linear logical forms. It is, in Freudian terms, the embedding of the id.

Of course it was possible that a dream might have a prophetic content, but Aristotle believed that this was mostly coincidental. In those rare cases where a dream might have a healing effect or prophetic effect on the dreamer, he wrote:

> Movements which occur in the daytime are, unless very great and violent, lost sight of. . . . In sleep the opposite takes place, for then even trifling movements seem considerable. . . . The beginnings of all events are small, so, it is clear, are those also of diseases and other affections.[11]

Thus it would be possible that small movements or the beginnings of a disease could be sufficiently amplified during sleep to cause a dream or, for that matter, set in motion a course of action that the dreamer, upon awakening, would follow.

Dreaming: The Line Between Divinity and Insanity

Although Aristotle's views concerning the negation of the divine origin of dreams had been presented, it wasn't until the sixteenth century that a dividing line began to occur in the world of dreams. This line marked the dream border as a crossing from divinity to insanity. Dreams began to be looked at as having diminished association with divine messages and greater association with insanity and irrationality in mental illness. Consequently, there was a shift to regarding dreams as serving as a diagnostic function in the same sense that one would look at wounds as indicating illness.

This marked a move from theology or spirituality to pathology. This milestone showed that the waking world was becoming more concerned with the rational function of the mind and less with the irrationality of the gods.

Dreams are no longer messages about the future; they are tied to the personal past—the link with the supernatural is severed. We are now reasoning. We are analyzing and separating "us" from "them"—those who dream irrationally and those who "forget" their dreams. We separate the orderly, logical "us" from the crazy and unreasonable "them." The same dichotomy also takes place in ourselves. Hamlet said, "I could be bound in a nutshell and count myself a king of infinite space were it not that I have bad dreams."

So we begin to maintain a "healthy" reasonableness as far as our outside image is concerned—our face to the world—but inside something else is going on. After this "scientific renaissance" the ability to own up to this irrational core of ourselves decreases as indicated by writers of this time. It wasn't that sixteenth-century writers who challenged the origin of dreams as godlike were attempting to single out this area of human concern. They were challenging everything else as well. They were just participating in the scientific discourse that began to arise in thought. But mental aberration quickly moved into the void left by the departure of the gods.

Thus the road is paved for the rational, and along came Descartes, who sauntered into the fray to enlighten us all. By the end of the sixteenth century madness was no longer a sign of the gods but a sign of a malfunctioning of a human brain. The same is true for dreams. With their religious or spiritual context undermined and their primary function of divinity or prophecy nullified or supplanted, a general separation occurs of luminal states of mental activity from any relation of transcendence. As divinity retreats and insanity advances, creativity becomes a bridge between these polarities and makes dreaming an important process in Western culture.

First Elements: A Physiology of Dreams

Aristotle's views, particularly the negation that dreams came from the gods, were acceptable until the midnineteenth century. Although the study of consciousness occupied the thoughts of humans from as far back as the early Greeks, by the midnineteenth century, the success of mechanistic thinking led European thinkers to engage in great rounds of speculative thought and, where possible, experimental investigation into mechanical solutions for what was called the mind-body problem and its relation to dreams.

The first elements of what we now call physiology emerged from a mixture of Newtonian mechanics, Maxwellian electromagnetic theory, mechanical speculations, and plain hard research into the nervous systems of the bodies of animals. These elements however led to experimental psychology.

In Germany and Austria, led by Wilhelm Wundt, a student of Hermann Helmholtz, a laboratory devoted to the study of physiological psychology was created in 1879 to attempt to bridge the gap between physiology and psychology. Wundt's work[12] led him to believe that during dreams the brain of the sleeping individual underwent marked changes in physiology. It is remarkable that this early speculation, although based on the studies of that time, has today been confirmed in modern physiology laboratories in the study of sleeping animals.

Wundt's chief discovery concerned certain deficiencies observed in dreams, notably the absence of consistent logic, the inability to remember dreams, and the seeming lack of good judgment during the dream. He predicted that the psychophysiological conditions of sleep, dreams, and hypnosis were essentially the same in that they all appeared to alter the ability of the person to maintain or have any willpower over the events that occurred or appeared to be occurring to the person. He believed that the brain must be undergoing some form of transformation during these "states" of consciousness.

Wundt's basic idea is called reciprocal interaction. It can be likened to a conservation theorem in physics[13] or perhaps to a cause-effect mechanical device. Basically it states that if some form of activity characterizes the brain during normal waking functioning, then if during dreams there is a lack of some aspect of that functioning and a surplus of some other characteristic functioning, then likewise a decrease in activity in one part of the brain should occur with the concomitant rise of activity in another.

For example, sensory data is often amplified during a dream. A sound in the room, if out of the ordinary, can sometimes appear in the dream as a great roar or possibly overwhelming noise of perhaps a passing train or falling waterfall from a dam. Thus Wundt would predict that the centers of the brain associated with sensory input would demonstrate greater electrical and/or chemical activity with a corresponding decrease in such activity in those centers associated with, for example, logic.

Physiological Mind/Body Research

In order to understand the dreaming brain and to grasp the startling hypothesis that the material universe dreams, we need also to look carefully at physiology, the study of the cellular-neurobiological-physical basis of living things. This requires us to look at the physical basis of the so-called mind-body problem. This problem has resulted in more thinking than any other philosophical problem that exists. Basically it asks, What is the relationship between mind and body or, if you wish, between the soul—sometimes taken to be synonymous with the mind—and the body?

I wish to focus on physiological studies of the brain and its relation to sleep and dreaming. In particular I want to look at a brief history of such studies up to the beginnings of modern neurobiology. In a later chapter we shall look at the current dream physiological research of such workers as J. Allan Hobson and his group at the Massachusetts Mental Center and Jonathan Winson and others at the Rockefeller Institute in New York, as well as mention other researchers.

Nineteenth-century workers studying consciousness would often find themselves dancing on the line that separates brain function and its organization from the structure and function of the psyche. Here I wish to make a clear distinction between experimental physiology and experimental psychology, particularly in the early days, although as we have seen, the two often overlapped.

An excellent study of the beginnings of scientific dream research can be found in *The Dreaming Brain* by J. Allan Hobson.[14] Part of the factual descriptions in what follows comes from this source.

Almost every science finds its roots in early Greece, and the study of the science of mind and matter is no exception. Probably the first question ever asked about the relationship of mind to matter was, Where does mind exist? The early Greeks debated the location of the human mind in the body. Although I am sure there were several likely candidates, the chief locales to emerge in Greek thinking were the brain and the heart. Aristotle (384–322 B.C.) believed that the mind lay in the heart, and it wasn't until experimental studies by Galen (A.D. 99–129) that the issue was seemingly decided. Galen, who was born in Pergamon where the ancient dream temples to the god Aesculapius (the god of dreams) were built earlier, convinced himself that the brain was the site of the mind, and therefore, consciousness.

Galen performed experiments on Barbary apes—quite crudely, I would mention, when compared with our modern scientific methods. He found that if he literally squeezed the heart of the animal the ape remained conscious, while if he squeezed its brain, it went unconscious. He also tied off the nerves leading from the brain to the animal's vocal chords and found that afterward the animal became incapable of making sounds. This led him to the idea that the brain was also the control center of speech. Thus from these early experiments, the seat of consciousness and the mind was discovered to exist in the brain.

Galen's discoveries and his theory that the brain was the seat of human consciousness, although based on the study of apes, were accepted throughout the Renaissance, as evidenced by the descriptions and drawings of the human brain made by Leonardo da Vinci (1452–1519) and careful dissection of the human brain by Vesalius (1514–64). Following this, study of the brain through dissection became standard procedure. Then came attempts to find just where in the brain consciousness could be located. This led to a number of theories and the study of phrenology, which ascribed specific aspects of human personality to specific areas of the brain cortex (the surface of the brain). Such attempts to localize seats of consciousness culminated in 1861, when Paul Broca correctly located the speech center in the left hemisphere of the brain.

The attempt of early neuroscience to map psychic forces in terms of physical parameters is echoed in modern research. Hobson points out that this attempt may be fraught with a mistaken conceptual basis. Today we are faced with a neurobiological search for consciousness that is largely based on classical mechanistic thinking. Hobson advises that neurobiology is still a long way from explaining psychological functioning. Thus such attempts must be governed by caution. I would echo this caution. I believe that we will not be able to understand the physical basis of consciousness without including the principles of quantum physics and a very new concept of what constitutes the action of observation. I will return to this question and its role in dreams and consciousness in a later chapter.

Humans Dream Electric Sleep

Here we may begin to ask, What is the main physical basis of consciousness that has been discovered? The answer today is found in the electrical activity of the nerves—a discovery that also has its history. The English anatomist Charles Bell (1774–1842) and the French electrophysiologist François Magendie (1783–1855), through their studies of the conduction of electrical energy as nervous impulses from the brain to the muscles and from the sense organs and skin into the central nervous system, were the first to point out that a reflex action was taking place.

Bell and Magendie's discoveries made a strong impact on theories of the mind as earlier exemplified by the German mathematician Gottfried Leibniz (1646–1716) and English philosopher John Locke (1632–1704), who held contrasting views. The question was, What happens to consciousness when one is asleep? Was consciousness just a result of sensation, and if sensation stopped, did consciousness also cease? Although these two died before the discoveries of Bell and Magendie, Locke and Leibniz tended to debate this issue and whether consciousness even existed during sleep, i.e., if it was suspended or continuous with waking awareness. Leibniz believed that there are innate ideas in consciousness that continued even into sleep, thus persisting without apparent sensation. Locke, disagreeing with Leibniz, believed that consciousness depended on sensations and asserted that sensations were experienced at a reduced level during sleep, thus still influencing the mind.

Even Isaac Newton (1642–1727) got into the fray with the idea that consciousness produced by sensation was carried by subtle vibrations of "spirit" along the nerves. Based on Bell and Magendie, this subtle spirit was first identified as electricity and later as the flux of ions traversing the nerve membrane. Thus as the nineteenth century commenced, a serious search for the brain-based mind had begun.

As in physics, we cannot leave out the contribution of the French philosopher René Descartes (1596–1650) to our understanding of the mind-body problem. On November 10, 1619, Descartes figured out just about everything there was to understand in the universe. He had locked himself up in a heated room during an unexpected snowstorm in Bavaria. He remained there for two weeks. According to him, he had three visions/dreams that linked together the understanding of the laws of the universe and the mind. He said, "I think; therefore I am."

I sometimes think that this statement is fraught with confusion. I would take it to mean that thinking or mind exists, therefore this implies that the body exists. The reverse statement, "I am, therefore I think," is not, however, true. Thus, according to Descartes, the body could exist without a mind to perceive it. But if there is a mind, then it cannot exist without a body.

Apparently, Descartes meant that he saw a clear distinction between the mechanics of the body and the mechanics of the soul or mind, which I believe Descartes took to be the same. Today he is credited with the theory of dualism—the separation of mind and body. However, in his day, the soul resided in a small part of the brain —the pineal gland, which is often thought of as the "third eye."

"Dualing" Cells

The question of dualism influenced the thinking of the Spanish neuro-anatomist Santiago Ramón y Cajal (1852–1934), a contemporary of Sigmund Freud's who is today considered the father of modern neuro-biology. He studied individual nerve cells and was the first to recognize the neuron as a discrete functional unit. This was the beginning of cellular biology of the brain. Although he was quite excited by the idea that the brain could be thought of as a colony of communicating electrically conducting polyps and that this realization could eventually emerge as the physical basis of consciousness, he was skeptical of the idea and remained a dualist believing in the separation of mind and body.

Cajal is best known for his work in drawing nerve cells using india ink and watercolors. However, it is his attempt to picture the human mind in terms of these communicating electrical polyps that lie above our nostrils that most interests us here in spite of his own skepticism. Consciousness somehow arose from this activity, and somehow information—the ability to think and feel—arose here. Thinking and feeling must, therefore, be reduced to the electrical-chemical activity of nerve cells. But how? Are the ego and the id of Freud's thinking to be found in the folds of the cortex of the brain? Would Cajal say, "I have a cortex, therefore I think I am"? Or does Cajal remain skeptical, clouded in the mists of the mind-body mystery, unable to penetrate the wall that separates the mind from its body?

What Do Little Neurons Do?

More followed. In the late nineteenth century at the same time that Cajal established the discreteness of the neuron, other workers were establishing the reason for the neuron—its function. The discovery here was the *action potential*—the electrical movement of a pulse along the body of the neural cell itself. Many workers contributed to this discovery, beginning with physiologists Luigi Galvani (1737–1798) and Alessandro Volta (1745–1827), who studied electrical nerve action in frogs. The galvanic skin response, a measure of skin resistance to small electric currents, is credited with Galvani's name, and the concept of voltage in electricity is named after Volta.

By 1875, Richard Caton was able to record the electrical activity of the brain and make the first *electroencephalogram,* now called simply the *EEG.* A cellular analysis of the so-called reflex arc and the interplay of excitation and inhibition of nerve cells was carried out by Charles Sherrington (1857–1952), who wrote the now classic *The Integrative Action of the Nervous System,* published in 1906.[15]

Although the exact processes of nervous electrical energy were just being mapped in the nineteenth and early twentieth centuries, today we recognize that the nerve cell conducts electricity from the cell body down its long tail called the axon. At the axon the electrical energy is converted into chemical messengers, small molecules that travel from one cell to another, thus stimulating the receiving cell to do the same thing or to inhibit it from doing so.

Thus, nerve cells communicate with each other by means of chemicals—called neurotransmitters—that travel from one cell to another. An action potential (a pulse of electrical energy) travels along the surface of the nerve cell from the main body to its axon. This electrical activity causes extracellular ions (charged particles that lie outside the cell body) to exchange with intracellular ions (charged particles that lie within the cell body) resulting in an electrical imbalance that supports the propagation of the signal. When the signal arrives at what is called the synaptic gap—a separation between the nerve cells—it causes the neurotransmitters to be emitted from small boutons contained on the excited side of the gap into the synaptic space.

When these molecules arrive after crossing the one-hundred-ångstrom distance (about one hundred times the length of a single atom), they create a condition in the other cell that either causes this cell to suck in extracellular ions, stimulating the cell to fire, or causes ions already in the cell to rush outward into the extracellular space, thus inhibiting the cell from firing. Sucking in is called excitation, and rushing out is called inhibition.

The question is: Does this reductionistic view say anything about consciousness?

Consciousness Is What Consciousness Does

It appears to me that the above subtitle has much to do with the physical basis of consciousness. Perhaps we are seeing not what consciousness is, but *what it does.* It alters probabilities of material events within the nervous system. If we can credit the physical basis of consciousness to electrical activity of nerve cells, then it would appear that if Eccles and I are right,[16] this activity is to some extent mediated or controlled by probabilistic events that are in turn modified by the role of observation.

Now what can be observing at the event scale of such a level as individual molecular vesicular emission is certainly another question. Many physiologists believe that such events are so rapid and random that human or animal consciousness could play no role in altering them. This of course puts a lower limit on consciousness in terms of space and time and effectively confines it to the spatial and temporal scale of ordinary events. However, there is today no real evidence that the mind should be only effective when it deals with inches and fractions of a second, although there is considerable debate on such things as subliminal awareness.

If mind could act on such a scale, what would that imply? First of all it implies that consciousness, whatever it is, can be looked at reductionistically—something that is also quite debatable. This means that our consciousness is somehow composed of subtle smaller units of consciousness—which, if correct, somewhat echoes the skeptical vision of Cajal.

Granting this hypothesis, then what does a small unit of consciousness do? The answer is, it chooses. But what governs that choice and what are the choices? Here we need to consider the integrative action of consciousness just as Sherrington considered the integrative action of the nervous system. Individual units would of course make very limited choices. They would consist of either noticing or not being aware of some change in the unit's environment or internal state. When we integrate all of the smaller units of consciousness, we arrive at a functional mind. This mind would appear to be making choices that are quite complex but would be made up of billions of smaller choices. A macroscopic choice would thus consist of a polling of these smaller units. In this manner, this macroscopic mind would make choices that are quite observable.[17]

The Ant Colony Model of Consciousness

The relation between microchoices and macrochoices would be reciprocal. These large-scale choices would then in turn affect the smaller units, which then respond and affect the whole consciousness, in much the same way that an ant colony affects the movements of individual ants and they in turn affect the movements and activities of the whole colony. Studying a single neuron to understand consciousness is somewhat like watching a single ant in order to grasp what the whole colony accomplishes.

Secondly, mind acting on a molecular scale implies that consciousness may exist at all levels of matter, even atomic and subatomic levels. Now, nothing in physics yet posits the existence of such units of microconsciousness. But it is just this aspect of consciousness that forms the bridge between the idea of mythic reality and physical reality and may be the solution of the mind-body problem if it does.

First Physiology of Dreams

I will leave this hypothesis and return to it in a later chapter. I wish now to continue with the physiological evidence of dreams, particularly in the early 1950s. First we will look at the early research of the discovery of the correlation between the rapid eye movements (REM) during sleep and dreams, including a brief history of the roots of this discovery.

As I mentioned, it was first the measurements by Richard Caton of voltages generated in the brain that started this line of research. Caton's research led to the work of German psychiatrist Hans Berger (1873–1941), who was able to amplify these tiny signals and analyze them in what we today call the EEG.

In the period between 1929 and 1933 Berger noted in a series of papers that the EEG from the scalp showed a ten-cycle-per-second rhythm (now called alpha) whenever a subject closed his eyes. Upon the subject's opening his eyes, the rhythm disappeared. Berger thought that the entire neocortex was involved in the production of the alpha wave. Later experimental studies at Cambridge showed that the alpha was generated in the primary visual cortex. But the significance of the alpha was still unrecognized.

Although these experiments were interesting, no conclusive evidence for what sleep was used for was found. I must emphasize that Berger actually performed such experiments on human subjects, a not-too-common procedure. When he published his results, the academic community was shocked. Many skeptics did not believe that these waves were actually generated in the brain but were an artifact of the recording device itself.

To convince his critics Berger decided to see if the recorded signals changed when the subjects changed their states of consciousness. His experiment was remarkably simple and convincing. He instructed his subjects simply to close and open their eyes for brief periods of time. When the subjects closed their eyes as a prelude to falling to sleep, he noticed an increase in their brain activity—particularly the appearance of strong rhythmic variations in the form of sinusoidal waves (simple repeating oscillations) of eight to twelve cycles in a second (eight to twelve hertz). As I mentioned, today this is called the *alpha* rhythm. When Berger's subjects opened their eyes, the alpha rhythm vanished. If this was an instrumental artifact, one would be hard-pressed to come up with an explanation of how it arose.

Next alpha was studied as subjects with their eyes closed fell asleep. Berger found that as the subject drifted off to sleep, the alpha changed into a bewildering pattern of other EEG patterns. Sometimes the EEG showed waking-state patterns and at other times there were spikes of 14 CPS lasting for about a second. Random patterns of 2 to 3 CPS also appeared. Berger's instrument showed that the amplitudes of the signals rose and the frequency slowed to what we now call *slow-wave* or non-REM (NREM) sleep.

What these patterns showed was that sleep was not a continuous state but several distinct states. This was objectively seen as spontaneous rhythmic electromagnetic waves emitted by the brain, which were picked up by applied scalp electrodes. These rhythms would seem to indicate that the brain is active even in sleep in the absence of strong sensory input, thus refuting Locke's original theory. With the occurrence of NREM signaling, most of Berger's critics were silenced.

Kleitman's Eyes and Aserinsky's Babes

Although more than twenty years had passed since Berger's work, and the EEG had become one of the major tools in the study of the human brain, it wasn't until 1953 that Nathaniel Kleitman and Eugene Aserinsky, a graduate student in physiology working under Kleitman at the University of Chicago, made a major breakthrough connecting the dreaming brain with its physical activity.[18]

Nathaniel Kleitman was a major researcher in dreams. He studied sleep in the 1930s and 1940s. At that time, although it was certainly known that dreams occurred during sleep, no one knew how long dreams lasted or how often they occurred. Kleitman measured whatever could be monitored, such as temperature, blood pressure, respiratory rate, and heart rate, during the waking-sleeping cycle.

The EEG was the most important tool used to monitor electromagnetic signals generated by the neocortex. This was done, as I mentioned above, using electrodes pasted to the scalp. Kleitman found by monitoring a person over several days that body temperature actually varied over a twenty-four-hour cycle and was lowest at midnight and highest at noon. Heart rate and blood pressure lowered during sleep.

Respiratory rates were found to vary. Some researchers found that the rate increased and others that it decreased during sleep.

Kleitman also attempted to alter the twenty-four-hour cycle. In 1938 he and others spent thirty-four days in Mammoth Cave, Kentucky, living on a twenty-eight-hour cycle. He found that some people altered their cycle to twenty-eight hours while others did not. In another experiment he deprived people of sleep to see what would happen. He found that people exhibited bizarre behavior, which suggested that they were hallucinating.

Aserinsky at first studied the slow rolling eye movements in sleeping infants. He wanted to correlate a relationship between deep sleep and eye activity. While watching the infants, often observing them for long painful hours, he noticed distinct periods when the eyes were quiescent and other times when they moved in rapid bursts.

One could say that Aserinsky stumbled onto the now well-known phenomenon of rapid eye movements or REM. What was interesting to Aserinsky was that during these rapid movements, the infants had little if any bodily movement. In fact it was the lack of bodily movement coupled with the rapid eye movement that alerted him that something new had been discovered.

Aserinsky and Kleitman then decided to study this phenomenon more systematically, this time with adults instead of children. Because adults usually have some trouble falling asleep in lighted rooms in a laboratory setting, they decided to monitor their subjects in the dark. They attached electrodes to their subjects and monitored eye movements and other electrical signals coming from the sleeping subject's brains using the EEG.

As expected, REM was also observed in sleeping adults, in clusters at particular times during the night. The first REM took place within an hour of falling asleep. A typical cluster did not consist of continuous REM but of spurts of REM interspersed with slow eye movements (SEM). The REM-SEM cycle lasted about ten minutes during the first REM period, with three or four other REM periods, each period lasting longer, as the night went on.

The findings confirmed Aserinsky's earlier observations: REM periods were interspersed with periods of no or slow eye movements. Aserinsky and Kleitman also found interesting correlations of the REMs with a number of other physiological responses including electrical brain-wave activity, respiration increase, heart-rate increase, and pulse increase together with irregular rhythmic patterns indicating that some kind of disturbance was occurring in the sleeping subjects. What could this disturbance indicate?

Kleitman and Aserinsky believed that these REMs indicated emotional disturbance and tested this hypothesis by waking the sleepers during or shortly after the REM period. The sleepers invariably reported that they were experiencing a dream during the REM period. It appeared that dreaming occurred only during the REM periods.

Their conclusion was at first speculative, but it appeared to be that emotional disturbances as recorded by instruments were correlated with the onset of dreams. This was the first time in history that the dreaming brain might be showing itself to outside instrumentation, or if you will, it was the first time the internal experience of a dream was being observed by objective viewers outside of the dreaming brain itself. Thus they postulated that when we dream, our eyes are moving in much the same way that they move when we are watching something occurring in waking life.

Later William Dement, a former student of Kleitman's, confirmed the hypothesis that REM during sleep indicated dreaming. When normal subjects were aroused from REM sleep, they invariably gave reports of visual activity indicating that they were dreaming. If the subject was aroused during a REM period when the eyes were moving less rapidly, the subject's report was usually less vivid. In contrast, when subjects were aroused from REM periods during the most active eye-movement periods, the subject usually reported more vivid details.[19]

There were a number of interesting questions to ask about the relation of REM to dreams. Was the early postulate that the REMs followed the actual passage of the dream person through the dream correct? Did the person in the mind's eye see visions that the real person's eyes were tracking? Was the variation of the other physiological functions also correlated with the action in the dream? For example, if I dream I am falling out of an airplane, will my heart rate and respiration rate increase as I fall imaginally in the dream?

What about sexual arousal? Researchers were soon able to notice that male erection and female vaginal lubrication occurred during periods of REM sleep. Did this indicate that the subjects were having erotic dreams?

If any of the above questions could be answered affirmatively, it would be an extremely useful way to observe dreams and their relationship to waking life. For example, would it be that some people suffered more anxiety dreams than others as demonstrated by the physiological functions? Could we tell where the dreamer's dream person was going by following the eye movements? If he looked up, did it mean he was moving upward in the dream? Perhaps we could determine that a person was flying or climbing stairs simply by watching the eyes in REM. Perhaps sexual dysfunction could also be studied this way, if indeed the erection or lubrication indicated sexual arousal in a dysfunctional person.

Well, there were a number of studies. But the answers are not definitive, although there were certainly indications of such correlations.

How Long Is a Dream?

Let's begin with time. Perhaps the length of the dream correlated with the length of the REM period. If so, this would certainly indicate some correlation between dreamtime experience and the movements of the eyes.

Probably one of the first reports describing the correlation of objective time (the time ticked off by clocks) with dreamtime was given by Alfred Maury (1817–1892).[20] Maury was a pioneer in the early-to-mid-nineteenth-century study of dreams and sleep. He was perhaps the first to attempt to analyze dreams by self-observation, in particular the effect of external stimulation on the dreaming brain. He was also particularly interested in the complex procedure by which visual images began to occur just at sleep onset. These are called *hypnagogic hallucinations.*

One evening in 1861, Maury had a dream that started people thinking about the relation of external time to dreamtime.[21] Maury's dream took him back to around 1793, the time of the French Revolution, and the Reign of Terror that took place in Paris. He reported watching a number of murders. Brought to trial by a tribunal, he was condemned to the guillotine. Then he was put into a cart along with other criminals and pulled through the streets of Paris past mobs of jeering people. Arriving at the scaffold, he was forced to mount the stairs leading to the "deadly lady." His hands were bound behind his back and he was laid on his stomach with his head through the stiles and on the block with the dreaded blade some tens of feet over his head.

Suddenly he felt the blade of the guillotine separate his head from his body!

Wow! Well, such a dream is not easily forgotten and Maury awoke from it with a start. He was, to say the least, feeling quite anxious. Then he discovered something quite astonishing. The top of his bed had come loose and fallen, striking him in the neck in just the place that a well-aimed guillotine would need to strike to separate head and body.

What are we to make of this dream and Maury's report? Did the dream occur in just those few milliseconds (thousandths of a second) when the bed top fell? Did all of those events happen in the brief time that the top was hitting his neck? Perhaps the bed top was loose and he noticed this just as he went to sleep. Maybe this had disturbed him and he had the thought that it might fall on him. This might have provoked the dream so that he had a normal dream that coincidentally ended just as the loose part fell. If so, it was a remarkable coincidence. How is dreamtime related to real time?

Freud, when hearing of this story, believed that this "dream" was really the report of a fantasy that Maury had thought about well before the dream and that the occasion of the falling bed top aroused this fantasy upon awakening.[22] On the other hand, Maury believed that the whole dream with all of its intricate and lengthy narrative parts was a flash in the brain that occurred in the interval between the blow and his awakening. He thus came to the conclusion that dreams are very short in actual time with many events squeezed together. Of course we know of stories that supposedly when a person is dying, his whole life flashes before him at the moment of death.

Ambrose Bierce in his story *An Occurrence at Owl Creek Bridge*[23] told of a condemned spy in the American Civil War who was to be hanged from a rope tied to the middle of a bridge over Owl Creek. As his body is dropping causing the rope to grow taut, the rope breaks and he falls into the creek. Dragged along by the rushing waters many hundreds of feet, he escapes his tormentors. He climbs ashore and begins a long adventure where he meets people, eats meals, sleeps several nights, journeys back to his home, and so on. But near the end of the story, he finds that something is wrong in the events he experiences. They begin to take on an eerie quality.

Suddenly the rope tightens, choking off his air and killing him. It was all a dream: a dying man's last look at the light of the earth, all in his mind and taking place in the few thousandths of a second it took his body to reach the end of its rope.

Do all dreams happen in a flash? Or do short dreams coincide with short periods of REM and long dreams coincide with long REM periods? Dement and Kleitman investigated this by awakening subjects either five or fifteen minutes after the onset of a REM period. They asked the dreamers if they had been dreaming for either five or fifteen minutes. Most subjects' reports coincided with the actual length of the preceding REM period. They also had more descriptions of dreams that occurred in the longer REM periods than in the shorter. Thus a person awakened after five minutes would tell the researchers that his dream was five minutes and not fifteen, and his dream would be of a shorter description, for example.

This might seem conclusive, but was it? Does this really show that the length of time of a dream is the length of time of a REM period? Philosopher Norman Malcolm argues that this is not a conclusive result. The length of time is determined from the description after the fact of the dream. It could just be, for example, that during a fifteen-minute REM period, there is a greater likelihood of having a short and incident-dense dream than in a five-minute REM period. In other words, the length of time of the dream and the REM time may be correlated but not the same.

In another experiment, reported by professor of psychology David Koulack, an attempt was made to correlate external stimuli with dreamtime.[24] The external world can cause dream events, as we have seen in Maury's report. Thus a splash of water on the face of a dreaming person, light enough not to awaken him, could induce a dream of wetness, or a water or liquid image. The experimenters measured the time between a stimulus and the awakening. In the case of ten subjects where the stimulus was introduced as part of the dream content, they found a correlation between the dream report and the length of time between the stimulus and the awakening. The researchers calculated that the dream action took the same time as if the dream events were real-life events.

In other words, suppose a person dreams of riding an elevator from the ground floor to the top of a twenty-story building. Suppose he dreams that he has wet feet (the researchers apply a water spray to the dreamer) when he gets in the elevator and that he jumps off the top floor at the instant when he arrives, thus awakening himself. The length of time between the wetting of the dreamer (the stimulus) and the jumping off (the awakening) would be found to correlate closely with the length of time it would actually take to ride an elevator from the ground to the top floor of a twenty-story building.

Koulack attempted to improve on this. He applied weak electrical shocks to the wrists of sleeping subjects after they had begun REM sleep. He then awakened the subjects either thirty seconds or three minutes after applying the shocks. In those cases where he could identify the presence of the shock in the dream report, he asked the subjects if in the dream they could determine the presence of the shock either thirty seconds or three minutes before he awakened them. In eleven of twelve cases where the stimulus was incorporated in the dream, the subjects judged the presence of the shock correctly.

This data would indicate that not only do we dream in REM periods but that the dream takes place in actual time and, from the random onset of the shock, that we dream during the whole REM period. Thus dreams seem to be lengthy rather than fleeting flashes.

But what should we do about Maury's report? And how do we answer all of these other questions regarding the correlation of eye movement and other neurophysiological data, such as respiration and pulse rates, with the events of the dream? Does a correlation exist between obvious sexual-organ physiological changes and dream content?

The Problem with Dreamtime Is the Dreamer

It would seem that all of the questions could be answered if the first could. In other words, it all hinges on the time that a dream lasts. The major problem in determining time is the dreamer him- or herself! The only way we find out about the dream is after the fact. We cannot get inside the dreamer's brain and watch the dream as it unfolds in spite of all of the neuro-correlates. The dream report may be a grossly amplified story of a flashing of events. It is even conceivable that during REM periods such flashes occur very briefly, perhaps for only a second or two, with varying intensities or brightness.

The number of flashes or the brightness of them may be greater during longer REM periods than during short ones. Consequently, most of the REM period may not be visual but may be an attempt to correlate the visual information with memory—in other words a kind of thinking or data-correlation process. When dreamers are awakened during a longer REM period, they are more likely to be awakened during the thinking process and attempting to remember the visual flash. Thus any external stimuli introduced during the thinking process would also be correlated with the attempted memory of the visual experience. That would explain the time awareness of these external stimuli and would explain Maury's dream.

Why do I suggest this in spite of the apparent data contradicting it? What, if any, experimental evidence would suggest that dreams are complete in a flash? In a later chapter we will look at the outrageous possibility that we don't dream at all! Are there any psychological data to indicate the duration of dreams? We will look at this question in the next chapters. There we will also look at modern neurobiological dream research and the remarkable hypotheses of Hobson and his activation-synthesis model and Winson and his evolution of the dreaming-state model based on his experimental evidence. But first we will look at the brain-mind problem in a slightly different light that will help us to understand that the role of time in the brain and its relationship to consciousness are far from obvious.

CHAPTER 5

THE MECHANICS OF CONSCIOUSNESS: THE WORK OF BENJAMIN LIBET

The world thus appears as a complicated tissue of events, in which connections of different kinds alternate or overlap or combine and thereby determine the texture of the whole.

—*Werner Heisenberg*
Physics and Philosophy[1]

So we have seen how the division of rationality from irrationality, so well put forward by the end of the sixteenth century, led the way to a mechanistic view of everything. Not only were we discovering mechanism in the outside world of physical matter, we were also seeking it in the inner world of our minds. We sought our minds in our brains and neurons as if they were cogs and wheels endlessly whirring on. Among other topics, we looked at how research attempted to correlate the dreaming brain's dreamtime with clock time, and we speculated on the possibility of a mechanism within the brain and nervous system that chooses specific outcomes from a field of possible outcomes resulting in awareness.

But that still left a mystery and several unasked questions. First of all, ever since Freud's discoveries we have been faced with the fact that we seem to do things unconsciously. Why? What purpose would nature have in evolving a human brain so that it processes information unconsciously? Dreams appear to operate unconsciously. At least we do not seem to be able to manipulate ourselves consciously when we are dreaming. But is that always true? What marks the border between conscious and unconscious processing of information? How does the consciousness work in the brain? The answer seems to be, paradoxically, unconsciously and retrospectively. Instead of "I think therefore

I am," it is now more evident that "I am and later I think about it or am even aware of it."

At least this is what we might conclude from the work of Benjamin Libet. Libet's data is so fantastic and yet so compelling, one often finds it difficult to talk about it without becoming embroiled in endless debate.

The next question refers back to Freud's concept of projection. What is meant by that process? Freud implied that wars occur because human beings project the death wish from their psyches out into the world. In a similar manner we project the life instinct out there every time we consider compassionately another's welfare. Is perception a projection from the psyche?

In this chapter we will explore Libet's remarkable results, which indicate that not only do we operate unconsciously most of the time, but we project our instincts and our perceptions "out there," and we may even be projecting the "out there,"—our sensual experiences of space and time—out there. I shall also offer some more speculation about what this has to do with the nature of our unconscious brains in their relationship to dreams.

A Brief History of Unaware Time

Libet's findings began in the late 1950s. Working with brain surgeon Bertram Feinstein at Mount Zion Hospital in San Francisco, Libet, a neurophysiologist, began by studying patients in the operating room who, for one reason or another, needed to have a procedure performed wherein their brains became exposed to a surgeon's knife. In order to monitor the postoperative patients, Feinstein implanted electrodes in the brains for some period of days. Later they were able to study the patients outside of the operating room, which was much more productive for Libet's research. Libet pointed out to me that Feinstein, who died in 1978, was a remarkable physician because he was willing to carry out such experiments with the consent of his patients. Often surgeons are quite fearful of doing anything to patients outside of the necessary surgical procedures dictated by their diseases.

By the time of Feinstein's death, Libet and his associates had completed the work for the now famous 1979 paper on subjective referral,[2] which I will be telling you about shortly. Libet continued with the study on volition afterward, which did not require electrodes in the brain, by working on people not requiring surgical procedure using scalp electrodes.

How We Create Time and Space in Our Brains

What Libet has found can be said simply, but I doubt if it will be believed simply. It is that our minds operate mostly unconsciously. This means that we make decisions and respond to sensations from the outside world totally unconsciously. We only become conscious of the outside world much later (about half a second later—a long time on the neural level), after the slings and arrows of our fate have already passed us by or struck us. But then there is an interesting twist: we refer the late moment of conscious awareness back in time to the moment of sensation and out in space to the location of a stimulus even if it is outside our bodies.

The first is called temporal referral, and the latter is called spatial referral. Spatial referral has been known for some time. For example, if the brain of a subject is stimulated in a particular area of the cortex, the person will feel sensations in the body. We all know that we see objects "out there" in space, and yet the mechanisms by which visual images are reconstructed are located within our brains, neural networks, and retinas. In a similar manner we reconstruct from sounds, that is, vibrations of our eardrums, the approximate location of the sound's source in space. That is why we look up when an airplane passes overhead. This is called subjective referral in space.

Libet's experiments had to do with time. Although one might expect some delay between the timing of the conscious awareness of some event, assuming that such awareness can even be mapped in time, and the time when a stimulus is applied, it was assuredly a surprise to find that the delay could be as much as a half second. A lot happens in a half second. A baseball crosses the plate in less than a half second's time, and yet the major league batter does manage to strike the ball for a base hit, at least around 20 to 33 percent of the time. An animal darts out into the street ahead of your car, and you manage to hit the brakes in less than a half second from the time the headlights reflected from the animal to your eyes. Yet in all of this, Libet would argue, the person involved is totally unconscious of the sensory signal at the time of reaction.

Libet refers to his theory of consciousness as "time-on theory" or subjective referral in time. His data show that a person, although able to react quickly to stimuli within a hundred thousandths (one hundred milliseconds) of a second, is not actually aware of what he or she is reacting to for several hundred milliseconds, up to a full half second.[3] Yet when interrogated about the time of awareness, a person responds as if he or she were aware at the time of the stimulus.

An example of this is a hundred-meter runner at a track meet. He leaves the running blocks at around one hundred milliseconds after the sound of the starter's gun has reached his cortex. Accordingly, some 400 ms later, he becomes conscious of the gunshot. By this time he is well on the way toward the goal, perhaps five or so meters from the starting blocks. Yet if we later interrogate him about his experience, he will say he was consciously aware of the shot at the time he pushed off from his blocks. As amazing as it may sound to us, Libet claims that it is not possible for the runner to be conscious of the shot even though he is responding to it as if he were.

Backward Through Time Experiments

Libet showed this result in a series of fascinating and carefully controlled experiments. It is important to understand his results as we attempt to build a model of consciousness, particularly as we come to the conclusion that the unconscious processes are far more important in our lives than we can even imagine and that a lot of our experience of the world is projected from our subjective "inner" worlds.

Now what happens in the brain when a stimulus is applied to the skin of a subject or when a shot is "heard"? Of course if the stimulus is so slight as not to be felt, nothing will happen. So we need to consider skin stimuli (SS) that are at the "threshold" of sensation. This is what Libet used.

To grasp Libet's findings completely, it is necessary to look carefully at the form of the signal as it is detected on the somatosensory cortex. One finds that it consists of four distinct "time zones." (See Figure 1.) The first time zone of the signal is a sharp electrically positive potential that arrives 15 ms after the skin stimulus and persists for around 35 ms (S1). Libet believes this pulse serves as a time marker, a referral signal for "apparent" conscious awareness. This is quickly followed by a deep and wide negative potential that persists for around 100 ms (S2). Thirdly, we find a low positive hump lasting around 150 to 200 ms (S3), followed, fourthly, by a shallow negative potential lasting for around 200 to 250 ms (S4). All together, the sum of intervals (S1 + S2 + S3 + S4), composing the complex signal, lasts for around 500 ms.

Libet showed that there is no conscious sensation of this until the full five-hundred-millisecond period of the total signal has passed. In other words, the brain needs to have all of this signal passing into the somatosensory cortex before any awareness of the skin stimulation is consciously felt. If, for any reason, certain parts of the signal are blocked out, say for example S1 is received but S2, S3, and S4 are not, the person will not be aware of the skin stimulus. In fact, Libet has shown that the S1 response is not even necessary for awareness. When Libet and his coworkers stimulated the cortical surface they found that people became aware even though no S1 response was present. Thus no one is aware of any stimuli until 500 ms have passed.

Earlier experiments by other researchers also established this. If you put a patient in deep anesthesia, signals S1 and S2 still tend to arrive with each cut of a surgeon's knife, but blessedly, the patient remains without any sensation of pain or awareness that surgery is going on. The anesthesia tends to wipe out the later parts S3 and S4. It is these later parts that must be present for consciousness of the patient to be achieved.

Further evidence that people are unaware of these skin stimuli when S3 and S4 are wiped out comes from using drugs such as atropine, which is directly administered to the brain. Finally the clincher of evidence comes when a train of electrical pulses is directly applied to the somatosensory cortex around 200 ms after the S1 pulse has already arrived. Again the person has no awareness of any skin stimuli and only becomes aware of the brain stimulus 500 ms after *it* has been applied to the brain.

Thus in the latter clincher, by the time the train of cortical electrical pulses is applied (200 ms after S1), both S1 and S2 will have already arrived. But S3 and S4 will be wiped out. In this case the person reports no sensation of skin stimulus.

Libet thus showed that conscious awareness only comes when a certain time period, around 500 ms, has passed. He calls this the time of "neuronal adequacy." If neuronal adequacy is not achieved, awareness does not take place. But what is amazing about his result is the subject's apparent report of awareness when it does occur. It appears to the subject that no delay in awareness has occurred at all. The subject reports awareness of sensory input within 100 ms of the S1 part of the signal. Of course this is coincident with the time "he should" be aware since it is coincident with the time of the stimulus.[4] But nevertheless, it is impossible that he could actually have been aware of a stimulus at the time of the S1 signal. This is the "subjective antedating hypothesis."

More evidence supporting this hypothesis comes from the neural delay experienced by subjects when Libet directly stimulated the cortex. When you stimulate the surface of the cortex, the form of the signal is radically changed. It consists of a train of electrical pulses around sixty or so in a second (CS). The strength of the train of pulses is adjusted to a threshold level so that the person feels nothing unless the train persists for 500 ms. If the train is on for less than 500 ms, the person reports receiving no sensation. If the train lasts for at least 500 ms or longer, the person reports perceiving the sensation. For such threshold signals, this would indicate that the person feels the CS only one-half second after it has been initiated. There is clearly a delay, and it makes sense that there should be a delay.

Here there is no S1 part of the signal present. In other words, you don't get the fast early signal at all. As Libet put it, "you are not stimulating the incoming pathways. So they don't have any [time marker] referral at all."

Now what happens if you compare two stimuli: the CS and the skin stimulus (SS)? There are three cases to explore.

1. Suppose for example, you begin with an SS and 200 ms or so later you stimulate the brain with a CS. As long as the CS comes after the SS by no more than 500 ms, the person reports no sensation of the SS, but if the train of the CS is sufficiently long, around 500 ms, he does report sensation of the CS. Conclusion? The CS wipes out the awareness of the SS.

2. Next, suppose you begin with a CS and 200 ms or so later you apply an SS. Now something apparently amazing occurs. Even though the CS was applied before the SS, the person reports feeling the SS before the CS. In other words he subjectively refers the SS back in time to the time of the marker signal S1 that came after the CS train was started. This result is perhaps the most important, and we shall refer back to it later.

3. Next, suppose you stimulate that part of the brain called the medial lemniscus (ML) with a similar train of pulses (MLS) as you did for the CS. The ML is on the direct pathway for the fast signal (S1). (Just in case you wondered about all of the electrodes sticking in people's brains, often in clinical procedures electrodes are inserted in the ML for the purpose of controlling pain.) Libet applied an electrical train of pulses to the ML similar to those that he applied to the surface of the cortex. He adjusted the intensity just to the threshold level so that it also took a half second of train to be felt. But in the case of the ML train, each pulse of the train generated a S1 fast signal that arrived at the cortex, just like the skin stimulus signal.

Libet's hypothesis predicted that, even though it would take a half second of stimulation, subjects should refer the MLS back to the beginning of the signal, unlike the cortical signal. The prediction was borne out. Since each MLS pulse contains an S1 early-evoked positive pulse as a time marker, a reference point in time is present. Remember the CS does not have such a marker. Thus if you turn on the MLS before the SS, the person reports that the MLS occurs before the SS, in the correct time order, with both signals being referred backward in time to their appropriate S1 markers.

There is other evidence. In experiment two above, Libet moved the time of the skin pulse down to the end of the half-second cortical train. The patient then says that the two signals are together even though the SS was applied 500 ms after the onset of the CS train. This is evidence that he is referring to the primary evoked potential, S1, because it is now coinciding with the time when the cortical train becomes adequate.

So if you stimulate the skin at exactly the time in which the signal being applied to the cortex is ending, becoming adequate, the person then says that the two signals are simultaneous, even though he is not going to know about the skin stimulus until a half second later as deduced from the other evidence. So he says in this case that both are occurring at the same time.

There is Always a Delay in Consciousness

Libet's findings suggest that there is always a delay between a stimulus and consciousness of the stimulus regardless of the presence of a timing S1 signal. All electrical activity resulting in eventual conscious awareness will take time to develop. Most signals won't be referred back in time. The only conscious experiences that are referred back in time are the stimuli that have primary timing signals, S1s. Nonsensory conscious experiences do not have a timing signal. It is only a special class of inputs that do.

In Libet's theory there will be a delay in conscious awareness all of the time. In another experiment, Libet worked with a patient who had suffered a unilateral stroke, only on one side. The stroke lacked the S1 signal to the somatosensory cortex. The patient could feel stimuli in her bad hand, but there had to be a great deal of stimulation to get her to feel it. In the experiment Libet and his coworkers matched the responses to stimuli to her good hand and the bad hand. They asked her which came first. She said that she felt the good hand first even though both hands were stimulated simultaneously. Only when they delayed the stimulus to the good hand by several hundred milliseconds did she begin to call them together.

Libet, following the work of others, also confirmed that the fast signal, S1, was not only necessary for temporal referral but also for spatial referral. Having established that the brain of the patient with the stroke was not able to perceive the S1 signal, and therefore was not able to refer the stimulus to the bad hand backward in time, Libet also noted that this patient was not able to determine just where in the bad arm a stimulus was applied. Thus Libet believes that, without a fast neural pathway reference signal, a person will not be able to correctly refer stimuli in space or time.

Time Enough

Libet's findings have been strengthened by some recent experiments that have attempted to determine the dividing line between perception and awareness. Perception is a difficult term to define. It may mean more than detection of a stimulus. Libet found a distinction between detection and awareness. It is possible for a person to detect an event without actually being *aware* that a detection has occurred.

Libet proposed that unconscious mental functions might simply be a matter of shorter durations of electrical brain activity. If the electrical train of pulses got long enough, what was unconscious would become conscious.

In the experiment electrodes were inserted in the sensory thalamus of the brain. The thalamus is located more or less at the base of the forebrain. It helps to initiate consciousness and make preliminary classifications of external information. Certain areas of the thalamus are specialized to receive particular kinds of information, which are then relayed to various areas of the cortex. For example, the thalamus houses the lateral geniculate nuclei, which are the first relay stations along the pathway from the eyes to the visual cortex in the brain for analyzing visual images. From the thalamus the signal proceeds to the primary visual cortex.

Insertion of electrodes directly in the sensory thalamus is used for many patients who suffer from intractable pain. It is not a normal procedure, and not many neurosurgeons do this. The technique is to anesthetize the scalp and surrounding area and then insert the electrodes. A subcutaneous coil is wired to the thalamus. An external coil outside the body is turned on, causing an electrical stimulus to go from the internal coil to the thalamus. This relieves the pain in many cases but not all.

The procedure not only relieves pain due to brain injuries, such as strokes in the thalamus, that produce thalamic pain, but also relieves pain from some peripheral injuries (as stated below). Yet even though it is the thalamus that has been injured, subjects don't feel the stimulus or the pain relief in the thalamus, but in other parts of their bodies. Other research discovered that even when there is not thalamic inflammation or pain, this procedure works well, as, for example, on many peripheral injuries such as broken backs and sciatic nerve injuries. Here the electrode insertion to the thalamus is used when nothing else is of help. The only other medicine that relieves pain is anesthesia.

Libet used such patients to examine the duration of the stimulus required for a conscious experience. He could control the stimuli with the electrodes in the thalamus, just as he did with cortical stimuli. He wished to determine whether or not an unconscious stimuli was still detectable, i.e., perceivable. In the experiment he would shorten the length of the time the stimulus was applied to the thalamus to the point where a subject could not feel it and hence was not aware of it. Then he would perform a test to indicate if it was still *psychologically* detectable.

In the experiment a subject was asked to choose or guess when his thalamus was being stimulated. To start the test a little warning signal was sounded. Next one light went on, then a second later another light went on. The stimulus was delivered in either one or the other of those lighted periods. The patient was then asked to indicate which lighted interval contained the stimulus.

Each stimulus was randomly located during the lighted period. Its duration was also random. The results of the test confirmed that subjects could actually detect information without knowing it. Some of the subjects felt nothing at all, establishing that the duration of the stimulus was too short to be noted consciously. The experimenters carried out a preliminary test to determine the level required for conscious awareness. Yet even when subjects felt nothing and were guessing, they got far above pure chance in their correct choices.

Even with trains lasting only one- or two-tenths of a second, well below the 500 ms required for awareness, they were getting well above chance correct in their "guesses." In these cases, the subjects never claimed that they "felt" the stimulus. They were simply asked to guess.

Other results were discovered when the stimulus was applied for around 400 ms. At this level some subjects would become conscious of the stimulus. Subjects reported what their choice was, and afterward they were asked what level of awareness of it they had. In some cases they said that they were aware even if the level of sensation was weak. In other cases they said that they were unaware and just guessing. In other cases they were somewhere in between.

The experimenters allowed for a large range of potentiality by including a button marked "1" to press if there was something felt, i.e., the subjects were conscious of something "there," and another button marked "2" indicating maybe there was something there. The number-two answers were hunches and rationalizations.

But even to get to this level of awareness, it turned out that the uncertain ones required at least 0.4 second on the average for train duration as opposed to feeling nothing and guessing correctly. Libet thus confirmed the theory that conscious awareness was a function of the time of duration of electrical signals and that briefer durations can result in unconscious detection.

The Quantum Mechanics of the Unconscious Mind?

What are we to make of these results? Here I shall not attempt to explain anything. I simply want to explore the mystery. The most important result is the fact that conscious awareness of the outside world, awareness produced through our five senses, requires two temporally separated events: a fast neural signal and a later achievement of neuronal adequacy. It would also appear from Libet's experiments that conscious awareness of the "inside world," as evidenced by the cortical stimulation, the world of our thoughts and dreams, does not require both events to be present.

I had earlier proposed in a paper submitted to the *Journal of Theoretical Biology*[5] that subjective referral was an indication that the brain-mind was operating in accordance to the rules of quantum physics. Consequently, I thought that the fast neural signal (S1) and the achievement of neuronal adequacy (S4) were indicating that a quantum physical message, a time-reversed echo, was transmitted.[6] S1 stimulates S4 to send a signal backward in time to S1.

Libet responded to my suggestion as follows:

> Your suggestion . . . would not explain why, in your quantum theory analysis, there is no echo back to the [start of the train of pulses] in a cortical stimulus (which in fact does not exhibit subjective referral). I.e., why should your echo select out the primary evoked response in a very specific way? Your proposal sounds a bit "ad hoc." It is only with the fast primary pulse that you get the referral.

In cortical stimuli and in the example above of the woman who suffered from a stroke, there was no subjective antedating, no referral of the awareness of the stimulus backward in time. Yet the person was aware of the "location" of the stimulus in some sense. In the example of the stroke woman, she knew that her bad arm was being stimulated, but she wasn't sure where the stimulus was being applied. In the cortical stimuli the person felt the stimulus where no stimuli were applied, but always at a specific body part associated with the appropriately stimulated somatosensory cortical region. Did these projections of experience indicate that we need the S1 signals to find our way in the world, just where we are and when we are there? Or was there something else?

I admit that I was puzzled by Libet's query. Why, indeed, if my theory was correct, did the referral only take place when there was a fast neural pathway signal, S1? Then I remembered watching a recent television show on the Learning Channel dealing with evidence of the "soul," recently produced by the BBC. During the program people who had suffered strokes many years ago, and as a result were unable to feel parts of their bodies, as the stroke woman above, began, after a period of time, to do a very strange thing. They separated their bodies into parts in their minds. They all universally referred to the unfeeling part of their bodies as not their own, as things "out there," separate from themselves. The unfeeling arm was an "it" and never spoken about as "my arm."

Could it be that we need the time-marker signal to tells us where the division between "out there" and "in here" is? Does the marker not only provide a reference, but also a self-awareness? Thus I began to think that the S4 signal was reflected backward in time to the S1 signal to provide the subject-object distinction. Even though the cortical stimuli, as most electrical activity in the brain and nervous system, do not possess referral time markers because there is no reason for them to do so, the projected location of the subjective sensation is just as precise as when the S1 signal is present. Perhaps the S1 signal marks a division between reality and fantasy. In the quantum model, all events send signals both forward and backward in time, but not all of these signals are reflected. Something else is required for reflection.

What could that be?

Apparently the S1 signal reaches into the future, reverberates off the S4 signal, and bounces backward in time, carrying with it S4-information that "awareness" has occurred and all is okay. But when the CS signal is applied, nothing like that takes place. The reason could be that the pulse shape of the SS signal is sufficiently different from the train-of-pulses of the CS.

The CS signal consists of a train of identical pulses. Although each of these pulses sends and receives quantum echo waves, there is nothing distinguishing about them. They are repeats and so no information is distinguished, much as if one were to send and then later receive a series of echoes of the sequence of letters "aaaaaaa..." They would appear identical and as long as the sequence was still being sent, the echoes would not be sensed.

This is not the case with the SS signal. S1 is different from S4 and so when S1 evokes S4 to send its echo backward in time, there is sufficient difference to be noticed. It would be as if a sequence of letters "abcdef..." was sent and what was echoed back was a modified sequence such as "fedcba..." or another permutation. The change in the echoed signal when compared with the signal being sent would be noticed. We need variety if we are to pay attention to the "out there." The "same old" "same old" is not only boring, but it is not even able to enter consciousness as "out there" experience.

This may explain why experiments in sensing the future fail when the sensor becomes too familiar with the remote sensing procedure. It also indicates that without variety of sensory experience, we not only become unconscious of the stimulus, but we may even consider the site of the stimulus to be not "out there" and not connected to us in any way. "If it's boring, it's not worth considering," cries our sensory apparatus. "It is an illusion or nothing at all."

In dealing with the outside world we all make decisions well before the time of neuronal adequacy. Could we conclude from this that the ability to veto an action requires the presence of a fast neural signal? Libet believes that all volitional activity is initiated unconsciously, but that before taking any action it is possible to veto the action even after the event reaches consciousness but before the brain sets off the "motor outflow to act." Perhaps this is the message of the Ten Commandments. Seven of them say "don't do this." Perhaps this is the necessary physical cause of human consciousness, and perhaps this is the dividing line between what we refer to as the outside world and the inner world of dreams: the ability to direct our actions unconsciously.

This is a difficult point to deal with—the question of awareness and choice. Libet believes that the ability to consciously veto an action is not the same mechanism as the ability to become aware of the intention to act. Thus it is possible to change the course of one's actions without the delay required for producing awareness.

In Libet's view, dreams are uninhibited activity of the brain. In the normal wake state when cortical arousal occurs, nothing bizarre seems to occur. One implication is that the inhibitory mechanisms that delimit the spread of activity in the cortex might not be there in the dream state. The explanation of psychoactive drug-induced awareness and the imagery it produces probably involves depression of inhibition.

Once activity gets going in the cortex, it may have certain rules by which it spreads. Without the normal inhibitory mechanisms to stop certain processes, bizarre images and thoughts may occur. In the case of epilepsy or spreading seizures there appears to be a focus in the sensory cortex of electrical activity. All epileptics who have that kind of focus will report the same kind of auras that precede the seizure. Activity spreads in the cortex in a characteristic way. This could result in the same imagery in different people.

Thus Libet suggests that it need not be necessarily that they all have access to a Jungian collective consciousness. There are potential neurophysiological explanations. Or perhaps Libet is pointing to how the collective consciousness actually functions.

Another mystery that Libet explores is memory consolidation. From a number of sensory inputs we build up a complete or consolidated picture of the outside world. Consolidation seems to be absent in dreams as evidenced by the fact that we don't remember most of them, unless we wake up and review them, i.e., consolidate. So obviously something about the functioning of the memory consolidation system during sleep is not the same as during wake.

Libet also questions how we integrate experience, the so-called unity of experience. When we are aware of anything at any given time, we tend to have a unified experience. We have 100 billion nerve cells firing, a great deal more synaptic junctions kicking off, but we

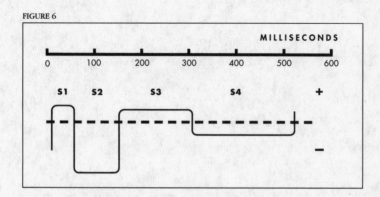

FIGURE 6

A rough schematic of the electrical signal response to a skin stimulus recorded on the somatosensory cortex

experience something that is unified. How does the unification take place?

Here I would suggest, and later I will attempt to show, that unification and consolidation take place quantum physically and are directly related to the ability of the human brain to form from a vast number of events the concept of an "I." The "I" is able to form largely through the activities of the dreaming brain acting through quantum physical synchronistic correlations: To dream, perchance to be.

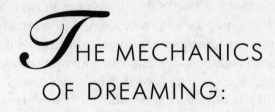THE MECHANICS OF DREAMING: PART I—WE DREAM TO INTEGRATE

The ultimate dreamer of the vast life-dream is finally... but one... and... the multiplicity of appearances follows from the conditioning effects of time and space. It is one great dream dreamed by a single Being, but in such a way that all the dream characters dream, too.

—Schopenhauer[1]

In the last chapter, we saw, largely through the work of Benjamin Libet and his coworkers, how the mechanics of consciousness takes place in the human brain. The mystery of the mechanism is how this leads to consolidation and integration of experience. The answer to this mystery may be found in this and the next few chapters where we explore the mechanics of dreaming.

We begin with some simple obvious questions. Why do we dream? And why are dreams so bizarre? Why are there certain themes in dreams that seem to recur? Since most of us have had dreams of doing the impossible, could these dreams be remnants of our early prehistory? In other words, are dreams simply echoes of our evolving brains?

Take, for example, dreams of flying. Carl Sagan in his popular book *The Dragons of Eden* has us consider that our nighttime dreams of flying and our daytime passion for flight are perhaps nothing more than "nostalgic reminiscences" of our primate brains for "those days gone by in the branches of the high forest."[2] In other words dreams are reflections of our prehuman history.

In this and the next two chapters we shall examine these questions and specifically how they may be answered by some of the research that has been carried out on the mechanisms of dreaming.

Jonathan Winson, a neuroscientist and presently Emeritus Professor of Neuroscience at Rockefeller University, in his book *Brain and Psyche: The Biology of the Unconscious,* and in an article, "The Meaning of Dreams," in *Scientific American,* explains that dreams may reflect a fundamental aspect of mammalian memory processing.[3]

Thus it might appear that we dream because we have a primate brain that still has aspects of a primitive structure. However, Winson points out that these brain-function aspects should not be called primitive. Upon examination one sees that the hippocampus (a structure in the brain) of lowly animals is the same except in size as that of humans. If the brain is primitive, then perhaps we are primitive. Perhaps better than primitive we should regard our behavior as simply the workings of the mammalian brain in which these ancient memory processes are still going on in us. Winson believes that the integrative scheme of processing memories that mammals have also constitutes our unconscious psychological structure. In other words we have an unconscious because we have a mammalian brain.

Today there are also scientists who take dreams to be little more than the unloading of useless information from the nervous system. Dreams are no more than the dump of the computer brain. For example, in 1983, Francis Crick of the Salk Institute in La Jolla, California, and Graeme Mitchison of Cambridge University, England, proposed that dreams were essentially garbage-information reprocessing dumps. They called the process "reverse learning." They hypothesized that rapid eye movements (REM) observed during sleep served to erase spurious associations that arose from vast amounts of information coming into the memory regions of the brain. Thus dreams were a running record of erasures. As Crick and Mitchison put it, "we dream to forget."[4] In the next chapter, we will look at the connection between Crick's hypothesis and the interesting work of network computer modeling. Some striking correlates indicate that dreams could indeed serve an erasure purpose.

Do dreams have any psychological significance? J. Allan Hobson and Robert McCarley of the Harvard Medical School proposed that dreams arose out of the random bombardment of signals from the brain stem (the part that connects the brain onto the spinal column) into the forebrain (thinking region). They suggested that dreams might at times have psychological significance, but in essence they were meaningless.[5]

Hobson, in his book *The Dreaming Brain,*[6] revised his earlier opinion and acknowledged the deep psychological significance of dreams. Hobson believes that each person imposes or projects onto these random signals an order that is interpreted as the dream. He also believes that the brain stem acts as a switch and simply turns on one dream after turning off another. In the third chapter (ch. 8) of the three dealing with the mechanics of dreaming, I will describe Hobson's work in more detail.

Are dreams truly meaningful and prophetic, or are they useless byproducts of an overloaded brain and nervous system? Or are they remnants of our earlier mammalian (perhaps reptilian) brain and serving some purpose of evolution that we still do not know? In these three chapters we shall look at modern dream research, its attempt to bridge the gap between physiology and psychology, and how it attempts to answer these questions.

Dreams of Animals: The Work of Jonathan Winson

Jonathan Winson began his career in science as an aeronautical engineer, graduating from the California Institute of Technology in 1946 with an engineering degree. He next completed a Ph.D. in mathematics at Columbia University and then began a business interest that lasted fifteen years. He had a keen interest in neuroscience and began to do research at Rockefeller University in New York, specifically in the area of memory processing during both waking and sleeping states. By 1979 he had become an associate professor there and although now an Emeritus professor has continued his research on memory and dreaming.

According to Winson, dreaming is the bridge between brain and psyche.[7] Dreams are associated with a physiological process in the brain that Winson and others have discovered. He believes that these processes are also the prime material which act in support of Freud's theory of the unconscious. Winson points out that man's nature is found to be an unusual product of evolution—a joining of a conscious intellect, present only in man, with an unconscious brain mechanism continually active in every individual awake and asleep. This joining has been inherited from our earliest mammalian ancestors.

Winson finds that REM sleep in animals (mainly in mammals) is caused by a basic physiological mechanism in which strategies of behavior based on an animal's experience are gradually constructed.[8] This mechanism is important for survival. He believes that his experimental evidence shows that behavioral strategies are set up in an animal's life during a *critical period* of early growth, and, in humans, set up in early childhood by a similar critical period. The result of setting up these strategies is the development of the unconscious: a complex of conceptions and misconceptions gathered in the earliest years that remain throughout at the "core of the human psyche."

Winson is convinced that the unconscious exists as hypothesized by Freud and later psychoanalysts, and his hypothesis affirms that it is indeed real—a product of evolution and the biology of the brain.[9] His concept of the unconscious as derived from brain function is different from that of Freud. Whereas Freud saw the unconscious as containing an Id *(das Es)*—a caldron of untamed passions and destructive instincts that were held in check by repression from the Ego *(das Ich)* —Winson finds the unconscious to be a cohesive, continually active mental structure that takes note of life's experiences and reacts according to its own scheme of interpretation and responses.

This reaction is reflected nightly in dreams. Winson ascribes a tenacity of unconscious thought even after psychoanalysis has dug to its deepest core. He believes that the sources of a human's irrationality lie in the interests of survival and that nature arranged to have such unconscious traits generally modifiable by experience early in life during the critical period.

Thus in Winson's hypothesis the unconscious is part of the physical structure of the brain. He believes, as well, that consciousness arises in the brain and is not separate from the brain as in spiritual theories such as that of John Eccles (who essentially follows the dualistic picture of Descartes discussed in an earlier chapter).

Welcome to the Hippocampus, the College of Memories

To grasp Winson's hypothesis and later my own hypothesis about the dreaming universe, which is based on a quantum physical model, we need to take a small detour and consider some basic brain anatomy.

First of all, just below the skullcap is a layer of material called the cortex. The cortex, about one-tenth of an inch thick, is like a convoluted rug covering the brain. It is composed of vertical columns that are arrays of neurons running from the top of the cortex to the bottom like tiny cylinders through a carpet. The diameter of each column varies between one- and two-thousandths of an inch. Each column contains roughly 110 neurons.

Each column functions as an input and output device. Although not all of brain processing has been observed, it is now known that columnar processing occurs with seeing in the visual cortex, with pressure on the body in the sensory cortex, and with hearing in the aural cortex.

In hearing, columns detect frequency of sound, in which ear the sound is heard, and the time lag between reception of sound in one ear after the other (this allows the hearer to locate the sound source). All in all, the whole neocortex seems to consist of similar columns, an estimated 600 million totaling approximately 50 billion neurons.

Hidden inside the brain's outer cortex, tucked under the inner wall of the temporal lobe—which looks like the thumb of a baseball catcher's mitt when the brain is seen from the left side—lie the hippo-campus, the amygdala, and the mammillary bodies.

The hippocampus is so named because it resembles the small, marine sea horse (*hippocampus* is the Greek word for "sea horse"). *Amygdala* means "almond" in Greek, and the so-called mammillary bodies are a twin pair of breast-shaped structures hanging from the front part of the fornix region of the hippocampus.

Mortimer Mishkin from the National Institute of Mental Health has researched the flow of information through the neural structures of the brain. Mishkin reports that all sensory systems send inputs to the amygdala, with each sensory system connecting to a separate part of the amygdala. Evidence indicates that the amygdala adds or creates an emotional tone to all inputs. Thus after input passes through the amygdala, the person feels something in an affective mode in regard to the sensory input.

Thus a song by the French singer Edith Piaf may sound sad to us because the amygdala has added a sadness tone to her already plain-tive melodies. Ultimately the amygdala sends all of its information to the hippocampus. All sensory systems also send signals to the entorhi-nal cortex—a region of the neocortex connected to a part of the hippocampus.

What has emerged from this research is that the hippocampus is a major component of the limbic system of the brain necessary for all memory processing. The limbic system was originally an anatomical designation given by Pierre Paul Broca in 1876 to a ring of brain tissue containing the hippocampus, amygdala, and other structures that formed a border (limbus) around a ventricle or fluid-filled cavity in the center of the brain.

The brain, excluding the brain stem, actually consists of two concentric shells surrounding this central cavity. The inner shell contains the hippocampus, amygdala, and other related structures termed the limbic lobe, while the outer shell is called the neocortex.

The term *limbic system* was introduced more recently by Paul McLean to designate the series of structures of the limbic lobe as well as others closely related anatomically. Together this system is composed of hippocampus, amygdala, septum, mammillary bodies, anterior thalamic nuclei, and the cingulate cortex.

It now appears that the limbic system's primary function is to tie memory to emotions. For example, male monkeys without limbic systems exhibit bizarre emotional behavior, approaching enemies that they would normally run from and spending endless hours masturbating or copulating with nearly anything near them. So much for monkeys, what about humans?

As evidence of the fact that the limbic system ties memory to emotions in human beings as well, Winson points to the case of a twenty-nine-year-old man whose initials were H.M.[10] In 1953, H.M., who was afflicted with epilepsy that gave him major seizures, was operated on at the Hartford Hospital in Connecticut. The attending physician, William Scoville, using an extended surgical procedure, removed H.M.'s amygdala, almost all of his hippocampus, and limited areas of his associated neocortex on both sides of his brain.

This radical procedure is hardly ever used today, but perhaps coincident with the McCarthy era of fear, this was the time of psychosurgery when lobotomies "were the rage." After the surgery H.M.'s epilepsy improved somewhat. He continued to have a pleasant personality, and his ability to reason and understand remained intact— virtually the same as before the operation. Although his epilepsy is now under control through medication, today his memory of events that occurred from the time of the surgery to the present is nearly totally absent. He cannot remember events that happened just a few moments ago. He fails to recognize people he has just met with whom he may have spent several hours. If he eats a meal, he doesn't recall having eaten it a few moments later. If you place another meal in front of him, he will eat it. He will read the same magazine over and over again, each time seeing it for the "first time." He is man without any recent past.

Does Winson Test Good Like a Good Theory Should?

Winson's hypothesis is that dreams reflect a basic aspect of mammalian memory processing. Thus information acquired during waking states of awareness are reprocessed during sleep, particularly during REM sleep. This information, Winson hypothesizes, constitutes what Freud called the unconscious.

Recent findings in Winson's laboratory and in other labs around the world indicate that dreams are meaningful, but not necessarily in the ways that Freud and Jung would have envisioned. Winson has mapped the brains of subprimate animals during sleep. He found that the *hippocampi* (which as we have seen are brain structures crucial to memory) and rapid eye movements of animals during sleep indicated that the animal was processing memory during dreams.

From his and others' research, an effect that is believed responsible for memory was discovered. It is called LTP, which stands for long-term potentiation. Timothy Bliss and A. R. Gardner-Medwin of the National Institute of Medical Research in London and Terje Lømo of the University of Oslo found changes in nerve cells that had been intensely stimulated with electrical pulses. Bliss and his coworkers applied a long series of intense high-frequency signals called tetanic pulses (TP) to certain nerve cells. After a long train of these tetanic pulses were applied, they then fired a single electrical pulse. There was much greater activity observed in those cells after the TP than had been observed before the TP. The heightened effect lasted for as long as three days, then returned to normal.

LTP is considered the basic mechanism for how cells accommodate memory or how memory is stored in the brain. There is a further mechanism for understanding how LTP works, although the exact details of the mechanism are not fully understood. For example, since tetanic pulses do not occur naturally in the brain, if LTP is the mechanism, how is it achieved under normal circumstances?

The answer had to do with a particular rhythm, called *theta,* found in the brains of mammals. This rhythm occurs at approximately six cycles per second and is apparently generated in particular neurons of the hippocampus.

But back to the original question: How does LTP occur in the brain if there are no TPs present? The answer came when Rose and Dunwiddie of the University of Colorado at Denver suggested that the occurrence of LTP in the hippocampus was linked to theta rhythm. They actually achieved LTP in cells in the rat hippocampus without using TP, but they were only able to do this when the pulses they did use were separated by the period elapsed between two theta-wave peaks—approximately 200 ms. The hypothesis is that theta rhythm is the natural means by which LTP takes place.[11]

Winson demonstrated the same thing in the hippocampus cells. Then Winson and his associates Pavlides and Greenstein demonstrated a rather subtle effect: memories occur—are recorded—only if they dance in step with theta.

This would give theta a major role in memory processing, yet, it is an interesting aspect that theta rhythms, discovered in many mammals, have never been demonstrated in primates, including human beings.[12]

Winson and his colleagues discovered by recording signals from the hippocampus in freely moving rats and rabbits that the source of theta rhythm was in the hippocampus.[13]

Their first findings were that theta rhythm occurs during specific behaviors that typify the species. It occurs, for example, in exploration in all animals that have been tested because a knowledge of space is essential for survival in all species. But space means different things for different species. For example, theta rhythm occurs during arousal in rabbits but not in rats. If an object moves and a rabbit observes it, a huge theta rhythm will occur in the rabbit's brain, but not in the rat's. Even if the rat is electrically shocked, nothing will happen. Only exploration induces theta in the rat.

Thus theta occurs in those specific behaviors most important to the survival of the species. Exploration is important to the rat, prey behavior is important to the rabbit, and predatory behavior to the cat; and in those activities, theta rhythm is observed.

In lower mammals, theta rhythm does not occur in all behaviors. It does not occur in a rat's feeding behavior even though the rat moves. It does not occur in sexual behavior, even though that involves motion. It does not occur in genetically programmed behavior.

An animal is genetically programmed to do a number of survival things. The one thing it is not genetically programmed to do is to incorporate new environmental information and determine how to use it. It has the structure to do it, but it can't be genetically programmed entirely because environmental experiences are continually changing.

The key to Winson's hypothesis or, as he put it, a first hint is that theta rhythm also occurs throughout REM sleep in the animals he observed. Winson believes that if theta is meaningful in dreams, it may indicate that information input in the waking state during these survival behavioral patterns is being reprocessed in REM sleep.

To confirm this, he first discovered that the sources of theta were two major cell fields of the hippocampus. He found that the rhythms were synchronous (the peaks and valleys in the fields were matched in step) but were phase-reversed (like watching two dancers facing each other, when one moves the left foot forward, the other moves the right foot back) in both cell fields. Winson suspected that this theta rhythm had a functional significance for memory processing. But how did it work?

In a carefully controlled experiment on rats he eliminated theta rhythm by making a lesion in the hippocampus. The result was that the rats lost spatial memory. This indicated that theta rhythm fulfilled a function: it was needed in the hippocampus to encode spatial memory.

In Winson's model of memory, sensory inputs, consisting of electrical signals, converge, moving downward from the cortex into the hippocampus in an awake animal. Theta rhythm partitions these signals into 200-ms parcels called bytes. This allows LTP to take place. For some reason a similar process occurs during REM sleep. Although there is no incoming information or movement during REM sleep, the neocortical-hippocampus network is also paced by theta rhythm.

Two researchers, John O'Keefe and J. Dostrovsky of University College, London, discovered that a rat's memories associated with particular places in the rat's spatial environment are associated with particular neurons in their brains. They called this discovery "place field." They noticed when the awake animal moved to a particular location, certain neurons would fire. They called the location to where the rat had moved those neurons' place field.

In 1989, Pavlides and Winson recorded from pairs of neurons in the rat that had different place fields. In other words when the rat was in one place, one of those neurons would fire, and when it was in another place, the other neuron would fire. They recorded from both cells simultaneously. After determining the normal firing rates in the awake and sleeping animals, they put the rat in the place field of one of the neurons and that neuron fired. They called that coding the space or mapping the location. The second neuron did not fire regularly when the rat was in the first place field, it just fired randomly. They continued to record the two neurons as the rat moved about and went into several sleep cycles.

They studied six pairs of neurons in this manner. They found that the place-field neurons—those that were coding space—fired at a higher than normal rate when the animal was asleep. There was no increase in firing in any of the other neurons if the rat had not gone to those neurons' place fields. The conclusion was that the reprocessing or strengthening of information encoded when the animal was awake occurs in sleep at the level of the individual neuron.

As I mentioned previously, Winson points out that theta rhythm has not been demonstrated in primates. He says that it may have disappeared as vision replaced olfaction as a dominant sense. But there might be an equivalent neural mechanism in the hippocampus that periodically activates certain neural receptors as he claims the theta waves do.

The conclusion is that since theta rhythm takes place in REM sleep, the purpose of REM sleep is to process memory. Thus REM sleep turns out to be an evolutionary factor, a development caused by the reduction of the prefrontal cortex area allowing dramatic reduction in size with evolution. Winson's hypothesis is that dreams reflect an individual strategy for survival. The subjects of dreams are broad ranging and complex but all reflecting strategies for survival.

So much for animals, what about human data and dreaming? Winson points out that from all the psychological data on dreaming, even though psychoanalysts are very loose with their ideas, something has been seen correctly: dreams do deal with psychological questions. Dreams have to be acted out for humans just as in animals. Dreams deal with survival issues—what our unconscious structure believes about survival. Thus, we dream in REM to survive and to refresh memories necessary for our survival. Our unconscious mind is the mechanism that accomplishes this. Thus, according to Winson, "Dreaming is part of the memory process that underlies and gives insight into the unconscious."

Winson's hypothesis offers some explanation for the large amount of REM found in infants. Newborns spend more than eight hours per night in REM sleep, while adults spend somewhat less than two hours in the same activity. Why? Winson suggests that REM performs a special function in newborns that is not fully understood at this moment. Yet by the time the newborn reaches the age of two, the REM sleep is reduced to three hours per night. It is at this age that Winson suggests, when the hippocampus becomes functional, that REM sleep begins to take on its interpretive memory-processing function. We will look at the dreams of fetuses in chapter 8 as we continue to gather evidence for the model that we dream to create our self-concepts.

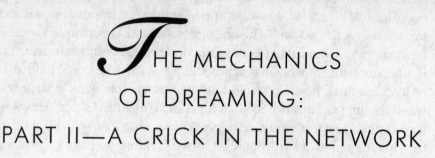

THE MECHANICS OF DREAMING: PART II—A CRICK IN THE NETWORK

There is but One Mind that underlies the dream.

—*Cherokee saying*[1]

The connections in dreams are partly nonsensical, partly feeble-minded or even meaningless or partly demented. The last of these attributes is explained by the fact that the compulsion to associate prevails in dreams.

—*Sigmund Freud*[2]

In their classic paper, Crick and Mitchison propose that the function of dream sleep, specifically REM sleep, is to "remove certain undesirable modes of interaction in networks of cells in the cerebral cortex."[3] This is accomplished by a mechanism called "reverse learning" resulting in a weakening of the unconscious dream trace in the brain rather than a strengthening or reinforcing of memory as Winson would put it.

When this paper was published, a lot of controversy surrounded it. As I pointed out in the last chapter, Crick and Mitchison (C&M) went so far as to say that "we dream in order to forget." In a later paper, they explained that this quote was really a slogan and not a precise definition.[4] They had hoped that the slogan would act as a mnemonic for their reverse-learning hypothesis. They later regretted this slogan since experience had shown them that people assumed far more than they had intended, namely that the function of REM was to delete all the elements of unconscious dreams from memory. This was not intended by them. Instead they would put it alternatively, "We dream to reduce fantasy," or, "We dream to reduce obsession."

Either way this sounds intriguing. Well, what is the reverse-learning hypothesis? Is it a kind of ecology of the mind, a reprocessing of mind garbage? In a sense it is. To grasp their concept we need to review the physiological basis and the computer-model neural-network foundation of their hypothesis.

Upon examination of minute areas of the neural cortex's anatomy, C&M were struck with the fact that the great majority of synapses (places where neurons connect to each other) came from axons (tails of neurons) that originated locally. That means that neurons in local regions of the brain tend to "talk" to each other within close proximity of each other rather than interconnecting "long distance" to neurons that are farther away. Furthermore they found that the majority of the cortical neurons were excitory rather than inhibitory. That means that these neurons tend to respond to input signals by sending out more signals rather than by closing down and not sending out any messages. So instead of receiving a message and not responding, these neurons tend to keep the message moving around, at least locally.

This fact suggested to them that the cortex has a great capacity for self-excitation. A little input stimulus produces a lot of output. This is a useful aspect for associative memory where a reminder evokes a whole memory. This is further supported by various neural conditions such as epilepsy and migraine as well as drug-induced hallucination in which parts of the cortex become so excited that the neurons swing into large-amplitude instabilities.

So what? Well, such a richly interconnected assembly of neurons is capable of being modeled with a computer program, and such models exhibit processes, at least mathematically speaking, that resemble what we would call associative memory. If a small number of "cells" in the model are activated, the network responds by exciting all of the "cells" in the model. Moreover the responses of the network tend to form a set of stable patterns, repeatable whenever a small input occurs provided the input contains a small part of the "memory" pattern. In other words the network "remembers" and reconstructs a whole pattern of "memory" based on a small piece of that pattern.

Such computer models of neural networks have been in vogue now for over a decade.[5] Let me explain how they work.

The model consists of units and connections between the units that can be numerically "weighted." Each unit is rather simple: it can take on one of usually two values, say 0 or 1, or −1 or +1 (there are models with multivalued units as well). Each unit is capable of changing its value depending on inputs through the connections to the unit. These inputs are numbers, usually a weighted numerical sum of inputs from the other units. For example, in the Hopfield et al. network, if this weighted sum is positive, the unit takes on a +1 value, while if the sum is negative, the unit takes on a −1 value.[6] Positive values could be said to model reinforcing or excitory neural behavior, while negative values could be taken to be weakening or inhibitory in real live neurons. Once the unit takes on a value, it sends out its value at random times (or specific times in some models) to all of the other units to which it is connected. Usually each unit is connected to every other unit, hence the name "network."

Now the "weight" in the weighted sum is nothing more than a numerical bias for each connection. For example the connection between unit one and unit two might be +10, while the "weight" between unit one and unit three might be +3. Thus unit one and two have a stronger connection than is found between unit one and unit three. Taken all together, these "weights" can be changed arbitrarily by the programmer, but usually the programmer is looking for a systematic way to alter them in order to produce a set of consistent, stable, and repeatable patterns found in the units.[7]

Furthermore, it was possible to "teach" the network via a simple learning rule in which the weights connecting the units were changed systematically. What resulted from this was that the network would tend to produce a stable array of values for its units. This was called a "memory." This "teaching" could be done several times, each time with a different set of input values for the weights, and the result was that each time the network would learn a different memory. Eventually, the network would "remember" all the patterns stored by changing the values of the weights.

Using this model, Hopfield found a number of stable patterns of unit values consisting of pluses (+) and minuses (−) (I've left off the "1"). Such a pattern of unit values would constitute a "memory trace." Hopfield and his coworkers found that certain memories were easier to access than others even though the patterns were of the same size. Also when memories were learned, spurious memories (resembling but not equaling the stable patterns) were created that weren't "taught." At times a spurious memory would be evoked even though a desired memory was sought. The appearance of these spurious pat-

terns signaled that the network was "overloaded," much like a student's brain crammed for an exam.

Specific inputs to the network via the learning mode could strengthen the desired patterns, thus producing something resembling one theory of brain memory, namely that memory lies in the efficacy or strength of the connections between neurons in the brain. By changing these strengths, i.e., interneural connection plasticities, memories could be reinforced. But, and this is C&M's point, specific inputs could also weaken memories.

Again let me explain this. Having "learned" all that it could, a particular memory is evoked by feeding in to the net any partial pattern contained in the units. For example, if a sequence of sixteen units constituting a memory contained the values (shown in blocks of four)

$$+ + - -, + - - +, (- + - +), + - - -,$$

and the values for cells nine through twelve, shown above in parentheses $(- + - +)$, were fed into the network while it contained a random pattern,

$$****, ****, (- + - +), ****,$$

it would eventually stabilize itself with the same memory pattern formerly shown.

However, if a different partial "memory" was fed in, the result would be another memory pattern. The ability of the network to reconstruct a true and faithful reproduction from a partial memory is what the modelers call associative memory and is the desired outcome. However, some memories were easier to access than others, and the spurious memories did arise from time to time. These "faults" constituted two problems for the modelers: how to make every memory equally accessible, and at the same time rid the network of unwanted bizarre memories. It turned out that one solution solved both problems.

Fantasy, Obsession, and Hallucination
in a Computer Network

At times the model nets exhibited three bizarre spurious patterns that C&M labeled fantasy, obsession, and hallucination. I believe that C&M

saw these behaviors as detrimental to the neural-net theory as a theory to explain brain processes, but I feel that they may actually illustrate common mental processes and disorders and thus should be considered a "success" of the theory. Be that as it may, C&M cautiously point out that although computer neural networks do exhibit properties that are somewhat similar to our brains, this is not conclusive that our brain operates anything like a computer or a neural network.

Let me explain the problem of neural-network overloading and its illness, consisting of spurious memories. Computer neural nets are quite finite—some examples used by Hopfield contained as few as thirty-two units—consequently they can become overloaded if one attempts to store simultaneously too many different patterns or associations of patterns, or if the patterns stored contain too many overlaps or similarities.

This is because the nets operate using a superposition principle—several patterns are capable of being generated by the connections even though the units are registering simple $+1$ or -1 values and the weights are fixed. When a net becomes overloaded, i.e., it is taught too much, it is likely to "get stoned," i.e., exhibit bizarre behavior. In a sense it knows too much and begins to relate everything to everything. Perhaps this isn't bad and is akin to some mystical states of awareness or exalted states of creativity. But if you need to cross the street, you will require the correct associations, not bizarre ones.

One bizarre behavioral network pattern is far-fetched associations or computer "fantasies." You feed in a small part of a pattern expecting the network to reproduce the correct total pattern, and instead the computer fills in the blanks with entirely different patterns. In the typical joke, the analyst asks his patient what a chocolate cake reminds him of. And the patient answers, "Sex." Then the analyst asks him what a flyswatter reminds him of. The patient might respond, "The moon." Overloaded neural networks caught in far-fetched associations are like the patient in the above story. Any input is likely to produce any output with seemingly no sensible connection.

A second bizarre behavior C&M call "obsession." No matter what input you feed to the network, it always responds with the same output. This is like the joke in which the son calls his obsessive mother on the phone and asks, "How are you?" The mother turns this into her obsession, "You don't love me because you never call your mother!" It wouldn't matter what the son had said at the beginning of the conversation, the obsessive mother would turn to the same response regardless. Hopfield et al. jokingly refer to this as the "50 percent of all stimuli remind me of sex" problem, meaning that when their nets were overloaded, 50 percent of all inputs resulted in the same output. No matter what you tell an obsessive person, he or she comes to the same conclusion, usually a negative one.

Finally C&M point out that certain model nets, particularly those that have feedback loops or connections that lead their outputs back into their inputs, exhibit what they call "hallucination." These nets respond to input signals that would normally not evoke any response at all, such as partially complete inputs. This is like the person who hears the wind outside slightly rustle and imagines that the house is being ripped apart by some monster or that the whole house is being torn apart by a hurricane.

How to "Correct" a Computer Fault: Murder It

I must say that I find these bizarre behaviors amusing, and they may be more important than the desired results that the modelers are seeking. However, they are considered to be "faults" of the model, and as such, they need correcting. I am reminded of the scene in the film *The Shining,* directed by Stanley Kubrick, where Jack is confronted by his hallucination of the former caretaker at the Overlook Hotel in Colorado. The caretaker reminds Jack that his child may need "correcting" because the child is far too sensitive to psychic influences. By "correcting," the imaginary caretaker really means murdering.

In a sense that is just what the computer modelers want to do with these unwanted "modes of neural network behavior." And indeed they found a way—by feeding into the networks specific "unlearning" inputs that poisoned the unwanted modes. They started with random states of the network, and when the network settled into an unwanted mode, they changed the "interneural" connection weights by adding slight negative biasing, causing that particular pattern to vanish. Furthermore, they found that the other stable patterns of "wanted" memories remained, provided that the bias they used was not too large.

For example, if the value for a normal learning input was 1, then the value for a "correcting" input would be of the order −.01. Larger negative inputs tended to wipe out good and bad memories equally.

Hopfield et al. succeeded in ridding the networks of the undesired spurious memories, and when the unwanted modes vanished, the accessibility of all desired memories tended to be equal. While in the "overloaded" condition, before inputting the "unlearning" bias, certain memories were easier to access than others. Thus they were able to solve both of their problems by feeding "poison" to the unwanted memories.

Unlearning in Our Dreams

Now there is quite a bit of support from neurophysiology for the "unlearning" theory. Hobson and McCarley (see chapter 8) have shown that during REM sleep major inputs and outputs are shut down, and the brain, like a lonely child locked in its room, is isolated. It is then given random spurts via the brain stem and shows a high degree of electrical activity. This activity results in dreams, which are normally forgotten and only remembered if the dreamer awakens.

These dreams are byproducts of C&M's mechanism. Dreams are "parasitic" memories evoked and witnessed particularly when the balance of excitation and inhibition to any neuron has been shifted to excitation. This disturbance is the negative feedback needed to "unlearn" the neural network.

The computer-model results of "unlearning" discovered in Hopfield's nets tended to support C&M's theory that unwanted "parasitic" modes would be eliminated in REM sleep and that what was actually occurring during REM dreams was "reverse learning." Thus the bizarreness of dreams can be compared to the spurious associated memories occurring in the neural nets.

During the day we take in a remarkable amount of data. We "learn" the world around us. Many of the inputs to our brains are of the type described by the neural networks—partial memories that evoke full memories. Some of these inputs, however, eventually cause the interneural connections, via the synapses, to overload.

When we enter REM sleep, our dreams are the products of neurons feeding back on themselves without stimuli coming in through our senses. As such, they are "negative" feedback loops, weakening the strengths of some of the connections with other neurons much as the negative weight biasing in the computer networks used by Hopfield et al. Thus our dreams turn into "erasure" modes helping us to become refreshed by making desired or important-for-survival memories equally accessible and ridding us of undesirable and bizarre memories—those that do not play any role in our survival. In essence this is the Crick and Mitchison model.

There are of course some objections to the theory. First of all it has been suggested, particularly by Winson and his coworkers, that REM in animals actually helps to strengthen their memories whereas reverse learning would tend to wipe them out. But, as we have discussed, the Hopfield model actually does strengthen the desired memories by ridding the brain of unwanted memories. Thus "unlearning" actually strengthens memory by making desired memories less confusing and of equal accessibility.

A major objection is found in experimental studies of people who are deprived of REM sleep for many nights, usually around one week. One might expect, based on the theory, that such persons would tend to exhibit increased episodes of fantasy and imagination, possibly even hallucinations. This is because if unlearning has not taken place, the unwanted memories would not be erased. Although there is some evidence for this,[8] by and large the general opinion of researchers is that when people or animals are deprived of REM, their behavior is not affected in any obvious or predictable way.

C&M suggest that before this criticism is taken too strongly one must look carefully at the experimental evidence. Waking a dreamer at the onset of REM tends to, after several nights, produce a rebound effect. It becomes more and more difficult to accomplish. By the end of a week's deprivation, the dreamer enters into REM states around fifty times per night, suggesting that in these cases the person may be snatching periods of REM even during the waking hours. Drug-induced suppression of sleep is not much better since drugs are known to produce many side effects that could mask the sought-for result.

Is there any experimental or biological evidence to support the "dream to erase" theory? Well, in a way, yes. Some animals, in spite of having larger brains, do not exhibit REM sleep. Hence we would conclude that they have no way to erase unwanted memories. Yet these animals, including the dolphins and the echidna or spiny ant-eater of Australia, have quite large brains. Why don't these animals REM? And why are the brains of these animals so large?

In comparison to the human brain—if we take the human brain weight divided by the weight of the human and compare this ratio to that of the echidna or the dolphin—we find that humans have a smaller ratio of brain weight to body weight. Possibly the relatively larger brains of these animals is connected to their lack of REM sleep because if you can't REM at night, you will need a larger neural net-work to "absorb" unwanted associations. This would tend to minimize overlaps in the networks of these animals.

Thus, by learning to REM we have adapted to having a smaller brain. We use our smaller brain differently by getting rid of unwanted memories through the "dream to erase" mechanism. Thus, the function of REM sleep is to make advanced brains more efficient and to allow these brains to be smaller than they would be other-wise.

An example of this may be found in the comparison of seals and dolphins. Seals have smaller brain-to-body weights than dolphins, and yet both animals live in similar environments. Seals REM and must be able to hold their heads up, out of the water, while dolphins do not REM and are incapable of supporting their heads out of water. Thus one might conclude there is less evolutionary pressure for dolphins to have small heads (since their heads are continually buoyed by water), while there would be considerable pressure, based on weight alone, for seals to have smaller heads than dolphins—it takes less work to hold up a small head.

Thus animals that have a need to have less brain weight would tend to evolve with smaller heads, but to survive they would need to develop REM. Although this does not prove C&M's theory, it is cer-tainly supported by it. Perhaps if we all were totally aquatic creatures, none of us would dream at all.

And then there is another aspect to all of this. First of all, does a lack of REM really mean that the creature is not dreaming? Something like dreams seems to be going on even during non-REM periods in human beings. In fact one might wish to make a case for erasure-mode operation during "shut-down" slow-wave sleep rather than during the much more active period of REM.

Could REM-ability be indicative of an evolutionary step in the animal kingdom aside from weight considerations? Could it be a requirement for space and time location? In the later chapters I will explore this possibility. Next we need to examine Hobson's theory of the dreaming brain.

THE MECHANICS OF DREAMING: PART III— A QUANTUM LEAP INTO THE LAND OF NOD

[The probability wave] meant a tendency for something. It was a quantitative version of the old concept of "potentia" in Aristotelian philosophy. It introduced something standing in the middle between the idea of an event and the actual event, a strange kind of physical reality just in the middle between possibility and reality.

—*Werner Heisenberg*
Physics and Philosophy[1]

John McCrone in the Science section of the British newspaper *The Independent* reported on the 1991 World Federation of Sleep Research held in Cannes, France.[2] The latest hubbub concerned a new view of sleep and dreaming, particularly the role of REM and dreams. Most researchers were now of the opinion that dreams are a "hangover" from our early womb time.

There are currently three physically based theories of REM dreams. It is commonly held in all of these theories that dreaming largely occurs during the REM stage of sleep. During the so-called slow-wave phase of sleep, there is some evidence of dreams, but the overwhelming data suggests that although thoughtlike processes are occurring, nothing like visual information is being experienced by the sleeper. To determine whether a sleeping person is dreaming or thinking at all, the researchers simply awaken the sleepers and ask them what they recall. We should note that there is no evidence of dreams per se. All we have as evidence are dream reports from awakened people. Certainly you may remember dreaming or not, but not usually during the dream. The one exception to this is, of course, lucid dreaming, which I will discuss in a later chapter.

The first theory states that dreams and therefore REM play a key role in memory processing as discussed in the previous two chapters. Dreams help us sort out and consolidate our day's experiences as in Winson's hypothesis, or they help in flushing away unwanted memories as in Crick and Mitchison's theory.

I mentioned in the previous chapter that the major problem with these theories is that experiments conducted on human subjects in which REM sleep was interrupted or, through the use of certain drugs, suppressed showed that people suffered no lapse in memory functioning as a result of lack of REM even though this interruption or suppression lasted for sometimes over one week. It is hard to do this for longer than one week simply because people begin to go into longer and longer periods of REM sleep on consecutive days following the onset of REM deprivation. It is true that people became more irritable as a result, and it could be postulated that if the period of time lasted much longer than a week, people might begin to hallucinate. This would actually support the theory, in that hallucinations would be taken to be unwanted memories surfacing into the awake brain.

A second theory suggests that REM dreams are caused by random bombardment of certain electrical signals originating in the brain stem and eventually landing on the neocortex, particularly the area known as the associative cortex. We shall examine this theory in more detail in this chapter. This theory suggests that although these bombardments are random and hence taken to be meaningless, the result of these bombardments on the half-aroused mind is for it to try to make sense of the random data. This is similar to what you might do in trying to find a particular shape or face on the moon or in a cloud.

As various hints flash before your mind (and of course we have no idea what this metaphor means scientifically, although we all know what the experience consists of), memories of experiences arise filling the mind with various images. The mind somehow brings all of these disparate images together and from them weaves a tale that we call the dream narrative.

These visual experiences are like hallucinations induced by drugs, hypnosis, or sensory deprivation. They appear lifelike because there is no competition from the outside world impinging on our senses. The slow-wave form of dreaming supports this theory. Most people feel that when they sleep, they are either out cold, i.e., unconscious, or dreaming. But data indicates that even in deep sleep the mind never really turns off. People awakened from slow-wave sleep report vague thoughts and images that appear to be drifting.

Normally we don't remember dreams. We must awaken ourselves from sleep in order to do this. Thus, it appears that sleep turns off long-term memory.

J. Allan Hobson and Robert McCarley have gathered a large amount of data supporting this second theory, which they call the activation-synthesis (A-S) model. At the conference mentioned above, McCarley and others presented new evidence for their theory indicating the complex electrical and chemical activity goes on when the brain stem begins to shut off the outside world during sleep.

We will look at the third theory at the end of the chapter. Next, we will look in some detail at the dream theory of Hobson and McCarley, who claim that REM dreams are caused by random brain activity as we come close to the boundary between wakefulness and sleep. This activity consists of bursts of electrical activity starting in the brain stem. While this mechanism has been accepted, by and large most researchers feel that it is just that, a mechanism. The question is, Why is it there?

Sense and Nonsense of the Dreaming Brain

To find out I went to visit J. Allan Hobson at his laboratory in Massachusetts. My description of his work follows both from his book and my visit with him and his coworkers in the Boston area. I found Allan Hobson to be a fascinating man with wide-ranging interests and a vast-searching and extremely quick mind that danced between hard science and the softer arts.

Hobson was born with a mixed cerebral dominance, being left-handed and right-eyed. He attracted the attention of a Hartford dyslexia specialist because he didn't seem to have any difficulty with reading, writing, and spelling. Such difficulties were predicted by the current theory of cross-brain wiring.

Perhaps it is the mixed dominance of his brain that accounts for the fact that Hobson is both a scientist and an artist (I'll tell you more about his artistic aspects later). I didn't really know what to expect from my visit. I was there to learn, but at the same time Dr. Hobson asked me to tell his group about how I saw quantum physics relating to the dreaming brain. I was only too happy to oblige, but I felt some reluctance. Would my speculative theories make any sense to these seemingly hard-nosed, materialistic scientists?

As a scientist, Hobson takes a neurobiological-mechanical approach to dreaming. He envisions dreaming as a brain mechanism[3] and believes that we will only understand dreams when we really understand the formal operations of the brain. So, he is interested in answering certain questions: What is the brain doing when the person is sleeping? How can scientists map it when it is dreaming? From that map, what can scientists say are the biological reasons for dreams?

But on the other hand, there is an artistic or creative aspect to Hobson in that he has been recording and analyzing his own dreams for many years and has created an art exhibition about the science of dreaming.

He points out that dreams are actually rational, even though they may not seem to be so. A dreaming mind can be said to be *hypermnesic*—which means that it has increased access to memory within the state of dreaming, which contrasts markedly with the virtual impossibility of recovering the dream product after the state is terminated.

Hobson points to five characteristic features of dreaming:

1. Strong emotions—so strong that they even tend to terminate or interrupt the dream.

2. Illogical content and organization wherein the usual aspects of time and space and even identification of persons, as well as the natural laws of physics, are suspended.

3. The experience of already-formed sensory impressions regardless of how bizarre those experiences are.

4. The uncritical acceptance of those formed sensory experiences as if those experiences were perfectly normal everyday occurrences even though they are bizarre and strange.

5. The difficulty of remembering any dream unless the dreamer attempts to record the dream immediately upon awakening.

These five cardinal characteristics of dreams may also be seen in a range of psychotic episodes including hallucination, disorientation, bizarre thoughts, delusion, and amnesia of patients with mental illnesses. These mental symptoms seem to constitute what would be called delirium, dementia, and psychosis. Thus were it not for the fact that they are asleep, people, having gained some moments of rational clarity, would think that in their dreams they were in a state of psychosis.[4]

Hobson concludes that the study of dreams is today a study of a *model of mental illness*—but not a study of mental illness itself. Thus a dreamer is not mentally ill, but the dream reflects what mental illness is.

He points out that dreams are strange because they seem to be involuntary, and so it is difficult for him to discern why there is such a long and continued popularity of the prophetic tradition of dreams as for example in the dreams of Joseph or in Joseph's interpretation of the pharaoh's dreams in Genesis. Dreams seem to challenge and deny the parallel notions of rationality and responsibility. To be responsible, one must be rational. In dreaming the dreamer appears to be irrational, and thus the dreamer appears to himself to lose his sense of volition.

Yet Hobson points out the reason for giving credence to the prophetic position—which complements the notion of an external agency that creates the dream, as say from gods—is that it comes from out-of-body experience (OBE) that occurs in nocturnal dreams or from the occurrence of hypnagogic images that occur in the transitional state between waking and sleep. He gives scientific evidence[5] that life events such as birth, death, and accidents, and dream events such as OBEs and precognitive experiences, are all in essence unwilled natural phenomena. They occur according to their own laws, in which determinism and chance are statutes. The associations between them are as much causal as the events themselves are causal. And are as acausal as the events themselves. Hobson does not believe that it is wise to regard their nonsensical aspects as hypermeaningful nor is it healthy and scientific to indulge in symbol interpretation.

Hobson is critical of Freud's theory of disguise-censorship in dreams. The key for this theory lies in the study of psychoanalysis, which Hobson points out is not really very scientific at all. The idea of some internal agency residing in a chamber of the psyche that is a constellation of drives that constitutes the id that seems to get released during sleep like an unchained madman seems unscientific to Hobson, at best. This internal agency is so unwelcome to the sleeping mind that its commands must be altered so that they can invade consciousness as dreams and disrupt sleep.

Hobson's brain-based theory runs deeply counter to the psychoanalytic theory of the interpretation of dreams. But he does not wish to imply that this means that he disagrees with its psychodynamic spirit. He differs with Freud in that he does not believe that dreams are obscure or bowdlerized but rather that they are transparent and unedited. His position echoes in a way Jung's notion of dreams as transparently meaningful and does away with any distinction between manifest and latent dream content.

Latent content refers to images or thoughts that are unavailable to conscious memory. To Freud this meant an unconscious wish that the dream was attempting to fulfill. If that proposition is invalid, it changes the whole ball game with respect to the way one thinks about content. While it may seem to be a bit of a cop-out to shy away from content and emphasize form, Hobson believes that the formal analysis impinges deeply upon content theory. It can even radically change the way one thinks about content.

As he puts it, "what passes for content theory is often carrying a lot of baggage that really belongs on the back of the horse of form." I'll go into this in the next part of this chapter.

Hobson builds a lot of his thinking on the research done by nineteenth-century French scholars Marquis d'Hervey de Saint Denise and Alfred Maury, and, of course, refers to Freud's classical interpretation of dreams in 1900. It is ironic according to him that Freud, while proclaiming a scientific approach to dreams, really relied mainly on subjective reports and failed to protect himself or his subjects from the effects of dream distortion—added information not actually contained in the dream—via suggestion.

He points out, however, that Freud, in an almost contradictory way, recognized the promise that brain science held for psychology and maintained that ultimately his theories would be replaced by the findings of neurobiology.

Hobson sees today's neurobiology or brain science as having been built to a great extent on the fundamental neuron doctrine of Freud's contemporaries, Santiago Ramon y Cajal being chiefly noted. He also credits the discovery of REM in 1953, and that occurred during sleep and seemed to accompany brain activation, as the first step in bridging the gap between subject and object. With the recognition that REM showed the onset of dreams during sleep, it was possible to study dreams in an objective way for perhaps the first time. Of course, before REM the early-nineteenth-century dreamers often awakened themselves just after dreams and recorded their impressions.

He points out that REM sleep was found to occur in nearly all mammals. This suggested that nearly all mammals dream. Or that even, possibly, dreaming is a mammalian phenomenon.[6] This meant that we could understand dreams in humans by studying dreams in animals. Humans report their experiences subjectively, while animals can be investigated at the level of individual neurons.

Hobson's Choice: To Jump or to Remain Where You Are

Hobson presents a psychophysiological theory of how dreams are formed. Specifically, the form of dreams is related to a form of brain activity in sleep. During sleep, the brain is first turned on or activated, and then as a result, it generates and synthesizes or integrates its own sensory and motor information. The sensory and motor information that the brain automatically generates are both the driving force and the thing that is being driven—the dream plot. The plot is synthesized in light of the individual's past experiences, attitudes, and expectations.

Hobson has a rather specific theory of how dreams work at the level of neurophysiology. He calls it the activation-synthesis hypothesis. He proposes that a specific brain mechanism is both necessary and sufficient for dreaming to occur. This mechanism is both more and less deterministic than previous theories, and it originates in the brain stem. It not only turns on the sleeping brain and turns off the waking awareness, but it also is capable of introducing abrupt patterns of electrical activity into the cortex during a REM period.

Hobson explained that if you analyze dream reports and ask what is peculiar about the dreams in these reports, the dreamers normally indicate the discontinuities. During a discontinuity the dream character, the action, or even the whole scene might change. The unities of time, place, and person we take as normal during waking awareness are, during dreams, extremely unstable. This aspect is characteristic of all dreams. This would suggest that these discontinuities are determined by physiology. Hobson has been attempting to model this process on a computer by working with neural-network and other models.[7]

As I explained in the previous chapter, neural-network models are mathematical structures easily programmed on computers. Hobson is quite keen on these models because they exhibit some familiar traits that characterize our nervous systems. For example, as I told you, a neural-network model appears to have a number of stable states differing from each other. Each state is characterized by a pattern in which a large number of the computer-modeled structures that can be either "on" or "off" fire periodically. In Hobson's work, random inputs to the model often cause the network to "jump" into one or another of these patterns. These jumps excite Hobson as much as they do the neural nets he explores.

Hobson explains that when watching living-animal neural activity, it is somewhat astounding to watch these real live "jumps" occur. "What causes them? What produces the jolt? What is hitting the net?" Hobson asks. The best candidates he suspects are the giant pontine cells of the brain. These cells are quiet during waking consciousness and most active during dreaming.

The sleeping brain during REM sleep appears to be jolted by specific EEG-recorded electrical waves at apparently random times. In fact REM is characterized by essentially two indicators: the REM that is visibly obvious and these jolt patterns seen with an EEG recorder. These jolts of electrical wave activity are labeled ponto-geniculo-occipital (PGO) waves. Hobson's latest research shows that these pontine cells are driven by the cholinergic system—neurotransmitter molecules that are capable of exciting neurons. Let me explain this further.

Cholinergic Jump-starting the Dreaming Brain

There are two chemical systems acting in the brain that most interest dream researchers. Known as the cholinergic and aminergic systems, these consist of molecules called neurotransmitters that are emitted in the synapses between neurons. In general, neurotransmitters either excite a neuron or inhibit a neuron from firing. The aminergic system excites neurons and turns on during our normal waking consciousness. We stay awake largely because of its effect. However it turns off when we sleep: when it starts to turn off, we begin to feel drowsy. On the other hand, the cholinergic system is normally turned off when we are awake and turns on when we sleep. Thus the two systems are in opposition to each other, leading to what Hobson calls a "war of nerves."

During waking awareness, the maintenance of a number of continuities, including, for example, the flow of conversation and/or the persistence or the development of ideas, depends upon the modulation of the cortex by the aminergic system—specifically the activity of two molecules: noradrenaline and serotonin. Shutting down the aminergic system during REM sleep is called *demodulation*.

Looking at the aminergic and cholinergic systems leads one to a two-pronged neurobiological-attack theory of sleep. On the one hand, neural nets become unstable when they are demodulated as a result of the aminergic system's shutting off. On the other hand, they are also unstable because they are being hit by these internally generated stimuli, PGO waves, when the cholinergic system turns on.

Is Hobson's Hop a Quantum Leap?

Are the PGO jolts also responsible for dream discontinuities? Dream discontinuities would seem to indicate that the dreaming system has received some kind of electrical jolt—something that sends the system into a different (but equally stable) state. Perhaps these jolts occur often enough so that the order of the dream becomes sufficiently scrambled to render the narrative of the dream extremely difficult to follow logically. This may also be why it is so difficult to remember dreams. We are continually being jolted by waves that disrupt whatever pattern of thought is required to enter the dream into memory. The brain is also continually being jolted from one scene to another.

When a narrative occurs, whenever we attempt to recall it, a meaningful line or plot seems to develop. Is this recall really a memory of the mind's record? Or did the dream all happen at once? Perhaps the ability to recall, to connect sequences together logically, requires the aminergic system to be turned on and the PGO spikes to be off. Thus we are able to construct a narrative logically when we are awake although there is no such thing as a dream narrative occurring when we are asleep. We need to be awake to provide continuity, i.e., narrative.

As we recall the dream, A follows B follows C follows D and so on. And then there seems to be a sudden leap. There appear to be pockets of stability and then a jump to another pocket of stability and then to another. Are these leaps recall of PGO activity? How often do these leaps occur?

The answer is that no one really knows. Nobody has really looked at this carefully. One problem in doing such research is the difficulty of getting really lengthy reports from dreamers. Hobson, however, has a graduate student looking at how long the coherent segments of a dream last.

The quantum leap of a dream requires a whole different way of connecting A to B. In one of my dreams, for example, I was walking out of a New York office building and I met Michael Douglas, the film actor/producer, who I happened to have met, very briefly, in San Francisco many years ago. The next thing I knew is that we were walking in Regent's Park, London. I remembered the whole thing clearly.

Dream researchers would say that my jump was a classic dream-scene-shift discontinuity. The spatial dislocations are not uncommonly that dramatic. Hobson believes that when something bumps the "orientation cognizer," a dream-scene dislocation occurs.

Hobson has been studying this problem. It could involve a whole run of pontine signals. Neural networks he has observed in the cat's brain don't jump out of one sequence into another unless they are hit by a run of signals.

Hobson believes that too much effort is placed on declarative memory because we think of dreams in a narrow linguistic sense. However, procedural memory is subnarrative; we know how to do things without articulation. All of our motor skills are strongly refreshed by doing without thinking.

Similarly, in dreams we seem to move about without thinking or forming words. This would indicate that motor-program generators are powerfully activated in REM sleep. Furthermore we know that dreams are conspicuously motoric. Hobson explained:

You and I are relatively sedentary critters, but we don't have dreams about sedentary activity. We have dreams about moving all over the place. Henri Beaunis called attention to that in the early twentieth century. Practically no one else ever noticed it. It is one of the most prominent formal features of dreams. It is very counterintuitive if you think that dreaming is replaying waking life. It is not. It is replaying a certain aspect of waking life, mainly that aspect associated with action. I think that action is a very important and good way to organize memory. It is very functionally significant.

In dreams we move. Often we move from place to place and notice the continual changes that take place around us. Why don't we just sit and meditate in a dream? Why don't we just wait for the world to come to us, as we often do in waking life?

Perhaps the question is academic. Einstein pointed out a long time ago that all motion is relative. I remember driving a car along a road at night in a particularly heavy snowstorm in New Mexico. I suddenly had the feeling that I was not moving, that the car was actually at rest on the road, and that the snow was blowing toward me in a blizzard. Whether I was moving from one place to another or everything around me was just flowing by while I was at rest was not discernible visually. Of course I felt my body making the effort of moving my muscles or I felt my body being jolted by the bumps on the road as I drove. This told me that it was I who was moving, and not the world moving past me as I sat still.

But in a dream, we are paradoxically "moving" while our muscles are paralyzed. But is it really true that we move through the dream landscape and that it doesn't move past us? I make this distinction to indicate that there really is no absolute answer. All motion is truly relative. Yet what is significant is that dreams are truly "motion pictures" regardless of who is really moving. What does this tell us about our nature? Later I shall recall this motion aspect of dreams in the holographic model.

The Dreamstage

I was certainly impressed by Hobson's research; now let me tell you about his artistic endeavors on the "dreamstage." During the 1970s, Hobson and some of his coworkers put together a rather unusual exhibit in the Boston area. They decided to form what they called a "dreamstage"—a living museum of what happens when a person "sleeps, perchance to dream." Hobson explained that it always seemed to him that one of the more important aspects of science that was underexplained was the phenomenology of science's aesthetic aspect. What appealed to him most about science was the perception of beauty at the level of phenomenon and at the level of modeling phenomenon. Hobson stated, "It is sensual in the deepest sense to do science."

He thought that this sensual beauty needed to be made clearer to people so that they didn't regard science as a dry, abstract, removed process. It seemed to him that one could consider designing a scientific exhibit that would be focused mainly on that aspect of scientific experience that would completely obviate the need to tell stories, to talk about results, or to use words at all. Part of his effort was to create an exhibit that was not cased in a panel, that had no labels, that was preverbal: "To convey the sense of wonder of phenomenon."

This sense of wonder arose from his daily life experience, which was to sit in the dark and look at an oscilloscope watching nerve cells. "The music and the sights of them and the microscope and the neurons, and all of that stuff, it just seemed to me that if I could just make a collage of all of that, then it might have a direct communicative appeal to people. The way that we decided to do it was to have a person sleep in public. Then we just let people watch."

But Hobson did more than just let people watch a sleeping person. They literally ran the exhibit out of the sleeper's brain by taking its electrical activity and broadcasting it all over the gallery. To make the exhibit more dramatic and visual they used a "laser oscilloscope." This works by using laser beams and scanning mirrors. Instead of applying the voltages of the brain to two electromagnets in a cathode-ray tube as is done in an oscilloscope, they put them onto the X and Y axes of a scanning mirror allowing them to make the laser beam produce a large trace across a wall exhibiting eye movements, muscle tone, and heart rate.

Not only light but sound was added for dramatic purposes by using a synthesizer so that the brain's electrical energy could be audibly experienced. Hobson said, "By playing with the synthesizer you could develop music algorithms for the various states. When you were in slow-wave sleep, there was a big basso. When you were in REM, the frequency would increase. We took all sorts of liberties in the way we programmed those frequencies. There was nothing unveridical about it although you could say that there was because we chose to represent a process symbolically in an arbitrary manner. But there was always the veridical signal at the root of the display."

Hobson Speculates

During my meeting with Dr. Hobson, I asked his opinion about the purpose of dreams, and whether dreams are, as he has often been quoted as saying, meaningless. As I mentioned above, Hobson believes that dreams are both meaningful and meaningless. In one sense they are almost hyper-meaningful in agreement with Freud's intent in that respect. However, Freud felt that the meaning of a dream was hidden, while for Hobson the meaning is transparent and revealed. Although dreams may be symbolic and metaphoric, he believes that the intent of the symbol or the metaphor, to the degree that it is present, is to condense a lot of meaning into a revelatory clear meaning. The symbol is not there to make things obscure; it is to carry more latent meaning with it.

On the other hand, he also thinks that dreams have a meaningless aspect. He finds that his critics as well as his public are often confused by his answer that dreams are "both/and." They want to know which it is. His point in his book, *The Dreaming Brain,* and in other writings is that the form of dreams is intrinsically chaotic. Therefore there are discontinuities that should not be thought of as meaningful in any psychological sense in that they reflect a process that is probably cerebrally driven. Since the discontinuities are probably an automatic or mechanical process, to struggle with interpreting that aspect of dreaming strikes Hobson as futile and pointless. He affirms that he doesn't believe that such an interpretation is meaningful. This was clearly his intent in the subtitle of his book, *The Sense and the Nonsense of Dreams.* Both exist in the dreaming brain and each has a different mechanism.

I asked Hobson about neurobiologist Francis Crick's erasure theory of dreams (discussed in the previous chapter). He welcomes this idea because people have mainly focused on the other side of the question: how dreams help people to remember. Computer simulations of networks indicate that nets could do both. It would then seem that the process could be both reinforcing of recent and/or charged inputs and letting other states that had become irrelevant fade or cancel out.

He agrees that the problem with Crick's theory is that there is really no strong evidence for it. There is some evidence for the positive effect on learning. This has been gathered by, for example, Winson's study of rats. Other studies showed that if rats were sleep deprived, they learned mazes much less well. One could say that they were sleepy. Studies showed that even so, if they were learning a maze, they had an increase in REM sleep. Hobson calls this increase a "bump." There seems to be a consistent time delay between the learning exposure and the bumps, suggesting that something lawful is going on. That strikes Hobson as one of the really interesting leads in the sleep-behavior literature.

In our conversation Hobson was careful to point out that this doesn't mean that the erasure theory is wrong. He welcomes it as an intriguing idea, but asks, "How are scientists going to get at it experimentally?" From a theoretical point of view both dream erasure and learning theories are possible.

Hobson believes that dreams have the same purpose as any other elaborative cognitive process. All cognitive processes determine the major dimensions of consciousness orientation. And all of these dimensions are measures of action for the observer. They include attempts of the observer to answer specific questions: Who is there? What's happening? What does it mean? What strength or valence does it have? What emotional significance does it have? What social significance does it have? All of these questions are dimensions of the cognitive process in any state of awareness, including REM sleep.

Hobson points out that dreaming is like cognition in any waking state in its attempts to share those intentions, those goals, and those organization properties. But in dreams, the cognitive process attempts to answer those questions in interesting ways that are qualitatively different from those in wake state. Yet it really is the same brain-mind trying to do the same thing.

Something New in the Land of Nod?

As I mentioned at the top of the chapter, there is a third theory now emerging. Jim Horne, director of Loughborough University's sleep research laboratories, says that the A-S model only explains the mechanism behind dreams. His research and others' now suggest a reason for dreaming, i.e., a purpose why the mechanism exists in the first place. These researchers believe that REM dreams are indeed the result of a bombardment from the brain stem but that this electrical barrage only serves a real purpose for the growing human fetus.

It is known that the human fetus spends about fifteen hours each day in what appears to be REM sleep. By birth, REM has dropped off to around eight hours per day, and by the time the child has reached full adulthood, the period of time is only two hours or less of REM per night. Horne believes that for the fetus REM is a form of rehearsing, an exercise for the developing brain.

The idea is that the fetus needs blasts of neural energy to tone up and activate its brain while it hangs suspended in the blackness of eternity—its amniotic fluid home. That is why these blasts result in REM lasting so long in the fetal stage. The fetus REMs to grow a healthy brain. As the child develops into adulthood the REM period is cut down but not out, leaving us with a hangover from early fetal time. By having the brain-stem mechanism at work in the womb, the developing child is preparing for entrance into the outside world.

This doesn't mean that the fetus experiences anything like a dream according to the experts, because there has been no input of data to constitute a memory, thus there is no information to provide dream images. Without memories, the fetus records, possibly, the bumps and knocks of intrauterine life, muffled sounds such as the heartbeat of the mother, and the movements it feels when it changes position in the womb or when the mother moves about.

The fetal REM periods are something like "look here" messages given to the fetus, possibly resulting from these stimuli, thus training its brain for its opening appearance into the world of sights, sounds, and other sensations after birth.

In adult life, we are filled with memories. These flesh out the program started in the womb, giving us the typical dream experiences we all have. This would imply that in adult life dreams have a limited purpose. Horne believes that we dream around ninety minutes each night (have REM sleep) to stop us from falling into deep slow-wave sleep. A person is easily aroused from five minutes of slow-wave sleep, but as the time lengthens, the ability to become fully alert takes an inordinately longer time. After forty minutes of slow-wave sleep, people need at least ten minutes to orient themselves. This would make early man easy prey in the supposed rough life-and-death world he inhabited. REM thus provides us with a quicker recovery from sleep when we awaken.

Thus our dreams are purely survival requirements in a world of uncertainty. How does this theory match with other dream concepts? In a surprising manner it fits with a whole other worldview of dreams. It is called "the dreaming" or the "dreamtime" and is the basis for the survival of a whole people—the Australian Aboriginals.

HE DREAMTIME

Aborigines believe in two forms of time. Two parallel streams of activity. One is the daily objective activity to which you and I are confined. The other is an infinite spiritual cycle called the "dreamtime," more real than reality itself. Whatever happens in the dreamtime establishes the values, symbols, and laws of Aboriginal society. Some people of unusual spiritual powers have contact with the dreamtime.

—*From* The Last Wave, *a film by Peter Weir*

The old man explained to me, "Your skin name is Tjongula. When you go into my country, you tell people that and you show them this drawing. They will recognize you." The drawing was my passport into the central parts of Australia—the land where large numbers of the Aborigine people now dwelt.

I had come to Australia to investigate what is known as the Aboriginal dreamtime. My contacts had led me to a house in the wilderness just outside Byron Bay, a seaside resort city on the east coast of that continent, just below the Queensland border.

The old man was a tribal leader, an elder, and a medicine man capable of many feats of magic. His name was Arthur. With him were two other younger Aboriginal men, Wayne and Graeme. We were sitting in the home of Wayne, Graeme, and Vicki, a young woman and business leader who is the program director of the Center for Strategic Leaders in Brisbane. I was there to learn. I wanted to know if dreamtime had anything to do with dreams and if what I learned from them would point to what I suspected about the dream of the universe.

From the previous chapter we learned that long periods of REM occur in early fetal development. Could this indicate that dreaming is a fundamental necessity of cognitive processing? In other words, does this evidence indicate that dreaming creates a concept of a universe and self? For without cognition certainly there is really no concept of universe possible. Could it be that we had much to learn about the relationship of dreaming to the universe by looking at the sophisticated but often-labeled "primitive" notions of dreams as given by Aborigines? I suspected that we had.

In his book,[1] W. H. Stanner refers to the concept of "the Dream Time" or *alcheringa* of the Arunta or Aranda tribe first immortalized by Baldwin Spencer and Frank Gillen.[2] Stanner prefers to call it "the Dreaming" or simply "Dreaming."

A central meaning of Dreaming is that it was a time of heroes when men and nature came to be as they are now. It was a time long ago as in "Once upon a time, there was . . ." However neither time nor history is actually being used in the meaning of Dreaming. Time as an abstract concept does not exist in the Aboriginal languages. The Dreaming cannot be understood in terms of history either. Dreaming means a complex state. A black "fella" may regard his totem or the place from which his spirit came as his Dreaming. He may also regard tribal law as his Dreaming. An "old fella" once told Stanner in a poem:

> White man got no dreaming.
> Him go 'nother way.
> White man, him go different.
> Him got road belong himself.

While resting at the home of my friends in Byron Bay, I watched a videotape about Aboriginal people. It described a man who went back to his land on an archaeological dig. When he got there, he realized that the stones of the land were connected to him and that he was connected to those stones. As a result of this he moved back to his own land.

Days earlier, after my arrival in Sydney, I met with Vicki, who invited me to her home, which she shared with Graeme and Wayne. She picked me up at the Brisbane airport. With her was Graeme, a full-blooded Aborigine from Mornington Island. I shook hands with Graeme. He looked at me with virtually no expression. I felt a sudden chill. What was I doing here? Graeme is a teacher, musician, and dancer who specializes in cultural knowledge and dances from his island.

The story of Graeme and Mornington Island is typical of the Aboriginal peoples. Mornington Island is situated in the southern corner of the Gulf of Carpentaria, northern Queensland. It is approximately sixty kilometers long and twenty kilometers wide and is the largest in a group of twenty-two islands. The traditional owners are the Lardil people.

The land is covered by low scrub vegetation with titree and swamp flats providing a habitat for many species of wildlife including migratory birds such as brolga, seabirds, varieties of ducks and cockatoo, and timid grass wallabies. There are windswept beaches lined with sea-oak trees, rocky outcrops covered with oysters, and cliffs that shine with the white ocher used as body decoration by dancers. The surrounding sea is abundant with fish and marine life such as turtle and dugong, which are the traditional foods for the Lardil people.

According to their history, the first three people on Mornington Island were Marnbil, Dhual-dhual, and Ghingin, who arrived by raft from mainland Australia some ten thousand years ago. They named all the places. Legends tell of the creation of the landscape and "story places." Laws and ceremonies came from Tuwartu (Rainbow Serpent) and Nyaranbi (Dingo). All the families and clans knew which special land areas were theirs to care for and to pass on to their children, how they should marry, and how they should share whatever they had. Their songs and dances teach them this history and inheritance. Many of the people living there still go to their traditional lands where certain "story places" or sacred sites are located and maintained for future generations.

The first European settlers were missionaries who arrived in 1914. After the First World War the island became a Presbyterian mission, and cultural "assimilation" began. In 1978, both Mornington and the nearby islands of the Wellesley Group were granted local-government status with a shire council and elected representatives of the community. The population is approximately 1,100 people, and the main community center is Gununa, which means "Enough!"

Graeme is a slender man with features seemingly typical of Aboriginal people. He is quite well versed in the traditional ways, and he explained to me that his "dream" comes from the Mornington Island. He told me that it is important to realize that the people of the land are vessels of the dream of the land. The land dreams through the people indigenous to the land, and when people tell their stories, it is important to know if they were on their land when they dreamed. The people of the land are the voices of the land's dream.

Dreamtime is a curious term, not original to the Aboriginal people. Instead it was coined by the English researcher Frank Gillen in 1896 and used by Gillen and Baldwin Spencer in their now classic work of 1899.[3]

Aboriginal people had many religions, not just one, before the coming of the white man. Instead of gods or a god they had ancestral spirits. These are neither human, flora, or fauna, and they do not relate to people personally with the exception of what are called "clever fellas," who are probably akin to shamans or medicine people.

Graeme walked over to the wall. He took a long spear, about six and a half feet long, from its attachments on the wall and showed it to me. It wobbled as I held it in my hand. Very flexible, it was decorated as if it were a snake with red ocher circles around its thin circumference. "This spear is a snake spear. It is thrown at grass height." He held it in his hand so that his hand was at the very bottom end of the spear. "There is a hole here for a sling.

"In war the hunter throws a lot of spears at his enemy. He throws them high in the air and the enemy must look up to dodge those spears. Then he throws the snake. It slithers along the grass as it flies, and it gets him in the leg just like the snake."

Graeme told me about the different boomerangs. Some of them are for throwing around a shield. They hit the shield and they bounce around, hitting the warrior behind the shield.

After talking to Graeme I suddenly saw the life of these people as it was and has been for thousands of years. I began to lose any sense of judgment, any sense of what was or is correct or civilized behavior, any sense of right or wrong when it comes to the taking of life, particularly animal life. It dawned on me that we are all the same people.

I reflected on my life in the United States. I sit at my home in Washington and I eat. I go to the market and I buy a salmon, already a dead fish when I bring it home. I don't even look at the salmon as a living animal. I only see it as "fish." When I think of fish, I think of how it tastes, not how it moves in the water. When I think of other animals I eat, I also don't think about how that animal was killed so that it could finally be brought to my table. It is only meat, a dead slab of beef or sliced and filleted red-meat salmon.

I eat this dead animal, but I don't feel it in my stomach. I am not aware of the animal as a living being. In my world everything has been safety-wrapped in plastic, and I have been removed from the "harsher" aspects of life. I have been safely tucked away from the fishing nets and the strangulation of the fish. I have been removed from the blow on the head to the steer from the slaughtering man or the electric shock from the machine as thousands of cattle are killed.

I am of the "civilized" world where death is hidden, and all there is is life and what I call reality.

"The Aboriginal lives in a dream world," Wayne says. He calls his life part of the dreaming. He lives in connection to the land. He hunts, and he kills. He eats the animals he kills. He kills kangaroos. He kills fish. He hunts, and he gathers where he goes. He is also infiltrated by me, the white "spirit." When white people were first seen by the Aborigines, they believed they were dead spirits. I am white skinned, so the reminder is ever present in their minds as they watch me. I have no color. I am dead.

Arthur is a "clever fella." He tells me his story. "There are many stories," "Uncle" Arthur tells me. There are stories about the dreamtime, which is the story of creation. There are stories about how man came to Australia and about the animals.

Man has to eat and live. Without animals to kill and eat, man does not survive. The Aboriginal knows this. He is not ashamed of killing the animals, of making spears out of flint, of cutting the flesh. He is part of the story. He is very aware of the thing he is dependent on. He sings the songs of the animals he hunts and kills. He respects them. The concept of the slaughterhouse is unthinkable, for why kill an animal if you are not going to eat it?

Why indeed? The Aboriginal never hunts the animal for fun. It is unthinkable, a violation of law. He hunts the wallaby for food. He hunts the land as the dream tells him. He dances the sacred dance of the animal he hunts.

My dreams come back to me. In one of them I am on an altar waiting to be sacrificed. I have chosen this. A Peruvian shaman tells me, "But you, too, must perform the sacrifice." I must learn to kill to be truly human. I must learn the sacred part of life that my Western culture has so well hidden from me: the meaning of death that is in life in food.

Mircea Eliade wrote about the coming into being of man and the actual world as seen by these people.[4] It took place in the dreamtime—the *alchera* or *alcheringa* time, to use the Aranda terms for the primordial and fabulous epic. When this happened, the physical landscape was changed and humans became what they are today. This was a result of a series of deeds by supernatural beings. Yet today, nowhere in Australia do these dreamtime personages impress us with their grandeur. As a matter of fact the majority of the central-Australian creation myths tell only of the long and monotonous wanderings of different types of primordial beings.

The dreamtime came to an end when the supernatural beings left the surface of the earth. But the mythical past was not lost forever; on the contrary, it is periodically recovered through the tribal rituals.

When all these earth-born supernatural beings had accomplished their labors and completed their wanderings, overpowering weariness fell upon them. The work that they had performed had taxed their strength to the utmost, thus they sank back into their original slumbering state and their bodies either vanished into the ground—often at the site where they had first emerged—or turned into rocks, trees, or sacred objects.

Initiates in tribal rituals today learn how to relive dreamtime through ceremonies. Eventually the individual becomes completely immersed in the sacred history of the tribe; that is, he knows the origin and understands the meaning of everything from rocks, plants, and animals to customs, symbols, and rules. As he assimilates the revelation in the myths and rituals, the world, life, and human existence become meaningful and sacred, for they have been created or perfected by supernatural beings.

At a certain moment in their lives humans discover that before their birth they were spirits and that after their deaths they are to be reintegrated into the prenatal spiritual condition. They learn that the human cycle is part of a larger cosmic cycle, that creation was a "spiritual" act that took place in the dreamtime and that although the cosmos is now "real" or "material," it nonetheless must be periodically renewed by the reiteration of the creative acts that occurred in the beginning. This renovation of the world is a spiritual deed, the result of a reinforcing communication with the eternal ones of the "dreamtime."[5]

Today, however, things have changed. Aboriginals are just within the last few years getting back their land. These Australians need to live in a *real* world. But this means something very different for them. It means a resourceful land formed, enriched, and consecrated by supernatural beings. Such a "world" has a "center" or a structure—and for this reason it is "oriented." It is not chaos—an amorphous, bewildering vacuity. The coming into being of the world of plants and animals and men is the result of a sacred history scrupulously preserved in the myths and periodically reiterated in the sacred ceremonies. This implies that the "world" has a history—a sacred history unfolding during the dreamtime—but also that man has assumed a responsibility for maintaining the world, by continuously reenacting the stupendous events of the beginning and by endlessly infusing the land with the powers of "dreaming." When man ceases to communicate with the dreamtime and to reenact his history, the world will disintegrate and life will wither and eventually disappear from the surface of the earth.

The Origins of Aboriginals

In the foreword to a recent book, Wandjuk Marika, OBE, explains that people today often discuss the origins of the Aboriginal people wondering just how they arrived on the Australian continent.[6] Many people have noticed the resemblance of the Aboriginal people to southern-India people and to hill people of the Celebes, suggesting that these people may have come from across the seas by boat or from a land bridge that long ago vanished.

But according to Aboriginal people, nothing like that seemed to have happened. Instead their story is always embedded in legend. Marika tells that his people, the Riratjingu, are descended from the great Djankawu, who came from the island of Baralku far across the sea, and that the spirits of his people therefore return to Baralku when they die. It seems that Djankawu came in a canoe with his two sisters, and they followed the morning star, which guided them to the shores of Yelangbara on the eastern coast of Arnhem Land. They walked across the country following the rain clouds. When they wanted water, they just stuck a stick in the ground and fresh water flowed. Djankawu and his sisters gave all the creatures names and are the source of the law.

Was the Dreamtime Ever a Real Time?

According to W. Love, early Aboriginal people, when they arrived here sometime between 40,000 and 120,000 years ago, were faced with flora and fauna that were so different from what they had seen in their own land that these life-forms gave rise to the stories and legends that now constitute the dreamtime.[7] For example, what Love calls macro-faunal creatures showed themselves in terms of their natural history. Observation of this history was then used to provide guidance, examples, or models of human behavior in daily living. As evolution proceeded, descendants of the original people used these examples as stories perpetuating the beliefs obtained. The macro-fauna "the Kadimakara" became in myth and legend the animals of dreamtime. Then species-specific patterns of behavior aligned to human thought and became enshrined ceremonial patterns.

According to another expert, Ebenezer A. Adejumo, in his master's thesis, dreamtime was not just a fantasy of Aboriginal people.[8] Instead it has as much meaning to them as we may find meaning in our dreams of today, particularly if we are psychologists or psychiatrists. The myths of the dreamtime contain records of history associated with geographic sites, sociological concerns, and personal experiences. Since the Aboriginals reenact the stories of the dreamtime, we can deduce that all of the past, present, and future are present now or coexist as if in parallel worlds of experience. All of this together makes up reality, in which our sense of present time is merely a small part.

Dreamtime is then eternal and timeless. And so are the spirits of people. These spirits also link with the dreamtime: they have existed in the past; they will exist in the future children yet unborn; and they exist now as the people of the land. By keeping track of the stories and legends, the spirit is in a real sense keeping track of himself—his path and pattern throughout historical time.

Aboriginals then see themselves as these spirits, and they see all human beings this way. There is no division between time and eternity, all time is essentially present. To keep this alive, songs must be sung, dances must be performed, and original creative acts must be reenacted by countless repetitions by the spirit's reincarnation in human forms.

We may ask why Aboriginal people believe this. The answer is apparent when we realize that the aim of this reenactment is a solution to the alienation of humans from their planet. They are utterly dependent on the land for their survival. They cannot adjust themselves by applied science since they do not possess a scientific way of seeing nature as our Western world does. Instead they see themselves as part of nature.

Time for the Aboriginal is quite concrete and based on the observance of natural rhythms such as the seasons and the lunar and solar cycles. Thus time is marked not by points on a line stretching from minus to plus infinity as in the Newtonian worldview but on a circle: they count recurrences of the cycles. Time of events on a daily cycle are marked by the position of the sun in the sky. Natives of central Australia mark time in sleeps. They will return to a place in so many sleeps or nights. Durations of time are marked by everyday processes. For example, one hour may be marked by the cooking of a yam. A moment would be the twinkling of a crab's eye. Longer times may be marked by the duration of a particular journey. Thus timetables are not definite. What is important is the concrete time of the "now." Aborigines thus find it difficult to stay on a clocktime schedule.

Aborigines also believe that spirits, particularly of cultural heroes after completing their creative acts in dreamtime, are often changed into rocks, boulders, or sacred trees. When neophytes are initiated, they are shown sacred objects called *tjurunga*. These object vary in size from about a foot in length to over six feet. They are often made of slabs of stone or wood. During an initiation the *tjurunga* will be rubbed on the body of the neophyte. They will be told:

> Young man see this object. This is your own body. This is the *tjilpa* ancestor who you were when you wandered about in your own previous existence. Then you sank down to rest in the sacred cave nearby. This is your *tjurunga*. Keep close watch over it.[9]

Another Time

Garrett Barden notes in his book[10] that the word for "dream" is commonly accepted as *tjukurpa*, which has two very frequent uses. As a noun it means "story" or "tale" provided that it is spoken and not sung. In the adjectival use the term actually refers to the time as experienced by the main character in the story. For example in the story *malu tjukurpa,* or kangaroo story, the storyteller is referring to the kangaroo who is the actor in the story, whose point of view we will be able to take distinct from the kangaroo that we watch as the object of a story.

Barden points out that we have several images of time in our world. For example, in the concept of duration there are two experiences. First there is duration of the perceived activity, and second there is the duration of the experience of the perceiver. For example, consider a dog crossing the street. The activity takes its own time: that is the objective component. There is also the subjective component, the awareness of oneself in the observation.

Barden refers to the relation of imaginal time to real time. He points out that imaginal time, the time, say, of the dreamtime, is true because it is sacred. As Eliade stated, *"les mythes sont vrais, parce qu'ils sont sacrés* [myths are true because they are sacred]."[11]

The imaginative scheme of Australian desert people constitutes a reality. But to what extent do these people consider this imaginative reality to be as real as their sensory world of reality? The answer is somewhat surprising. These people believe that the imaginal world is more real than the sensory world. It is the world to which the sensory world must look for guidance. From its viewpoint the sensory world is to be criticized.

Now how is a myth such as the dreamtime to be considered real? Is it to be considered historically accurate? The problem here is subtle. When dealing with mythical themes or events, there is a sense of time that is very different from chronological time—the time that we experience as clocktime or in duration division, that we undergo when we compare the rising of the sun with the movement of the earth about the sun or to the photo-decay of a cesium atom in a laboratory in Paris.

We all have a natural way of distinguishing past from present. We believe that there is a difference between the past of a few moments ago and the past of several years ago. Thus we tend to take the dreamtime as the story of a time in the far distant past such as millions of years ago. We relate to legendary time as we would to our own sense of time past. Thus my childhood took place earlier than my adulthood. And thus the time of legends took place a long time ago.

On a time-line I could symbolize my life as:

where *C* refers to childhood, *A* to adulthood, and *N* to now. In such a symbolic reference we might consider a sacred event such as symbolized in dreamtime stories by the following time line:

The asterisk marks the time of the dreamtime in history, the break in the time line symbolizes that the line is extremely long, and the *N* again refers to now. Thus the sacred event happened a long time ago, if we mark that event as fitting on a historical graph.

But there is another sense of time we need to deal with here. That is the subjective time of our experience. There is a sense here that the time of the dreamtime as past is not essential. The notion of the events of the dreamtime as fitting within the scheme of passing time is also not essential. Instead we are looking at two contrasting images. There is the image of an origin marking an event and of one progressing farther and farther away from that origin along a line. Then there is the image of duration that does not stretch on to infinity. If we think of time as experienced as a sequence of oscillations between polar opposites, then the past has no real "depth" to it. For example, if we think of a day existing between the polar opposites of the rising and the setting of the sun, then yesterday is the same in depth as the day before yesterday and the day before it. All days are the same, equally deep, in that they are all in the past equally far away from the present.

Mythical time shares in the second way of perceiving time. All events in the "past" are equally deep, equally far from the present. That they are not to be taken as events of chronological time means that they are not to be put on a chronological time line as we may put the events of our lives. They are therefore not to be put graphically on a historical-time basis. That doesn't mean they are not real or that they didn't happen or for that matter are not happening now.

If we consider sacred events as historical events we would have to draw them on the time line as:

****

and not as:

*———

That is, they are ever occurring in the present and not once occurring in some distant past. This different sense of time affects the Aborigine in his dealing with the white world. White man sees time as being spent within the framework of the time line, whereas the Aborigine does not. Duration is not governed by the clock but by the business at hand.

Dreams and Dreamtime

The next day I rode into town with Graeme. We sat silently for some time. After a while, I asked him about his dreams and about the dreams he has when he is not on Mornington Island. What do those dreams mean?

Graeme explained that it depends on what you mean by *dream*. His people have their normal dreams. He explained, "The proper dream is the dream you get when your song is given to you through a dream by a relative. Or you see a story place that has significance and something will tell you about that area. My people have actually dreamt songs and stories in other people's countries. They take the story as it comes with their own language."

He then told me that dreams were always important. Many times he wanted to get out of them. One doesn't always have big dreams or visions, one must dream the small ones, too. One time before his grandfather died, Graeme dreamt that he was sitting in a circle on a big sand dune. Other people were sitting in the circle, and they were looking toward the middle of it. One man was standing in the middle talking. Graeme looked toward the right, and he was suddenly in another country called Marion. In the distance he saw Sydney Island. He saw a dark pool on the tidal mudflats. He was looking down on it as his body hovered over it. Then he saw a dugong sitting in it with half of its body on the mud and the other half in the water. One half was flesh and skin, and the other half was dry bones. That vision told him that his grandfather was dying.

He then explained that seeing the dugong in the dream was the important clue. His grandfather had taught him how to hunt the dugong. The other clue was seeing Sydney Island in the distance. That told him that he was in Marion and that the dream was an interpretation of what was going to happen.

Graeme explained, "People of the land are put on the earth to carry out the laws of the land and protect their earth. When you die, your spirit goes back into the land again. Before you are born the spirit comes in and takes the form of you. If a man and woman who is pregnant see a snake before she knows she is pregnant, that snake will be a sign of the coming birth, and the snake will be a spirit totem of the child. The child also has the spirit totem of the mother, which is its major totem. We are just a spirit that is covered over with flesh and bones."

Dreaming Today: Journey to the Center of the Universe

After I left Byron Bay I returned to Sydney. I made plans to visit the center of Australia, particularly Uluru, also known as Ayers Rock. Some weeks later I left Sydney with a friend who wished to return to central Australia to visit with his children—part Aboriginal and part white. We were to make the journey across New South Wales through Broken Hill then on to Port Augusta through to the town of Coober Pedy in South Australia and up to Mount Ebenezer across to Uluru.

The journey across the red lands of the Northern Territory left me bewildered. But when I saw the "rock," I was captivated. Its shape changed with each passing moment. Next I hoped to reach the Pintupi people west of Alice Springs.

Today the Aboriginal outlook on life and the universe is still shaped by the Dreaming. Yet, the relationship between Dreaming and life remains a problem. First, Dreaming must be considered a phenomenon. It is "that which is." For the Pintupi people who live in central Australia it is a framework for human behavior. What it means is another thing. Dreaming (tjukurpa) has many meanings. It is a projection into "symbolic space" of social processes, and it must be related to individuals' lives. For the Pintupi, living as they do, precariously, in central Australia, it must also be related to something that transcends everyday life.

Dreaming among the Pintupi represents this paradox. How the Pintupi live in space and time is reflected in their Dreaming. The Pintupi thus live at two levels: within and outside of space and time. Within they have their vision and without they have their society. Their constructs of "family," "social life," and "country" are linked to their Dreaming.

Dreaming is basic to Pintupi reality. The difference between Dreaming and everything else is vital to their view of the universe. The people and the country are thought of as arising from the Dreaming. For example, the Pintupi people living near the Kintore mountain range see a large hill in that range as the body of a monitor lizard, *Ngintaka.* This lizard traveled from the west. When the lizard came upon a group of women and children dancing at Kintore (in the middle of Australia), he raised his tail and killed them with it. Then he raised his head, and his body took the form of the hill and turned to stone. Today the hill is called *yunytjunya* in reference to the throat of that lizard, which was exposed when it raised its head.

Dreaming then refers to both specific stories and the whole creative epoch to which all the stories refer. Thus the story of the monitor lizard is called Monitor Lizard Dreaming.

Pintupi people do make a distinction between what they call the sensory world, *yuti,* and the Dreaming, *tjukurpa.* Any event that could be seen or has been seen by a person can be called *yuti* by the Pintupi.

The important distinction between *yuti* and *tjukurpa* seems to be one of objectivity. If it is a possible event in the world of space and time, it is *yuti* or objectively provable in some sense. Events that really happen are called *mularrpa,* meaning true or actual. Yet if something is obviously a lie or story, it is not *mularrpa* and at the same time it is not *tjukurpa.*

But *mularrpa* and *tjukurpa* are not opposites either. There is some overlap in which a story can be both. Some events are capable of being witnessed and are thought of as arising from the Dreaming, so that what is *mularrpa* can actually be seen as arising from *tjukurpa.* Thus the lizard mountain is both *mularrpa* and *tjukurpa,* that is, it is both true and from the Dreaming. The Pintupi thus say that from the Dreaming reality arose.

The Dreaming can be said to transcend the space-time of the immediate. The landscape is seen as tracks of the totemic animal spirits that once walked the earth and, indeed, by becoming stone themselves, became the earth. Just as everyday animals leave their tracks on the ground, these totemic being/animal/spirits left theirs. Certain areas such as the great Ayers Rock in central Australia are known as sacred grounds called *Yarta yarta* because a power can be felt there.

The Pintupi believe that nothing was or is created by humans; it was all there from the beginning arising from the Dreaming. The conception and birth of an individual also arise from the Dreaming. Before conception, a person is said to be "sitting as a dreamtime being." This process is thought of as a transformation from the Dreaming into the actual.

Dreaming links everything together. Thus a person is linked to a place. The Dreaming provides an identity for the person, an identity that has existed before the person's birth and will exist after. Thus Pintupi come from the Pintupi land, which is their Dreaming.

Dreamtime and the Dreaming Universe

The Pintupi do distinguish between dreams and the Dreaming. Some dreams are of the Dreaming and some are not. Conventional dreams are not considered to be important. But there are dreams that the Pintupi describe as "seeing the Dreaming." I would call these "big dreams."

When a person dreams, his spirit is said to leave the body and observe things that are outside of ordinary reality. Sometimes the spirit will encounter spirits from the Dreaming. What one sees in these encounters is believed to have always existed. Thus one may take the view that these dreams are showing us another parallel reality in perhaps a different dimension.

Should we consider these "Dreaming" dreams as real? It depends on what happens next. If the dream portends some events and the dreamer eventually realizes them, then the dream is thought of as "real." However an important part of this is gaining the acceptance of others with whom the dream has been shared. Thus dreams become "more real" if they are accepted by the community of the dreamer. But dreams can be interpreted in many different ways. So one cannot be sure about their meaning. To validate a dream, one must share the dream and find acceptance with others.

In a sense this is not unlike our present view of quantum physics. There is a basis of belief in quantum physics that is shared by the physicists that use this science in their work. Yet there is quite a range of beliefs concerning the interpretation of quantum physics that lies outside the work of the community of physicists and is not universally shared or accepted.

In his book, *The Secret of Dreaming*,[12] Jim Poulter tells a story of how the universe and all life began from nothing, nothing but the Spirit of All Life. This Spirit began a Dreaming. At first the Spirit dreamt of Fire. Next came a big Wind and then Rain. A battle between Fire, Wind, and Rain raged on until there was a Dream of Earth and Sky. Then Land and Sea. But the Spirit grew tired of the Great Dreaming and so sent his own Life Spirit into the Great Dream, first appearing as the Barramundi or fish. The fish swam in the sea. From this point on the story of evolution continues. The fish dreamt of land, waves, and wet sand, but did not understand the dream for it only lived in the world of constant surrounding water. But the fish passed the dream on to the spirit of the turtle. Then the turtle climbed out of the sea into the very world dreamt of by the fish.

The turtle spirit dreamt of the lizard, who lived on the land. Then the lizard dreamt of the eagle. The end of all of this dreaming was the human being, who dreamt of all that the Great Spirit dreamt.

The story is really a dreamtime recounting of evolution, but this time evolution has a purpose that transcends mere survival. For each animal in the Dreaming dreams of something beyond itself. Poulter believes that this capacity to see beyond oneself, to see into the future, to imagine possibilities that do not seem to exist in our immediate environment, is the unique mark of our human consciousness. In the story, the basic driving force of the universe is this capacity. The Great Spirit brings about existence through this ability to go beyond what is to what could be. In other words, to dream.

But for what reason? The answer for Poulter lies in responsibility. The crucial Aboriginal concept is the belief that as the Big Dream continues, we are actually waking up to a greater sense of care and responsibility for the future. All humans yet to be are waiting in the dreamtime for their births. It is our responsibility to bring children into the world through our directed actions and to let them know about the Big Dream. Gradually, as we evolve further, the responsibility will become clearer that we are all part of a bigger Dream of a bigger Spirit and that we must share this responsibility for caretaking with each other.

Thus in the previous chapter I pointed out how dreaming, at least the precursor of dreaming, REM, occurs early in fetal development.

The development of the fetus is a microcosm of the development of the universe itself. It is said that the fetus goes through every stage of life, beginning with the single-celled animal, passing through the fish stage, complete with gills, all the way up to our present human form.

Perhaps we need to see this as a vital clue to what I shall call the "meaning of matter." It is to communicate all possibilities to all existence so that a responsible and loving unity of spirit and matter is fully realized. This is the Dream of the Great Spirit.

$\mathcal{Q}$UANTUM PHYSICS AND DREAMS: A PRELIMINARY SEARCH FOR THE I

Meanwhile, outside of time and space, Llixgrijb started working on its greatest achievement: a universe with height, width, depth, and time . . . a universe with the illusion of chronological history. And it created imaginary entities for its entertainment . . . imaginary entities like yourself, *patient reader! . . .*

But Llixgrijb was afraid.

"Suppose my creatures discover that they are only phantoms," wondered Llixgrijb. . . . "Suppose they learn that I am the only reality . . ."

—**Wim Coleman and Pat Perrin**
The Jamais Vu Papers[1]

So why do we dream? According to the latest research, dreaming is necessary in fetal development. It prepares the child for the world to which it shall be introduced postuterus. Our dreams, once we are in the world, are reflections of that early development. Now bring in the theory of dreams as presented by the oldest peoples of the world. According to Aboriginal thinking, dreaming is necessary for our recognition that we belong to a whole greater than our mere individual selves. It is a reflection of the future and our responsibility to continue as a species and as caretakers for the universe. Thus the universe, like the fetus, dreams to survive. In chapter 11 we will examine this more fully in the work of Montague Ullman.

Yet we are still perhaps missing something in all of this. The fetus dreams to survive in the world. The human being dreams to survive as part of the greater whole. But what about the "I"? How does that precious distinction arise that says, "I am I, Don Quixote," or whoever I am?

For it would certainly seem that we do develop our senses of individual selves or egos as we grow and mature. Do dreams play a role in that? If we dream to survive in whatever way we survive, doesn't it seem that our dreams may reflect on ego development?

The major purpose of an ego is to distinguish a self from the nonself. Survival certainly seems to depend on that. We must be able to distinguish what will harm us from what will nurture us. Thus we have our fears. Jumping for a moment from the individual self to the whole universe, if the universe dreams to survive, then what is it afraid of? Can the universe die? After all, the universe is everything that is, so what is there outside of it to be afraid of? Yet we all know that dreams do reflect strong emotions, particularly fear. Could fear arise from matter itself?

Look, I am only asking. Perhaps these questions are not scientific enough to be asked by a scientist.

Could it be that as we evolve, we will lose our fear for we will realize that we are part of a larger whole? Will this realization eventually reach to the edges of the known universe?

Who am "I"? Where am "I"? What am "I" doing? What does it all mean? These questions are at the basis of cognition whether we are awake or asleep and dreaming. They are going on all of the time. It is just that in dreaming one has little externality to anchor the process, and probably there are also these intrinsic electrophysiological and chemical changes that determine the discontinuities and other aspects of bizarreness of the dream.

The emotional intensification found in dreams should also be mentioned. In my earlier conversations with Allan Hobson (see previous chapters) I asked him what he thought about some of these matters. He believes, although it is not rigorously established, that dream cognition is fraught with considerably more intense emotion than is most wake-state cognition.

Yet, I recalled, when I am having a dream, I am not aware that I am feeling anything intensely. It is only when I recall the dream that I feel the emotions associated with the actions of the dream. So I would say I feel when I am awake. When I dream, I have potential feelings, but I don't really feel. In a lucid dream I once had, I remembered feeling fear. But did I in the dream manifest in my body all the chemical changes associated with fright? Or was the fear only felt upon awakening?

Hobson explained that with young subjects who were instructed to make a clear distinction between emotion after the fact and emotion in the dream itself, there was a lot of emotion that they believed they felt in dreams. Some of it was intense and tended to be unpleasant with a lot of anxiety. On the other hand, there were also reports of pleasure, elation, and hypomanic giddiness.

Perhaps emotions are highly evolutionary in their nature. As young people we dream perhaps more emotionally. As we grow older and hopefully wiser, perhaps we dream less emotionally. How did emotionality fit into dreams? Were emotions part of the dreaming universe?

Quantum Dreams

After talking with Hobson, I was still impressed with the jumps and discontinuities in dreams. I was beginning to suspect that the dreaming brain could be a "dreamstage" indeed of quantum-physical processes. Hobson's data was leading me to possibly a new model.

I asked Hobson if he believed that dreams were an altered state of conscious awareness. He answered most emphatically, "Yes, certainly." This was somewhat of a tricky point, however, since one needs to redefine consciousness in order to answer the question. He explained that some definitions of consciousness are restricted to waking-perception processing. If you restrict the definition to only that, then the answer is no. But Hobson thinks that consciousness is a kind of awareness that may not be only awareness of the outside world but also its representations in the brain. If so, then dream consciousness is definitely an altered state of consciousness, a very interesting alteration indeed, in which the focus of awareness is internal representations and not outside ones.

Here I want to explain how quantum physics may apply to the dreaming brain. Quantum physics is clearly the only theory that successfully explains most if not all of the physical world. Quantum physics has made possible modern electronics, computers, television, nuclear energy, lasers, and space communication. It deals with the behavior of matter and energy particularly on the scale of atoms, molecules, and subatomic particles, and lately even with objects that are as far apart as thirty feet! Today, it is still the cornerstone of our understanding of the physical universe, and if, as I speculate, this is so, it may be the basis for understanding the human mind.

As I explained in chapter 3, quantum physics has introduced a new form of order into our thinking. In the old order, events were connected by the law of cause and effect. From a given cause the effect was determined. In quantum physics this is no longer true. Instead order arises as a meaningful, often instantaneous, pattern wherein events happening at one place and one time influence, but do not cause, other events. Later in this chapter I'll provide some examples. Usually this pattern is recognized in hindsight, wherein even if all of the separate events did not happen at the same time nor even at the same place, they were yet observed to be correlated in a specific manner. This correlation is not causal and it is not teleological, yet it is highly meaningful.

The explanation of this order offered in this chapter is somewhat preliminary. More of it will come later. It is time to get just an inkling of how quantum physics may apply to the brain. This explanation arose from my conversation with Allan Hobson and his associate Robert Stickgold about my theory of the "I" and how quantum physics establishes a possibility that the "I" arises from the brain through a particular quantum-physical mechanism called quantum correlation.

Several clues led me to this theory. The first was the recognition that quantum-physical events may be occurring in neural tissue.

In a recent paper Sir John Eccles, the distinguished Nobel laureate in physiology, who also believes in the mind-body dualistic picture, postulated that small boutons, which house the neurotransmitters, emit packets of neurotransmitters called vesicles into the synaptic space probabilistically.[2] That means in a random manner, seemingly uncontrollably. Eccles believes that vesicle emission is a quantum-probabilistic event and that therefore the mind enters the body in such events by altering these probabilities in much the same way that an observer alters the probabilities of events by observing them.[3] In an earlier paper I offered the same hypothesis, only I looked at the gating mechanisms within the neural wall.[4]

In quantum physics we know that observation plays more than a passive role in determining the outcome of an experiment. But before you jump to any conclusion about this we need to consider this statement carefully. We need to look at what has now come to be called in quantum physics the observer effect.

A quantum system usually exists in a superposition of states. This means that there is a relationship between the various possibilities of an outcome in a quantum physical experiment. Each outcome is called a state. And before any observation, all possible states are said to exist simultaneously. Upon perception, observation, recognition, or cognition—the words interchange depending on whom you are speaking to—or upon making a record on a magnetic tape or in a computer memory, suddenly a superposition of states becomes a single state. That is called "the reduction of the wave packet" in the quantum physics jargon. There are many interpretations of what is happening when a reduction occurs. It is not clear what is happening.

The problem is that there is at present no physical-mathematical way to model that process. It takes place in a completely nonphysical manner. By that I reemphasize that we have no understanding of how it can take place. This reduction bothered Einstein very much and led him to believe that quantum physics was an incomplete theory because there was no way to model this effect.

More than that, quantum physics is based on a mathematical framework of nonobservable entities. The fundamental entity of quantum physics is the *quantum wave function*. The first thing about this "wave" is that it is very strange if we look at it as a physical wave. Because of certain "quantum rules," such as the Heisenberg uncertainty principle, the wave must be represented mathematically as a complex-number function. That means that it has two distinct mathematical parts: a so-called "real" part and a so-called "imaginary" part.

The use of these terms *real* and *imaginary* comes from the study of complex numbers, which also consist of real and imaginary numbers. The fact that the waves have these two parts seems to indicate that the waves cannot be objective since no one has ever "seen" an imaginary number.

It may be a rather suggestive "unconscious" or "collectively unconscious" metaphor that we must have all quantum waves composed of both real and imaginary parts, i.e., composed of a part that could be pictured as a real physical wave and a part that only exists in our imaginations. I say this because the wave appears not to be entirely real itself and is sometimes thought of as a product of the physicist's imagination altogether. In other words, the wave is not quite "out there." (In a later chapter we shall see that physicist Wolfgang Pauli was also struggling with this concept in his attempt to bridge the gap between physics and psychology.)

However, whether they are real and objective or not, all physicists must think of quantum waves "as if" they were out there in space and moving in time like any common waves you might witness, in order to give meaning to their computations of the correct mathematical probabilities of specific events in space and in time.

And there is another imaginative factor here. To arrive at a numerical probability function that specifies how likely a specific event is to occur at a specific location and time, one must multiply this wave by another wave that is similar to it but different in one essential way: it runs backward through time.[5]

This idea that one multiplies two counterstreaming waves together, one coming from the present and one coming from the future, is called the transactional interpretation.[6] What is new here is the idea that events, even those that haven't yet occurred, can generate these waves.

If true, then our notion of time needs some revision. One now has to look at events in a new light. From relativity we have learned that events can be mapped on a space-time grid and that time order in the grid is not absolute but relative to how an observer describes any pair of events. If, for example, the events are separated in space, it is not completely clear how they are separated in time, particularly if those events are the end points of a signal that travels faster than light. The time order of the events is strongly dependent on the speed of the observer.

If we draw an event map on a sheet of paper, the wave would appear to spread out on the sheet much like the wave produced by a small pebble dropped in a pond. Only this time the wave would show itself as having motion both forward and backward through time (also sideways through time; see fig. 7).

Now, when such a wave encounters another event, it stimulates that event to do the same thing. The strength of the stimulated wave depends on the wave that stimulated it, consequently the second event also sends out a quantum wave that travels both forward and backward through time. Now if the second event is somehow very dissimilar from the first event—they are off resonance so to speak—then the response to the stimulus will be weak, and little strength will be mustered by the responding event. But in any case the responding

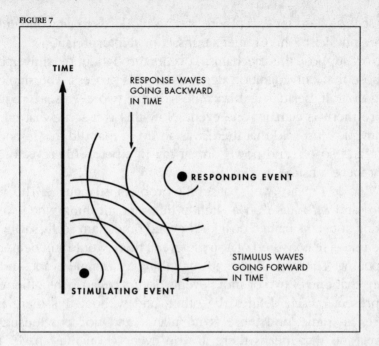

FIGURE 7

TIME

RESPONSE WAVES
GOING BACKWARD
IN TIME

● RESPONDING EVENT

STIMULUS WAVES
GOING FORWARD
IN TIME

STIMULATING EVENT

event will be a response to the offering event echoing backward through time, a kind of shaking hands across time.[7]

If we looked at all events in consciousness in this manner, we would be looking down on a pond that has many pebbles bombarding it and is sending out many, many waves. Now if we look at any two of the pebble sites, i.e., events, something rather marvelous happens. The waves tend to reinforce themselves in the space between the events and during the time between the events. They then cancel each other out in the space outside these events and before the initial or offering event and after the final or echoing event. The degree of cancellation depends on how similar the offer and echo waves are to each other. The greater the match, the greater the reinforcement between the events and the greater the cancellation outside of the events. Such is the magic of these waves. And this is in fact exactly what we need to make sense of the probabilities of events occurring.

The echo event can be seen to be nothing more than a modulating wave riding the back of the offer wave in much the same way that a radio-station wave is modulated by the information that is put on it from the broadcasting studio.

This produces the probability field of quantum physics. Now all physicists know that you must multiply these two waves together modular style as described, yet there was no model as to why one did this before physicist John Cramer's transactional interpretation.

Now suppose this mechanism occurs throughout the universe and suppose that our cognition depends on this process. The significant thing of it all, besides its bizarreness, is that two events are required before there is actually one event. Now this is a somewhat circular argument. I just said that there was an event that did this to another event and so on, and now I am saying that before there is a single event there must be two events.

What do I mean? Well, part of the problem is language. The words *before* and *after* take on a slightly different meaning when we are looking at events from a position beyond time. I am really saying that if the universe consisted of a single event, there would still be nothing happening. There would be no such thing as a single event. And that means that one of two or more events occurs because the other event is "present." Each defines the other, and without this there is no reference frame, and there is no matter and no consciousness of events, and that means there are no events. You must have "two" before you know you have "one." This is quite paradoxical to describe, as you see.

A single event, wherever it occurs, in the brain or anywhere in the universe, will not constitute an event of consciousness. You need two events. Consciousness is the relationship between two events via this offer-echo quantum-physical mechanism. The higher the probability, the greater is the awareness of the initial event. The greater the probability, the more aware is the event. Thus I suggest that the consciousness field is the product of these two quantum waves (U^*U), and this product appears as a probability field that exists everywhere, not just in the brain, but everywhere.

The richer the number of neural events there are, and this now gets into the neural-network models, the more meaningful the initial event becomes. Thus a rich probability field is built up around an outside stimulus, and that density of the probability field is what we mean by consciousness, provided that a second event is occurring that can correlate with the primary event. This is what constitutes an act of consciousness.

Now I would also suggest that the current neural-network models will not be able to replicate this simply because they don't take into account this future-to-present action suggested by quantum physics.

No binary network model will take this into account, and certainly no model that doesn't include the participation of the future into the present will take this into account.

Another key here is the notion of quantum wave superposition. The dream state is representative of superpositions of brain-generated quantum waves or quantum states. These states, although present in the waking state, are masked by the input of waking data much as sunlight masks the starlight during the day. Thus it is necessary to look at neural networks using quantum states rather than Boolean binary states.

One may ask if this quantum idea is appropriate to the waking brain as well as the dreaming brain.

It is appropriate to the waking brain, it is just that the process is overwhelmed by the input of external stimuli. Only when the outside world is shut off can the quantum superpositions be experienced directly. After all, the outside world is hazardous and requires all of the neural correlates that can be mustered to deal with it. When you have many such correlates occurring, the effect is to wash out the subtle effects of the brain-generated superpositions. The wolf at the door is not a superposition of Red Riding Hood and grandmother as it may be in the dream state.

The Freudian Ego: The Structure of Consciousness

After reading Freud's *The Ego and the Id,* I was struck by Freud's vision and drawn to make comparisons of Freud's psychical apparatus and certain concepts from classical physics. You might wonder why I am not continuing directly into Freud's model of dreams. It is because I believe that Freud's basic model of awareness is more important than his study of various dream analyses, and it is through Freud's basic theoretical constructions such as the ego and the id that I believe a better understanding of dreams is possible. Put in another way, I want to lay a groundwork of commonality between Freudian concepts of the psyche and quantum physics, particularly as it regards consciousness.

In *The Ego and the Id,* Freud has us consider the question of what we mean when we say "making something conscious." To answer this question he then introduced three psychical structures or terms: conscious (Cs.), preconscious (Pcs.), and unconscious (Ucs.). Freud wrote:

> Consciousness is attributed to the surface of the mental apparatus. All perceptions which are received from without (sense perceptions) and from within—what we call sensations and feelings—are Cs. from the start.... Internal processes represent displacements of mental energy effected in the interior. ...Do [internal processes] advance to the surface...or does consciousness make its way to them?...There must be a third alternative.[8]

It is the Pcs. that is of special interest here. Freud gives to the preconscious the attribute of latency—that of existing in a dormant or static state. The Pcs. is capable of becoming Cs. at any time. It is invoked commonly as a memory, such as where you left your car in the parking lot. The Pcs. is a "middleman" along the path between the Ucs. and the Cs.

Freud continues:

> How does a thing become conscious? [It] would thus be more advantageously stated: How does a thing become preconscious? And the answer would be: Through becoming connected with the word-presentations corresponding to it. These word-presentations are residues of memories.[9]

Thus through the interposition of word-presentations, internal thought processes are made into perceptions. Only something that was once a Cs. perception can become conscious again. Anything arising from the Ucs. (apart from feelings) must be transformed into external perceptions before it can become a part of consciousness. These word-presentations arise as latent images or memory traces derived from auditory perceptions.

Are there any constructs in quantum physics that are analogous to word-presentations? Not only do I think that there are, but I believe that by postulating that such an analogy exists we will understand why it is that dreams are essentially in picture form and not in the form of words or thoughts. I will make this clearer at the end of the book.

I would suggest here that in the language of quantum physics word-presentations constitute a set of commuting mathematical operators[10] that determine what is observable in the outside world. Assuming that the brain operates by following quantum rules, then physical operators exist that can alter the probability functions and cause differing memory impressions to appear. These operators must be invoked in any physical observation. They are coded sets of rules and are stored in a latent condition on the surface of the Pcs. Freud labeled this surface the perception-consciousness (Pcpt.-Cs.).

Feelings, on the other hand, do not become Pcs. They are either conscious or unconscious. I wish to suggest that feelings constitute a complementary way of experiencing the world. Just how these complementary experiences arise will be discussed in the last chapters of the book. I will only point out here that levels of self-reference are important in understanding how images are turned into feelings and into thought forms. Feelings are complementary to thoughts and therefore constitute a set of observables that do not "commute" (are not simultaneously knowable) with the operators that make up word-presentations. Moreover, these operations do not exist on the Pcpt.-Cs. Consequently when these operators are invoked, the Pcpt.-Cs. is bypassed.

However it is from the Pcpt.-Cs. that the ego arises. It is that part of the unconscious field that has taken the brunt of external world influences. This brunt has occurred through the intermediary of the Pcpt.-Cs. In turn the Pcpt.-Cs. is the surface of the ego, which covers the unconscious. Remaining below the ego surface is the id (about which I shall say more later). But not all of the id is so protected. The ego does not totally envelop the id. Whereas the id seeks to satisfy the needs of what Freud called the pleasure principle,[11] the ego is driven by the needs of the reality principle,[12] which asserts itself incessantly through the sensations.

Freud portrays the ego riding horseback on the id. The horsey id with its brutal and strong sexual energy must be held in check by the rider, who, lacking strength, must use his intellectual prowess to direct the horse. But like the inexperienced rider the ego must sometimes act as a steersman taking the horsey id in the direction in which it wishes to go.

The word *id* arises from the Latin *it,* the neuter form of *is* or *be.* In old English its root is *gif* relating to our word *if.* One also finds roots connected to our words *item* and *identify.* If we put these together we come up with *id,* representing two conflicting concepts: something that could exist, and something that does exist. We also have the surprising concept of identity contained in the id. Somewhere here is to be found the process we call our identity. Freud will call this the ego out of which the *superego* develops.

Quantum Freudian Id

The unconscious is most likely the ground where the superposition of quantum states occurs. That is what Freud had in mind when he said:

> The id contains everything that is inherited, that is present at birth, that is laid down in the constitution—above all, therefore the instincts which originate from the somatic organization and which find a first psychical expression here [in the id] in forms unknown to us.[13]

Most important to achieving a physics of psychology is Freud's statement:

> The logical laws of thought do not apply in the id . . . . Contrary impulses exist side by side, without canceling each other out or diminishing each other.[14]

The alogical structure of the id is like the alogical structure of the *Hilbert space* of quantum physics. This space is not necessarily a physical space, it is a space of *ideals,* concepts that are yet to be realized and are thus potentially available but not actually present. One creates experience from Hilbert space by observation in physical space. What I observe depends on the network of possible ideal observations existing in the Hilbert space. My observation is made up from the choices that are available in my Hilbert space. If my observation is not sharp, I pull up from my Hilbert space several, and possibly conflicting, ideals representing to my mind the experience of what is "out there." A sharp observation gives a clear and unambiguous view.

The id is a shadow land of possibilities that are somehow real! All possibilities exist as *vectors,* extended lines with specific directions, in

Hilbert space, much as the four directions of space exist as vectors on a map. This space is spanned by ideals representing any possible observation conflicting or not.

There is further evidence to support the theory that the id is a Hilbert space. In quantum physics, time (t) plays a peculiar role. It cannot be represented by a physical process or observable. Similarly the id does not know time. As Freud put it:

> In the id there is nothing corresponding to the idea of time, no recognition of the passage of time, and (a thing which is very remarkable and awaits adequate attention in philosophic thought) no alteration of mental processes by the passage of time. . . . Naturally the id knows no values, no good and evil, no morality.[15]

The Timeless Personality

Now, as I mentioned above, in quantum mechanics physicists have realized that time is not an observable. This means that we cannot observe time passing. What we observe when we say we are observing time, as on our wristwatches or in the sense that we are older, is not time—it is motion, experience, and memory. These are not the same, nor are they equivalent to time in itself.

In quantum mechanics we have discovered that to every physical observable in the universe there must correspond a mathematical operator. Let me clarify this further. The operator is a symbolic representation of the observable. This symbol is the means by which knowledge of that observable is gained. For example, the observable of position in space is representable in quantum mechanics by the operator q. The movement of an object through space is represented by the operator p and is called the momentum of the object. The energy-mass of an object is represented by an operator $H,$ etc.

In the language of quantum physics, word-presentations constitute the set of operators that determine what is observable (not what is felt) in the outside world. These operators are stored in a latent condition on the surface of the Pcs.—the perception-consciousness. These operators represent the way we go about observing the universe.

Their latency means that we can call them up to consciousness in a certain manner. To use them we must have material for them to operate upon. This material arises from the id without any time sense —without a time or t-operator. These are the timeless ideal vectors of Hilbert space.

Going back to quantum physics, there is no t-operator in Hilbert space. In quantum mechanics time appears as a parameter that does not separate past from future, but does separate ideal from ideal.

Repression: A Quantum Physical Model

I have always wondered how the mind was able to repress thought in the unconscious. Repression must occur if we recognize it as the principle of complementarity in action. As Freud put it, "the essence of repression lies simply in turning something away, and keeping it a distance, from the consciousness."[16]

Repression pushes any potentially anxiety-provoking concept into the unconscious. It also requires a constant vigilance to maintain the stasis of burial. Later we will look at the vigilance aspect of not only repression but how vigilance operating through continual observation actually alters the physical atomic world.

The Creation and Division of World

Following Freud, experience is divided into three parts: sensation, perception, and conception. Conception consists of a pool of symbolic representation of all sensation. Perception is a projection from the symbolic pool out into the external world where the sensation is experienced. Sensation is purely mechanical in its action and without thought or feeling. I view all sensation as part of the classical mechanical worldview.

Just as we divide the "tions" into "sensat." "percept," and "concept," we also divide reality into three parts: classical (corresponding to the senses), semiclassical or semiquantal (corresponding to the perceptions), and quantal (corresponding to the concepts). The quantum world is purely symbolic. The classical world is purely sensational. The borderline world where the symbolic and sensational meet is the perceptional or semiclassical. This is the realm of the ego. The unconscious and the symbol reference world are the same.

The Timelessness of Dreams

With quantum physics as a metaphorical basis, we can provide a new insight into the timelessness of dreams.

Nearly totally unconscious, the processes of the id include mental forms that have never been observed as well as memories that have been repressed—pushed down into the murky id. These memories, like the unobserved mental forms, influence the mental and physical life of the individual. But she or he has little control over them. They just pop up from time to time like mushrooms. I would also suggest this popping up from time to time results from a desire to see the world through the Pcpt.-Cs., i.e., through word-presentations. The well-known word-association tests used in psychoanalysis would indicate that words just seemingly pop up in association with any given word mentioned by the analyst. The words that pop up are similar to the appearance of physical attributes in quantum physics. We cannot predict ahead of time, for example, where a particle might appear in a given experiment. We can attempt to search for it, which corresponds to using the position-in-space operator, but the result is indeterminant.

During a dream experience or during a shamanic experience, particularly taking place in the dark, you shut off the outside world. That is when you are likely to see bizarre superpositions. This is a view into the Freudian id or, if you wish, the unconscious mind. I would imagine that there are people walking around in mental hospitals who do not differentiate all of the time between the outside world and the mental world of quantum superpositions. Perhaps they are in quantumland.

Dreaming is like observing an interference pattern in the famous double-slit experiment in physics.[17] And waking is like adjusting the distance between the slits so that the interference effects begin to wash out.

The Quantum Mechanics of Dreaming:
The Bridge Between Objective and Subjective Experience

From the quantum physics point of view we are trying to objectify everything. Yet we are led through our perceptions to our subjective experience. Thus from my quantum physical perspective I am led to studying objectively the subjective experience of observation—which is somewhat paradoxical. I want to have a direct experience of whatever I write about. I become the laboratory and the experiment as well as the experimenter.

From my experiences in altered-state awareness, I have been developing various theories about how consciousness works. The major question we all have in consciousness studies is: Where is the subject? Where is the "I" that witnesses all that is going on? We can map very clearly, as, for example, in Hobson's work, what is happening at the neurological and cellular level, and eventually even at the molecular level, what is happening when an event enters consciousness, or when a person enters a dream state. But where is the observing "I" that is recognizing the pattern of the visual and sensual light-show that is going on?

But before I attempt to answer that, let me briefly answer the question suggested in chapter 1: How does the I/not-I separation occur? The new answer is through *spacelike quantum physical correlation of events.* It is this correlation of events that gives rise to the experience in space and time of the self and the not-self.

Let me take the answer apart to explain the meaning of this. There are three key words combined here: *events, spacelike,* and *quantum.*

Now we all have some idea of what events are. As I see them, they are specific, locatable in terms of space and time, experiences, requiring some form of object-subject distinction to result in an experience. Thus something becomes an event when it is noticed. Now before you claim that I am arguing in a circle, for after all I am attempting to explain how experience arises in the first place, let me complete this line of reasoning.

The word *quantum* comes up here. It refers to the rather specific way in which possibilities are changed into actualities according to the laws of quantum physics. Briefly, a possibility becomes an experienced event—an actuality—when it is an observed event. Again notice the circularity implied in this action. I am attempting to define how this happens in terms of a process that already states that it does happen. And again I ask the reader to bear with me. This is no easy job, and I'm still only in the preliminary discussion of quantum dreaming!

The third word is *spacelike*. This word arose in the early history of Einstein's special theory of relativity. It refers to the way two events may be related to each other simultaneously in space and time. If you imagine billions of fireworks all exploding in separate parts of the sky at once, and that in some way these explosion events are connected together (correlated), then you have the idea of spacelike connections. In the model proposed here, the self exists "out there" in the space-like network of all events capable of being correlated.

In this "spacelike" view, you are aware of the world around you because your self actually extends into that world. A self primarily concerned with sensations is skinbound.[18] Skinbound consciousness is a necessary step in the growth and evolution of awareness. But it does not lead to self-awareness. Or perhaps better put, it leads to a self-awareness that cannot differentiate between self and skin sensation. Not to put this down. It is a necessary development of evolution.

These spacelike connections are not what you might expect; they require quantum physical correlations in order to develop the self. This is the key concept.

Peter Russell in his book, *The Global Brain,*[19] points out that all creatures evolved through communication between individual parts. As the parts connected, they developed an extended self-awareness. The process can be seen in biology. The cell's self-awareness is limited. If it limits itself too much, it becomes cancerous. The cooperative behavior of cells produces organs. Organs produce beings. And if those beings dream, the beings develop self-awareness.

Limited self-awareness, what I call skin awareness, is incapable of correlating with stimuli outside the skin. To go beyond this limit, we dream. Paradoxically, we shut off the outside world to correlate with the universe.

Does the "I" Exist at the Molecular Level?

How does "I" appear? "I" seems to be arising in the density of the probability field occurring at all of the sites correlating with the stimulus, regardless of time, and in fact seemingly beyond time.

Synchronistic acausal connections, those that I called spacelike quantum physical correlation of events, produce awareness. And these connections occur everywhere. There is "I" present in all the universe. We won't find any little being inside of ourselves. There is no homunculus. Thus we have to look at the process itself and its meaning as a physical phenomenon. Out of this concept the "self"-concept arises.

And yet paradoxically, I have concluded that there is no "I." The processes of "I"-realizations, like the realizations of the Eastern mystics, is the whole. Thus one may conclude: therefore, I am not.

In a sense this is true. Or in another sense "I" am all that is. So if you throw out the subject and say one doesn't exist, and that all is objective, then in some funny way that we don't yet fully understand, you have to come to the conclusion that all processes are alive and cognitive. They all have cognitive latency.

This has been a preliminary look at some data and some theory and some speculation. Before you reach the end of the book, we will attempt to look at this again in terms even more specific to dreaming and to how the dreams provide the correct laboratory setting for the subtle quantum physical experiment that the "Big Dreamer" is concocting, the realization that "I" am the whole universe, if I choose to evolve enough to see it.

*T*ELEPATHIC
DREAMS AND SPECIES SURVIVAL

———

Now I know that it is not out of our single souls we dream. We dream
anonymously and communally, if each after his own fashion. The
great soul of which we are a part may dream through us, in our
manner of dreaming, its own secret dreams, of its youth, its hope, its
joy and peace—and its blood sacrifice.

—*Thomas Mann*
The Magic Mountain[1]

Today we know, scientifically speaking, that there are three principal
states of consciousness: waking, sleeping, and dreaming. I am sure
that there are more, but these three are well documented scientifically
and are certainly obvious to most of us. An electroencephalograph
(EEG), an instrument that records electrical brain activity, detects
three distinct characteristic patterns or brain waves during these three
states. Yet, during REM periods, the EEG pattern is similar to the
waking state pattern. Could there have been an earlier primal state of
consciousness that has passed through the halls of time and evolved
into the present three?

In much the same way that we presently conceive of the universe's
beginning, starting, as it were, from a single point, possibly there was
such a single state of consciousness before there was the present
three. Current thinking about physics suggests that when the universe
began, things were, in a way, simpler. There was only one force in the
universe. But as it evolved, that force broke itself up into the four
known forces[2] we are familiar with today. Perhaps a similar thing
happened in consciousness.

Is there any evidence of this? In other words, does there exist
anything in present brain research that would suggest that dreaming,
waking, and sleeping were somehow merged into one state of con-

sciousness? If there was any evidence, it would necessarily involve information that is normally received or experienced in one state of consciousness being available when the recipient was in another. For example, a dreaming person would become aware of events taking place in waking life. Could a person while asleep and dreaming somehow become aware of events that were taking place in the outside world? It is this question that will concern us here as we delve into the work of Montague Ullman and others regarding telepathic dreams and the role of dreams in species-connectedness.

Telepathic dreams include dreams of prophecy, links between a dreamer and an awake person, dreams that connect one dreamer with another, and dreams in which an awake person attempts to send a picture to a dreamer.

Ullman points out that precognitive dreams are distinguished from telepathic dreams and that even though both are paranormal, telepathy normally refers only to paranormal contact between one's mind and other minds present or past but not future. He also explains that most paranormal dreams are precognitive (dealing with the future) rather than telepathic (dealing with the past or present). Consistent with my description in chapter 10, wherein it is possible for quantum waves to travel forward, backward, and sideways in time, I have used the term *telepathic* to include both Ullman's definition of that term and the notion of precognition.

In the previous chapter I explained how the brain possibly operates through quantum physical correlations, events that are meaningfully connected synchronistically but not necessarily causally. I pointed out these correlations may be necessary for the development of a sense of self and not-self, i.e., an ability to differentiate self from the rest of the universe. Here we shall explore these correlations in more detail from a quantum physical point of view showing how dreams may be the state of consciousness that is necessary to strengthen and at times weaken these correlations.

The quantum physical aspects arise because quantum physics itself does not deal with the "outside world" of matter but, instead, with ghostlike clouds of overlapping possibilities, essences that are in a very real sense dreamlike. In a nutshell, by controlling these ghostlike possibilities, one gains some control of the real world. How and to what extent control arises may be due to just how much is correlated and how many sensory experiences are involved in the appearance of the events.

Ordinary or nontelepathic dreams differ from telepathic dreams in only one way: the data that is correlated during the dream. Ordinary dreams usually correlate the day's remembered experience (daily residue) with past associations and/or future expectations contained as memories. They can also introduce anticorrelations as a mechanism to wipe out memories that do not serve the survival of the individual or of the human species (see chapter 7). Telepathic dreams are quite different in that they tend to correlate feelings and emotions with space-time events.

Closely connected to telepathic dreams is the related issue, as theorized by Dr. Montague Ullman, that dreams serve to help the human species survive with survival of the individual as a secondary, but necessary, issue. Dreams seem to originate in a manner that escapes our ordinary waking selves. We tend to dream of things that we may never have even thought we had any concern with. Our waking awareness is concerned with space-time-matter issues. We organize our daily experiences according to our coordination with time, space, and matter. Not so in our dreams. There we seem to link events, not according to space and time, but to feeling and emotion.

Why would our dreams do this? Ullman suggests that dreams are concerned with the "assessment of damage to, repair and enhancement of our connection to others."[3] While awake we operate fairly self-centeredly, fragmentedly, and with concern for individual survival as deemed through sociological pressures. During sleep and in dreams we seem to rearrange the daily residue of wake life according to different priorities. The dreaming self is concerned with anything that interferes with its connection with other human and sometimes nonhuman beings. This is accomplished chiefly through visual metaphor.[4] Ullman refers to dreams as metaphors in motion.

Dream metaphors tend to link feelings and emotions with visual imagery. How we connect a feeling with an image is unknown, although I will offer a speculative theory based on quantum physics in chapter 20. It is amazing that we do this unconsciously or perhaps during our sleep. It happens so quickly. We have a dream image, and we feel something stirring as a result of that image. While most imagery arises from the previous day and the past, occasional images arise connecting the dreamer with the future or with events that are not part of the person's local or past environment.

Perhaps we are putting this question of connection of image and feeling the wrong way round. It may be that image and feeling are already joined, and during waking, self-centered life, we dismantle the connection, cutting it in two. We all too often cut asunder our feelings from our sensory experiences. The movement of the self through waking life, although telepathy does occur, may be the process of separating feeling from space-time; while during dreaming life, we refresh the connection, we heal the cut. Telepathic dreams are in this sense healings that must occur, reestablishing our connection with others through our feelings.

Thus dream telepathy is a corollary of human survival. We communicate telepathically through dreams to keep ourselves informed of threatening forces and to communicate with other members of our species about these concerns, regardless of the source of these threats. In waking life we seem to know what is the cause of all of our problems. It is "that guy" out there. But in dreams, the distinction of "out there" and "in here" is not the same.

Indeed, the problem of survival is strongly dependent on the boundaries we put between ourselves and the rest of the universe. Just where do I leave off and you begin? To what extent am I a part of humanity and at the same time an independent being? This question is constantly being asked, constantly being surveyed, as each of us encounters time and moves through space beginning and ending relationships with others and our environment. Where we sense our boundaries, how far we are extended in space and time, is largely determined during our nightwork—the business of our dreams.[5]

Now this notion may seem strange. Most of us consider that we are no more than our bodies, particularly if we follow classical science. To even think that I may extend beyond the boundaries of my own skin seems to be sheer fantasy.

But is it? If you remember Libet's data (see chapter 6), we tend to refer experience right back to the site of that experience even though we "know" that each experience is "in here" registering in our brains. Remember that Libet showed through his experiments that subjects refer experience back in time to the origin of the stimulus even though the brain did not show that the stimulus had evoked a conscious awareness until half a second later. In a similar manner, he pointed out that we also refer visual experience right back to the site of the vision, rather than to our retinal nets.

This is perhaps a clue that objectivity is largely dependent on the subject and that the "out there"/"in here" division is somewhat arbitrary. What I propose here is that dreams serve as a necessary mechanism that provides us with the ability to place that boundary. Usually we have no problem with this when we are talking about sensory experience. But what about experiences that are quite external to our skins? Is it possible that an event happening "out there" quite far away from me, both in time and space, could have a meaning for me?

Well, yes, it could. But not in the ordinary sense of meaning as the provocation of a causal link between two events, an event in the physical world and an event in the consciousness of the perceiver. The meaning would involve our feelings and possibly our emotions.

But then, how would that event become part of my consciousness? It is here that we make a radical change in our view of the universe. The normal view is that the universe consists of separate objects that *must* interact with each other through the exchange of some material agent. Given this exchange of a material agency, *both* objects involved in the transaction suffer a change in movement. Here, Newton's third law of motion dictates the reason: when an object exerts a force on a second object, the second object exerts an equal and opposite force on the first.

Take away the material agency, and the objects go about their own business as if the other object failed to exist. Newton's law of inertia is the prime axiom of this thinking: an object in motion or at rest tends to stay that way unless acted on by an outside force.

However, quantum physics seems to be pointing in a very different direction from that indicated by Newton's laws. Instead of separated objects acted on by forces through material agencies, we have potential objects, ghostlike images of objects that appear like out-of-focus images, arising out of a sea of possibilities. We have potential interactions that not only indicate the movements of these potential objects but also the potential movements of these potential objects.[6] Thus objective qualities appear to arise from some deeper order, an order that resists definition in any objective sense. David Bohm calls this the *implicate order*.[7]

Taking Bohm's intuitive concept in tow, we see the universe as one essential and potential *whole* in which separated parts arise as a result of some deeper action. This action produces not only the material universe but the means by which the material universe can be appraised: mind-consciousness. From this point of view, wherever there is a material event, there *must* be some form of consciousness to perceive it. Now how this happens is still a mystery. A big clue, I suggest, lies in the dreaming brains of humans.

Perhaps all so-called external events arise from this deeper action in the implicate order. Just as no two electrons differ in their fundamental properties, no two mind-sets that perceive these electrons differ in their fundamental properties. Just as we could postulate that all electrons are the same electron,[8] all mind-sets are the same mind.

Taking this perspective, I suggest that external events are already part of one consciousness and that the problem is not how to make them fit into the mechanical local model of individual self-consciousness, but to see that we must do something to "turn off" outside "extrasensory" experiences and "turn on" or "tune in to" normal sensory experiences because they appear to be essential for our individual survival.[9]

Ullman goes farther in suggesting that we dream to survive not as individuals but as a species. Thus we would turn on awareness of extrasensory experiences to the degree that they affected the survival of our species. This would suggest that whatever we are doing during the dreaming we are only partially successful in tuning out those events that are external to our individual survival. It would also suggest that when events become catastrophic, threatening our survival as a species, we all would sense them in our dreams.

What are we doing during the dreaming phase of our existence? I suggest that we are doing two complementary things. We are correlating data synchronistically (quantum physical spacelike[10] separated events) and causally (classical physical timelike[11] separated events). Just how we draw the line is perhaps a mystery[12] However we make the distinction, I suggest that we accomplish the training to do just this during the nightwork we call dreams.

Telepathic dreams are essentially no different from ordinary dreams except that they tend to correlate data involving events that will occur in the future and/or are occurring simultaneously with the dream that are nonlocally[13] connected to the dreamer. None of this "science-fiction-like" correlation could be understood if the mechanism for it were not already a part of quantum physics.

Nonlocality or actions at a distance are commonplace in quantum physics today. These refer to meaningfully connected events that are happening at the same time but at different places, a necessary attribute for telepathic connections. What about meaningfully connected events that are happening at the same place but at different times? Certainly this would be necessary to explain using quantum physics precognitive connections between events.

In a series of experiments carried out in 1967, Physicists R. L. Pfleegor and L. Mandel at Rochester University in Rochester, New York, were able to demonstrate that a single photon (particle of light) somehow emitted from independent sources[14] of light could produce an interference effect (see the footnote in the previous chapter discussing the double-slit interference pattern) in a target area. This occurred even though only one single light particle was present in the region at any given time.[15] Two lasers would emit light sporadically, and photons would arrive in the target region at different times. By the time a second photon had arrived at the target, the first photon would have been well absorbed, so that one could not explain the interference as the result of having two (or more) photons present simultaneously at the target area. Instead, each photon was arriving at the target area as if "it knew" that it could arrive there both/either earlier and later and be emitted by both lasers!

Each photon had two different pathways through time to reach the same place. Thus it interfered with itself. The future possibility for the photon can be viewed as communicating with itself in the possible past in some way. This is a quantum physical precognition effect and, as we shall see shortly, could be an explanation for precognition.

Later I will tell you about holographic dream images. Here I want to point out that holograms are capable of storing images taken at different times with the resultant single image showing interference effects. Thus a past image superimposed on a present image will distort the present image. If this process is quantum physical as well as holographic, then the future possibility will send "ripples" back in time to the present, creating a distorted dream image. This may be the reason why it is so difficult to see into the future.

Dream Telepathy

Are telepathic effects seen in dreams? The only difference between telepathic and nontelepathic dreams is the extent or locality of the data "field" being correlated. While ordinary dreams appear to be correlating local data, the field of everyday life, and telepathic dreams, nonlocal data, the field of events outside of our normal environment, the mechanism is the same.

The only reason any of us find any difficulty with this is the belief that only local events are capable of being related to each other. It is precisely this point that is refuted by quantum physics. Any two events, no matter how far apart they may be, no matter that they are not connected by any physical signal, are capable of being correlated.[16] This means that meaning arises from their correlation. This meaning results in an experience of self different from something "out there" as nonself.

The process of differentiating self and nonself is fundamental and is what we mean when we say that an event occurs, when we see an event occurring, when we label an event's attributes, when we describe events, and in general, when we have an experience of the world.

Thus the self/nonself split is responsible for awareness of the universe as "out there" and awareness of "in here" or the "I." The two are the same experience, for one cannot be aware of "out there" without simultaneously being aware of "in here."[17]

Now the dream is the experiment that sets in motion where that boundary between I and not-I is to take place. The wider in space and time that boundary is, the greater is the extended sense of self. If we were to be telepathic at all times, we would not feel that we were living inside of our skins. Our senses would include "direct experience" of being well outside. Thus if I were in telepathic communication with all events in the universe, I would be all of the universe, in much the same way that I am in telepathic communication with all of my body, and therefore I am my body.[18]

What Does Dreaming Have to do with Ego?

Now why is the dream so special in this process? We need to consider this question in light of the Freudian model of ego and id. I suggest that these constructs are still useful today if we regard them in the light of quantum physics. From the new point of view I take here, the ego is that construct that is in the business of causality—linking events in a causal manner, seeing cause/effect relationships, determining which events "out there" are life-threatening; while the id is that construct that is in the business of synchronicity—linking events that are perhaps meaningful, dealing with feeling and intuition, but not related in a causal manner. Thus the ego links events in a time-ordered timelike fashion while the id links events in a spacelike non-time-ordered, feeling, synchronous fashion. There is really no separation between id and ego, only a complementarity.

The dream is the id's domain.[19] The work of the id is to attempt correlation of events (hence the bizarreness and ordinariness of dreams). Any events are correlated, that is any events that are deemed survival worthy. Now what is survival worthy gets us into questions of evolution and Darwinian survival of the species. Both mysteries are resolved at once when one sees that quantum waves travel backward through time warning us what not to do.

The timelessness of the id is remarkable. If taken literally, the id contains all that we know that has been suppressed or in some sense "forgotten," i.e., the unremembered past going back in time, if I may speculate, even before the birth of the individual, all that we can know as a result of uncontrollable actions we take, and all that would be the future.

This is my interpretation of Libet's discussion of the Ten Commandments described in chapter 5, and why they essentially tell us "don't do that." They are God's messages, the "Big Dreamer's" messages from the future. We have received those messages and are continually receiving them. When we fail to pay attention to them, we get in trouble. Our bodies work like machines, but we have this voice inside that comments on our actions all of the time, if we care to listen. That voice that you hear warning you, that feeling that you have not to do this, comes from your future.

If you don't like God telling you what to do, then forget this metaphor and believe in Darwin and quantum physics. Either way you are evolving toward something, and your dreams are the school ground where you learn about the future that you are evolving to.

Now what would make one person capable of telepathic dreams while another feels lucky if he has any memory of dreams at all? I would suggest that survival schemes built up over the life of the individual are vital in this regard. If a child "needs" to see beyond his or her skin, he or she will do so. Such a need could have developed as a result of early childhood trauma. I'll return to this in a later chapter.

Experimental Dream Telepathy

Dream Telepathy, the major work on the subject, was written by Montague Ullman and Stanley Krippner, with Alan Vaughan.[20] The authors have recently revised their book due to the large growth in interest in such dreams, especially dreams that are shared by people in close personal relationships.

It is perhaps surprising that although some attention has been paid to such dreams, little of the data so patiently accumulated over twelve years has reached mainstream psychology. Much of this work was put on solid scientific ground when Dr. Stanley Krippner and Charles Honorton joined the research effort originally proposed by Dr. Ullman when he was the director of dream research at Maimonides Medical Center in Brooklyn, New York. Krippner was chiefly responsible for producing the quantitative experiments that the team accomplished over the twelve-year period.

Altogether the team did twelve formal experiments of which nine were statistically significant. In the revised edition of their book, Ullman et al. included an article by Dr. Irvin Child, who analyzed all of the critical reports in the literature of their results, showing that they indeed had valid evidence for telepathy in dreams.

Child was concerned with the fact that the psychological community did not pay attention to these results and yet he could not find any flaws in the work. Child pointed out that the psychological community has a scotoma (a blind spot in the retina) about it. What they cannot control and predict as far as psychology is concerned does not exist, a commonly held belief in other scientific circles as well. The belief is that if you cannot control the phenomena and you cannot predict them, they cease to exist.

Such concerns, as echoed in modern research, are really not new. Anomalous dreams have been dealt with over a long range of history. Even in the days of the glory of ancient Rome, the Roman orator Cicero complained that dream divination was sheer superstition. Yet there are many accounts of spontaneous telepathic dreams that are seldom described in journals, simply because of their spontaneity and lack of reproducibility.

Consider the following example taken from Ullman et al.'s book. One of the authors, Alan Vaughan, had watched an interview on television of the author Kurt Vonnegut, Jr. A few nights later he dreamt of

Vonnegut and then wrote to Vonnegut about the dream on March 13, 1970: "You appeared in a dream I had this morning. We were in a house full of children. You were planning to leave soon on a trip. Then you mentioned that you were moving to an island named Jerome. As far as I know, there is no such place, so perhaps the name Jerome or initial 'J' has some related meaning."

Vonnegut's answer to the letter was dated March 28, 1970. "Not bad. On the night of your dream, I had dinner with Jerome B. [an author of children's books], and we talked about a trip I made three days later to an island named England."

Clearly there was a connection between Vaughan's dream and Vonnegut's experience, all happening the same night, although it is probable that the discussion between Vonnegut and his friend Jerome took place before the dream. But the connection cannot be considered to be causal or local since there was no signal between the two events. One would have to consider this a spontaneous telepathic dream containing the facts of the conversation mixed in a capricious manner, typical of such dreams.

A series of experimental dream-telepathy episodes were also reported in Ullman et al.'s book.[21] Laura A. Dale, a research associate under the direction of Dr. Gardner Murphy from the American Society for Psychical Research, who had been a subject in a series of experiments since 1942, and Dr. Ullman decided in early 1953 to record their daily dreams and check for telepathic communication appearing as correspondences in their dreams. The theory was quite simple: tell one person of a pair in telepathic rapport a key idea or word, and see if the second person dreams about that key. For example, tell person A the word *dog* and check to see if person B dreams about dogs. The second might dream about something associated with a dog, for example, "bite, bark, or bone" might be dreamt of.

Ullman and Dale modified this approach. They decided to use a nonsense word and present that word to both dreamers as a shared stimulus. They set their timers to present the tape-recorded nonsense word to both at the same time (usually around three A.M.), while the two slept twenty miles apart.

In the two-year period of their experiment, Ullman and Dale met weekly and compared dream notebooks, and a number of correspondences and precognitive dreams were recorded. In April 1955, Dale demonstrated that telepathic communication was possible from one dreamer to another. In her dream of April 2, she reported:

I went to see a doctor. He turned out to be a seedy little man with a shabby office. . . . I waited for a long time for my turn, then the doctor saw me. I was shocked by his ungrammatical English. I don't recall my complaint, but he said nothing was wrong with me and called the next patient.

Dale associated the dream with her visit to a doctor the month before, and her being told that nothing was wrong with her. This "real" doctor was, however, quite respectable and showed none of the "seedy" characteristics of her dream doctor.

However, the same evening of April 2, 1955, Ullman dreamed: "I seemed to be trying to recall the name of a doctor I interned with who went into the navy and then into psychiatry."

Given that this was an example of dream-to-dream telepathy, Ullman explained that since he did not like his "navy" doctor, it may have been the case that Dale's dream doctor was put in a negative light by Ullman's antipathy for his doctor.

Later in June 1955, another correspondence appeared in their dreams. On June 15, Dale dreamed "something about being in a summer resort—small hotel or boardinghouse—Atlantic City?" while Ullman dreamt "something about being on a beach." The next night Ullman reported, "I was walking on a boardwalk."

A month earlier on May 4, 1955, Ullman reported:

There was a tattered slip of paper. Something about an interview with the FBI in Atlantic City. The words on it said, "He will talk." I was going there on the subway and going into a hotel in Atlantic City. They would be surprised when they saw that I put up a stand.

The key feature of prophetic dreams or for that matter any reports of divination or telepathy is that the dreamer appears to know something that has not been communicated to him via any normal timelike causal sequence of events. The chief difficulty with research into prophetic dreams is that they occur spontaneously.

Let me clarify this. For an event to be known it would seem, from the point of view of causal science, that the event had to have occurred in the past, and that the event had to have had some way of sending its message to the perceiver, and moreover, that message could not travel from the event to the perceiver faster than the speed of light.

All this constitutes what is called a timelike connection between the event in question and the perceiver of the event.

Remember, timelike connections are the backbone, as it were, of causal science, i.e., causality. They are the framework for locality—that no influence, other than local influences, can reach a given event. This means that if two events are connected and they are spatially separated, one of the events, the prior, had to send a signal to the other event, the latter, by emitting a particle of one kind or another. Thus the latter event is only disturbed locally by the presence of this emitted particle and by nothing else acting at a distance. In a nutshell, if something happens here, it had to have a previous cause there. And "there" cannot be any farther away than the time it would take for a light signal to reach from "there" to "here." This is due to the fact that physical forces, all of them as we know them in physics, take a finite time to propagate from one point in space to another. The fastest propagation speed is the speed of light, and the messenger in this case is a photon.

Given then that telepathic dreams do occur, then what are we to make of them in the light of causality and locality? Such dreams provide the dreamer with information about the future or about events that are happening simultaneously or with information that is not locally connected to the dreamer—that is, no signal was sent. Clearly these events in the future or in the immediate nonlocal environment of the dreamer cannot be connected in a causal timelike manner to the dreamer. Although one could say that the dream may be a reflection of memories, there is clearly no way that a dream could reflect what is happening nonlocally or what is to happen in the future.

Neural Nets and Quantum Nets

How do telepathic dreams occur? How do they fall under the hypothesis that we dream to develop the self and the corollary hypothesis that matter itself dreams? Here we need to consider again the neural network models of the previous chapters. Our brains and neural-network models of our brains operate associatively. Events in one part of the net stimulate the rest of the net to reproduce a particular pattern. This results in a recall of a memory that was created in the first place by the plasticity of the connections in the interconnecting matrix.

However, these nets operate causally: the neuronal units of the net are interconnected through a matrix that will respond in time, i.e., given enough time. Thus a change of value in one neuron will be sent over the connecting matrix to the other neurons, ultimately causing them to change values, after a while. All of this happens over time as the network "interrogates itself" over several cycles in attempting to reconstruct the whole truth from a piece of the truth. This would explain the normal sense of a time delay as we attempt to remember some event based on another associative event.

Quantum mechanical nets, if they are ever simulated with a computer, will operate differently. Neurons throughout the net will not be connected by anything like wires or a mathematical connecting matrix. Nor will they have definite values. Instead they will be "quantum physically correlated," and each will be in an indefinite state. As a result of any one neuron's taking on a definite value, the other neurons in the net will instantaneously take on values as if the connection between them were superluminal. The result of this "beyond time" interconnection produces a range of "popping-on" neurons acting simultaneously, giving rise, I believe, to a distributed "sense of presence" that I label as the self.

Thus, in the model I propose, the dreaming brain is capable of correlating events occurring elsewhere and "in here." Normally the awake brain does the same thing, but the overwhelming "out there" data swamps any hope of correlating the "in here" events with such events as those that will occur in the future or those that are occurring out of normal causal range. But the dreaming brain is shut off from the overwhelming causal data field of the outside world. Thus it would seem that it could on occasion "read" events that would be considered paranormal. It would not read this data as unusual any more than your awake brain reads the rustling of a tree or a bird's flight as unusual.

But for this to happen there would have to be some previous event that set up the quantum state of correlation or, as some physicists have discovered,[22] some event in the future that will correlate the events in question. Given that this correlation mechanism can generate a correlation of events in the past or the future, it would at least appear that the same mechanism that explains the rise of the self also explains psychic or telepathic dreaming. All that is necessary is that something happened in the past or that something will actually happen in the future that involves the dreamer's brain and the outside world.

Wholeness, Telepathy, and Species Connectedness

Ullman in his paper, "Dreams, Species-Connectedness, and the Paranormal,"[23] makes an interesting point about consciousness being nature's way of making humans behave cooperatively. In Ullman's view, consciousness is not just our personal recollection or reflection.[24] It is not a property of a brain in isolation but of a brain in communication with other brains. Thus we are conscious because we are in communication with other human beings. Even though it appears that our being is centered in our brains, if consciousness is the relating of one brain with another, then one's being is centered not in one's self but in the relation between one's brain and others.

Maybe we are missing the point in looking for consciousness in individual brains. My consciousness is changed every time I am in relationship with anybody. Thus it may be that my consciousness does not exist just "under my skin" but also out there.

Now why should "my" consciousness exist in such a bizarre manner? Perhaps the answer lies in the survival value of having consciousness exist as an extended field out of which both space-time-matter and thinking-feeling-intuiting all arise. Following this line of thought, events arise. They have components, aspects that manifest both as measurably evident in space-time coordination and immeasurably evident but equally significant as feelings and intuitions. During dreams we reexperience the wholeness of the events of our lives. This process involves interference patterns of quantum physical correlations in our brains. If the patterns reinforce, the dream is integrated. If the patterns interfere or reinforce in destructive interference, the pattern is erased. Either way, we learn to survive.

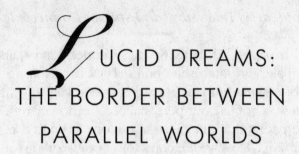

CHAPTER • 12

LUCID DREAMS: THE BORDER BETWEEN PARALLEL WORLDS

―――――

SOCRATES: *What evidence could be appealed to, supposing we were asked at this very moment whether we are asleep or awake?*

THEAETETUS: *Indeed, Socrates, I do not see by what evidence it is to be proved; for the two conditions correspond in every circumstance like exact counterparts.*

—*Plato's* Theaetetus

For a long time dream researchers believed that dreaming was only possible when a person was asleep, and by asleep they generally meant not awake or unconscious. To be sleeping and be conscious or awake was a seeming non sequitur. An awake dream was nearly an oxymoron. But all of that has changed in recent times. Starting with the work of Dr. Keith Hearne in England and continuing with the work of Dr. Stephen LaBerge, Dr. Jayne Gackenbach, and many others in the United States, a new field of dream research has opened.[1]

We now know that it is possible for people to be fully conscious while remaining asleep and dreaming at the same time. In fact, although until recently this area of dream research was not a popular one scientifically speaking, it has been known for a long time, since the days of Aristotle, that so-called *lucid* dreams are possible. Even more recently lucid dreams made their way into the laboratory for study.

The term *lucid dreams* was coined by Frederik W. van Eeden,[2] a Dutch physician who described personal experiences of luminous phenomenon in such dreams as far back as 1913. But well before van Eeden's dreams, Tibetan Buddhists worked with many forms of dream states of consciousness including what we now call lucid dreams. Stephen LaBerge in his book[3] points out that Tibetan Buddhists have practiced lucid dreaming since at least the eighth century and believe that they are extremely important for "self-discovery." Tarthang Tulku describes lucid dreaming as beneficial for changing attitudes, becoming more flexible, and bringing forward new dimensions of reality.[4] This practice is called dream yoga.

With practice the Tibetan dreamers were literally able to "dream anything into existence" in their dreams. Through their techniques they believed that they were able to see an essential truth of the mind's existence throughout the universe. Thus what they experienced in "waking dreams" or lucid dreams was parallel to what was experienced in their waking life.

Tibetan Buddhists are taught to realize that everything in the universe is in a constant state of change, nothing is permanent. Indeed the nature of the universe is impermanence. All matter and forms of matter, whether they are cosmic scaled, human scaled, or subatomic, are subject to the will of the perceiver.

One requires training to perceive this. Lucid dreaming provides a necessary step in this training of the intent of the practitioner. Through practice the student sees that form in the dream state is nothing more than the plaything of the mind and is as unstable as a mirage. Further practice enables the student to see that all forms of sensation in the waking world are equally as unreal as those in the dream state.

What are lucid dreams? Having experienced them on several occasions, I thought I knew. However, after talking with many researchers about the subject, I am not so sure. In fact this has been one of the major blocks in attempting to do dream research on lucid states. Gackenbach defines a lucid dream as "a dream during which one knows one is dreaming while the dream is ongoing."[5]

My Own Lucid Dream of Flying

I'll never forget my first lucid dream. Talk about flying, I really took off. I found myself flying through the ruins of ancient English castles, although at the time I was in California. Later, I actually went to the west coast of Wales and discovered similar castle ruins. Was my dream prophetic? Or did it have another hidden meaning? What was different about this dream?

The outstanding difference between this dream and others like it that I have had, and ordinary dreams, was the extreme sense of reality I felt. It was a three-dimensional dream, and I was flying in it and sensing the environment around me as if the experience were actually occurring. And, most important of all, I knew that I was dreaming when I was flying.

From my own experience, lucid dreams are quite different in both dream content and experience. The major factor is the awareness that one is dreaming while the dream progresses and the vivid details that one can remember after the dream. Upon awakening, the dreamer has immediate recall of the dream and the recall that during the dream one felt in control of the events of the dreaming entity. I use the word *entity* because, although I know the entity is "I," it feels different from my normal waking persona in several ways. The awareness of being split into two conscious minds is the most striking difference. There is the sleeping person "at home in bed" and there is the person experiencing the dream and knowing all along that he or she is in bed at home.

A Brief Review of Lucid Dream Research

In her recent review[6] Gackenbach pointed out that there have been essentially two research approaches to lucidity in dreams, psychological and psychophysiological. Using a psychological approach, researchers have attempted to classify such dreams as a form of information processing wherein lucidity is seen as a cognitive tool. Thus when we dream, we are attempting to utilize the same processes we use when we attempt to understand the world "out there" in waking life. Just as we utilize models of the world in discerning what is real from unreal in waking life, we attempt to do the same things when we are dreaming. The fact that most of us seem to fail to have lucid dreams or to remember them may be due to our failure to model our experience as a dream.[7]

Other psychological approaches see lucidity as another form of self-reflectiveness. Susan Blackmore in particular places a strong emphasis on how the model of a self in the world gets constructed. As she puts it:

> We create all the time a model of self in the world. It is continuously built up from and checked against sensory information and backed up by memory. The result is that we seem to be a person located inside a body, perceiving a stable external world. In other words, we have an effective "model of reality."[8]

Charles Tart, a well-known researcher in parapsychology and altered states of consciousness, attempts to develop the concept of lucidity in a broader context that he calls "lucid waking."[9] In a review article he wrote, he described lucid dreaming as:

> an altered d-SoC (discrete state of consciousness) characterized by the lucid dreamer experiencing himself as located in a world or environment that he intellectually knows is "unreal" (or certainly not ordinary physical reality) while simultaneously experiencing the overall quality of his consciousness as having clarity, the lucidity of his ordinary waking d-SoC.[10]

For most of us the ability to distinguish what is real from unreal is a major concern. Consciousness is in a sense an ongoing battle in which an attempt to model reality correctly fights against our penchant for creating illusions. For Tart this battle is an illusion. Tart notes:

> Psychologically . . . we tend to regard these [battles] as "tricks" of the senses, as mechanical breakdowns, rather than drawing the most profound lesson that *all* perception is constructed and not necessarily accurate.[11]

This point of view is similar to Buddhist and other Eastern spiritual practices that indicate that we all "live in illusion." It does not indicate that the physical world is unreal, however, only that our perceptions are fraught with "unreality." Thus from this viewpoint dreaming involves, perhaps, a higher degree of unreality. This is lessened when the dreamer "wakes up" in the dream, and the dream becomes lucid.

For Tart, lucidity is the booty to be won in the battle for clarity, whether one is dreaming or awake. This prize is constantly being sought through the practice of meditation and conscious living: a greater sense of personal presence and awareness with little lapses into fantasy and daydreaming or wasteful thinking. Instead of seeking the outside for satisfaction, one is satisfied just in *being* regardless of what state that being happens to be in.

Of course, a number of other researchers in the field have other viewpoints. I refer the reader to the excellent review article by Gackenbach mentioned above. In a later chapter I will describe how lucid dreams may be pointing to a fourth state of consciousness and possibly an evolutionary jump.

Psychophysiological approaches have shown that lucidity is somewhat of an effort for the brain and that a more aroused REM sleep experience occurs while one is lucid. Still further, some researchers have attempted to model lucidity in terms of neural networks (see chapter 7).

For example, LaBerge has studied lucid dreams in the laboratory and has found that they require an unusual degree of brain activation. To dream lucidly one's brain must be in good condition. In many cases the brain might not be up to a lucid dream. In studies LaBerge conducted he showed that if a subject was showing delta brain waves, the subject turned out to be less likely to be conscious of what is happening in the dream. REM distinctly is both tonic and phasic.[12] In the last eight minutes of a REM period there is tonic REM with suppressed muscle tone mixed with variable frequencies. During a REM period the eyes move and then don't move. REM is a measure of the general activation of the brain, and that is not constant. Periods of intense eye movement are called phasic.

In a number of lucid dream studies LaBerge and his coworkers averaged the EEG patterns during REM and found an elevation of the overall EEG thirty seconds before a lucid dream. Without this elevation before the dream starts, dreamers don't become lucid. The brain has to be strong enough to support this elevation to become lucid. To recognize that one is dreaming requires a high amount of cortical excitation.

Jayne Gackenbach and Jane Bosveld, in their book *Control Your Dreams,* explain how lucid dreaming helps one to uncover hidden desires, confront hidden fears, and explore the frontiers of consciousness. Jayne is a well-known dream researcher and has put together, besides her book, a journal called *The Lucidity Letter.* Several years ago, she interviewed me about my lucid dreams in one issue and, in a later issue, published an address I gave at the Second Lucid Dreaming

Symposium, held in Washington, D.C., in June of 1987.[13] In both of these articles I explained that I felt there was a connection between lucid dreaming and quantum physics that may be explainable through the model of a hologram.

Holographic Dreams and Reality

Although I will explain this more fully in a later chapter, let me tell you a little about my theory. A lucid dream is, I believe, a time-resolved hologram or, if you will, a series of holograms following each other as the dream unfolds. The hologram is created in the brain, and certain elements of the construction of the hologram and the dream make this hypothesis more tenable. To grasp this we need to look at how a hologram works.

The idea that the brain is somehow creating a hologram when it is dreaming or when it is awake may seem incredible. Why a hologram? What is the difference between a hologram witnessed during a dream and during wakefulness? These questions ask us to look at the model of a hologram not only as it may apply to the dream world, but to the world at large as well.

Implicit in the holographic model is the notion that what we sense as out there in the physical world is not as it seems at all. Instead we are sensing something else, images, as it were, of something far less material than it seems. Grasping this idea is not easy. It helps to consider the Buddhist idea of impermanence. Nothing out there is fixed and permanent. Everything changes. Solid objects are not really solid at all, they only appear to be such to our senses. Thus everything that we sense is only a passing instance, a glimpse of reality.

So how is reality glimpsed? Before I even attempt to answer this, let us consider a hologram's operation and construction. An optical hologram consists of a glass plate upon which a thin photo-sensitive film has been deposited. When light strikes the film, it darkens as any film emulsion does. Next, when light is allowed to strike the film, it comes from two coherent sources. A main source called the reference beam strikes the film unhindered. The secondary source that strikes the film is the light reflected from an object illuminated by the first source. This second source of light carries a jumble of scattered waves. Since the object is actually shining reflected light coming from the primary source to the film, the light waves coming from the two sources are coherently related.

When the two sources simultaneously illuminate the hologram, the light waves interfere with each other producing a complex pattern of dark and light places on the plate. If one then develops the film, one sees a wave pattern much like a moiré pattern that occurs when you look at a fine lace curtain folded over itself through a brightly illuminated window. Examining the pattern on the film in no way gives one any evidence that it is anything other than what it appears to be: a film emulsion. But if one shines the original light source, usually a laser beam, through the film and views it from the correct position, one sees, in addition to the light coming from the illuminating source, light waves scattered from the hologram in exactly the same form as the waves scattered from the object that was previously illuminated; in other words, one sees a three-dimensional image of the object.

In this way the film contains the object in all of its visual aspects. Indeed if one continually changes one's viewpoint during the illumination of the hologram, one gets a continually changing view of the object, exactly the same experience that one would get if one were viewing the original object "out there" in space. Indeed the image of the object is fully three-dimensional. To all intents and purposes, at least visually speaking, the object is really out there. But in actuality it is "enfolded" within the complex interference patterns contained in the hologram and only experienced as "out there" when you attempt to look at it using a light source.

If one breaks the glass plate into pieces, shattering the hologram, and then views a hologram piece using a light source, one actually sees the same object once again. Only this time what one sees is a highly distorted and vague image of the object. One does not see just a piece of the object as one would do if one tore a photograph into pieces. Each part of the hologram contains the whole image for which it was constructed in the first place.

The World Is a Ghetto

Physicist David Bohm is well-known for his holographic theories of the world. In particular Bohm believes that the world of matter, energy, and mind exists as a single unbroken *whole* like the hologram. He calls this the implicate order. When ordinary matter and energy is observed, two things happen. The unbroken whole unfolds, becoming matter and energy "out there" and an apparently separated mind "in here" observing that matter and energy. When this happens, he says, the implicate order contained as an unbroken whole becomes explicate in terms of the appearance of the material world and the mind that perceives it.

Bohm imagines the unbroken whole as a hologram that becomes explicate when the actions of observation take place. In Bohm's view, the universe is something like this hologram, perhaps in a higher number of dimensions. Our viewing of the world of solid matter is something like our viewing of a holographic image. It is not really "out there" but is created "out there" by the process of observation, i.e., through the operations of our senses. In some sense our distorted views of reality are somewhat like the distorted views we would have upon viewing a piece of the hologram instead of the whole.

What the hologram teaches us is that reality as we perceive it is not just out there in space and time but is somehow *projected* into space and time through our actions to perceive an "out there" reality. Again I caution the reader that this does not mean that there is no reality. It just means that our experience of whatever reality is takes an action that we must initiate in order to get a perception of it, whatever it may be. Going to the analogy of the broken hologram again, we must keep in mind that all we have to deal with are broken pieces of that ultimate reality, and so our views of it tend to be distorted.

Now is there any evidence of this bizarre aspect of the way we sense the world around us?

The Evidence Unfolds for Itself

There is. Experimental work described by physician Karl Pribram indicates that the processes occurring in the brain that we label as internal, such as feelings of love or hate or sensations like hunger, are no different from the processes that register as our senses of the outside world. These senses ultimately are projected from our brains and possibly nervous systems "out there." Pribram wrote:

Clinical neurological experience tells us that the localizing of a perceptual image is not a simple process. The paradoxical phenomenon of a phantom limb after amputation, for example, makes it unlikely that our experience of receptor stimulation "resides" where we are apt to localize it.[14]

Even though we apparently feel with our fingers and toes, the evidence is overwhelming that the locations of those sensations are not taking place there. In a similar manner, as I mentioned in chapter 5, we see light that impinges on our retinas and hear sounds that strike our eardrums, but we place the sources of those disturbances "out there" back in time and stretching through space to their appropriate locations. We do not localize starlight at our retinas but thousands of light-years away. We do not localize the music of a Mozart sonata at the basilar membrane of the cochlea, but at the fingers of the pianist on the concert stage or at least in the speakers of our stereo system at home.

The outstanding exception to this is listening to a concert with earphones. Then the music appears to be coming from somewhere inside our heads. However, an Argentinean physiologist, Hugo Zuccarelli, recently developed a new recording technique that reproduces sounds listened to through headphones that appear to be coming from outside sources in much the same way that we hear ordinary "out there" sounds with our ears. He calls his invention "holophonic sound."[15]

I have experienced a Zuccarelli tape recording through headphones and confess that the experience is remarkable in that I heard sounds seemingly coming from in back of me, in front of me, and experienced the sound of having my hair cut even though I was clearly not in a barber's chair. All this while I was sitting with my eyes closed and my attention riveted to the sounds coming through a pair of earphones.

Zuccarelli believes that his invention is based on the emission of a reference sound wave emitted by our ears and that he has been able to reproduce the "out there" experience of sound by somehow causing these waves to interfere with the recorded "out there" sound waves. Accordingly when we listen to the recording, our own reference sound waves interfere with those coming from the tape recording and give us the holophonic experience. Michael Talbot in his book *The Holographic Universe* reports that Zuccarelli believes that his recording has nothing to do with stereophonic recording technique but is based on this emitted reference wave.

Although I doubt this explanation, it is perhaps not difficult to explain the remarkable stereo liveliness of the Zuccarelli recording.[16] I believe that the recording has nothing to do with sounds emitted by our ears (indeed, if there is any evidence of this), but is due to the placement of the microphones when the recording was made. Instead of the placement of stereo microphones several feet apart, as in a typical recording studio, each track of the stereo recording was made from sounds entering an appropriately located microphone. Probably each microphone was placed in a similar position as a human being's actual ear so that when the recording is played back through earphones, the sounds entering the ear are as close as possible to the actual sounds that reverberated in the microphone that recorded them. I would imagine that this recording must be done quite carefully.

The only reason that ordinary stereo recordings do not reproduce this three-dimensional quality of sound is more than likely due to the placement of the recording microphones. Usually, as I mentioned above, they are placed several feet apart and in no way are they placed in "ear" positions. Consequently, with ordinary stereo recordings we hear sounds in our heads as if our ears were projected to be several feet apart. This probably accounts for the lack of some aspects of three-dimensional reality to the sound and the sensation of the sounds lacking precise localization.[17]

With holophonic sound recordings, the sounds are interpreted by the brain in much the same way that we interpret ordinary sounds around us. It is likely that here the holographic metaphor needs to be applied. It is in the brain that a holophonic three-dimensional sound is "heard" and projected to be "out there."

This ability to project experience "out there" not only occurs with our senses of sight and sound, but also with touch! For example, data gathered by Nobel Prize–winning physiologist Georg von Békésy indicated that subjects deprived of their visual sense would actually feel sensations in a space where no parts of their bodies were present. He explained his experiment as follows:

> For this study a pair of vibrators stimulate two [adjoining] fingertips. . . . Each vibrator is actuated by the same series of clicks, and [there are] . . . equal magnitudes of sensation on

each fingertip . . . The setup includes a means of varying the time delay between the clicks [given to each fingertip]. If a click is delayed for more than three or four milliseconds, a person feels separate sensations in the two fingertips. . . . If . . . the time between clicks is reduced to about one millisecond, the two-click series will fuse into one, and the vibratory sensation will be localized in the finger that receives each click the earlier. If the time delay is further decreased, the sensation for a trained observer will move into the region between [the] two fingers [closer to the "earlier" finger], and if then the time relation between the two click series is reversed, the click will move to the opposite side. . . .

The interesting point in this experiment is that for the condition in which there is no time delay, the vibrations are localized between the two fingers where no skin is present. If the fingers are spread apart, the same effect is found, and when the amount of time delay is varied, the sensation will move correspondingly in the free space between the fingers.[18]

In another experiment, he placed vibrators on the knees of subjects and asked them to spread their legs apart. As he had discovered with the fingertip experiment, when the time delay was varied, the sensation would appear to jump from one knee to the other and would then appear in the space between the knees.

According to these experiments, the sensation of feeling something "out there" in space is no more mysterious, if we adopt a holographic model, than the sensation of seeing something "out there" in normal vision. We construct reality from the data inputted to our senses. What we actually sense is coded reality re-created as "out there" experiences. The information received at the sense organs is sent to the brain, and there it is somehow decoded.

Dreaming Holographic Virtual and Real Images

We decode and reconstruct reality by making a sensorial hologram in our brains from our sensory input. Now, how this is accomplished is explained in a following chapter. Here I want to get to what this all has to do with dreams!

A hologram is remarkably similar to a lens in that it can make both virtual and real images. The words *real* and *virtual* have special meanings here. Virtual images are created as illusions of objects. The light that we see when we view a virtual image appears to be coming from the image, but it actually is not. The image of an object seen through a magnifying glass is an example of a virtual image.

Real images are different. The light that we see from a real image actually comes from the image. The image exists in real space. For example, the image seen of a movie on a screen is a real image. The light rays coming through the lens come to a focus on the screen forming the image. You can always focus a real image and project it on a screen. You cannot do this with a virtual image. You could imagine trying to shine the image of a small object coming through a magnifying glass onto a screen. It won't work. You won't be able to see the image on the screen because the image is not formed there.

Consequently, real images are sharp and capable of being focused. Virtual images are diffuse, diverging, and are not capable of being focused.

Ordinary dreams, I suggest, are created as virtual images of the hologram. They are diffuse and made from diverging rays of light. When one views a virtual image through a hologram, it always appears blurry. In a similar manner, when having an ordinary dream, the sense of witnessing is often confused and blurry. Virtual images tend to diverge. In a similar manner, the sense of presence is diverged in the ordinary dream, and there is no ability to focus one's "presence" and become aware of one's self in the dream.

Lucid dreams are made from converging real images of the hologram. That is why they appear so vivid and three-dimensional. Using the analogy then, when one is having a lucid dream, the sense of presence is focused. One is aware of the distinction of self and the dream environment. This sharpened awareness allows one to be awake in the dream experience. Following along with the neurophysiological evidence, it takes some work to bring this about in the brain. Probably this work amounts to using a focused reference "beam." I shall attempt to explain what this reference beam consists of in a later chapter. However, whatever the mechanism consists of, it is clear that lucid dreams carry with them an enhanced sense of self whenever they are occurring.

Do Lucid Dreams Model the Self?

Lucidity in dreams marks a paradigmatic shift in consciousness research. Although they have long been known in Eastern traditional practice, it is really in the West that the concept of fitting these experiences into a scientific paradigm has arisen. In the East, we could say that the concern of the "I" is of a lesser degree, so the "So what?" aspect of being awake in dreams would appear to be less important. The concern in the East is knowing that reality is primarily witnessed as "unreality." While in the West we want to know the "truth" about reality as evidenced through our scientific methods.

In lucid dreams we are attempting to answer the same age-old questions that we all have to in order to survive. Where am I? Who am I? What am I doing here? The question of survival is strongly connected to the question of self. Where I am and who I am depends on the line that distinguishes me from the other, from the rest of the universe. In mindful waking, one becomes less concerned with this division and more, simply put, alert.

In ordinary waking consciousness, the mind tends to play tricks with us constantly. Why it does this is perhaps not discernible. Maybe it has to do with the broken-hologram analogy. It can't help but play tricks because it is constantly dealing with fuzzy images. Yet, there is hope. One can train the mind to go beyond fuzziness into some experience of what Buddhists call "clear light."

The division of lucidity from ordinariness is a question of where the "I" exists and how it is distributed throughout the brain and body and universe at large. It is a question of viewpoint. It is a question of viewing the hologram from one central, focused viewpoint at the place where a real image is formed of all of the sensorial input available during sleep and during wake or remaining unfocused and unaware. Clearly an effort is required to come to a focus, to come to one's center. And when this happens, one becomes, paradoxically, the whole universe. This is perhaps when the universe stops dreaming and a fully awakened state of oneness is achieved.

In chapters 19 and 20, I will return to the study of lucidity and how the hologram is created in the brain and how the sense of "I" is developed or arises from what I call neural automata in the brain. Next we want to look at how the sense of "I" arises throughout the body and in particular via something we can call the dreambody.

CHAPTER 13

THE DREAMING UNIVERSE: THE DREAMBODY AND THE WAKING DREAM

———

Outside our time and space, Llixgrijb was still dissatisfied.

"I have created a world full of imaginary creatures," said Llixgrijb. "And yet I am alone. How can this be?"

Despite the populousness of its illusion, Llixgrijb could only watch its lovely universe from the outside. It had not forgotten its own suffering and loneliness. It was not fully a part of the creation it had made.

"I must become a part of my illusion," considered Llixgrijb. "And to do that, I must don a costume, I must wear a mask. I must forget myself forever. But what—or who—shall I become?"

—Wim Coleman and Pat Perrin
The Jamais Vu Papers[1]

To dream the impossible dream, that is my quest.

—Don Quixote

What emerges from my study of the physics of the dream state of consciousness is the "self" itself as it deals with the world. It appears that to make sense of the world, the self must deal with two lives: the sleeping/dreaming life and the waking life. We dream to make sense of the world, to form our maps. We awaken to experience the world, to test our maps by going out into the territory. But the division between dreaming and waking is not as clear-cut as it would seem. In some ways the forming of maps is itself a voyage into territory.

Our dream images, even if we don't remember them, invade our waking awareness as patterns. By these patterns we live. By not recognizing them, we live unconsciously. By recognizing them we live consciously, or as Charles Tart put it, we live in a state of "lucid waking."

To experience the world, we invent ways to move about in time and space, to change matter into energy, to turn chaos into order; to survive. When we dream, we are programming ourselves for successful survival and meaningful experiences, or we are eliminating scenarios that do not satisfy those purposes. Dreams are therefore important to us, even if we forget them. But, they are more important to us if we choose to make the effort to remember them.

To a large extent we walk this planet as if we are dreaming even if we are already seemingly awake. To awaken completely takes discipline and desire. But in every path we take to gain discipline, every way of life that we master, we eventually find ourselves in some form of dream once again.

The way of a physicist is an example. He attempts to determine what is real in a disciplined manner. But to do so he must form a model of the world. Any model requires images and/or words. From dream images we invented number.[2] Mathematics is just another form of words and images relatable ultimately to scale and number.

In physics we ultimately attempt to explain everything in terms of just three basic scales or measurements based on number. These instruments consist of the pendulum, by which we measure time; the balance scale, by which we measure mass; and the straight ruler, by which we measure distance. Through just three concepts, time, mass, and space, we attempt to model everything in the universe.

Of course, one could point to the folly of even attempting to measure anything nonexistential such as the mind or its contents, consisting of thoughts and emotions, with such instruments. Certainly one should not expect to measure anything like a dream with rough instruments based on such concepts as space, time, and mass.

And yet, we are doing just that, even if we think we are not. Our dreams reflect our lives, our thoughts, and our emotions. Life is survival and more than survival. It is also an experience. This experience can be rich or poor in content and either way we could survive.

We invented physics for the purpose of survival, at least survival as we see it being the heir of the Greek's vision of a rational universe. Could the universe survive without physics? As I looked into this question from many different cultural points of view, I saw that every culture dealt with physics in one way or another. The only differences seemed to be in what were considered to be the elements upon which the physics was based.

So-called "primitive" cultures used a form of magic to deal with change and insecurity that ultimately resulted from change. They called this magic by many names and believed that it was the basis of the universe. This magic we might label universal energy.[3]

Typically the physicists of such cultures were shamans or medicine people. The dream quest of shamanic initiates was the search to understand and ultimately control or use this vital universal energy to explain and illuminate the questions of life, the universe, and everything.

Our culture, following the Greeks' vision of a rational universe, used space, time, and mass as basic elements but ultimately came to see the universe in terms that went beyond these elements. Mass turned out to be energy, and energy turned out to be ultimately undefinable.[4] Space and time became entwined, interpenetrating, and ultimately inseparable. Mass, too, became part of that entwined fabric. With the quantum physical discovery of the effects of the observer on subatomic systems, the mind became part of the universe entwined with mass, space, and time.

Today, our position is close to the one discovered by basic tribal peoples. The concept of universal energy in our language might be called the "universal quantum wave function" or "matter wave" or "probability wave" of quantum physics. This "wave" pervades everything, and like the universal energy, it resists objective discovery. It appears as a guiding influence in all that we observe. Perhaps it is the same thing as the "clear light"—the all-pervading consciousness without an object—of Buddhist thought.

Why do we come up with such concepts? The problem is that humans need to model experience to survive and find meaning in their lives. And modeling experience is a sword with two edges, one that cuts and enlightens and the other that dulls and causes us to fall into the illusion of our own thought and dreams. Often, survival models deny the essence of universal energy—the enrichment of experience. And often the attempt to enrich our lives denies us, the human species, its very survival.

Modeling Reality: The Waking Dream and the Dreambody

Thus we come to how the dream shapes the universe. In this chapter I will discuss the work of two eminent "dream" researchers, psychologists Catherine Shainberg and Arnold Mindell. Both researchers have shown that dreams go far beyond the Freudian and Jungian models. They are overlaps into the physical world that model it and shape it. Catherine Shainberg describes her work in terms of the concept of the *waking dream*. Arnold Mindell describes his research as working with the *dreambody*.

Shainberg now lives in the United States but has done much of her work in her native land of Israel, particularly with patients who suffered during the many wars that Israel has had to fight to survive. Mindell, a key figure in the revolutionary field of dream and body work, is a psychotherapist, analyst, and founder of the Center for Process-Oriented Psychology in Zurich, Switzerland, and Portland, Oregon.

According to Shainberg, the waking dream is a specific technique that looks at the images of a patient's night dream. Although the process for creating these images is not just a fantasy, it seems to involve the same kind of mechanism—the imaginal mind fabricating images.

This can often lead to misleading interpretations. In visualizing these waking images you often see a lot of psychologists guiding the fantasy of the patient, which Shainberg tries to avoid doing. For her, this is not what revealing waking dreams should be. It is instead a probing to a much deeper level at which the person sees the pattern for himself.

For Mindell, symptoms of illness, tension, or pain are voices speaking from the unconscious in the language of body. Accordingly, just as the unconscious speaks to us in our dreams through its images, it speaks to us in waking life in our bodies through its aches, pains, illnesses, and physical symptoms. Mindell discovered, via his studies of theoretical physics (he has a M.S. degree in physics from MIT), Jungian psychology (he also holds a Ph.D. in psychology), and his work with patients, that the body's symptoms were just as much a reflection of the patterns of the person's life as were his dreams. Thus for Mindell, there is no clear separation between dreams and the body, hence the coined word *dreambody*.

Mindell has authored several books.[5] In his recent work[6] Mindell has gone beyond the concept of the dreambody to what I might call the "dreamuniverse." He now sees that global myths, patterns, and ideologies have created our present planetary crises in much the same way that our images revealed to us in dreams and through our body symptoms have created our own illnesses. He sees that planetary "dreams" organize the behavior of groups, networks, and nations.

Both workers realize that the patterns of a person's life are reflected in the dream and in the events of a person's life. While there is clearly some overlap in their work, it is perhaps clearer to look at their work separately.

Working with the Waking Dream

Catherine Shainberg has been working with the concept of the waking dream for several years. She has literally worked with hundreds of people, helping them to live a fuller life through recognition of their lives' patterns revealed to them through their dreams. Her process involves the merging of the dream and the waking-state awareness. Her research has shown an immediate link between a person's daily behavior and his night dream. During her sessions with people, she gets them to experience the link between the night dream and the waking life—to show them that there is no separation. They learn from their night dreams that their dreams are a continuation of their life in the day.

Often what we experience in the day unfolds as patterns that we are not aware of if we are not trained to look for them. If we begin to become aware of our dream patterns, we actually begin to realize that these patterns exist in our waking life.

As a simple example, suppose someone dreams that he finds the apple that Paris gave to the three goddesses in an old legend. The next day he thinks that an apple would be a wonderful gift to get for someone. Later, he walks into a shop and finds the apple he dreamt of, even though he was not expecting to find apples in that particular shop.

Such events could show the prophetic aspects of dreams, or it could be that the pattern causes the person to be "attracted" to situations in waking life that will reveal the pattern. There may not be any causal reason for the revelation to occur. It could be a synchronicity, possibly explainable by my model of quantum correlation in this book, or it could be that no present theory of physics will explain this. And then again there may indeed be causative factors leading the person to his destiny.

However, Shainberg's work does not indicate that some kind of destiny is "out there" or "in here" and we are just actors acting out roles in that pattern. Catherine believes that, instead, our bodies are following images that continually unfold and change.

At first an image starts to unfold when the material body becomes "aware" of it in some manner, possibly through an illness or some healing occurrence. In the body, cells unfold and develop in a certain order and pattern according to that image, regardless of its benefit to the body. As the cells develop, the image becomes stronger, and we continue to fabricate these images in our dreams.[7]

What would happen if we did not have such images coming to us in our dreams? Catherine explains that if we were not dreaming, we would become ill. As proof, she points to experimental studies on people who were denied their dreams when they were awakened from REM sleep. As I explained in an earlier chapter, after people have been interrupted from having REM sleep for four or five days, when they finally go to sleep, they almost immediately go into REM sleep for a long period, seemingly making up for what they have missed. This could indicate that dreams are indeed necessary for creating the images of our daily life. Without those images we would get lost and possibly ill.

Returning to the example of a person who dreams of the Paris apple and then goes into a store and purely "accidentally" finds the apple, Catherine explained that there are many stories of a person who goes out into the world and searches for some treasure that he actually has inside of himself. In the conclusion of such stories the person has to come home to find the treasure. In the apple story we have a different conclusion. The person actually finds the apple out there.

Catherine refers to the people she works with as students, not as patients. She has had students whose dreams are more like the apple story. One of her students, a young girl, was hospitalized and quite ill, so ill that her doctors thought she wouldn't pass the night. Her mother called Catherine and asked her to go to the hospital to see if she could do anything. When Catherine arrived, she found the girl in a comatose deep sleep. She then did "a very short piece of imagery work with her."

Catherine told me, "If you want to change something, it has to be very quick." She told the comatose girl that she would go into this vast open space and that the space would be enough to keep the girl comfortable. Catherine did not tell her what the space would be like or what she would see in the space. Catherine was leaving it open so that something could happen purely initiated by the young girl herself.

Shortly after this the girl sat up, opened her eyes, and said, "The frog jumps." Then she lay back down and went to sleep.

Catherine told me, "And you could see the difference. The next morning she woke up completely on the road to recovery. Meanwhile I had gone home and then had come back to the hospital very early the next morning because I wanted to see her before I went to work."

Catherine went into the gift shop in the hospital to find her a stuffed toy frog, fully believing that one would be there. She continued, "And indeed there was a big frog, which I bought for her. I found the frog, which I knew I had to find, but I hadn't dreamt it, she had. I gave it to her because she needed something very concrete to recognize that her image had brought her back to life."

Later Catherine discovered that this frog had a long history involving healing sick children and was given to children who needed to believe in life.

Shainberg believes that there is an internal pattern that has empathy with an external pattern that breaks all the bounds of time and space. Usually there is some emotional connection between what you are dreaming and what you desire in real life. She told me a story about her two-year-old son that illustrated this.

Her son was madly in love with fire engines and firemen and talked about them constantly. He played that he was putting out fires when listening to the musical piece "Slaughter on Tenth Avenue." Catherine and her husband had to play the recording many times during this love affair with firemen. One day Catherine and her son went into a bookstore up the street, where he had never previously been. Catherine was showing him several children's books suggesting that maybe he wanted one of them. He insisted, "No, Mommie, I don't want that book. *I don't want that book.*"

"What do you want?" she asked him. He said, "I want to go down there. I want that book." Now "down there" was a long aisle between shelves of books. From where they were standing, he could not see down to the aisle's end. Yet, he wanted to go down there nevertheless. When they got to the end of the aisle, the child said, "I want that book," pointing to a specific book. That book was a book about firemen.

Shainberg believes that the child's dreams of firemen and his desire were connected to the bookstore where the book on fireman existed. In fact, wherever they went, there would probably have been a pattern recognition going on in the child that would produce an experience of fireman on the scene, whether real or in books, television shows, etc. Somehow the child would have telepathically discovered the connection and would sense what to do to produce the revelation. For example, he might suddenly turn on the TV set at home just as a program about firemen was airing.

Of course there is no way that a causal connection could exist between the dream world and the real world. The pattern is there and the connections are there, but they are not causal connections.

Patterns of the Unus Mundus

How can such a pattern exist in the world? How can our dreams connect with physical reality? How indeed. In her book *Number and Time,* Marie-Louise von Franz describes how she began work on the project that resulted in her book. It was after C. G. Jung had completed his work *Synchronicity: An Acausal Connecting Principle* that he offered the conjecture that a unity between psyche and matter could be found in researching the archetypes of natural numbers. Two years before his death he suggested that von Franz look into it.

For the next two years she did nothing about this project. After Jung's death, the project haunted von Franz. She then consulted Nora and Arnold Mindell, who helped her clarify her thoughts. Later she consulted with Dr. Mokusen Miyuki, who gave her information about number theories worked on by a Chinese scholar, Fa-tzang, that turned out to be a synchronistic event in itself.

Before she met Miyuki, when she thought she had completed the book, she had a dream in which she was at an exhibition of antique Indian art. She saw a showcase with figurines of demons, approximately thirty centimeters in length, which were crying. She knew this was related to a story from the life of the Buddha, in which he was killed by demons, who, when they saw what they had done, wept and were then converted to a more human attitude.

She then noticed that some of the figurines were missing because a young male scholar had taken them to show during a lecture. She looked into the lecture hall, but found it pitch-black. The young savant (unknown to Dr. von Franz) then emerged from the room. Next, Jung approached him and they began an animated scientific conversation. Jung signaled von Franz to join in. She realized that the young scholar (whom she believed represented her animus dealing with her spiritual and mental side) knew something that might possibly concern her already-completed book. But he was reading in the dark, so she interpreted this as that his knowledge lay in total obscurity.

Since she had no idea how to pursue this knowledge any further, she did nothing about it. A few weeks after the dream, she met Dr. Miyuki in completely different circumstances. During a pause in their conversation, she mentioned her dream to him. Miyuki then informed her of an esoteric science of numbers in Hwa-yen Buddhism, a written (in Chinese) transplant of Indian Buddhism to China. The passages he was referring to, written by Fa-tzang, had not been translated for von Franz. Miyuki then took the trouble to do so.

To her surprise, the ideas of Fa-tzang paralleled hers. Her unconscious, she claims, was thus aware of information that, rationally speaking, was impossible to have been known previously. Fa-tzang's ideas indicated that there was an all-embracing unity of the archetype of the Self that she herself described in her manuscript, and included other speculations that she had not included in her work.

Von Franz's experience indeed paralleled her own investigation into the relationship of psyche and matter via the concept of what Jung called the *unus mundus*. As she put it:

Whenever the human mind confronts an unknown, it invents symbolic models, drawing on a preconscious process of projection. In the history of mankind we therefore find numerous symbolic representations of the *unus mundus*, ... this "one world" as a continuum consisting of images, as a geometrical continuum, or as a numerically structured system.[8]

Physics has long delved into the unity concept in attempting to understand the universe. Einsteinian relativity deals with the unification of space and time into the one arena of space-time, an all-embracing continuum. With Einstein's general theory of relativity, mass becomes part of space-time and is unified with energy through the famous equation $E = mc^2$. The idea here is to see all of physics as a geometrical continuum, paralleling Jung's "one world" concept.

In their book, *Margins of Reality,* Robert G. Jahn and Brenda J. Dunne posit a role for consciousness in the establishment of material reality.[9] Their book indicates a number of experimental studies of psychic and telepathic phenomena that would suggest that mind does influence matter in an acausal manner. This would suggest that the idea of *unus mundus* is, as revealed to us through unusual mind-matter connections, not far-fetched at all, but is in the real spirit of scientific inquiry.

So far, science, in its attempt to look at all processes in the universe in a rational manner, has failed to grasp how the material universe could be affected by processes that resist measurement based on space, time, and mass. Yet we clearly see that human behavior is often determined by the images that people carry with themselves. In quantum physics, we have at last come to the edge where the material world and the dream world are overlapping. If we are to take the idea of the *unus mundus* seriously, then we must investigate this border area, this "neutral zone" in the area between rationality and irrationality.

Working with the Dreambody

This has been the area of investigation of Arnold Mindell. Illness had affected Mindell to the degree that he realized he could not deal with his own body problems in a purely intellectual manner, a technique that had been successful when he dealt with dream material of his patients. Instead he began to see that the body was a mirror of the person's life patterns and that these patterns would appear in dreams as signals from the body and that the dream's concerns are magnified in the body.

Thus a body's symptoms are not to be dealt with purely mechanically as pathologies. Symptoms are not just sicknesses that must be healed, repressed, or cured. Instead, symptoms are potentially meaningful and purposeful conditions signaling a fantastic phase of life or bringing one closer to the center of existence. As Mindell put it, "they can also be a trip into another world, as well as a royal road into the development of the personality."[10]

Mindell has discovered in his work that every physical manifestation of the body is expressed in a person's dreams. This includes all physical gestures, the tone of voice, the way one moves one's arms, how one walks, the way one holds the shoulders when talking, facial expressions, and all physical diseases. Relationship problems are also reflected in dreams and carried in the body.

Mindell discovered that he couldn't find any reason for his illness. He studied everything he could, but in the end failed to learn what his illness was telling him. He then carefully watched patients who had obvious physical illnesses or disabilities. He noticed that a person with severe eczema would start to scratch and actually make the symptoms worse. When someone had a headache, he would shake his head about; if someone had an eye ache, he would press on the eye; if someone had a stiff neck, he would bend the neck, intensifying and amplifying the pain.

In general Mindell saw that people would do just the opposite of what one might expect. If one was suffering from pain, instead of soothing the pain, the person would try to make the pain even worse. In this manner Mindell discovered that amplifying the body's symptoms resulted in giving the patient the true significance of the illness.

In one particular story from his book *Working with the Dreaming Body,* he told of a patient suffering from stomach cancer. He told Mindell that his stomach tumor was giving him unbearable pain. Since the normal therapies weren't working for this patient, Mindell went to see him and asked him what he could do to make the pain even *worse!* The patient said that when he pushed his stomach out, the pain got much worse, so Mindell had the patient stand up and push out on his stomach muscles. This continued and the pain increased. Finally the patient screamed that the pain was so bad that he felt he was going to burst. Then the patient broke down and cried and explained that all of his life he had felt that he could not express himself adequately.

Even though the cancer was severe, by working the patient in this amplification-of-pain technique the patient began to express himself more fully than he had before and actually lived for two or three more years before dying.

Shortly before this patient had learned of his inoperative cancer, he had dreamt that he had an incurable disease and that the medicine for it was like a bomb. Mindell concluded from this patient's illness that the cancer was the expression of his unexpressed desire. It was his lost expression that could only come out through the cancer. He had to explode.

This was where the idea of the *dreambody* entered Mindell's mind. The dreambody is both a dream and the body at the same time. Mindell claims that, in all of his cases, he has not found one where the person's dreams did not reflect the body's symptoms and vice versa. So for Mindell, dreamwork and bodywork became synonymous.

The dreambody can be related to the physical body in much the same way that the quantum wave function that gives the probability of a particle's state can be related to the particle's physical state. In quantum physics we do not deal with physical matter because we have no way of controlling it.

Instead we deal with expectancies, tendencies, and probabilities as if they were fields floating "out there" in space. These fields, I'll remind you again (see chapter 10), are represented by complex numbers, numbers that have two components: a real number and an imaginary number. Thus even though physicists picture these probability fields as represented by complex numbers, no one has ever seen such a field. The greater these numbers are, at any particular point of space and instance of time, the higher is the intensity or propensity for the physical particle to manifest there and then.

We deal with these fields in a mathematically exact manner, and in many circumstances, the field's intensities are so marked that we have as close as possible a control of the "symptoms" of the manifestations of the particle as we deem necessary. Thus in many physical circumstances, those that we call "classical," we believe we have control and understanding of the physics of the phenomenon.

Yet in many other circumstances such control is clearly impossible. For example, we cannot determine the precise location and momentum of any subatomic particle. Thus we fail to make predictions about the movements of such particles where such information is desired.

Even though we know this in physics, we still tend to look at nearly everything in the universe as if such knowledge was at our beck and call. This prevailing mode of thinking, which has produced technology, has also filtered into the work of the psychologist and medical practitioner.

Mindell's work, if we take the dreambody to be the analogy of this probability field, has the same relationship to the body as the field has to the particle. Just as there are many classical situations where it isn't necessary to invoke the field concept to explain the particle's behavior, there are also classical situations of healing in dealing with the physical body. But there are clearly cases where this does not seem to work. Diseases such as cancer and possibly autoimmune diseases may not be classical; they are not curable as just body symptoms. Instead we need to deal with the dreambody to see to what degree any control can be attempted.

The comparison may be more than mere analogy. For the moment, suppose that it is true that we are dealing with the dreambody when we are dealing with quantum wave functions of probability. Since the dreambody is the field that tends to manifest as the body according to intents and purposes (whose intents and purposes we will look at later), it would follow that intent and purpose also is at work in the field of all physical matter. In other words, just as the body is the manifestation of the dreaming body, the universe is the manifestation of the dreaming universe. Just how this all works we will see in the next chapters.

$\mathcal{G}$ETTING TO THE BIG DREAM

Know all things to be like this:
A mirage, a cloud castle, a dream, an apparition, without essence, but
with qualities that can be seen.

Know all things to be like this:
As the moon in a bright sky in some clear light reflected, though to
that lake the moon has never moved.

Know all things to be like this:
As an echo that derives from music, sounds, and weeping, yet in that
echo is no melody.

Know all things to be like this:
As a magician makes illusions of horses, oxen, carts, and other things,
nothing is at it appears.

—*the Buddha*[1]

In September of 1989, I received a phone call from my friend Lawrence N. Koss inviting me to be a panel member for a forum that was to be held the next month in Aspen, Colorado, on "Close Encounters of the Fourth Kind (CEIV)." Larry's intent was to create a public dialogue around the unidentified flying object (UFO) phenomenon that he hoped would "move into a new arena of understanding." He specifically asked me if I would present some thoughts concerning the phenomenon based on the new physics.

We have all heard about the close-encounter phenomenon, especially since the appearance of the successful Hollywood movie *Close Encounters of the Third Kind* and a number of books dealing with the subject.[2] Just what are close encounters, and, even more relevant, what do they have to do with the subject of this book?

So far ufologists, researchers interested in UFOs, have classified encounter phenomena into four classes: (1) sightings of UFOs at a distance (CEI), (2) sightings of UFOs close up (CEII), (3) sightings of beings from UFOs that have landed (CEIII), and (4) abductions of people by the UFO beings (CEIV). Together these CEs compose what are called UFO phenomena.

In this chapter we will examine CEs, other UFO phenomena, and a range of what we might call "imaginal realm" (IR) appearances that have been investigated by a number of researchers, notably Jacques Vallee, Michael Grosso, and Peter M. Rojcewicz, in an attempt to define the parameters of the IR. Having looked at the data of the IR, I will attempt to form a physics of the IR in the next chapter; and in the chapter following the next, I will continue this train of inquiry by including the work of Kenneth Ring, Michael Persinger, Paul Devereux, and others, who have carried out major research efforts concerning near-death experience (NDE), and its relationship to the IR, particularly UFO CEs.

I believe that NDE, UFO, and other phenomena that border into the world of folklore and fantasy are elements, possibly archetypal "real" images, of a dreaming consciousness and that the rules of quantum physics may be applicable.[3] These elements are foreign to our Western way of science. If, indeed, these imaginal-realm phenomena are aspects of a dreaming consciousness, we simply have no idea how it is that something we dream could in any way manifest as "real" objects. That is where quantum physics must enter if it applies at all.

Yet, if we are to believe people who have had such seemingly bizarre experiences as meeting with people from flying saucers and the like, we are forced to attempt some kind of explanation. We need to look at how such phenomena could ever occur and perhaps come up with a scientific model.

Well, how could they? The answer, I believe, must lie in a realm of physics that borders on psychology, a realm that is perhaps halfway between objectivity and subjectivity.[4] My late friend and author Michael Talbot, in his book, *The Holographic Universe,* called such experiences "omnijective"[5] rather than subjective or objective. I will attempt to clarify this as we go along.

If I am correct about the existence of a middle realm halfway between material and mental reality, then we may be witnessing something like a collective intent manifesting in individuals as waking dreams or, as I would label them, "big dreams."

Big dreams are not always pleasant or benevolent. Nevertheless they are possibly indicative of the existence of another realm of reality, possibly a parallel world that overlaps our own and that has some objectivity. My friend and professional folklorist Peter M. Rojcewicz told me that his speculations about men in black (MIB), mysterious beings dressed in black who come into a person's home or vicinity and often threaten the person, are exactly along those lines. As he put it:

> Here we have a collective image . . . a collective dream of the bogeyman, of the fear of being hijacked or abducted, of big brother watching. These images represent the dark part of the psyche and are psychically kindled during times of extreme anxiety and of concern. If there is anything to this notion of the physical powers of the *imaginatio,* that is, the "imaginative faculty" of the soul, it seems reasonable that a mental image can coalesce and stabilize in the material world, however briefly. So that we, in fact, are dreaming on a collective level and actually encountering something of that hybrid reality in a personal way.

Rojcewicz's statement eloquently expresses the omnijective character of imaginal-realm experiences that seem to have both objective and subjective realism, for short moments of time, and then seem to vanish. If I may make an analogy, the imaginal-realm experiences are fleeting bits of reality somewhat like short-lifetime subatomic particles.

We have in physics a range of what we call stable fundamental particles. These are subatomic "objects" that persist for relatively long periods of time. The electron exists forever; it does not decay into pure energy. The proton also exists practically forever and does not decay, although there are some theories that predict that it will decay after 15 billion years or more. But there are far more "fundamental" particles that do not last as long as one second of time, and yet we believe they are "real" also.[6]

But we have come to see short-lived particles in the laboratory. Is there any scientific evidence of the existence of IR experiences (IREs)? Good question; where should we look for data? Remember, these experiences are not only difficult to capture objectively, but their very character borders on fantasy.

Even though in the Western world we fail to account for such experiences or often even to believe in them, Eastern spiritual practices see IREs as significant. If we look into the history of Tibetan Buddhist practices, we find that Tibetan yogins practiced a form of lucid dreaming in which they were able to gain mastery of the contents of their dreams (see chapter 12). The division between dreaming and waking disappeared for the Tibetan yogin. He remained awake during the dream state and was able to see the illusory quality of all things.

Peter M. Rojcewicz told me that some Tibetan Vajrayana Buddhists practice the creation of *tulpas*—materialized thought forms.[7] The students attempt to visualize a solid object based on an image in much the same way that an architect envisions a three-dimensional building from drawings, renderings, and blueprints. But the process goes further. In the Tibetan yogic tradition the yogin practices visualizing some icon over a period of time until it goes through three stages of materialization:

1. First the initiate will meditate upon every aspect of the icon until he or she can clearly see it entirely in the mind even while performing everyday activities.

2. The image is actually "projected" outward like a holographic image that can be seen by others.

3. The image becomes material.

Peter explained that in some of these cases the tulpoidal "objects" are meant to survive the life of their originator. In other words, even after the yogin has died, other persons will still be able to see the materialized object. In his 1987 article,[8] Rojcewicz told of the tulpoidal experiences of Alexandra David-Neel, a remarkable Frenchwoman known for her books on Tibetan Buddhism,[9] while she was living in Tibet. David-Neel traveled in Tibet in disguise, lived in Tibetan monasteries, and spent considerable time alone living in the mountains of that country. She died at the age of one hundred in 1969. In one of her accounts of her Tibetan Buddhist life she described her success in creating a tulpa, which after some time became malignant and bold, escaping her control.

A Walk in the "Vallee" of Science

Yet, in spite of the impressive display of mind control exercised by Tibetan Buddhists, I would hardly call this scientific evidence. Probably the most scientific inquiry into such phenomena has been conducted by Jacques Vallee. In his book, *Dimensions: A Casebook of Alien Contact,* Vallee critically examines the issue of IREs from a new perspective.[10] The usual perspectives on UFO phenomena fall into two camps: the sheep and the goats, i.e., the believers and the skeptics.

Believers tend to regard UFOs as physically real phenomena. Typically such beliefs follow a trend. Spaceships really come to our world. They are solid objects. They flew here or transported to us via some form of superphysics beyond our technology, faster than light. The creatures aboard them are superintelligent and are literally capable of what we would see as miracles. For example, spaceships are seen to undergo accelerations that would rip apart any vehicle made of terrestrial materials.

Skeptics point out that the vastness of our universe would preclude the possibility of any intelligent life coming here. How would they find us in the vast sea of space? Even if they did, assuming that these craft are subject to the same laws of physics that we presently believe exist everywhere in the universe, a voyage from the nearest star to us would take thousands of years at worst and, even if the ship were to travel at the speed of light, several years at best. Since no material object can exceed or even reach light speed, this would preclude visits from material beings.

Vallee takes a new approach, one that we should look at carefully. He does not believe in extraterrestrial spacecraft because this belief is not supported by the evidence of UFOs. The first piece of evidence that UFOs are not caused by spacecraft is, surprisingly, that there are far too many verified unexplained sightings! Vallee has himself documented over two thousand cases reported over the last twenty years. While this may not seem overwhelming in number, Vallee reminds us that this list only includes *reported* sightings.

Most if not all of the reports suggest that these sightings were happenstance, purely at random. Taking this factor into account and the fact that most sightings, particularly landings, occurred after six P.M. with activity peaking at around ten-thirty P.M.,[11] and then, significantly fewer reports until an increase again occurs at around six A.M., one would conclude from this that sighting and landing activity is mostly a nocturnal affair. But then why do the sightings drop off at around midnight? Simply because most people go to sleep, and since there are fewer witnesses, there would be fewer sightings. It does not mean that there are fewer events.

Taking all of the mathematical factors into account, Vallee concluded that the number of events occurring would reach the staggering number of over three hundred thousand in the last twenty years rather than two thousand. But there is still more to the story. Why do most of these sightings only occur in unpopulated areas, far from people's homes and dwellings? Perhaps it is the lighting of cities that makes the events unobservable, but putting that aside, clearly one would expect based on randomness and numbers of people living in cities that there should be more city sightings of events simply because there are more people.

Following this line of reasoning, it would follow that if the earth's population were distributed evenly instead of concentrated in cities, there would certainly be more "country" reports. Taking into account the unpopulated areas of land involved and even possibly the vastness of ocean areas, where there are few sightings because few people are out there, bumps the estimate of events up to over 3 million in the last twenty years.

Vallee suggests that this number is absurd. An orbiting probe the size of a beer keg would, in a few weeks, be able to capture a wide range of scientific data about our planet. Taking the enormous amount of radio and television transmissions into account, such a probe would, pretty well, tell any extraterrestrial beings a lot about us. So why should there be so many visits? One or two or perhaps even fifty would be enough. Why do the visitors keep coming back? Perhaps they like to visit us as we would return to see an old movie over and over again; or perhaps there is a different explanation.

So random visitations do not explain UFO sightings. The visitors must either carefully select their witnesses for psychological or sociological reasons, which is a possibility (one must wonder how they are able to do this and why they would choose the witnesses they do), or they are not coming in spacecraft. Whatever the reason is, the visits are planned and, as Vallee puts it, *staged* and therefore not random.

UFO Superphysics and Creatures

Looking at a wide range of sightings, Vallee concludes that in nearly every case, the spacecraft did not move by flying away, it simply vanished or faded away like Alice's Cheshire cat. In several cases there was a white cloud left behind, and in some cases there was the sound of an explosion. Looking at the physics of material objects, one would conclude that such spacecraft are to be locked up by the cosmic police for violation of the laws of universal physics.

How could such disappearances occur? Do we need some form of superphysics to explain them? Do the ETs possess superphysics technology? Taking a minimalist approach, one must conclude that the behavior of all such sightings follows the laws of filmmaking, movie projectors, and holographic image projection rather than the laws of material objects moving in space. In other words, what is being witnessed is a *visual* phenomenon, not a material phenomenon. The sightings are of "real" images, not of real objects.[12]

What can be accomplished with images is even more amazing than most sightings report. Take any modern film studio's ability to create magical images, and you have a far richer source of magical images in films than have been seen in sightings.

From this I would conclude that sightings are some form of image phenomenon, not necessarily optical imagery, and that one does not need a superphysics to explain them. I'll return to this at the end of the chapter.

Why Do the ETs Look the Same to So Many Contactees?

In CEIVs we have a range of astonishing similar-looking creatures, humanoid, and yet in many cases highly emaciated with long faces and thin bodies. Here we have a number of contactees in different parts of the world reporting similar images. There are also cases of several people near each other seeing similar images.

Michael Grosso, in his article entitled "UFOs in the Myth of a New Age," describes that on April 23, 1971, he watched an unidentified cluster of lights hover over the dome of Our Lady of Pompeii Church in Greenwich Village in New York City.[13] These clusters of lights moved in impossible aerial maneuvers and then streaked north in a zigzag movement, vanishing over the Empire State Building. Michael was not alone. He saw this with two other people, and they all had similar reports. Were they "out there"?

Grosso is the author of *The Final Choice,* a book that examines the dangerous split between high-technology intelligence and what he calls our underdeveloped moral consciousness.[14] In his article he explored the thesis that UFOs and other extraordinary phenomena are actually manifestations of a disturbance in the collective unconscious of the human species. This disturbance is caused by the violent impact of modern science on human life and the ecology of the earth. This idea resonates with Montague Ullman's concept of the collective unconscious manifesting in dreams and producing images that support the survival of the species rather than the survival of the individual (see chapter 11).

Grosso told me that Henry H. Price, Oxford professor of logic and onetime president of Britain's Society for Psychical Research, once stated the view that every "idea" is inherently psychokinetic.[15] Every idea has a tendency to materialize itself in some shape or form. Grosso points out that if our ideas interact telepathically so as to produce group thought processes, then the group thought processes might have even greater psychokinetic potential. This would imply that a myth such as the UFO that was understood in a fictional sense might objectify itself temporarily under certain circumstances in space and time and assume certain commonly experienced physical characteristics.

I would add that this concept could have some basis in the quantum physical idea of observer-created reality. By observing, one creates a state from a possible superposition of states. If more than one observer is involved, some form of amplification may occur wherein several people have the same or similar images of an event. I'll return to this point concerning vigilant observations at the conclusion of this chapter.

Grosso points out that the UFO experience is part of the making of a New Age myth. He makes three basic points in this regard.

1. We have to look at the whole of UFO phenomena, not just separated, isolated cases of one type or another such as alien abduction versus contactee stories.

2. We have to look at connections between UFOs and other possibly related anomalous phenomena, such as the Big Foot visions or the visions of the Virgin Mary, near-death experiences, poltergeists, channelings, and others.

3. We need to consider the phenomenon historically. There is an evolutionary dimension to the data dealing with the IR of UFO experiences.

The key point of Grosso's article is that the Western world is haunted by a hope and expectation of a new age. He points to the reports of the visual appearance of UFO aliens—they seem to be fetal-like, looking like children, often very sick children with thin arms, bulging eyes, and large heads, like the starving children you see in the countries where famine and war have decimated the land.

Is it that the UFO alien is a vision for all of us of a collective dream, a reminder that we are like—Schopenhauer's idea—all part of a bigger dream? Does this big dream indicate our lack of responsibility in taking care of the children of our planet? Maybe this reflects our concern about the future; after all, the child is the harbinger of the future.

Hardly a day goes by when some television show doesn't have a program dealing with child abuse. The abuse occurs through starvation in Africa or sexual abuse in our country, particularly by fathers and stepfathers in the home. We watch these shows or we read about abuse or hear about it on news programs as we drive home from work. In one way or another, the images of abused children haunt our unconscious minds. Perhaps these images resonate in all of this, producing some form of memory that boils up, either in our dreams at night or on some lonely stretch of highway as we move along the road in our cars.

Could this explain the persistence and the similarity of the images of aliens as they appear to us? Are we witnessing something akin to a "big dream," a survival dream of the human species that manifests in some of us?

Sex with the Fairies: Contact with Images
Throughout Time

Yet there are different images and they have appeared in different guises throughout time. When you look at most of the reports of UFO aliens, they come in a variety of shapes and sizes. There are dwarfs with large wraparound eyes, hairy little creatures, tall, thin Nordic types with long arms and legs, and mysterious men and women in black clothing. So why are they so different? Why are they here at all? These creatures, if we tend to see them in such details, are not just there for us to see, but also to have contact with us. "They" want to communicate with us.

Throughout our history there have been images of beings from other realities who have contacted us physically. In the British Isles sexual liaisons between humans and nonhumans have been reported for several hundreds of years.[16] From the days of Shakespeare, the fairy folk have been dallying with us in many amorous interplays. In recent times, a Brazilian farmer from the state of Minas Gerais reported being abducted by UFO aliens who stripped him naked and spread over his body a clear, odorless liquid that served as an aphrodisiac. A little later a female alien, naked and attractive in her humanoid form, entered the chamber and had "normal" sexual relations with him, numerous times!

Rojcewicz in his article[17] gives several other reports of sexual liaisons with alien creatures. Yet as physical as these fleeting contacts are, in a later article[18] he explains that fairies, UFOs, and their occupants possess quasi-physical natures that seem to violate what we would experience as the laws of physical reality. They appear to pass through solid objects, materialize and dematerialize, and to split into two complete twin objects, then re-form into single objects.

Even if there were no physical aspects to the contacts, just purely visual ones—although such reportings seem to be bizarre when we hear them—I'm sure that few of us have not seen such phenomena, nearly every day of our lives! Just turn on the television set and watch any commercial program. What do we see? We see automobiles fly through the air and vanish. We see people travel from one continent to another without moving. We see cars turn into cardboard images. We see people materialize and dematerialize. The list is endless.

Recent films use a process called morphing in which one object continuously shape-changes into another. The film *Terminator II* exhibited this process with remarkable visual and financial success.

But all of the sightings and contacts between otherworldly folk and us are not television images, you might object, sensing the direction I am going in. If they are not TV pictures, then what are they? I will attempt an explanation of these encounters. My explanation is based on two aspects of my life: my experiences with such "folk" and my hypothesis of the dreaming universe. These aspects indicate to me the existence of a third realm of reality.

Dialogues in the Tertium Quid

In the spring of 1991 I met with Peter M. Rojcewicz and Michael Grosso at a café on the noisy Upper West Side of New York City. Michael Grosso is an artist-philosopher who teaches at Jersey City State College and is well known for his research in UFO studies. Peter M. Rojcewicz, Ph.D., is Co-Chairman and Professor of Humanities in the Department of Liberal Arts at The Juilliard School in New York City. Peter is well known for his work in folklore.

Although our meeting and discussion often took on the typical form of a coffee-klatch, back-table, theoretical speculation, certain themes emerged with clarity. One of them was the recognition that scientists need to expand their concept of reality. One of the few modern researchers who took this seriously was C. G. Jung in his notion of the *psychoid*. Jung's notion suggests that there is a realm of being on the borderline between the physical and the psychical.

Peter pointed out that we could call it the IR as Henry Corbin did in his book.[19] The IR is between the earthly mundane and the completely abstract world of concepts. It is real but not physical, and as such it is not unlike Jung's notion of the psychoid archetype and a related alchemical idea he calls the *unus mundus* (also see chapter 13). It is a place where psyche and nature manifest with a dual aspect not resolving itself into either of its two aspects.

Peter explained:

The psychoid nature of the unus mundus (one world) is a blurred-reality genre. The psychoid realm raises questions of perception and epistemology. In our materialist tradition we are trained to develop a monocular vision and see only the physical. If we happen to see a blurred-reality genre, that is, something in an ambiguous ontological state, most of us would likely see only the most conspicuous physical aspect of it. Some of us would fail to see anything at all. As far as we know about the process of perception, the brain intercedes from moment to moment, matching up and synthesizing what is occurring out there with what it has already recorded. Psychoid phenomena raise the question of whether or not an event takes place in an intermediate realm which doesn't manifest exclusively in a physical objective way or leave a trace.

How do events occur? Where do they occur? Most of us believe that physical events occur in space and time, "out there." We also believe that mental events also occur in space and time "in here," in our brains. We tend to locate events as either in or out. But psychoidal events are different from the mental world, the world of subjective ideas and impressions, and the physical world, the world of things. Psychoid events are occurring in a realm of reality that does not fit into material physics. Yet, psychoid events have both a partial and temporary physical manifestation.

Perhaps we are making an error in thinking about events as occurring in space and in time. Perhaps all events are psychoid and we have learned how to project many of the events "out there" as a survival technique. Other events, so-called IREs such as UFO sightings, are perhaps less life threatening. I remind the reader I am speculating.

This discussion then led my two friends into describing their witnessing of psychoid events. I already mentioned Michael Grosso's sighting of a UFO. Grosso then told me about one of his students who was apparently able to reach the psychoid level. In 1975, while Grosso was teaching, he had a very strange student whom he kept in close contact with. During one of the classes, this student described a classical archetypal child dream. She dreamt she saw a child with a white cape appear on a black stormy shore. In the dream, her family and friends told her, "Don't touch the child." But the child beckoned to her to save him from the storm, a classic motive of the endangered-child dream. She then felt pity for the child and reached out and touched him. When she awoke, her right hand was covered with a mysterious black substance.

Grosso interviewed two people who were with her at the time and saw this. They swore that this was a true account. The dream recurred several times, and the black hand covering appeared every time she had this dream. Later on, she told Grosso that she had a dream in which she was going to be in an auto accident. After the dream, she had an auto accident. A week later she walked into his class with her right arm in a sling, and Grosso saw that her right hand was black.

Her hand never healed. For one year she struggled with this hand. Part of the story is that the magical child instructed her to become an artist and told her to paint a picture of him. Whenever she tried to paint, her hand healed. But whenever she listened to the advice of her parents, who were superstitious, or her boyfriend, who wasn't too bright (Grosso knew the boyfriend because he was also Grosso's student), things would go haywire and the black hand would return.

Because of her unusual ability to manifest psychoid phenomena, Grosso decided to test her himself. He led a meditation in her class and invited the students to dream. He wanted to test her ability to become aware of real, hidden objects, which she claimed she could do in her dreams. Grosso had selected as an object a target that no one had seen before. The following morning he found in his office a report, that he still has, of her dream. It was an *exact* description— every detail of her report fit the target. No one in the rest of the class even got close to it. She had dreamt that target and described a number of specific details such as the presence of cobblestones.[20]

Grosso still isn't sure if he believes her story about the black hand. The point of the dream-child experience is that there was something that manifested as reality for her. Not listening to her guide, which came in the form of a dream child, turned out to be bad news for her whole life. At the end of the year Grosso lost contact with her.

What can we conclude from this story? I suggest that there is a rationale that applies to the materialization of events through dreams that I believe was hinted at by Werner Heisenberg in his book *Physics and Beyond,* as a middle realm between hard objectivity and soft subjectivity. Heisenberg wrote about the mystical and the scientific experience of the world as being joined in some way. He said that somewhere between the object and the subject is a middle realm, a concept that is receiving increasing interest among physicists today. It appears to me that this middle realm is Jung's psychoid realm, the tertium quid.

Perhaps being influenced by Heisenberg and Bohr, I came to this conclusion as a result of dealing with quantum mechanics. It is perhaps strange, but quantum physics actually describes the possible objective qualities of things in this realm rather than either objects or subjects. Quantum physics doesn't describe the realm of subjective experience or the realm of objective experience.

Quantum physics was the "great white hope" of science—the dream to see everything in terms of objective experience. But, as it continued to battle for supremacy, it became blacker and blacker as the subject was thrown into the mathematically and geometrically shaped arena. Instead, quantum physics describes the realm of imaginal experience that is potential material experience.

Here we are faced with subjectivity simply because we are faced with our inability to specify exactly what is going on. For the moment, let me assume that reality is not fuzzy, that the fuzziness we experience of reality must be due to us. Result? We experience fuzzy reality. Now let me assume that reality is fuzzy. Then reality is not solid as we, in our attempts to model reality and survive in it, think it to be. Result: we experience fuzzy reality.

Which is true? Either way, we're forced to the mathematics of probability found in the wave motion of Schrödinger's equation.[21] This wave does not move in the "real" world. It moves strictly in the IR, and yet it conforms to the real world, or, perhaps better stated, the real world somehow follows its form, but only probabilistically rather than ballistically as Newton's equations described the classical real world.

There is something else about this wave of the IR. In mathematics we talk about two kinds of numbers, real and imaginary. It appears to make sense to say that we observe real numbers in the real world. Actually we don't even do that, for number itself is a concept arising from the IR or perhaps, as von Franz suggests, arising as an archetype. But let that sleeping dog lie. At least we say that the things of the real world, the bits and pieces in it, are numbered as the proverbial hairs on your head or days of your life.

So much for real numbers. But you cannot describe a quantum physical wave without representing it in terms of both of these kinds of numbers. And they don't mix. If you leave one of them out, you get the wrong answer. The fact that you need both real and imaginary numbers is a clue, maybe, to the "reality" of some psychoid level, a middle realm, a twilight zone. The fact that we use the term *imaginary* to represent these numbers is also significant and perhaps arises from some unconscious process pointing to the IR.

In philosophy, Michael Grosso explained, we normally discriminate between the physical and the mental world. Some philosophers fully acknowledge the existence of a mental world but base the mind in the physical world. This point of view is called materialism. Others, called idealists, think that the physical world is derivable from the mental world. Where does the psychoid event fit? With this phenomenon the distinctions between materialism and idealism evaporate.

Grosso calls this third realm the *tertium quid* of being. It deals with concepts such as the astral level, IR, psychic awareness, psychoid phenomenon, and ultradimensional existence, that is, areas of thought that science is not able to define or pin down with exactitude.

This realm encompasses anomalous experiences and dreams. Most dreams seem to be purely subjective in terms of our common understanding of the universe breaking down into the above two categories of being. But, as researchers are seeing, there are subcategories of being, some of which seem to suggest other possibilities—anomalous dreams that bleed over into the realm of psychoid experiences emerging in waking reality.

Grosso's strategy for investigation of this realm is simple. Try to describe this world, be as truly descriptive as you can. For example, some ghosts have been photographed and then they are witnessed disappearing through solid walls. That means they have both characteristics: imaginal—they pass through walls—and physical—they leave a photographic trace.

Grosso has investigated Marian visions—images of Mother Mary, especially the one that took place in Zeitun, Egypt, in 1968. It clearly seemed to be a psychoid projection—an apparition of the Virgin Mary that was photographed.

Peter M. Rojcewicz pointed out to me that some of the UFO photos are like the Marian vision. In some photos you can see the UFO, and yet you can also see through it to the tree behind it as if it were in the process of materializing. While the same thing could indeed be simply produced by a double exposure, if one takes it as genuine, then it has both light and dark areas as if it were both light-releasing and light-absorbing.

Whether these phenomena fall on either side of the border between the objective and the subjective may depend on consciousness; on the observer, if there is a kind of interaction; or on something to do with the percipient's experience. Studies show that we often do not see something unless we truly believe in it. Peter finds this interesting from a neurological viewpoint; there may, however, be some percipients who encounter UFOs simply because they possess a wider range of the visual field and have different thresholds.

Rojcewicz explained that he has been researching, for several years, the realm of folklore, looking seriously at different folk ontological systems, and has come to the conclusion that there is something fundamentally true even though no one takes a fairy tale or a myth to be literally true. For example, societies that have strong taboos against incest or violence have violent and incestuous folktales. Why do these stories persist? Peter believes that this persistence involves something more than just fantasy. These stories have some pragmatic value for these societies. They materialize unique ways of seeing and experiencing reality, bringing various mindsets out into the physical world where we encounter them. Or perhaps they reflect the dark side of our consciousness.

Granting this, we could consider that the religion of today is science. For a while we had several people telling us that nuclear power plants were dangerous. There was the movie with Jack Lemmon, *The China Syndrome*. And then shortly after that we had the Three Mile Island and Chernobyl incidents. Were these cases where the psychoid world extended into the physical world? In the next chapter we will explore the physics of this possibility.

$\mathcal{T}$HE PHYSICS OF THE IMAGINAL REALM

Looking at what people with shamanic traditions say about dreams, one comes to the realization that, experientially, for these people dream reality is a parallel continuum. . . . I suggest [we] take seriously the idea of a parallel continuum, and say that the mind and the body are embedded in the dream and the dream is a higher-order spatial dimension. In sleep one is released into the real world of which the world of waking is only the surface in a very literal geometrical sense. . . . We are not primarily biological, with mind emerging as a kind of iridescence, a kind of epiphenomenon at the higher levels of organization of biology. We are, in fact, hyperspatial objects of some sort which cast a shadow into matter. The shadow in matter is our physical organism.

—Terence McKenna[1]

My conversations with Peter and Michael in the West Side café in New York City continued throughout the afternoon. It was refreshing talking with them. Most science researchers have a hard time keeping an open mind about the imaginal realm (IR). Yet as we saw in the previous chapter, some scientists, such as Jacques Vallee, have hinted at its existence and spoken about it as something that is ontological. At some point we all begin to wonder at the strangeness of our experience of the universe.

Yet it is important to recognize the simple limit that is enforced on us by our attempts to describe experience. Many people believe in the existence of objective reality as simply being "out there," not requiring anything additional. We see what's there, nothing more and nothing less. Others believe that our sensory experiences are limited, and that is why we fail to see the whole picture. We see only parts of reality.

Yet none of the above is quite true or complete. Experimental data does not exist without a theory of the meaning of that data. Einstein once remarked that it was the theory that determined what we can observe. Without a theory of reality, no observation will have any meaning, and without meaning, I contend, there is no observation. We need meaning to observe.

For example, we may take as meaningful the idea that the universe is a great thought from a great mind. Or that the universe is a machine. Or perhaps we believe that the universe is consciousness or that space itself is conscious. Such statements appear to be meaningful, but they border on fantasy. By fantasy I mean that eventually the idea reaches into a realm of fuzzy definition, open to several, sometimes conflicting, visions. Indeed any idea about the universe borders on fantasy. Does this mean that we simply cannot talk about the universe meaningfully?

For example, take the idea that the universe is a great machine. Newton's laws and the observation that the planets follow these laws of motion would support the idea. But if it is a machine, then it would mean that life is a machine also. It would also mean that someone built the machine. And that the machine existed in space. But the universe encompasses all of space, so if it is a machine, it is a machine that built itself out of itself. What does that mean?

Take the idea that the universe is conscious. But if you ask where that consciousness resides, you have to say everywhere or nowhere because space-time location of consciousness is not measurable. For example, we cannot even find a seat of consciousness in our brains, no less in the whole universe. The mind does not fit into space-time, or it has no space-time coordinates, or it has them all. Is this meaningful?

The Physics of Meaning

Thus in order to understand this limit of attempting to talk about reality, to make meaningful statements, we need to know what we mean when we speak about meaning. So far it is impossible to define meaning without going in a circle. David Bohm in his book *Unfolding Meaning* points out that when we communicate with each other, we know what meaning is without defining it.[2] Bohm theorizes that meaning arises always in connection with matter and energy. He would put it that meaning enfolds matter and energy, and that matter itself points to energy and meaning, and that energy signifies meaning and matter. In other words, any of the three terms *matter, energy,* or *meaning* signifies the existence of the other two.

I will attempt to define *meaning* as an experience that arises whenever any two or more events, happenstances, or random occurrences are quantum mechanically correlated.[3] Thus in my model meaning arises from such a correlation and, most importantly, is *experienced* as conscious awareness. Thus it takes two to tango. A single event not only has no meaning, it has no existence, and it is not even observable!

I am indicating here that an observation of an event in and of itself is impossible without a referral, that is, another event. Physics deals with observables. Today we know that any mechanistic model of the universe that does not include how quantum mechanics deals with observables is bound to be wrong. However, observables refer to an observer, and this ultimately refers to a perception of something, an act of consciousness.

The question is, how does consciousness perceive? Without knowing what consciousness is I know what it has to do. It has to act. And if such actions are meaningful, these actions must encompass two or more events. But we need to make a framework for these events, a space where the action takes place. This space, the IR, contains the actions of consciousness. From the imaginal into the actuality of space-time, a sudden movement occurs wherein we find ourselves as observers separated from the "out there" observing the world as if we were suddenly dematerialized and rematerialized in another location.

Bohm would call this action the unfolding of the implicate order making it explicate. If we put these actions within a framework of space and time, "out there," then one event in the IR leads to two or more events in space-time. The space-time events can be separated timewise or spacewise or both. The two events could, for example, be simultaneous. This would be a single event of synchronicity or psychic awareness.

Although I state that you need at least two space-time events, you can have more. The more events you have, the stronger is the sense of the event in consciousness. Thus, sitting in a room, you are bombarded with billions of events in the space-time of your brain and body, all constituting a single event in conscious awareness occurring in the IR.

Consciousness does not fit into a space-time matrix. If one tries to do this, one finds oneself making paradoxical statements such as: It is everywhere at all times or nowhere at any time. The idea is that quantum-correlated pairs of space-time events are experienced as single events in consciousness. Any two events anywhere in the universe at any time produce an associative quantum probability that, depending on the strength of that probability, will be a conscious event. The degree of consciousness is determined by the intensity of the connection between the events. In other words, the more probable the connection, the greater is the awareness of the events.

But why does consciousness seem to occur in my brain? The answer seems to be intensity or numbers of events that are correlated. For example, looking out the window and seeing something correlates with firing events in my striate (visual) cortex. The "out there" also correlates with firing in your striate cortex, so we "see" the same thing. However, the "out there" is connected to the "in here" when we become aware of the "out there." Thus the observer of the "out there" is actually as "out there" as "in here." The IR encompasses both "out there" and "in here."

To look for the observer inside the brain is futile. When you have a dream, is the retinal net firing? I would say yes. Who is witnessing the event? Everything is. The quality of seeing the event is part of the pairs of the events themselves. They cannot be separated from the space-time events. *Ding an sich*. It is a thing to itself.

Once this concept is grasped, and I know that it is difficult to grasp fully what I am saying, we can see how a process of "dense" observations, made in temporal sequence, not only leads to enhanced awareness of the object of that observation and therefore a meaningful objective view of the reality of the object, but to the actual creation of the movement of that object along a pathway that it may or may not have taken if those observations were not carried out. Now what happens if a sequence of observations is carried out over time?

Psychoid Physics and the Vigilance of Intent

Let me put this in a framework. Consciousness is a field that exists in an arena called the IR. The objective world "out there" and the subjective sense of "in here" are by-products of that IR. The qualities of these by-products are matter, energy, and meaning. In Bohm's terminology, matter, energy, and meaning unfold from the implicate order into the explicate order. Thus the IR and the implicate order of Bohm are one and the same.

This implies that there is a deep connection between the observer and the observed. So deep, in fact, that we really cannot separate them. What causes us to feel that they are separated is an illusion, a necessary illusion, a lucid dream of the universe.

Now in lucid dreams of human beings, this becomes most evident as we will or intend something to happen and then witness it occur. To the degree that we take responsibility for the actions of the dream, we find ourselves gaining greater and greater power over the contents of the dream, even the power to do magical acts.

Let me give you an example. On December 16, 1992, I had a lucid dream. I was riding a bicycle in a park and came upon a group of people. I then realized that I was having a lucid dream. I carefully controlled the dream so that I would not awaken. I then rode on and came up to some people standing outside a house. I spoke to them and they responded. I knew in the dream that this was an opportunity to inquire about the world I had entered. I asked them where we were, in what country. They asked me into the house and showed me a map, pointing out just where we were. I noticed that the map of the country looked very much like a map of South America. I read the map and saw that we were inland near the northwest coast. They told me that the name of the country was Angola or Auburn or something like that. I asked them for the address of the house, and they told me that it was 644 (or possibly 144) Fitzroy St.[4]

I then left them and decided to test my powers of intent. I returned to the park near a small outdoor café. I went up to a tree and decided to move my hand right through one of its branches. I felt that the tree was solid, but this did not deter me. I "knew" that I could pass my hand through it. I did and was delighted. I noticed that children were there watching me. I could see that they were amazed that I was able to do this. I told them that I was not from their world and that I could do many magical things.[5]

I then thought of Uri Geller and decided to do a number of metal bendings with spoons and forks that were on one of the café's tables. I bent the hard metal objects as if they were soft malleable tin. I didn't bend them with effort; I just held each implement in my hand

and the metal bent by itself following my intent. It was easy to do. I then felt myself awakening, and I could not control the dream any longer.

Now I bring up this dream because it raises the question of intent. How does intent work? Is it a physical process? In a later chapter I will explain how intent works in a model of neural self-observing automata. The idea is that intent can operate in the dream world as it does in the physical world by altering the observed state of that world. The fact that intent affects the physical world reflects a recent discovery of quantum physicists Yakir Aharonov and M. Vardi. They have shown that the old proverb "A watched pot never boils" may have a range of validity previously unsuspected. They have discovered a paradoxical situation that arises when a quantum system is watched carefully. As they put it:

> Namely, if one checks by continuous observations, if a given quantum system evolves from some initial state, to some other final state, along a specific trajectory...the result is always positive, whether or not the system would have done so on its own accord.[6]

If a quantum system[7] is monitored continuously, we could say vigilantly, it will do practically anything. For example, suppose you are watching a quantum system and attempting to determine just when it undergoes a transition from one state to another. To make this concrete, think of an imaginary "quantum pot of water" being heated on the stove. The transition is for the water to go from the calm state to the boiling state. We all know that pots of water boil, given a few minutes or so. You would certainly think that the watched pot would also boil. It turns out that, because of the vigilance of the observations, the transition never occurs; the watched pot never boils.

Another theoretical example is the decay of an unstable atomic nucleus. On its own it would decay in a few microseconds. But if the nucleus is watched continuously, it will never decay (I don't know if this has ever been experimentally observed). All vigilantly watched "quantum pots" never boil, even if they are heated forever.

All of this might be considered just quantum physical speculation. However, in 1989, physicist Wayne Itano and his colleagues at the National Institute of Standards and Technology in Boulder, Colorado, actually experimentally observed the "quantum watched pot," and indeed it never boiled![8] Their experiment involved watching some five thousand beryllium atoms confined in a magnetic field and then exposed to radio waves of energy. The atoms were the equivalent of the pot of water and the radio waves the equivalent of the heat applied to the pot. Under such circumstances the atoms will "evolve" into excited atomic-energy states as they absorb the radio energy. Nearly all five thousand will reach their excited-state goals in little over 250 milliseconds (ms), i.e., a quarter of a second.

To check this, the physicists observed the atoms after 250 ms by shining a short pulse of laser light into their midst. Excited atoms do not absorb and immediately reemit any of the selected laser energy. Atoms that remain in the unexcited state do. By observing the laser light after it passed through the trapped atoms, the physicists were able to determine just how many atoms remained unexcited.

Virtually none were after 250 ms. We could refer to this as the unwatched pot that naturally evolved to the boiling state in a quarter of a second. But then the scientists became slightly vigilant. They decided to look at the atoms halfway along, after 125 ms had passed. So, an eighth of a second after starting the experiment the laser pulse was turned on, and then at the 250 ms mark the scientists looked again and found that only one-half of the atoms were excited. They repeated the experiment by looking in at 62.5 ms, 125 ms, 187.5 ms, and 250 ms; in other words, they divided the one-quarter-second interval into four equal parts and were surprised to find that their enhanced vigilance produced a result of only one-third of the atoms making it to the excited-energy state.

They next redoubled their vigilance by looking in sixteen times, thirty-two times, and finally sixty-four times during the 250 ms interval. In the final experiment where they watched their tiny atomic "pots" in sixty-four equally spaced tiny time intervals, virtually none of the atoms were ever found in an excited state, even though 250 ms had passed. They all remained frozen in their ground or original states just as they were when the experiment began. In each experiment, mind you, the "heat" was on—the radio waves were continuously being sent in to the magnetically trapped beryllium atoms.

How does this work? If the system was unobserved, it would certainly undergo the physical transition. The pot would boil. The decaying system would decay. It is the observer effect that causes the anomaly to occur. Let me explain. When the system is first observed, it is seen to be in its initial state. When it is observed just a smidgen of time later, well before the time in which it should change, the system is observed with more than 99.99 percent chance to be in its initial state. In other words, the system is found to be exactly where it was initially. Now repeat this measurement again and again, each time just a tiny bit of time later, and with a very high probability the same observation occurs: the system is found in its initial state.

But time marches on, and eventually we pass all reasonable time limits for the transition to occur, and yet it still doesn't happen. The system "freezes" in its initial state. The only requirement to freeze the motion is that the observer must have the intent to see the object in its initial state when he looks.[9] The old adage comes up: you will see it when you believe it.

Suppose he doesn't watch vigilantly or suppose that he does but with the intent of seeing it evolve naturally, then what? Take the pot. If he looks only intermittently, expecting it to boil eventually, the pot will follow its natural unobserved course and will boil as Itano et al. proved. Or if he intends to vigilantly observe the object evolving along its natural path of evolution, then he will observe that instead. In other words, a watched pot boils, if you intend it to.

Finally there is even another bizarre element to this. Suppose that the system could be observed to evolve along a bizarre path, an impossible mission so to speak. If the intent to observe that occur is vigilant enough, then the object will actually follow the bizarre path of evolution. You can make things happen simply by intending them to happen, if you observe what you intend with great vigilance. That means with intense observation occurring over very short time intervals, more or less continuously but along a new, unexpected track. A watched pot boils on a cake of ice, if you intend it to.

I need to point out that intent and intentions are not the same. Intent refers to a vigorous action of vigilant observations along a specific path of evolution. It matters little what you hope for or even what you expect will happen passively. The direction of evolution is determined as you go and depends on where you focus your observation. Thus intent requires a quantum physical basis. Intention, on the other hand, is a classical mechanical concept. One sets in motion a certain expectation and then hopes for the best. The old line "The best-laid plans of mice and men often go astray" tells the whole story.

Our brains may be composed of quantum systems, and consequently the physics of dreams, particularly lucid dreams, may be governed by the "pot watched with intent" theory. Thus this may be the physics of the imaginal realm, or how it is that what is dreamt of, manifests. Maybe we have caught the "Old One" in his magic act after all.

RANSPERSONAL DREAMING AND DEATH

What mysteries this vision contains!
  Someday a great Sage will come and explain it to us, but that may not be until ten thousand generations have come and gone.
  Still, for us in this dream, it will only seem like the passing of a single morning or afternoon.

—*Chuang Tzu*[1]

Let us assume the abduction experience is an extraordinary type of dream. The coherence of the experience shows it's not a private but a collective dream. A dream, perhaps, of the species mind. Produced by the species mind, like any dream, it is about the dreamer. Perhaps about the dreamer's future.

—*Michael Grosso*[2]

After my meeting with Michael Grosso and Peter Rojcewicz in New York City, I hopped a train for the short trip to Hartford, Connecticut, to meet with Dr. Kenneth Ring, a major researcher in the rapidly developing field of near-death experience (NDE), and professor of psychology at the University of Connecticut. Ring was noted as the first researcher to offer scientific validation for these remarkable experiences that had been anecdotally described by Elizabeth Kubler-Ross, Raymond Moody, Jr., and others.

Ring explained to me that an NDE exhibits a typical pattern. It is the result of an individual's undergoing and surviving some kind of life-threatening, near-death crisis, often, but not always, involving a cardiac or respiratory arrest, or something of this sort.

In his latest book,[3] Ring established a connection between NDEs and UFO abductions (described in chapter 14). He proposed that people who have either of these experiences fit a certain psychological profile that he labeled "encounter-prone." He in no way suggested that these individuals are less capable of coping with reality, but on the contrary, that they are distinctive, spiritually sensitive, and possess visionary psyches that may be signals of an evolutionary trend—a new stage in human development.

What is this new trend? Here I wish to suggest that the development is the recognition that mind is not confined to individual and separated persons, but is universal, singular, and beyond any conceptual limit we enforce, such as the notion of space-time confinement. Thus I am suggesting that NDE, UFO encounters, and a range of other imaginal-realm (IR)[4] bleed-throughs into our normally seemingly separated minds are an evolutionary trend leading us to a single, one-mind experience of our SELF, the whole universe and nothing less.

From this point of view an NDE is an awakening experience, a recognition that one's mind is everywhere, and it is also a recognition that each of us can experience this one mind continuously even after an NDE as if it were a heightened awareness or lucid state of our separated and partitioned self. From this lucid state of awareness, the sense of separation, the feeling that one is alone and separate from others, appears as an illusion. I hope to offer scientific evidence for this, in this chapter.

If this is so, then self-separation is a dream within a larger one or "big dream" of the universe. Just why the dream exists in this form, and why we feel that we are separate from each other, appear as nothing more than conditioned responses, a natural historical development of the Hindu concept of *maya*.[5] Let me now look at the evidence.

Discontinuities in Time

Such thoughts that we are currently undergoing a rapid evolutionary development, possibly leading to a new concept of self, resonate with the work of Grosso and Rojcewicz described in chapter 14 and the theory that Montague Ullman suggested in chapter 11. A key insight that I hope to establish here is the connection of imaginal-realm experiences and certain experiences occurring both physiologically and psychologically in the dreaming brain.

The first piece of evidence that leads to this evolutionary conclusion is one of the points that Ring makes: the discontinuous character of both UFO encounters and NDEs resembles that of similar phenomena in dreams. To Ring's point I add that discontinuities in these IREs resemble the experimentally observed behavior of quantum physical systems. In looking over his own research and scores of other researchers' documented accountings, Ring noticed that the stories people told were punctuated by such expressions as "the next thing I knew" or "what I remember next was" or "suddenly I blacked out" and so on.

Such quick shifts in story lines are quite familiar, if one remembers one's own dreams. In them we are often faced with discontinuities, rapid scene changes, and temporal and spatial distortions as if one were "beamed up" in a Star Trek transporter. Ring is not, however, suggesting that these experiences are dreams per se; no, indeed; they are more like, as he states,

> dreams that one has *awakened into* and that, in some unknown way, have come to interpenetrate ordinary reality, resulting in a kind of double vision, which, eventually, returns to normal. If these experiences are some [form] of dream [they] must be some sort of *collective dream* since many people are reporting similar, and similarly bizarre, encounters.[6]

The discontinuities in the experiences and the disparities in time flow suggest that some kind of quantum physical mechanism is as applicable to the way our minds work as it is to the world of matter and energy. Before the discovery of quantum physics all objects in the universe were believed to be in motion following continuous trajectories from the past into the future. Accordingly, for every effect, every change in movement that an object underwent, there had to be a prior cause. Matter and energy followed the Newtonian God-given rule of physics: all change is continuous change.[7]

With the realization that matter at the level of atoms and molecules did not follow that rule, the "new physics," quantum mechanics, was developed. At first Niels Bohr came up with the idea of the "quantum leap," which was not only a break in the continuous movement of atoms, but also a break with traditional physics. Bohr had put discontinuity into the realm of physical matter in order to explain how atoms emitted and absorbed energy. Later Erwin Schrödinger came up with a master equation that explained atomic motion and the remarkable stability of atoms and molecules. Although Schrödinger's equation showed that the *probability* of observing the energy of an atomic system developed continuously, it was still necessary, in order to explain how atomic matter changed energy, to assume that it suffered quantum jumps—leaps from one place to another in a completely discontinuous manner.

At first no one knew what was causing the jumps. Schrödinger's equation gave a map of smoothly changing possibilities that only applied to unobserved quantum systems. But observed quantum systems did not follow those equations when they changed energy discontinuously. Later it was suspected that it was the observer that was causing the jumps. But the observer effect on matter did not fit into a continuous mathematical description.[8]

Nor do dreams and NDEs. In terms of clocktime, some NDEs seem to last only seconds. Others can take place over an extended time. But usually the individual will say, "I didn't have any sense of time. It could have been a minute or year or ten thousand years." In this state, Ring told me, the "voyager" seems to be outside of time and time seems to be spatialized somehow.[9]

Thus, what is actually occurring in time as perceived by the person during the experience is unknown. In brief, all we have are the reports of the person after the fact indicating that the experience was discontinuous in time, but afterward when the person describes the experience, that description appears ordered in time. Ring told me that it is important not to confuse the description of the experience with the experience itself. The description is in words and in time and of necessity following some form of a linear sequence.

In much the same way, we have the mathematical description of atomic behavior following a continuous linear time progression while the experimental evidence indicates that atoms change energy states discontinuously subject to an observer's intent.[10]

Ring also believes that the NDE is holographic[11]—the whole experience displayed all at once. In making an analogy he explained that when we are looking at something in a room, we are more or less looking straight ahead at some object. However, while doing this we actually have panoramic vision encompassing a whole scene. Although all of the objects in the room are all around us, they are not in any specific arrangement. But when we focus on a particular object and then another and another, we will tend to recall the experience of the room in terms of a linear sequence. "I saw the lamp and then I saw the picture on the wall, and then . . ." and so on.

In a certain period of clocktime one could say the "voyager" experienced a much longer period of time. An example of this occurred in the film *Jacob's Ladder* in which the hero experienced a rather long period of days in what was just a few minutes as he lay unconscious between life and death.

NDEs are situations in which the person appears to exist outside of time. There are events, but they are not necessarily in sequence. But when the person comes back from the experience, back into his body and clocktime, the experience can seem as if it took place over a long period of time even though by clocktime it was only a minute or so.

Thus Ring believes that the NDE is not in time and that it is misleading to interpret the words *and then* as if they implied a sequential progression. Only after the recovery, when one is back in time, does the narrative form emerge. Unfortunately and consequently, these experiences are usually talked about as if they happened in linear time.

UFOs and NDEs: Discontinuities and Electrical Brainstorms

In chapter 8 I explained how Hobson's mechanism was based on electrical PGO jolts in the nervous systems of sleeping persons and that these jolts may be the cause of dream discontinuities. UFO researchers Paul Devereux and Michael Persinger have found a similar connection between electrical activity in the brain and both NDE and UFO close-encounter abduction (CEIV) experiences.[12]

Devereux has found that people usually report observing unusual light phenomena near fault lines, power lines, transmitter towers, mountain peaks, isolated buildings, road and railway lines, and bodies of water including waterfalls. In many instances these lights seem to emerge from the ground and either swiftly dissolve or hover, sometimes touching down to ground again and then rising several thousands of feet in the air. They have also been seen during daylight hours and appear metallic. Light phenomena also tend to reappear in certain regions of the world so often that local people have incorporated them into folklore and superstitions. Devereux believes that such light phenomena are characteristic of high-amplitude electro-magnetic disturbances.

Michael Persinger, a Canadian professor of psychology and a clini-cal neurophysiologist, has carried out numerous studies, along with his colleagues, on the relationship of electromagnetic phenomena to tectonic stress. He and Devereux believe that UFO phenomena are natural occurrences producing high-amplitude electromagnetic pulses that are direct products of stress relief in tectonic plate move-ments of the earth's crust.[13] Persinger's statistical studies show that seismic events are clearly related to UFO reports. In other words, during seismic events more UFO sightings will be reported.

Well, suppose Devereux and Persinger are correct in their obser-vations. What does this tell us about the reality of CEIVs and NDEs? If a person is sufficiently far away from a tectonic stress release and its concomitant electromagnetic energy burst (EMEB), the person may describe seeing a light show typical of CEI and CEII reports. If the person approaches the light or if he happens to be standing near enough to it, he may be close enough to the EMEB to feel its effects. These could include the raising of hair on the body and head, skin tingling, goose bumps, and other signs of nervous excitation. Follow-ing this line, deeper immersions could lead to brain disturbances resulting in psychological disturbances and hallucinatory images.

Persinger suggests that the temporal lobe in particular is sensitive to such electrical disturbances—a finding that is quite consistent with other research. Probably the most research in this area was done by Wilder Penfield, the late neurosurgeon and writer. Penfield noted that the temporal lobe has convolutions that are apparently new evolution-arily and are not committed to motor or sensory function.[14] When a child is born, these new convolutions appear uncommitted and unconditioned as to function. During the initial learning stages of childhood some of these convolutions seem to be devoted to interpre-tation of present experience in terms of past experience. This part of the temporal lobe has today been labeled the *interpretative cortex.*

During surgical procedures on patients suffering from temporal-lobe seizures (epileptic seizures caused by electrical discharges origi-nating in the temporal lobe), Penfield and his colleagues stumbled upon the fact that electrical stimulation of the interpretive areas of the cortex occasionally produced what John Hughlings Jackson—the British neurologist who in 1872 introduced the concept of increas-ingly complex levels of function in the brain—has called "dreamy states" or "psychical seizures." The patient's conscious reports during the surgical procedure often signaled surgeon Penfield that he was close to the cause of the seizures. Penfield reported that during the procedure, in the early days of temporal-lobe surgery, electrical stimulation was a helpful guide for the surgeon in locating the causative areas of the brain that needed excision.

It was clear to Penfield that these "dreamy states" were not dreams. They were electrical activations of sequences of records laid down during the patient's earlier conscious experiences. The patient "relived" all that he had been aware of during an earlier period of time. He was having a moving-picture "flashback."[15]

Penfield's descriptions of patients' reports are quite amazing. The range of sensory experiences, including sight, sounds, finger tinglings, tastes, smells, emotional feelings, in essence the whole gamut of human sensory experiences, could be recalled by electrical stimulation of appropriate areas of the temporal cortex in these patients. However, the major responses were in the visual and auditory senses.

In each case the patient reported a story line as if the person were witnessing the experience all over again. For example, a young man reported that he was sitting at a baseball game in a small town watching a little boy crawling under the fence to get into the stands. Another patient was in a concert hall listening to music. He explained that he could hear the different instruments and what each was playing. In these cases the stimulated memories were unimportant events.

Neurophysiologist Persinger has discovered that all of the major components of the NDE, including out-of-body experiences, floating, being pulled toward the light, hearing strange music, and a profound sense of meaning, can be duplicated in a laboratory setting by using minimal electrical-current induction administered to the temporal lobe.[16]

Based on the above findings, there seems to be no doubt that imaginal-realm experiences are produced by electrical disturbances in the temporal lobe. These can be induced by anomalous electromagnetic phenomena, such as those that accompany tectonic stress relief in the earth's crust and brain surgical procedures, and even under laboratory settings. But what about you and me? What about so-called normal people who, through seemingly no fault of their own, experience such phenomena when no added electrical stimulation is present?

Here Ring suggests and Persinger concurs that some individuals may be "encounter-prone." Such individuals, for perhaps a number of different reasons, are unusually sensitive to normal temporal-lobe electrical activity. Ring made a study of the characteristics of two categories of people: those who had NDE or some kind of UFO experience (UFOE) and, as a control group, those that did not but were interested in them. People that report one kind of UFOE or another are quite similar to one another; however, Ring found that NDErs and the UFOErs were not more fantasy prone.

One might suspect that fantasy-prone people are more likely to have imaginal-realm experiences (IREs). Psychologists have indicated that certain kinds of people are susceptible to inner worlds of fantasy. These fantasy-prone people become so deeply absorbed in fantasy that they can't distinguish between fantasy and reality.

But Ring and his coworkers did not find fantasy-prone individuals any more susceptible to IREs than those who were not fantasy prone. But he did find that as children, encounter-prone individuals were more likely to say that they were sensitive to alternative realities. These are the kinds of people who say things like, "As a child I was able to see nonphysical beings while I was awake. I was able to see other realities that other people were not aware of." These same people also claim to have had psychic or paranormal experiences when they were young. Ring emphasized, "They are not, however, more fantasy-prone, but they are seemingly more susceptible to alternate realities."

What would make an individual more sensitive to alternative reality as a child as distinct from fantasy? What is it about these people as children that would make them more prone to these kinds of experiences? The answer is disturbing and illuminating. There appears to be a high correlation between child abuse and imaginal-realm sensitivity. Ring explained, "These people come, not from the ranks of the fantasy-prone, but with histories of child abuse that include sexual and psychological trauma, neglect, and family dysfunctionality."

Ring explained that children who are abused tend to be more dissociative—able to split off from ordinary reality and go into alternative reality. A family history of child abuse and trauma promotes dissociative response as a psychological defense. If you grew up in a home of unpredictable violence or sexual abuse or other forms of trauma, you would be motivated to tune out that situation. As Ring put it, "They can do anything to your body but you, the 'real' you inside, will go elsewhere. Once you learn to dissociate in response to the trauma, you are much more likely to become sensitive to alternate realities."

Therefore, when in later life you are exposed to an NDE, because of your history in dealing with trauma by psychological escape, you are more likely to split off into a dissociative state of consciousness that gives you access to an imaginal realm.

What about people who experience near-death trauma but do not have an NDE? Many individuals suffer traumatic experiences in which they become unconscious and lapse into near-death, but they come out of it with no memory of anything at all. Ring explained that somebody who doesn't have this early child-abuse history is not as likely to have an NDE. His studies indicate that only one out of three people having a near-death experience remember having the NDE. A similar argument can be made for people who have UFO experience.

Thus Ring believes NDErs and UFOErs have a distinctive psychological profile. I had made the same observation in 1989 at the Close Encounters of the Fourth Kind (CEIV) Conference in Colorado described in chapter 14. Present at the conference were a number of people who had experienced UFO CEIV abductions, including Betty Hill, Travis Walton, Charles Hickson, Rosemary Onato, and others. After listening to each of them describe their experience, I had observed that these individuals all had certain similarities. They were all amazingly cogent verbally, able to express themselves and describe their experiences quite well in spite of a quite varied educational background. I would describe them all as remarkably intelligent.

But there was a disturbing sense of loss in all of them and a certain lack of joie de vivre. They seemed quite unspontaneous and lacking in personal drive or motivation. Their descriptions were also similar. In each case the described CEIV experience was one of powerlessness, of being taken into a strange surrounding and physically abused with probes inserted into parts of their bodies. Whitley Strieber in his best-selling books also describes quite well and, similar to the above description, how unpleasant the CEIV experience was.[17]

After hearing their descriptions, I had the intuition that they all were unhappy children and were all reliving and describing their early childhood abuse. Of course they were all adults and my speculation could be quite in error. But following my insight, I can only surmise that as abused children they were not able to talk about the abuses, but later as adults, and assuming that they are more sensitive to temporal-lobe electrical activity than most of us, these experiences either resurfaced from memories (only now it was more acceptable to describe them in terms of UFOs), triggered by electrical temporal-lobe excitation, or they were indeed "visits" from imaginal-realm beings.

Ring tends to concur with this line of reasoning. However, he told me that this explanation has met with a lot of resistance from people doing work in the CEIV abduction area because it tends to make it less than it is. Persinger suggests that the physical abuse may have a physical effect on the brain, opening it for these kinds of activities. This is not the only factor involved, but it may be causal in these cases.

A Typical Description of an NDE

I asked Ring to describe for me a typical NDE. He told me:

> The first thing is a tremendous feeling of peace, like nothing else you have experienced. Most people say like never before and never again. People say [that it is] the peace that passes all understanding. Then there is the sense of bodily separation and sometimes the sense of actually being out of the body. There are studies that show that people can sometimes report veridically what is in their physical environment, e.g., the lint on the light fixtures above themselves. They could see in a three-hundred-sixty-degree panoramic vision. They had extraordinary acuity. Often when they went further into the experience, they went to a dark place that is sometimes described as a tunnel, but not always. They usually feel that there is a sense of motion; that they are moving through something that is vast almost beyond imagination. And yet they feel they don't have the freedom to go anywhere. They feel as if they were being propelled.

> The extreme sense of motion often seems to be one of acceleration. Some describe that they have felt as if they were moving at the speed of light or faster. One NDEr described this as superluminal—moving beyond the speed of light with tremendous accelerated motion through a kind of cylindrical vortex, and then, in the distance, the

person describes a dot of light that suddenly grows larger, more brilliant, and all encompassing.

Ring continued:

> At this stage of the experience there is an encounter with light.
> It seems to be a living light exuding pure love, complete accep-
> tance, and total understanding. The individual feels that he is
> made of that light, that he has always been there, and that he
> has stepped out of time and stepped into eternity. This feeling
> is accompanied by a sense of absolute perfection.

Being out of time introduces another aspect of the experience: a
sense of destiny. Ring explained:

> Then there is a panoramic light review in which you see every-
> thing that has ever happened to you in your life. Not [only] just
> what you have done but the effects of your actions on others,
> the effects of your thoughts on others. The whole thing is
> laid out for you without being judged but with a complete
> understanding of why things were the way they were in your
> life. The best metaphor I can suggest for this is: as if you were
> the character in someone else's novel. There would be one
> moment outside of time where you would have the perspective
> of the author of that novel, and you have a sense of omni-
> science about that character. Why he did the things that he did,
> why he had affected others, and so on. It is a profound moment
> outside of time when this realization occurs. You see the whole
> raison d'être of your life. You may also see scenes or fragments
> of scenes of your life if you choose to go back to your body. In
> other words, it is not only that you have flashbacks but you also
> seem to have flash-forwards of events that will occur almost as
> though there is a kind of blueprint for your life. And it is up to
> you at that moment. You have free choice because it is often
> left to you whether to go back to your life or to leave it behind.
> The people we talk with of course always make the choice to
> go back or sometimes are sent back.

Getting Near the Big Dreamer

UFOEs and NDEs have similarities with dreams and significant differences. The similarities and the differences may be pointing to what I call the "big dream" experience and to the realization that the dreamer is part of what we might call the "big dreamer," the universe itself.

As I mentioned above, time shifts and discontinuities are similarly experienced during these "dreaming" experiences. Many dream researchers assume that because REM persists over time the dream is also passing through a similar time sequence lasting as long as the REM movement. This would imply that the dream takes place in clocktime like our experience of the "real" world. However, there is also evidence that this isn't the case.

It may be the case that REMs are indicating something very different—possibly they are a form of eye-brain correlation wherein the brain is attempting to interpret the discontinuities of the dream. The dreamer is attempting to look around the event space of the dream in much the same way that Ring described the holographic report of an NDE. The dream scene is an ongoing, holographically illuminated single scene of great complexity. In other words, the viewer is looking around the hologram, not moving through his dream as we do in waking life. The random character of the dream is then caused by the randomness of the scanning procedure accompanied by the electrical-jolt discontinuities observed in dreaming brains by Hobson and his coworkers.

There is another possibility. The dreamer could be experiencing a rush of holographic imprinting—image flashes of a whole. Each flash could be of a different scene, even from a different viewing point, lasting for a brief period of time followed by a longer period of darkness. My shamanic experiences[18] with waking-dream consciousness showed me that the scenes lasted for only one second or less. My eyes were closed, and I remember distinctly being in a lucid three-dimensional scene, much like experiences I have had during lucid dreams, and yet my "experience" of the vision clearly lasted much longer than one second. By that I mean that during the scene I did much more than I could possibly do in one second of "real" time.

Thus the REM could be indicating a means for coping with the on-off experience rather than a straightforward continuous scanning of a single scene. The scanning REM might be taking place in the dark, so to speak, during the transition period between scenes. During these periods, thoughts may be occurring, not pictures, and these thoughts may be the dreamer's attempt to make sense of the experience. During this darkness period, the dreamer is in thought much like the thoughts that are chiefly described during slow-wave sleep.

But then the dreamer relates the experience as a story in time lasting much longer than the scene lasted. Tibetan Buddhists suggest this kind of explanation, not only of dreams, but of life in general. Tibetan *thonkas,* typical spiritual paintings, show the life of the person in a circle surrounding a Buddha figure in the center, as if the person's life were all happening at once. Yet if you look at the individual pictures in a sequence, you see a story unfolding in time.

Following this line of reasoning, the ability to control the scan requires some form of lucid awakening during the dream. Thus, controlled scans may be what is needed for lucid dreams. The dream may not be in time, but the "I" seems to be in time due to the linear accessing of the holographic scenes.

Ring told me that Freud had thought that dreams were outside of time. Ring explained that from this point of view, you are exposed to a field of information as presented as a kind of image. It is like a flash of something real and intense that is difficult to describe metaphorically as just an image. Perhaps it is like the experience of looking at a desert scene when there is a sudden flash of sheet lightning and the whole panorama is illuminated. The next instant it is gone. Then you have to try to make sense of it. You talk about the image as if it consisted of a sequentially arranged set of images in which you are moving from one place to another. Yet the whole thing was just one flash.

There is one other similarity between dreams and UFO-NDEs. I have had many lucid-dream experiences while sleeping and lucid-awake experiences during shamanic ceremonies. I noticed that at the end of these experiences, when I "awoke," I felt an extreme sense of bliss and well-being as if all of my material cares, difficulties with relationships, and other aspects of waking life were just dissolved away.

As described above, Ring has found that NDErs seem to express a similar feeling after their experiences.

So much for similarities; what about differences between dreams and NDEs and UFOEs? The major difference that Ring and other workers have discovered between dreams and these imaginal-realm encounters is found in the people themselves. They unanimously report that while they know that the experience was an inner or imaginal experience, it was not a dream. They will say that the experience was more real to them than the present reality they find themselves in now. In other words, the experience was more "real" than life itself.

It may be more analogous to a lucid dream in this respect. People report that the experience was so real, so "extremely" real, that when they came back to "reality," it was hard for them, at times, to experience that this world was real in the same way that they had thought about it before.

Ring explained that having sojourned in the other world, they have a dual citizenship; they live in this world, but they are not fully of it. They still feel that the real world was the world they entered into when they were close to death, as though "real" life blinded and shut off their senses. In the NDE world they can really see. It is this aura of lucidity that suggests to Ring that it is like the imaginal world that is revealed when the sensory systems no longer operate.

Both Ring and Michael Grosso also point out another difference between these imaginal-realm encounters and ordinary dreams. Again it involves the time dimension and the experience of "flash-forward" to the whole panoramic vision of the person's life: what his life has been to this point, what his life is now, and what it might be after he decides to return to his physical body. Unless an accident has brought about the NDE, the person usually has recall of his whole life including future possibilities. When the person recalls the NDE, it does not tend to fade away. It remains vivid, and a person will say, even though the experience happened twenty-five years ago, that it seems as if it happened yesterday. It remains powerfully etched in the person's psyche.

The Big Dreamer Awakens

What do these experiences tell us? Let me summarize. NDE/UFOEs are characterized physically by a disturbance, an electrical storm in the temporal lobe—that part of the brain that interprets experiences and attempts to make sense of the world as it is sensed. It is called temporal because making sense of the world means putting our experiences into a time sequence, arranging things logically. These experiences are profound and hypermeaningful. Yet, there appears to be some element of trauma in them. Either the trauma takes place at the moment as in NDEs or it took place before as in UFOEs, as for example through child abuse.

The result is that the time-ordering sequencer of the temporal lobe is thrown for a loop. Things that happen, happen willy-nilly, seemingly out of control of the experiencer.

If we now look at the range of experiences including lucid dreams, UFOEs, NDEs, and other imaginal-realm experiences wherein the dreamer is lucid while the experience lasts, we find that the outstanding quality that persists is the shining sense of lucid reality. We also find, although this is controversial, that time does not seem to "flow" as it apparently seems to in our ordinary clocktime universe.

Lucid Experiences and Temporal Discontinuities: A Parallel Worlds Theory

At this point, I want to offer an explanation based on quantum physics of both the lucidity of the experience and the temporal discontinuity. My speculation is that the mathematical structure of quantum physics, particularly the parallel-worlds hypothesis, can encompass both of these experiences.

First of all, according to the parallel-worlds interpretation of quantum mechanics, a quantum system can exist in a superposition of states. For example, an electron can exist as if it had an infinite number of locations in the vicinity of an atomic nucleus. As another example, an electron can spin clockwise and counterclockwise. It can also spin in both directions simultaneously. Now suppose that your brain is a quantum physical system capable of existing in a superposition of many possible states.

When an observer looks at a physical system, seeking out information about which state the system is in, he experiences an answer. According to the parallel-worlds idea, he experiences a definite answer for each of the possible states the system is in. In other words, his mind splits into separate conscious experiences, seemingly cut off from the others. In each conscious experience, each world, he feels quite cut off, quite alone with his single bit of information.

Now he can do one of two things. One, he can reinterrogate the same system he has just looked at. What he finds tends to reinforce what he has already discovered. He sees that the system is exactly the same as he saw it before. If he does this continually, he experiences the system remaining stable. He can do this with one system or any number of similarly prepared systems. Each time he examines a different but similarly prepared system, he may get a different answer. The second system may not be in the same state as the first system after he looked at it. As he repeats this line of interrogation using a different but similarly prepared system each time, he assembles a statistical sample and pieces together a story that is consistent with his findings.

For example, suppose he is looking at three "quantum" coins in the fountain.[19] He may find them in one of the eight equally possible distributions of heads and tails (HHH, HHT, HTH, HTT, THH, THT, TTH, TTT). Each distribution exists in a separate but parallel world and so does the observer's mind. As long as the systems (coins) are not changing, he will repeat his observations seeing just what he had seen before. This takes place in each of the parallel worlds, further confirming that he is in a real world, for there is no trace of the other possible worlds present. In this case there are eight worlds, and no matter how many times he looks at the coins, there are still eight worlds, and in each of those worlds he finds just what he found at the previous observation.

Or he can look at other physical systems that, although they are prepared identically to the first system he looked at, are capable of evolving on their own. Now suppose that each system is capable of changing due to environmental circumstances, disturbances of one kind or another. Each system, originally in one superposition of states, then observed to be in one of those states, now tends to evolve into another superposition of states. This would mean that in the above example, at first each coin was in a superposition of states (symbolized by H$\oplus$T), then was observed to be heads, for example, and then evolved once again to another superposition of H$\oplus$T. In other words, suppose that each coin in the fountain when not looked at evolved from being in a state of heads (or in tails) to a superposition of heads and tails.

Now again suppose the person takes a look at the coins. He will again see them in one of eight possible arrangements of heads and tails. However, he also has a "memory" of what the coins looked like before he looked at them a second time. Remember, as far as he is concerned, he merely looked at the coins twice. Since the coins could "evolve" into superpositions between observations, there are actually now sixty-four (each of the eight worlds can split into eight worlds) different observational possibilities. (For example, one possibility is HHT could change to THT.)

All the person knows at the end of the second observation is that the coins have surprisingly changed. In each of sixty-four worlds there is now a memory of what the coins were before he looked the second time. The question is, which world was the real world at the time of the first look? At the end of the second look, all he has is a memory of what existed during the first look, but the first-look world has passed away.

This is where classical reality and quantum reality part company. In the classical world, he would know which state the coins were "really" in at the first observation. In the quantum world, he is not privy to this knowledge. All he knows at the time is that the coins are in a state and were in a previous state. Which of the eight possible previous states they were in, he does not really know. As far as he knows, he is in one of the sixty-four possible worlds, and in any of them data confirms that the coins were in a previous state and are now in a new state.

If the three coins once again do their thing and evolve and he repeats his observation a third time, he will be consciously aware in one of 512 possible worlds. With each evolution and following observation the number of worlds multiplies by eight. In each world there will be a memory trace, but it will be impossible for him to know just which world "he" was in at the previous observation.

This point is crucial to quantum physics. In each world, there will be a memory; however, there is no guarantee that the memory is "his" memory. It could be that he is remembering the state of the previous systems as they were observed by an alter ego. Each world exists this way, and in each world everything seems natural and normal. His memory is consistent even though it was created at the moment of the last observation. He won't feel this jolt of creativity even though his whole life in regard to the coin experiment was created all at once. He will feel instead that the memory is really his own.

If this evolution continues following some causal law of motion such as the law of falling bodies, even though the number of worlds is multiplying, the overwhelming number of worlds in which the sequence of states follows the law of gravity is most likely to be observed. In other words, the observer is most likely to be aware of a normal, causally developing world.

Suppose that now we take it that our brains are like the "three coins in the fountain" and that consciousness is like the observer in the above example. During normal, waking awareness, the world and our brains operate classically. This is much like the observer observing the coins over and over again, confirming that they are as they were. Even though consciousness is developing in alternative worlds, nothing seems out of the ordinary because of the causality development in the outside world. The sensory overload of external experiences by far overcomes any "unusual" developments.

But during dreams and during these imaginal-realm encounters, the brain, operating quantum physically, deals with experiences that are not following a causal material law. An unobserved evolution of the brain takes place during temporal-lobe electrical excitation that causes the brain to shift states as in the coin example above. Then periods of introspection take place just after each electrical disturbance.

I suggest that the quality of what is perceived depends on the path of perceptions taken by the observer, by consciousness, even though there is no actual memory of anything like a path of perception. There is only a flash of memory in each world at each perceptual moment; in each parallel world there is a memory of how the coins were and how they are now, then a flash of how the contents of the brain were, and how they are now, then a flash of how the contents of the brain were, and how they are now, and this sequence of flashing continues always repeating, but never repeating the same view to the same mindset, regardless of how that brain was "really" in the past.

In the imaginal realm there is no anchor in material reality, no laws of classical material physics governing the connection between flashes. Thus each experience, each flash, is new and somewhat startling. Consequently the observer in all this is apt to pay attention as he need not do in a classically perceived world of repeated similar experiences.

Given this, what makes ordinary dreams, the kinds we are not likely to remember, and imaginal-realm dreams (including UFOEs and NDEs) differ? To understand that we need to look at the holographic model once again in chapter 19. But next we will explore how such flashes have entered into ordinary consciousness. We call them "art."

CHAPTER • 17

*O*VERLAPS OF THE IMAGINAL AND THE REAL: DREAMS IN ART, MYTH, AND REALITY

———

To devote oneself to puzzling fictions does not mean to be an artist, but being an artist means enduring the wind from the worlds of art which are altogether unlike our world, but tremendously influencing it. In those worlds there are neither causes nor consequences, neither time nor space, neither the corporeal nor the incorporeal, and these worlds are innumerable.

—*Alexander Blok* [1]
Russian poet

[The many-worlds interpretation of quantum mechanics reveals a universe that] is constantly splitting into a stupendous number of branches, all resulting from the measurement-like interactions between its myriad of components. Moreover, every quantum transition taking place on every star, in every galaxy, in every remote corner of the universe is splitting our local world into myriads of copies of itself.

—*Bryce S. Dewitt* [2]

The artist is the antennae of the race.

—*Ezra Pound*

If the imaginal realm (IR), the realm of the big dreamer, is ontologically real, which means that it has objective existential quality as Henri

Corbin put it,[3] then why is it that only a few persons have encountered it? Why don't we all see it? Well, in some real sense we have all had IR experiences (IREs), but simply didn't know they were "real" happenings or believed that what was happening to us was fantasy, hallucination, or some obsession. (You may remember that computer-model neural networks suffer these anomalies from time to time, so why not us?)

Before I explain how an IRE would appear to us "normal" folk or what constitutes an IRE, we need to consider what Henri Corbin, a deep student of mystical and visionary experience, and other researchers who have dealt with the IR both as subjects and as observers have to say about it.

For Corbin the IR is more irrefutable and coherent than the world we experience with our waking senses. Beholders of the IR who reported to him upon returning to this world were perfectly aware of having journeyed "elsewhere." These voyagers were not schizophrenic or mentally ill. The world they had experienced was not a fantasy. It was a world with form, dimension, and even other life-forms; in short, there were people living there.

Yet this IR is certainly not normally sensed as real for most of us. Instead reality seems so clear to us. It consists of the things we see and feel with our senses. Speaking for each of us, if it's real, I can see it, I can taste it, I can hear it, I can smell it, I can touch it. I may not want to do any of the above, but nevertheless my senses are my means by which I ascertain reality.

What if something appears to us and only engages one of the above senses? For example, you suddenly taste something. Since you haven't eaten an apple, and yet you taste it, you would probably dismiss the taste as imaginary, a memory or hallucination. The same would be true for any other sense experience if that experience was singular. Suppose that two of the above senses were involved. Then what? Did the experience indicate that the object of the senses had objective reality to the sensor? How many senses do we need before we put a sensed object into the "reality" camp?

Now add to this the possibility that we have more than five senses. Corbin refers to the additional senses as "psychospiritual." In my book *The Eagle's Quest,*[4] I wrote about the five imaginal additional senses of the IR that shamans all seem to possess but which sadly elude most of us. Taking Kenneth Ring's work into account, that people who have

NDEs are not fantasy prone, but are "encounter prone," means that they may be people with psychospiritual sensory awareness.

Why do some of us have this ability, if it is real, and seemingly most of us don't? Perhaps the overlap of the IR into "reality" is an evolutionary change and some of us are not as evolved as others. What would it be like to experience an evolutionary change? Perhaps the change would reflect in our dreams. In chapters 4 and 6, I pointed out Carl Sagan's consideration that there is a connection between dreams and evolution. Sagan, remember, suggested that perhaps early prehumans lived their waking lives in a state of consciousness akin to what we would call dreams. Also in chapter 4, I described Julian Jaynes's point that early humans had no real consciousness and that they walked around in an automaton state of perhaps trance consciousness akin to some form of dream state.

If this was true, then obviously something happened. Consciousness evolved. How did that happen? Did it happen in a minute, an hour, a day, a decade, perhaps over a century or two? Longer? A millennium? Does consciousness just take a quantum leap every so often and then rest after its ordeal? Are we, today, on the edge of a transformation, another quantum leap of consciousness? Could the IREs be suggesting an evolutionary change? This seems to be the opinion of a number of researchers, including Kenneth Ring, Michael Grosso, Peter Rojcewicz, and Terence McKenna. I have already told you about the research and ideas of Grosso and Rojcewicz.

Terence McKenna bubbles with evocative phrases completely turning our brains upside down as he explains the impact of the imaginal on the marginal mind. Primarily a researcher in the study of shamanism and psychopharmacology and its impact on spiritual development, McKenna is the author of several books and audiotapes.[5] Speculating most elegantly about "wild and zany elf-infested spaces," he characterized the richer reality of the imaginal realm as a "crackling, electronic, hyperdimensional, interstellar, extraterrestrial, saucerian landscape, filled with highly polished curved surfaces, machines undergoing geometric transformations into beings, and thoughts condensing as visible objects."[6]

McKenna points out that shamans see dreams as evidence of a parallel world or continuum overlapping into the "real" world. McKenna believes that the mind and the body are embedded in the dream and that the dream exists in a higher-order spatial dimension.

Present scientific view, based as it is in materialism, sees mind as an emerging biological phenomenon. In this view, mind and matter are both emergent as partial realities.

Michael Grosso also sees that we are in a period of rapid evolutionary growth.[7] Since 1985, a number of researchers such as Peter M. Rojcewicz, Ken Ring, and Grosso have observed a relationship between different categories of IREs—allegedly other- or parallel-world types of encounters. Grosso noted at least sixteen different categories of IREs with one common characteristic that he calls "ontological ambiguity."

These ambiguous encounters have the appearance of being real at one level and then unreal at another. For example, UFOs leave gear marks and soil changes, but then the UFOs disappear. No one ever catches one of these machines that has left the mark. In NDEs one often has a veridical out-of-body experience (OBE). But other NDEs seem to blend with the veridical part of the experience, then seem to shade off into a parallel or purely imaginary universe.

These experiences, including Marian visions (visions of Mary, the mother of Christ), encounters of diabolic attack, men-in-black visions, a variety of UFO experiences, and reports of alien animals, such as Bigfoot and lake monsters, are assuredly highly visual and sometimes tactile. People see things "out there" while they are apparently awake. Sometimes several people see them at the same time. Grosso's descriptions of these seemingly objective but yet not quite objective experiences are for me very close to experiences I have had when I am admittedly experiencing a lucid dream.

One of my many lucid or conscious dreams leapt into mind as I wrote this. I was living in Paris in 1974 and had taken a room on rue de Condé in the center of the city across the street from where the infamous Marquis de Sade had lived. It was a small room on the sixth floor of a rather old building (at least two hundred years old). I had a number of bizarre dreams there.

One balmy summer night, I had my room window open as I fell asleep. Paris is filled with wonderful memories, but its streets are noisy. As it was hot, I wanted the windows open, but I had put earplugs in my ears to shut out the sound. Living amidst Paris's architecture constantly reminds one of the past. One receives daily stimulation by that ancient city's past. Such stimulation is also a message from the IR. A quick tour of the city acquaints you with the belief structures of

French pre-Revolution minds. At least we see how the architects of that time thought and dreamed.

I was impressed with the gargoyle statues that were all around my apartment. In that oldest part of Paris, many buildings have such figures. In particular I found myself visiting Notre Dame Cathedral nearly daily just to gaze at the variety of gargoyles perched high on its arches.

In the middle of that balmy night, something flew through my window into my room and landed on my bed. I could feel its presence on my bed. I felt it go thump when it landed, and I was concerned. I thought, "My God, something is in the room with me." But then I noticed that I was in a state of sleep, a kind of lucidity, and yet I was awake, but at the same time paralyzed. It may have been a lucid dream; however, I do not remember it as such. I was not seeing things nor hearing them, I was feeling them, sensing them, my tactile senses were awake. My lucid "dream" had not taken me elsewhere; I was in my room. I then thought to myself that whatever was on my bed would disappear if I just roused myself. I then woke myself, and I could feel it dissolve gradually as I came awake. When I was fully awake, it was gone.

The "thing" that flew in my window had for me the same type of quality that Grosso discussed, ontological ambiguity. It was real for me although I never saw it. It reached my tactile sensory awareness, but not my visual or auditory sense. It seemed to exist between objective reality and pure fantasy.

Ontological ambiguity is slippery. It doesn't quite fit into reality as we perceive it normally, and it isn't fantasy. Perhaps it is an indication of a deeper reality, one that we are evolving senses for as pointed out by IRE researchers. Michael Grosso's belief resonates with the theme of this book. There is a "mind at large," an oversoul that appears to us as a force of evolution, a new level of conscious awareness. It is, as it were, as if a dreamer, the "big dreamer," were awakening from a nightmare. This nightmare is evident if we just look around us. We might call it the nightmare of abuse that indicates that we are becoming aware of something beyond our material existence.

Today, there have been more indications, more television shows, more media reports in general, more books, dealing with abuse than ever before. We are aware that we humans not only abuse ourselves, in war and peace and in selfish forms of conflict, we abuse our children and our planet.

Okay, so what? you might say. You are not a child abuser, nor were you abused. You did not murder anyone, and you are not evading taxes, the law, or the local loony bin. Perhaps you do on occasion abuse yourself one way or the other, overeating, undereating, drinking, drugs, other self-afflicting harmful habits, but, you rationalize, "I'm okay. I'm normal."

Perhaps you have at times abused somebody, your wife, your husband, your employee, and well, there was a time when you may have struck your child, your friend, your lover, but you are not "really" an abusive person.

Yet there are these weird things happening all over the world. Nothing seems as secure as you "remember" it was. Gosh, people sexually abusing their own children? Child pornography?

Well, let's suppose that you are at the moment asleep and dreaming and all of the above is just some kind of bad dream. I know that you feel completely awake and are presently reading these words holding a solid book in your hands. But humor me. How could you awaken yourself from this dream? The first requirement is to realize, as we do in lucid dreams, that this, too, is a dream. To awaken from it, to bring your control into it, you must realize that it is a dream. But the dream has too many characters in it, you argue, and they behave in very typical "human" ways. For example, for some weird reason everybody in your dream is suffering. Why is that?

For some reason, since you are having this nightmare, you are also suffering. Why is that? Oh, you don't feel any "stinking suffering." You are happy. You have everything you need. Well, you will die one day. Does that thought cause you any suffering? Oh, you also see that many people in all parts of the planet you live on in your dream are suffering from all kinds of abuse. Does that make you feel any suffering? You feel sorry for them, but that is their lot, and you have your life and you insist you are not suffering anyway.

Carry on. Humor me. What is the problem with your dream? The problem is the character you are playing. He or she is unconscious of the dream or unfeeling of the "reality." But suppose you begin to recognize that not only your character but all of the other characters in the dream are none other than, the big prize is coming, *ta ta* (hear the trumpet sound), YOU! Now what? That means that everyone you meet, everything you touch, is nothing more than your dream creation.

But, you say, you don't feel that to be true. You feel that you are alone and separated and that everyone else is "out there" independent of you, minding his or her own business, which is what you should be doing right now, instead of reading this nonsense. Besides, this nonsense is making you feel a little uncomfortable. You have enough trouble just keeping up, just coping.

Don't put the book down yet. Hang on for a little while longer. If you are the dreamer of this whole thing and the creator of everything in your dream, that puts you in control of a lot more than you could ever imagine. It means that you are the "big dreamer." Let me wax academical.

Arnold Mindell in *The Year I* and in his other books[8] suggests that the whole world can be thought of and experienced as a global information network. This vision has been also introduced by Peter Russell.[9] The idea is that our planet is a living conscious entity. Now that is not a new idea. It has its roots in mythology and, as we have seen in the example of the Australian Aborigines, in cultural belief systems as well. Is there any solid evidence of the "big dreamer's" presence?

Evidence of the Oversoul: The Overlap

Most likely that evidence has reached us through the eyes of the artist. Leonard Shalin, a California surgeon and author who lectures widely on the history of science and art, pointed out that even though the worlds of physics and art appear to be dealing with seemingly opposed points of view, they have run remarkably parallel courses of discovery and vision.[10] Just at the time the abstract concepts of relativity and quantum physics were emerging into the consciousness of the proverbial "everyman," artists were evoking surrealism and relativistic distortions of space, time, and matter on their canvases.

People experiencing the new physics for the first time were baffled. And the same befuddlement occurred when the abstract surrealist movement in art struck the observer's eye. Picasso's cubist paintings seem weird to most of us when we first encounter them, but I assure you, once having taken LSD, the pictures seem quite real. Picasso always said that he was not painting the bizarre, but attempting to show what he saw.

The new physics was pointing to an invisible landscape, one that had an order and a meaning that eluded common sense. The surrealist painters, including Picasso, Giorgio De Chirico, Salvador Dalí, Marc Chagall, René Magritte, M. C. Escher, Jackson Pollock, Jasper Johns, and many others, all attempted to picture this landscape, even though it was hardly a conspiracy of common minds working together.

Perhaps the similarity exists only in the mind of the perceiver who is versed in both new physics and modern art. But I don't think so. It seems more likely that the experience of the imaginal was bursting into the dreams of the physicists and the artists at about the same time, and both were attempting to reach into the other's visionary camp, perhaps without even knowing it.

In today's literature and television shows, science fiction is emerging stronger than ever. Today's science fiction writers amazingly are dealing with subtle themes of time travel, the future, space travel, and consciousness as it exists in humans and nonhumans alike, in a manner that at first seems to counter the rules of physics. But, as I have pointed out in my book *Parallel Universes,* there is actually little contradiction. Although science fiction writers are usually versed in science, it is not the science that makes for a good story, it is the situations that the characters must deal with that keeps us reading and watching.

And yet the seeming paradoxes of science fiction seem to echo the very same paradoxes that physicists dealing with new physics are faced with. Who is following whom? Does science fiction lead physicists into science "faction" or is it the other way 'round? Kenneth Ring has shown that extraordinary encounters (EEs), be they UFOEs, NDEs, or OBEs, have a form and possibly even content that resembles the science fiction stories of the time in which they occur. The influence of science fiction on EEs is not a curiosity. Researchers such as Jacques Vallee and the French writer Bertrand Méheust have shown in a number of case studies the connection between early science fiction stories and contemporary UFO reports.[11]

For example, the events in the outstanding case of the UFO abduction of Betty and Barney Hill show a remarkable similarity to the events depicted in the film *Invaders from Mars.* Ring gives a number of other case studies in his book,[12] and I shall not repeat his findings. However, I need to point out that, although to any reasonable skeptic it would appear that I am suggesting that EEs are no more than fantasies and recalls of fictional events as seen or read about, I am not saying this. I am suggesting that there is a parallel course in which the

IR is managing to impinge into our waking consciousness. Not just the waking consciousness of "encounter-prone" individuals, but of artists, physicists, writers, musicians, architects, and in general, creative people wherever they happen to live.

Now I bring us back to the oversoul, the universal mind, the big dreamer. The self-reflective mind that knows that it knows. The universal mind knows everything, anything, and perhaps surprisingly it knows nothing. Its nothingness is described by Buddhist philosophers and practitioners as the state of pure awareness, consciousness without an object of consciousness. In it, moments, events, fly by as ephemeral flashes like fireflies, but nothing is adhered to, nothing is given any value. Everything is seen as a dream.

If the universal mind is a composite of our minds, then how is that composite mind integrated? If the process is akin to a superposition of quantum states of awareness, then the result of that superposition will be another state that does not share in the qualities of the separated states. For example, if in one mind I know that a coin is heads up after it is flipped, and in another mind I know that it is tails up, the net result of both minds together will be no coin appearing at all! Because if the minds are combined in sympathetic resonance,[13] the result is a third state not characterized by the possible outcomes.

Only if the minds are decoupled, only if there is something that keeps the patterns in the superpositions of the minds from merging, will there be anything like an objective quality emerging in any single mind, at all. Thus it is important to realize that the separation of consciousness into observers is a requirement for the appearance of any objective reality. But carrying this further, given the reality of the oversoul, then the mind separations that produce the results of objectivity are an illusion, and as such, the reality of the oversoul will from time to time "pop" up into the individual minds.

How does that happen? It happens as described above, as EEs, and it happens to creative minds everywhere in forms that are acceptable to these minds. Always the rational mind attempts to minimize the extraordinary events, to put them in serial order, temporal order, spatial order, energy order, or logical order. Thus it attempts to explain how it knows in terms of the context in which it believes and senses its own existence as an ego, a separated self. It is, as if highly conditioned to belief and social pressure, asleep. This sleep is found in group awareness, in religious orders, in political systems, and is a root cause of all suffering for it tends to maintain the nightmarish quality of the dream, as if the dreamer were separated from all other sentient beings.[14]

Artists and scientists, writers and architects, and many others deal with the big dream in a different manner. Their dealings are akin to the dreamer having a nightmare and wishing to awaken.

Russian Dreams: To Awaken into the Impossible

During the writing of this book, I spent three months in St. Petersburg, Russia. I wanted to go to Russia to experience how a change in consciousness, as reflected in the massive political changes occurring there, was being experienced by its people. A revolution in a country is the big dreamer turning over in his sleep. This nation was awakening from a dream that had lasted a long time. I was looking for what you might call evidence of the Russian form of the big dream, and I found it.

My journey to Russia was for me a return to the home of my ancestors. Both my maternal and paternal grandparents were born in Russia. They left that country and came here, like so many immigrants, between 1900 and 1910. Although they died many years ago, I, of course, remember my grandparents and remember feeling how strange they seemed to me. My maternal grandmother, in particular, lived to be in her nineties, so I had ample time to get to know her as I grew up. Her Russian Jewish accent always amused me, and I would imitate her.

Perhaps that gave me a desire to learn languages. The idea was to imitate the way people speak around you, and you will soon be speaking their language. And I was soon hesitantly speaking Russian. The language felt familiar to me, but I was having troubles. These troubles were part of my big-dreamer discovery.

As a child, sometime around the age of eight or so, I must have suffered some form of trauma because I began to stammer. At first it was hardly noticeable, but in the years that came, I suffered a severe speech impediment. My mother did what she could. She took me to see brain surgeons, psychologists, and speech therapists. Each expert had a different way to deal with my "problem." The brain surgeons wanted to open my head, the psychologists wanted to talk to me on a regular basis, and the speech therapists wanted me to take part in classes that included other children who suffered from a range of speech problems, including children with cleft palates, ones with hearing disabilities, stutterers and stammerers.

The key to my being "cured" (actually I am not cured, I am still a stammerer, but you would never know it) was working with my mother on such techniques as breathing, meditating, and altering my consciousness. I learned that when I sang a song, I did not stammer. That meant that if one changed the way in which one observed one-self, the result could seemingly be miraculous. I found that by increasing my vocabulary, I was able to substitute one word for another when I spoke, so that if a particularly difficult word for me came up, I would substitute another.

Today I not only write, I also speak for a living. I successfully lecture and lead workshops and seminars in various parts of the world each year. But what has this to do with Russia and the big dreamer? Today I speak several languages, none of them with great fluency except English. I have learned these languages by living in the countries where those languages are spoken. Russia was no exception, but it was only there that I saw a connection between my speaking a foreign language and the imaginal realm.

It happened one evening as I made my way down the dark streets of St. Petersburg. I had been out walking during a cold winter day and marveling at the architecture. It was a particularly bright cold day. The sun rose around ten or so in the morning and would set by three-thirty that afternoon, hardly making its way higher than a mere raise of the eye. Wherever I walked, I sensed a dreamy eerie feeling in the air that was further enhanced by the long shadows of the winter sun. Ancient Russian legends proliferated the buildings. One of these legends contains an answer to a fundamental mystery: how the city of St. Petersburg arose from a dream.

According to this legend, there once was a city called Kitezh, which was miraculously saved during the invasion of Batu Khan. The invaders missed the city when it vanished from view in a great fog (some say it was submerged underwater). Even the church bells were not heard by the invaders. But any righteous man could still hear its church bells tolling from the shores of Lake Svetloyar. The "invisible city" became a symbol of people's faith in good and justice in the face of oppression. This legend persists today as the image of St. Petersburg: the sleeping or dreaming city.

Fyodor Dostoyevsky referred to St. Petersburg as "the most fantastical city with the most fantastical history out of all the cities on the globe." This European-style city sprang up almost as a miracle under the will of Peter the Great. Today, as in the legend, it actually exists on a boggy marshland and has become a major source of bizarre and fantasy-prone themes in both literature and art.[15]

Everywhere you walk in the city you will find evidence of dreams in the architecture, evidence of the dark side of the night, the unconscious mind attempting to deal with the reality of rationality, attempting to sweep it away. According to my Russian friend and art historian Aleksey Kovalev, a longtime resident of St. Petersburg, such architectural styles are prevalent in St. Petersburg and in the north of Russia, Finland, and some Baltic states. This style is not filled with baroque images but of images of ancient paganistic Slavic, Finnish, Baltic, and German mythologies with different Teutonic animals, especially vultures, bears, eagles, owls, eagle-owls, lynxes, and lizards.

As I walked, I looked up at the top floors of the buildings. Often you can see strange figures of mysterious knights or warriors who sleep resting their heads on the handles of their swords. What does this mean? It reflects the spirit of the place. It reflects the land itself, perhaps the pre-Christian spirits, spirits of warriors that wearily rest on their swords but secretly beg to be awakened.

Soon the early darkness began to descend, and as I knew I was near the major marketplace in the city, I decided to shop. However, I didn't exactly know where the market was, so I decided to ask. I stopped a woman in the street, but I found myself stammering as I attempted to speak in the "mother tongue." Soon I was able to make myself clear, and the woman took my arm and walked me to the market.

Her generosity was typical, I found. Russians are hospitable to foreigners. After shopping, as I made my way toward the metro (the underground subway system) and back home, I reflected on my plight. Why was I stammering in Russian? My memories of childhood rushed back to my mind, and I recalled how I had overcome my stammering by always finding substitute words for the difficult ones. I was frankly both disturbed and amazed that I had begun to stammer once again. I was stammering because I had no choice; if I wished to be understood, I had to speak the few words of Russian I knew. I knew no substitute words. I was in a corner, so to speak.

Then the symbolism, the IR, appeared in my mind. I had come back to "mother Russia" to learn to speak Russian. Just as I had returned to my mother to learn to speak. I had gone back to my Russian roots. The connection between my mother and languages was reflected to me in the country of my ancestors.

It was a connection that I could label synchronistic and meaningful to me. The IR had made its mark deeply in early childhood consciousness. My experiences in Russia were as meaningful to me as any dream. "Out there" in the space-time of my Russian experiences were my emotional conflicts of childhood and the connection of my mother to my emotional problem.

For each of us, the same reminders of the wholeness of nature, the experience of the big dreamer, are present, not only in dreams but in the world we construct around us. We build that world based on information arising from the imaginal realm, the dream imagery of the one mind.

Now as I walked the city, I began to look for more evidence of my discovery. Those most sensitive to the big dreamer were the builders of the city, the architects and the artists.

The Blue Rose and the Jack of Spades

When I returned to my apartment, I met with Aleksey and did some research. He provided me with some insights and background information. At the end of the nineteenth century and beginning of the twentieth, a number of fine artists in St. Petersburg established a revolutionary enclave called the World of Art. This group of artists published a magazine in opposition to the established academy of art, which they found to be too conservative. They fought with the political realism of the nineteenth century. The leader of the group was Alexander Benois, who illustrated a famous poem by Alexander Pushkin— *The Copper [Bronze] Horseman*.

The poem is about one of the greatest and most disastrous floods in St. Petersburg, in 1824. A great number of houses in the western part of the city were destroyed, and many people died. The hero of the poem was a poor official who lost his family in the flood. He was in despair and wandering across the city when he came to the monument of Peter I that stands on the bank of the Neva River. This monument had become a majestic symbol of the city, and at the same time it was one of the city's dark, mystical signs.

At the moment he looked at the monument of this founder of a city on the Finnish floodlands off the mainland of Russia, a city in the world of Finnish pagans and devils, lizards and owls and other animals symbolizing the night hours, he understood that this city would always be ill and possessed by evil forces. Grief-stricken, he shouted abuses at the czar. But then the monument turned its head and looked at him. It then left the pedestal and began to chase him through the city.

This monument, still standing today, is one of the best examples of protosurrealism. At the climax of the poem Pushkin reflected on a main theme of Russian literature: the struggle of the little man against the state power.

Nikolai Rörich was another artist of this same group. In 1920, he either defected to the East or was sent there by the secret service. He lived for a time in Tibet and India. His early paintings, connected with northern art nouveau, were devoted to the theme of the sleeping land of Russia. One of his pictures, called *The Celestial Battle,* shows ancient burial grounds, a sleeping earth below, and the dynamic sky above.

Another of his paintings, *The Eternal Waiting,* has an eerie, dreamlike quality and shows a number of peasants looking out at a landscape and waiting. Waiting for what? The great northern country sleeping and dreaming of what? Its great past, its future?

All during this period, a time of revolution, many artists were seeing a different vision. This was a time of hard materiality and survival—dialectical materialism. But still another group of artists, appeared at the beginning of the twentieth century, calling themselves the Blue Rose. Their name was symbolic of their program since the blue rose didn't exist in nature. The Blue Rose was a response to the hard material symbolism of their time.

A third, and probably the most controversial, group of artists called the Jack of Spades also appeared during this time. As the revolution proceeded, many people were put in prison. Prisoners had to wear clothes distinguished from ordinary dress, with symbols on them marking their crimes. Political prisoners wore symbols shaped like the spade on playing cards. In Russia today the symbology still exists in the language. A "spaded" person is a man who is done for. When a person accepts this name for himself, it means he feels finished with life.

The Jack of Spades artists were followers of Paul Cézanne and primitivism. One of the most famous Jack of Spades was Marc Chagall, who later became world famous in France. But in Russia, he was just one member of Jack of Spades. Chagall depicted a range of themes all dealing with the dream world or the imaginal realm. They were certainly of Russian Jewish themes such as a dream of a messiah. In one of his pictures you can see a woman who has just borne a child but feels tension, which can be understood. The child may be a messiah.

In another painting, *The Clock,* a huge wall clock with a pendulum, a table, and a woman are seen. The table and the clock are of normal size and shape, but the woman is tiny. The surrealism of the images indicates that time, represented by the clock, is a huge and powerful force. It is as if when you look at the picture, you can hear the sounds of the ticking clock but they are not comforting; they are loud gongs.

Remarkably, Chagall only painted his native land of Russia from memory when he was living in France. These paintings included the same motifs of little wooden houses in Belorussia, young people, and other images. In 1973 he returned to Russia to visit his hometown, but the Russian authorities did not let him go there. No one knows why they refused him. But it was fortuitous that he did not go, because his native village no longer existed, having been ruined during World War II. Perhaps the authorities wanted to save him from a terrible shock. The Russia of Chagall's paintings only exists in the imaginal realm.

Fantasy in Russian Art

During my stay in St. Petersburg and Moscow, thanks to Aleksey, I had many opportunities to see how Russian artists were depicting the dream world in painting and architecture. Why is fantasy so prevalent, not only in Russian art but in painting in general? Perhaps the answer can be found by looking at the art of a society that has undergone so much stress in this century, in much the same way that individuals are "encounter prone" as a result of suffering childhood trauma. I suggest, as Ezra Pound put it in the quote at the beginning of the chapter, that artists are the first to tune to evolutionary changes.

Fantasy has existed in Russian art for as long as Russian artists have painted, sculpted, and designed buildings. Many of the works of Slavic artists from prehistory, which include ritualistic sculptures, relief designs on metal objects, and cave dwellings reflecting animistic spirits, are completely fantastic and have an eerie, dreamlike quality.

Like many prehistoric peoples, Russian ancestors depended on nature's whims, so that every movement of nature held its tale. The wind in the grass, the movement of clouds overhead, the splashing of water, and the rolling of thunder were all signs of great forces in motion.[16]

Spirits, goblins, mermaids, and dryads existed as images of these forces. In the sky dwelt gods who held puny humans in their powers. After all, they could hurtle down lightning strikes, cause hurricanes, floods, or gentle rains and soft sunshine. One could today rationalize these beliefs in terms of mere anthropomorphism, but let me continue.

In fairy tales we have quite a variety of Russian mythological creatures. These include the imaginary beast *kitovras* (who resembles the half-man, half-horse centaur of Greek myth); the mysterious glittering firebird (well known in Stravinsky's musical suite by the same name), who symbolized dreams of happiness; the multiheaded serpent Gorynych the Dragon, the embodiment of evil; the horrible wizard Kashchei, the Deathless; the famous witch Baba-Yaga; the beautiful swan-princess (made famous in the *Swan Lake* ballet by Tchaikovsky); and many more.

Hops and Beats in Evolution

It is perhaps surprising, given the strong materialistic, atheistic element that existed in Russian political systems, that such images persisted throughout the art age in Russia and are still present today in modern architecture and paintings. Why should such themes persist?

Evolutionary changes result when the human spirit integrates the inner and the outer elements of reality. This takes place in quantum steps. First there is a vision, and the artists attempt to capture that vision for the society in which they exist. In primitive societies these visions were captured by the shamans, and the people of the shaman's tribe followed those visions in order to survive. When a particular vision takes over a society, one aspect of the mind-matter dialectic takes over at the expense of the other. We could call this the "resting stone" phase. Picture a person hopping across a stream from stone to stone as he attempts to get to the other side, and you will get my metaphor.

These hops and beats are reminiscent of the discontinuities in time and space found in our dreams. Perhaps we are witnessing changes in the big dreamer's dream and our dream discontinuities are holographic pieces of that big dreamer's dream.

The vision guides the hop, but once the society arrives at a given stone, it mistakenly "thinks" it has arrived at the end of its journey. The society, like each of us, falls into the trap of illusion created by the desire for security. It then attempts to build its image in the world around it. Triumphant images of success begin to appear. After all, we made it so far, so why not celebrate the "truth" of our survival. The society sets itself up as a standard for the rest of humanity, believing that its vision is the correct one for human survival over all. We all go along with it because the big dream is like our own little dreams.

Triumphant images of success appear all around the city of St. Petersburg. However, the journey is not over, the triumph has an ever-false ring to it, and the artist-shaman of the society is the first to point out the lack of clothes on the newly refurbished emperor.

The Dream Arch

At the end of the eighteenth century many examples of dream images appeared in Russian architecture in both St. Petersburg and Moscow. Aleksey told me that in St. Petersburg there is a little island surrounded by canals called the New Holland. Peter I was interested in nearly everything that existed in the world and had lived some time in Amsterdam, Holland, where he saw canals and buildings. As a result he ended up establishing a New Amsterdam and a New Venice in St. Petersburg, in contrast to the old capital of Moscow. He also established the Russian navy and introduced in it Dutch terminology. This is probably why he called this island the New Holland.

Today it still exists and this name persists, although on the island all that remains are many old and uninteresting common red-brick buildings used for storage. By the end of the eighteenth century, a French architect, Jean Batiste Valin de la Mot, designed and had built an arch across one of the canals that separates a private inner basin on the island from the outside entrance. This arch is quite mysterious because it has no obvious purpose nor any reason for being where it is.

St. Petersburg has many triumphal arches. Arches hail the triumph over the Turks and over the French. But is this arch one of those? It stands above a quite narrow passage and is surprisingly low. It hardly seems adequate to let battleships of that time pass through it into the basin. Yet the arch was designed in the form of a traditional triumphal arch of Europe with columns and other typical ornamental elements. But for what reason? What triumph could be celebrated in such a prosaic, quiet place? And why is it so popular among artists of St. Petersburg today? A famous artist once painted a large drawing of the arch, calling the drawing "my altar."

This arch has become one of St. Petersburg's nonofficial architectural symbols. Each great city has its symbols of successful survival and life, such as the Moscow towers, American skyscrapers, the Eiffel tower in Paris, etc. While such traditional symbols in St. Petersburg as the bell towers of the Fortress of Peter and Paul or the spiral design of the Admiralty present the awake, hopeful, perhaps masculine consciousness of the city, this arch seems to present the city's darker unconscious, or even its feminine aspect. Maybe these symbols are complementary.

One can feel something somnambulant when one looks at it. It is not an active arch. It appears to invite one to enter it not in triumph but in exhaustion. This is perhaps an arch of a dream of a triumph—not of Russia's present triumphs but triumphs from a remote past.

Looking at the arch on a sunny winter day, I realized that each structure in St. Petersburg demands an appropriate time of season and day to be seen. The senate square demands a sunny winter day. The arch of New Holland demands a white night of summer.

Political Architecture

Russian cities are filled with images of the dreams of the people and the society. During the early revolutionary years 1918, 1919, 1920, and 1922, architects drew up architectural drawings and plans that were never carried out. What did these architects dream of?

The answer was Red power. The symbols, having to symbolize a power that emerged from the earth and reached toward the sky, were figures of ziggurats, pyramids, and obelisks of ancient Egypt and Mesopotamia. These structures became the official designs of the Bolshevik party.

But there is a mystery. Why would Lenin and Trotsky envision the construction of such buildings? Far from expressing dialectical materialism, these symbols are mystical links between ancient times and these times.

There were approved plans of the so-called Tower of the Third International to be built in Moscow. The tower was never constructed. The plans of the Palace of the New International Red Power looked like something from a Franz Kafka story. These plans contained a building with twisting curves ascending like a Tower of Babel with a nightmarish quality. It also was never built.

One of these symbols was constructed in Moscow by Alexie Shusav. This pyramid is now the mausoleum of Lenin. Yet it is remarkable that the father of materialism lies asleep in a structure that greatly resembles the ziggurats of India.

In Vladimir, a small Russian town, there once stood an isba—a wooden house where Lenin met someone. The isba no longer exists and in its place stands a memorial with the inscription, "Here was Lenin." But interestingly enough, around the memorial are some logs symbolizing the wooden isba forming the image of a pyramid.

As another example, the facade of the local headquarters of the KGB on Litany Prospect in St. Petersburg looks like the temples of Egypt.

In Moscow a Christian church, built on the banks of the Moscow River in the middle of the nineteenth century to celebrate the victory over Napoleon, was pulled down in the 1930s. An old Russian proverb says that a holy place can never be empty and will always be occupied by people. In place of the destroyed church, the Communist Party decided, in the 1920s before the old one was torn down, to erect a temple of their new religion. The new atheistic temple for large congresses, to be called the Palace of Soviets, was designed to hold twenty thousand people in a lower meeting hall and five thousand in an upper hall, with many smaller rooms and halls.

The Communists arranged an international competition for designs, and two hundred architects contributed plans, mostly Soviets but even some Americans. The winning design was a combination of ziggurats each 230 meters high.

A picture by Brueghel the elder of the Tower of Babel shows the same design. The final plan was a tower that stood 415 meters high with a statue of Lenin at the top 80 meters high. It would have been the highest ziggurat in the world.

In some Russian spiritual opinion, this monument could not exist because God exists. To these thinkers the designers didn't understand that the temple was a moral perversion—an affront to God. Other, more scientific, thinkers realized that the statue of Lenin, because it was so high, could not be observed without distortions. It would have needed to be built with distortion in order to make it observable without distortion. But which point of view would be correct? Would some viewing points be forbidden?

The cost of this temple would have been enough to build a few small towns. Like the construction of the Tower of Babel, the project was endorsed and the builders began to build by first making a huge hole for the foundation. In 1941, the second year of construction, work was halted with the outbreak of World War II. As the war went on, the idea was abandoned.

However, by the end of the war, the hole remained and was used as an open-air swimming pool. Ironically, instead of a gigantic Babylon tower scraping the air, the builders created a gigantic depression in the ground filled with water. However, the evaporation from the warm water was so intense that it began to destroy paintings in the museum of fine art nearby. Today the giant pool is dry. A dry-bottom hole still remains in Moscow instead of a Babylon skyscraper, and many people in Russia wish to restore the original Christian church on this ground.

Gorky and the Dream Museum in Moscow

As I mentioned, in the twentieth century a style of art representing dreams, known as art nouveau, began to appear in architecture, sculpture, and painting in many countries. It also made its appearance in the Soviet Union, where it was forbidden as bourgeois by the official Soviet government and accepted by other nonofficial workers as anti-bourgeois style. Art nouveau became the style of early capitalism. Western architects used art nouveau in the design of banks, trade houses, new plants, bridges, and so on.

While it represented the glories of a golden-dawn dream fantasy, it also had its darker shadow images. These images could be seen as an escape from one fantasy into another, or as a realization that the golden-light concept embedded in political-religious systems had a dark halo. Perhaps the artists were sensing the illusion surrounding them in political systems and slogans and realized that these systems, designed to "stamp out" the dark side, get rid of crime and evil, share the wealth, the American way, truth, justice, and . . . , workers unite, world Communism, etc., were worse fantasies than the dark contents of their own dreams. And perhaps the dark-side dreams of these artists were messages from the imaginal realm, reminding them that the world that has been created by Western culture is an illusion that like all other systems will rot at its base.

The artist as antennae will always be there to bring us to our imaginal senses when the going gets rough or too smooth. This is why we come across the theme of dream, vision, and fantasy in so many sculptures, stained-glass windows, frescoes, and the facades of buildings.

We might wonder how a culture, blinded as it is in its dream of social-political-spiritual perfection, could tolerate any upstart counter-cultural vision. Thus when my friend Alexsey, in St. Petersburg, told me about the Gorky museum in Moscow, I was immediately fascinated and decided to take the overnight train to spend some time there.

The building, although Russians call it "designed in modern style," is not modern at all. It was built by a gifted Russian architect, a German by birth, named Fyodor Shektel, who worked in Moscow. Shektel designed the house for Nikolai Ryabushinsky, a Russian millionaire who before the revolution supported artists and the fine arts. During the revolution many millionaires, including Ryabushinsky, disappeared from the USSR. Of course all private property was confiscated, and consequently, soon after the revolution the house became (what else?) the first Russian Psychoanalytical Institute under the orders of Leon Trotsky.

In the late 1920s psychoanalysis fell out of fashion. The house was then given to the great proletarian writer Maxim Gorky, but Gorky never liked his new home. He felt the marked contrast between the golden-light ideals of the revolution and the dark unconscious content of the house. Yet he lived there until his mysterious death. To this day no one knows how he died.

Today the house still stands near the center of Moscow on a small street, Ulitsa Kachalova. No one lives there anymore and it's known as the Gorky Museum. The afternoon after my arrival in Moscow, I decided to visit it. As I approached the building on this typical cold winter day, I noticed that it had many asymmetries. The right side of the house is not in any way a mirror image of the left as is the rule for most houses. Every window has a different shape. The balcony over the entrance has a spider's web banister. Ancient Egyptian and baroque styles are placed in opposite parts of the building.

As I approached, I knew why Gorky was so unhappy in his new home. It wasn't a house of dialectical materialism at all, it was a house of dark dreams. When I entered, I immediately noticed the staircase, probably the most famous staircase of all Russian architecture. The balustrade is designed as an imaginal ghostlike wave. I saw quite clearly that the wave character of the balustrade wasn't like anything I had ever seen before. Although it appeared more as an archetype or motif of a wave, as I ascended the staircase, I felt an eerie sense of displacement as if I had become seasick.

Clearly the architect hadn't meant this to be a real wave. It was a wave from the land of dreams: perhaps the designer was anticipating the idea of the quantum wave of possibilities. As I went up the stairs, I saw a torch design standing a full seven or eight feet tall at the beginning of the stairwell. But as I walked up and around it, its shape continually changed. At first it appeared to be flame rising upward and then a figure of a woman or girl. The shape changed like a dream image as I moved around it. It seemed to have a flow as if each element dissolved into the next as I changed my viewpoint.

I came back to the stairwell just as the museum was closing to see it in twilight. Again it changed. Sometimes the image appeared as a nightmare, a shriek or crying out from a lost soul.

At the top of the stairs I found a dreamlike door leading to the dining room. The ceiling in the dining room was even more dreamlike. It appeared that even though I was looking up at it, the scene I saw was as if I were flying over a seascape looking down. One can see seaweed floating on the ocean and then a deep cavern. The cavern appears to be an abstract face of a cat. It also looks like a ship.

After I left the "museum" I had a realization about the imaginal realm existing as an evolutionary force, even perhaps a voice from the future.

Dreams Appear Even If We Don't Want Them

Gorky's experience, and indeed the current changes overwhelming the former Soviet Union, illustrate that in spite of our need to find resting stones, to take time to praise ourselves for surviving, the battle is not over. The jump to the next level is coming, whether we want it to or not. The imaginal realm seems to have its own plan, and that plan tells us that just at the moment when we think we have found the answer, and we believe we have arrived, we are to take the journey all over again.

The Buddhists tell us that all is impermanence and we, in our attempts to hold on to the illusion of a reality we create, grasp, in addiction, to whatever we can take hold of. But all becomes sand vanishing through our clenched fists. The dreamer goes on, and we being the dream of the dreamer have still another stone to quantum-leap toward. If we don't take the leap, the discontinuous nature of the dream will force us to anyway. Our future beckons to us. For what purpose, we can only surmise.

In the next chapter we shall see how the IR blew the mind of one of the world's greatest physicists and taught him that physics without spirit is as empty as a clenched fist of sand.

HE SPIRIT OF MATTER

Scientists went a little too far in the seventeenth century.

—Wolfgang Pauli[1]

The Self is not only the center, but also the whole circumference which embraces both conscious and unconscious; it is the center of this totality, just as the ego is the center of consciousness.

—Carl G. Jung[2]

Physicists are supposed to be rather cool characters when it comes to the questionable relationship between spirit and matter. Most physicists will not talk about this relationship, believing that it does not belong within the province of science at all. Yet recently some new wind seems to be stirring as we leave the twentieth century behind us. We physicists are coming out of the mystic's closet, so to speak. And the reason why this emergence *must* take place is well known.

For a long time now, a serious problem has existed in our understanding of the most fundamental laws of physics: quantum mechanics (QM). This problem runs deeply against the grain of mechanical science. It violates the basic paradigm of science: the ability to predict and control nature. The first inklings that we physicists had discovered something about the material world that didn't quite fit in with the mechanical scientific paradigm occurred as far back as 1927 when Einstein and Bohr, the giants of their time in physics, began to debate the meaning of quantum physics.

It was as if the two giants represented the two halves of our brains, or perhaps the mystical and the rational, or maybe the feminine and the masculine ways of perceiving the world. Their debate acted on our brains like a yin-yang yo-yo that seemed to defy both gravity and the string that held it in its orbit. The general conception of that time was that Einstein was a realist (he grabbed for the yo-yo saying it was there even if we failed to catch hold of it), while Bohr was perhaps a logical positivist (he flung it out there into the nothingness saying to speak of its existence when it was out of his hand was an error).

Realism meant that Einstein believed that there was a real objective world "out there," while logical positivism meant for Bohr that we cannot speak about things that are in principle incapable of being observed. Some philosophers of science point out that perhaps Bohr, too, believed in objective reality, but he also believed that we humans were incapable of describing it. So for Bohr, QM was our "best shot" at description, while for Einstein, QM was sadly incomplete.

Their argument had to do with the nature of observation. It seems that a quantum mechanical system such as an atom or a subatomic system (later this was quite generalized to include large objects as well) undergoes a rapid and unpredictable change whenever it is observed. This rapid change cannot be encompassed within the equations that describe quantum systems. It lies embarrassingly outside of the domain of mathematical representation. Somehow the very act of observing something causes an irreversible and uncontrollable change in the system, and this change effects and, for that matter, affects the relationship that exists between the observer and the observed.

Wolfgang Pauli, the discoverer of the famous Pauli exclusion principle and Nobel Prize winner, later entered into this debate in a somewhat mysterious and even perhaps alchemical manner. The epigraph quote was Pauli's way of saying that we have adopted a far too rational approach in our attempts to understand nature. Pauli, later working with Carl Jung, became deeply interested in the psychological aspects of the physicist's view of physical reality. When physical research is carried out, measurements must be made and are the result of psychic actions within the brains of the experimenters. So also are the concepts and theories that are invented by physicists to describe nature.

Pauli became convinced that the unconscious was far more instrumental in making theories about matter than most physicists would have even contemplated. Thus he was convinced that a new conception of reality had to include matter and spirit as complementary aspects of one world.

Thus for us today, and in this book, it is extremely important to look at Pauli's views. These views run close to my own and to the ideas expressed in this book: specifically, that matter is capable of consciousness and of dreaming. I only recently became aware of Pauli's views and was shocked to realize that most physicists, including myself, had no idea that his thoughts were running along the edge of matter and spirit.

In this chapter I will also look at Pauli's dreams and his relationships with psychologists Marie-Louise von Franz and Carl Jung. These relationships as shown in his letters indicate that Pauli was a troubled man—troubled by his irrationality coupled with his brilliance as a physicist. Pauli was not ordinary in any way. He was one of the few who made brilliant contributions to our understanding of nature. The most important discovery was in the rather abstract notion that sub-atomic particles possess an ability to "exclude" each other so that no two of them can enter the same quantum physical state.

Now a quantum state is a very special thing. It is a structure of a system consisting of a physical object or objects that enables a physicist to say all that can be said about the system consistent with Heisenberg's wishes: i.e., the Heisenberg uncertainty principle.

Pauli believed that reality had both a rational and an irrational aspect. Many scientists find this objectionable. However, the reality that is being considered by Pauli and us here is richer in content than just physical reality; it includes mental or psychic reality as well. And if we are to look carefully at the issue of observation, we must eventually realize that, as physicist John Wheeler colorfully put it, "there is no reality unless it is an observed reality." Thus taking it for granted that humans do operate irrationally from time to time, there can be no doubt that irrationality plays a role in reality.

Pauli was convinced that the rational view of reality was essentially incomplete and that mysticism and physics were complementary aspects of a single reality. On the other hand, Wittgenstein believed that if one attempts to speak about one world containing both matter and spirit, the result is absolute silence and a "closing of all doors." This point of view has affected physics at its roots. However, recently Pauli's "irrationalities" have come to light, and many physicists are entering the domain of discourse concerning the relationship of mind and matter[3] I welcome this, having been at the frontier of this subject for the last twenty years or so and frankly feeling a little lonely there.

Pauli's Dreams

After World War II, Wolfgang Pauli attempted to find a unified framework for quantum mechanics and depth psychology. His letters and some recent research now seem to show that he was motivated by what we may call alchemical considerations.[4] Pauli died in 1958, a relatively young man only in his fifties. An aura of mystery seemed to follow him both in life and in death. Many people who knew him found him to be a rather difficult and unpleasant person, often severely critical of other physicists' work or apparent slow-wittedness.

He was gifted with an extremely quick mind and a sharp tongue. Rumors persisted that whenever Pauli was visiting a town in which experimental work in physics was being carried out, the experiments would fail the instant Pauli arrived in town, much less at the lab. This had occurred so many times that experimenters called it "the Pauli effect." If an experiment failed on a given day, they would sometimes inquire if Pauli happened to be visiting town that day.

Perhaps not surprisingly, a silence concerning this brilliant mind has existed for more than thirty years following his death. But in 1988, the Finnish physicist K. V. Laurikainen presented a serious study of Pauli's later "alchemical" views of matter and spirit.[5] Pauli actively corresponded with his friend and former research assistant Markus Fierz. Fierz had been Pauli's assistant at the Polytechnic in Zurich and was then a professor of theoretical physics at the University of Basle.

Pauli had written about the seventeenth-century controversy between astronomer Johannes Kepler and physician Robert Fludd in an essay that was later included in a book by Jung and Pauli.[6] Fludd was an alchemist in opposition to Kepler's quantitative views of the universe. Pauli wrote to Fierz, "I myself am not only Kepler, but also Fludd." The controversy between the two antagonists also raged within Pauli. Pauli sensed that his unconscious tried to reconcile the seemingly unreconcilable viewpoints of alchemy and physics by producing images in his dreams of their unification. He wrote in the same letter to Fierz:

My search is for the process of conjunction, but I have only partially succeeded in this. Nevertheless first an exotic woman (slit-eyed Chinese) appeared in my dreams. Later also a strange, light-dark man who seemed to know something about the unification of opposites which I sought.[7]

Van Erkelens in his article[8] refers to Pauli's two dream figures as indicating how Pauli was attempting to reconcile the seeming divorce between matter and psyche. Pauli had dialogues in his dreams with these characters, and they are quite amazing in content. In Pauli's mind, the spirit of matter, seemingly long dead and buried with the Greeks of antiquity, and perhaps reburied with the Newtonian revolution, struggled for resurrection. I shall follow Van Erkelens's presentation in telling you about these dreams and the dream conversations.

Pauli and His Shadow

When Pauli returned to Switzerland after a stay in the United States just following the end of World War II, he was depressed and had lost his zeal for modern physics. During this severe depression, he dreamed of a character that he called "the Persian." This "Persian" appears to tease Pauli and wants Pauli to help him get admitted to the Polytechnic Institute in Zurich. First Pauli sets the scene of the dream, which occurred in December 1947:

I arrive at my former house. I see how a dark-skinned young man in whom I recognize the Persian is putting objects into the house through the window. I make out a circular piece of wood and several letters. Then he approaches me in a friendly manner and I begin a conversation with him:
Pauli: You are not allowed to study?
Persian: No, therefore I study in secret.
Pauli: What subject are you studying?
Persian: Yourself!
Pauli: You speak to me in a very sharp voice!
Persian: I speak as someone to whom everything else is forbidden.[9]
Pauli: Are you my shadow?
Persian: I am between you and the Light, so you are my shadow, not the reverse.
Pauli: Do you study physics?

Persian: There your language is too difficult for me, but in my language you do not understand physics![10]

In a dream that took place several years earlier when Einstein and Bohr were discussing the completeness of QM, Pauli dreamt about a man who looked like Einstein. The dream Einstein showed Pauli that QM only describes a one-dimensional intersection of a more fully developed two-dimensional reality.[11] If you recall the story *Flatland,* the character in the story is a two-dimensional square that is suddenly transported into the world of three dimensions, where he sees how two-dimensional life can be merely an intersection of three-dimensional beings with a two-dimensional surface—sort of like observing that a circle arises in a plane when a sphere is pushed through it. Pauli realized that the second dimension referred to by the dream Einstein was a metaphor indicating that something was missing from QM—the unconscious and its archetypal contents. Pauli thought that not only can these archetypes structure and order mental images, they can also structure matter itself.

As the years passed, Pauli tried in vain to find a new language that would enable him to bridge the gap between physical and psychical occurrences. He believed that this language needed to be neutral with respect to any distinction between psyche and matter.

But in the Persian dream Pauli realizes that this "second dimension" is not merely a theoretical physicist's attempt to add fuel to intellectual fires—to go beyond QM into a new, broader physics that includes the psyche—but is a hidden dimension that appears as a being. This being tells Pauli that he knows about the secret workings of nature, but he is unable to understand the difficult language of QM. He also tells Pauli that Pauli would not understand his language. But this "being" wants admittance to academia. He feels a need to enter into the dialogue of modern physics, perhaps to learn that language so that he can reveal his secrets to physicists. He pressures Pauli. This being is the spirit of matter and the hidden dimension that Pauli was seeking.

The Light-Dark Stranger

In another dream, which occurred in November 1948, the spirit appears to Pauli once again. But this time the dream figure is a superposition of two images, the Persian and a light-skinned blond man. This time the "stranger" embodies things that are unfamiliar to Pauli. His second encounter with the light-dark man took place in a dream of October 1949. Here the stranger tries to drive Pauli by means of a fire out of his field of mathematical physics:

> I am with colleagues on one of the upper floors of a house where a local conference on mathematics and physics is being held. I see that under my name a course of cookery is announced: "Start: December 15." Surprised, I ask a young man near me why the course begins so late in the year. He answers, "Because then the Nobel Prize will be granted."
>
> Now I notice that a fire has started in the adjacent room. I take fright (affect), run down a staircase along many floors (hurrying-panic). Finally I succeed in getting outside. Looking back, I see that two floors of the house, where the colleagues were gathered, are burned down. I walk across the level ground and enter a garage. I see that a taxi is waiting for me and that the taxi driver fills the tank with petrol. I look more closely, I recognize "him," the light-dark "stranger." Immediately I feel secure. "Probably he has lighted the fire," I think without saying it aloud. He says to me quietly, "Now we can refuel, because upstairs there has been a fire. I will take you where you belong!" Then he drives me off.[12]

Van Erkelens interprets the dream as a transformation. Pauli is attending a conference on mathematical physics. The conference is held on an upper floor, indicating that it is a world that has lost contact with the ground floor of reality but has become the only admitted means for contact with matter via the theoretical physicists' interpretation. But Pauli has to give a course on cookery—a symbolic reference to the concrete world of matter in which the fires of the stove transform the raw materials of matter into the materials of modern technology, not a theoretical seminar.

Then the fire takes off after Pauli, driving him out of his second-story "ivory tower" head. He must flee to the ground floor of reality where a taxi driver awaits him. He recognizes the driver as the symbol of the psyche-spirit. Pauli then relaxes and gives up his theoretical-physics life to follow the driver, to go with him wherever the driver takes him, presumably to the land of the spirit. When Pauli awoke from the dream, he said, "I awoke with a feeling of great relief and it seemed to me that essential progress had been made."

This spiritland is home for the stranger, and now Pauli must enter this land, too. But Pauli is still too much a theoretical physicist. In a letter to Emma Jung, Carl Jung's wife, he remarks that the dream stranger is ambivalent—a spiritual light of great wisdom and a chthonic (underworld) spirit of nature. The stranger's actions are always decisive, his words are conclusive though often incomprehensible. He regards his surroundings and people as ignorant (including Pauli) in comparison with himself.[13]

Pauli in this dream has acknowledged that the stranger is an alchemical light known as the *lumen naturae,* the light of nature that is found in the unconscious. A pupil of Jung's, Erich Neumann, called this light the light of eros—a light that springs from strong emotion, from what Jung would call feeling-tone constellations in the unconscious.

Thus this light is not the light of logos, and its appearance in Pauli's dreams tells him that his worldview is far from complete. Pauli was known by his colleagues as "the conscience of physics." But Pauli now knew through his conversations with the stranger that he was incomplete in this knowledge and, as the dream figure suggested of him, "totally uneducated."

It is then that eros fully enters Pauli's life. A dream woman enters. She is the dark eternal woman—an unknown symbolized to the Western mind as a "slit-eyed" Chinese woman who takes him to himself, through his transformation into a whole being.

Pauli and Eros

In January 1951, Pauli fell in love with Marie-Louise von Franz, a coworker of Jung's. Von Franz was then thirty-six years old and had succeeded in developing a deep understanding of the unconscious. Before his feelings for von Franz had developed, Pauli was attempting to create a neutral language to enable him to unify the concepts of modern physics and psychology and include parapsychology as well. He finds through his feelings for von Franz that this, too, must fail. He cannot follow the abstract dictates of modern logos. He feels the need of something else: eros.[14]

Even though von Franz had worked with Pauli and helped him to translate Latin fragments of the works of Fludd and Kepler, and in spite of the fact that Pauli was a physicist and von Franz a psychologist, this working relationship between them was not enough for him. It would appear that his relationship with her became more than professional. But this becomes too much for Pauli. He felt that his love for her had a deeper spiritual significance. This eventually drives Pauli to wish to change their relationship to a more spiritual kind of love rather than an *amor vulgaris*. Pauli seemingly wants out of his love relationship with von Franz, and she in turn has reservations about her relationship with him.

But why the change? What is driving Pauli? Why does he seemingly wish to change his love for von Franz from physical love to purely spiritual love? Again we need to look at the light-dark stranger in Pauli's dreams. He is a masculine figure, a messenger perhaps like the ankle-winged Mercury or the god Hermes. This godlike figure tempts Pauli. He brings Pauli to him on the knees of his desire through eros, but asks him to raise himself to see the light that surpasses all matter, the light of the spirit.

Pauli is still driven by the male-like logos. During the three years of his relationship with von Franz, Pauli remained loyal to his feeling side, but he still persisted in his intellectual discourse: he wanted to *understand* the lack of soul in the modern scientific worldview. He finds that meditation is more suitable to express the soul than his desired neutral language. In a letter to von Franz, he writes:

> For a long time I have wanted to write to you in order to communicate a certain mood in which a kind of unified view begins to assert itself in me. In order to give it expression I have to write in a curious way, half fantastic, half rational. In this way a kind of "meditation" is developing which also contains two dreams you do not know yet.[15]

Pauli then writes his "meditation." It is a strange piece of work dedicated to his friendship with von Franz, and it contains in a meditative and imaginative manner the answer to all of the problems he had been wrestling with. The figure of the "stranger" is now called "the master." Instead of a collision with this masculine master-figure, a woman appears. She is a piano teacher and she mediates between Pauli and his master, his higher self. He calls his work *Die Klavier-*

stunde—Eine aktive Phantasie über das Unbewusste[16] (The Piano Lesson—An Active Fantasy about the Unconscious).

Piano Lessons beyond Space and Time

In this dream lesson, Pauli seems to be in a world that exists outside of time and space. Here he meets a female piano teacher who is dependent on the master and is used to following this master without question. But with Pauli arriving to take piano lessons, she is given the opportunity to develop more independently and to act as a go-between for Pauli and their master.

The piano is especially symbolic here. In the world, it symbolizes creation. But this world is split in two. Scientists grasp the words of creation but not the music. They read the notes but fail to listen to the song. The woman playing the piano symbolizes the feminine side—the music and not the logical arrangement of the notes.

Pauli understands the logos of music but cannot play the piano. He reads sheet music, he knows the logical arrangement of notes as vibrations, but he cannot express this as beauty and sound. So he must take piano lessons—he must develop his feminine, feeling side.

The piano teacher is of course Pauli's *anima*—his feminine soul. She looks like Marie-Louise von Franz, some of the time, but most often she is the slit-eyed Chinese—an exotic or hidden part of Pauli. She seemingly lives in his unconscious safely away from his rational, logical masculine ego. Her Chinese face also symbolizes the mysterious East—the other half of the yin-yang. Pauli often referred to China as "the realm of the middle." This meant to Pauli the central part of the Self-psyche referred to in the quote by Jung in the chapter epigraph.

In the studio, Pauli talks with his teacher. Together they help each other. They work out how the world can be both a mathematical equation of seemingly cold logic and a sensory, feeling world of meaning, purpose, and emotion.

But at the end of his conversation with his "lady," Pauli again feels sad. Pauli like Moses sees the land of his master—his spiritual homeland—but is afraid that he will never enter it. He promises his lady that he will try to communicate the language of physics to his master. Then Pauli hears his master say in a friendly voice, "That is what I have long waited for." Pauli now wants to leave the piano-lesson room. He bows to the lady, but the master says to Pauli, "Wait. Transformation of the center of evolution."

And Pauli says, "In earlier times one said, 'Lead transforms into gold.'"

The Ring of the Imaginaries

The piano lesson ends as follows:

> At that moment the lady slipped a ring from her finger which I had not seen yet. She let it float in the air and taught me: "I suppose you know the ring from your school of mathematics. It is the ring i."
>
> I nodded and I spoke the words:
>
> "The 'i' makes the void and the unit into a couple. At the same time it is the operation of rotating a quarter of the whole ring."[17]
>
> She: It makes the instinctive or impulsive, the intellectual or rational, the spiritual or supernatural, of which you spoke, into the unified or monadic whole that the numbers without the "i" cannot represent.
>
> I: The ring with the "i" is the unity beyond particle and wave, and at the same time the operation that generates either of these.
>
> She: It is the atom, the indivisible, in Latin . . .
>
> With these words she looked at me significantly, but it seemed to me unnecessary to speak Cicero's word for the atom aloud.
>
> I: It turns time into a static image.
>
> She: It is the marriage and it is at the same time the realm of the middle, which you can never reach alone but only in pairs.
>
> There was a pause, we waited for something.
>
> Then the voice of the master speaks, transformed, from the center of the ring to the lady:
>
> "Remain merciful."
>
> Now I knew I could go out of the room into normal time and normal everyday space.

When I was outside, I noticed that I was wearing my coat and hat. From afar I heard a C-major chord of four tones, CEGC, apparently played by the lady herself when she was on her own again.[18]

What the Ring of the Imaginaries Represents: Dreams and Realities

This is perhaps the turning point in Pauli's search for the ultimate reconciliation between matter and spirit: the ring i. I have already told you a little about this ring, although I didn't refer to it as such. The ring is actually a mathematical symbol representing a movement that occurs in the complex plane of real and imaginary numbers. You can think of this plane as being crossed by two axes, perpendicular to each other. Their crossing point is the number zero. The axis that stretches horizontally across the plane marks the realm of the real numbers, those that run both positively and negatively from zero. The axis that crosses the real-number axis marking the number zero is the realm of pure *imaginary* numbers symbolized by the letter *i*. Any point on the plane, then, is marked by two values, a real number and an imaginary value. The real number measures how far the point is from the imaginary axis, and the imaginary-number value tells you how far the point is from the real-number axis.

This is no more complex than a map that tells you how far you are from the center of a city. The axis that runs north-south crosses the axis that runs east-west, marking the city's center. Any point on the map, say an address, is given in terms of so many numbers or blocks east or west of the north-south line, and so many numbers or blocks north or south of the east-west line.

The ring in this complex plane represents a transformation. If you draw the ring with a radius of one unit centered about zero, this ring will cross the real axis at the points plus one and minus one, and the imaginary axis at the points plus i and minus i. As a point moves around the ring, the number it represents always has the same magnitude—the radius of the ring—but it changes in phase as the point moves. This means that it changes in the amounts of real and imaginary components that make up its total value.

The ring can also be thought of as a wave motion. As the wave goes through its complete cycle, its phase changes, marked by the movement of the point on the ring. In chapter 19 I will tell you about Schrödinger waves, consisting of ionic currents that may exist in the brain cortex. The brain hologram could be made from these waves, and the phase of these waves is important in determining the ability of the hologram to reproduce memories. That phase can be pictured as the movement of a sweep second-hand on a clockface. Now that picture is completed by noting that the movement of the sweep second-hand on the clockface is actually the movement of the point around the ring of the imaginaries in the complex plane.[19]

Although the interpretation of the wave-particle duality is still being discussed, all physicists recognize the need to require complex probability amplitudes in the description of nature. The fact that imaginary numbers are not "observed" as physical fields or particles is indeed bothersome. However, it may just be that the field of imaginary numbers runs outside of the logical consistency of our logical minds. They are a rude, perhaps feminine "anima" spirit that we physicists find necessary and vital in order to make "sense" of the physical world. We need the imaginary numbers, but we don't know what to make of them.

As a mathematical symbol the ring i is as powerful in science today as the cross is in Christianity. Indeed there may even be a suggested relationship in that the horizontal arm of the cross marks the physical world while the vertical bar of the cross marks the ascendancy of the spirit. In a similar way the horizontal line of the real numbers marks the physical "reality" while the vertical line marks the world of the spirit represented as the imaginary numbers.

The ring then marries the two and makes them inseparable, if we wish to grasp the meaning and significance of life. By having his anima present him with the ring, Pauli is given a vital clue to his search and possibly the very answer. The ring i reconciled the wave and the particle. Could it also reconcile the psyche and matter—the spirit and the material? Pauli learns about the ring from his unconscious. He is given the same symbol that he knew brought quantum physics into harmony.

Niels Bohr believed that the complementarity that existed between the wave and the particle aspects of nature were indications of a much deeper complementarity in which irreconcilable pairs of opposites need not be contradictory. As he once said, "the opposite of a small truth may be a lie, but the opposite of a great truth is also a great truth." Thus the ring i may be a symbol of the reconciliation of complementary parts of the whole.

It can also be more. For to Pauli the ring also symbolized the feeling tones that were absent in his search for a neutral language. Thus the ring symbolizes a new realization: nature need not be conquered by our need to objectify all experience. After all, this need can be seen as rising from our early Greek heritage to masculinize nature and her gods, to force her to submit to revealing her secrets in a language that only a rational, logical mind can deal with. Pauli realized this in a letter to Fierz. He wrote:

> It appears to me that the ignored "after-effects" of observation will yet enter into the picture (as atomic bombs, general anxiety, "the Oppenheimer Case," for instance) but in an undesirable form. The famous "incompleteness" of quantum mechanics (Einstein) is still factually present somehow-somewhere.... This has to do with integral relationships between "inside and outside" which are lacking in contemporary science (but which alchemy has suspected, and which may also be detected in the symbolism of my dreams, symbols that I believe to be typical for contemporary physicists).[20]

The master in Pauli's dreams has also been transformed. He now speaks from the ring i and seems to have lost his threatening power. The center of the ring is perhaps symbolic of Pauli's center. And perhaps the stranger/light-dark man has come to rest there. Perhaps the piano-teacher/anima has served Pauli by teaching him to listen and play the music, not just compose and read the notes.

We will never know. Pauli never completed his work in this regard. His death in 1958 may mean that now he really knows the truth about existence. In the next chapter I will attempt to complete Pauli's inquiry and bring us all to the cross of the real and the imaginary.

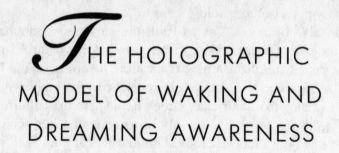 THE HOLOGRAPHIC MODEL OF WAKING AND DREAMING AWARENESS

If we ask, for instance, whether the position of the electron remains the same, we must say "no"; if we ask whether the electron's position changes with time, we must say "no"; if we ask whether it is in motion, we must say "no."

—*J. Robert Oppenheimer* [1]

Dreams reflect the fuller development of the self. They tell us something about ourselves that we are neglecting to look at in our waking life. We saw how Pauli's dreams eventually led him to realize that he was missing half the universe in himself.

In this chapter I will attempt to define the dream at last in terms of a physics model based on the hologram. Yet dreams are elusive, and like the above quote they can't quite be defined as easily as we define an electron. In fact, as Oppenheimer points out, we cannot even define an electron as we expect it should be defined. Perhaps there is no such thing as an electron. And perhaps,

There Is No Such Thing as a Dream!

Now that we have had the chance to explore some basic ideas concerning consciousness and dreams, we are still left with some rather fundamental questions. First of all, when we are having a dream, exactly what is it we are doing? By this question I mean, how is that we see images or, perhaps better put, believe upon awakening that we indeed remember seeing such images? It would appear that we are aware of something, that we have a knowing, self-reflecting sense of ourselves participating, as it were, in some world stage or scene, albeit an environment made up by our minds, as imagery.

But some researchers suggest that this may not be true. That, for that matter, dreams may not even consist of images in the same sense that we see them when we are awake. If dreams aren't really perceived images, as some neurophysiologists and philosophers suggest, then what are we doing when we are experiencing a dream and what is actually being experienced?

Although modern lucid-dream research indicates that such philo-sophical considerations are erroneous and that indeed during a dream we not only experience imagery but are capable of sensing time and even apparent solidity of dream objects, and we have looked at this research in a previous chapter, it is useful to look at these counter-arguments carefully for they may contain a clue to how consciousness behaves and what dreams really are. Let's first consider the idea that in a dream we aren't doing the same type of thing—perceiving images self-reflectively—that we do when we perceive the outside world. As strange as it may seem, for certainly we all apparently "remember" seeing dream images, there is some substance to this argument.

For example, philosophers Jean-Paul Sartre, Norman Malcolm, and Daniel C. Dennett all hold to the idea that there is no such thing as dream perception in which vision, touch, or even thought occurs![2]

Sartre points out that there cannot be a dream perception of a life world because to him perception alters the content of consciousness and thus changes the dream. Much like the observer effect in quantum physics, to think about what you are dreaming destroys the dreaming process, whereas in a real-life waking awareness perception is reflec-tive—the perceiver knows that he is perceiving an external reality and, via this reflection, is capable of taking a willful action. In a normal dream, putting lucid dreams to the side for a moment, this simple volitional aspect of choosing what to perceive and what to do, and to know simultaneously that one is doing this, seems to be absent.

Why? For two apparently unrelated reasons. Firstly, put simply, the dream objects of perception are not really objects, but are generated by the brain. So what does it mean to see an object "out there" if there is no objective reality "out there" to begin with? Secondly, as J. Allan Hobson points out, dreams are involuntary. Dreams seem to challenge and deny the parallel notions of rationality and responsibility. To be responsible, one must be rational. In dreaming the dreamer appears to be irrational, and thus the dreamer appears to himself to lose his sense of volition and responsibility.

Thus it would seem that we "encounter" dream objects unreflectively. What happens if we do reflect upon the dream content? Sartre says that we then disrupt the dream. This disruption of the "observable" by becoming aware of self is enough for Sartre to stop the dream from progressing. A typical example of this is the sudden apprehension that can occur when a dream becomes "scary" and the dreamer awakens.

Granting that there are certainly exceptions to this, again in particular the lucid-dream experience, what is happening when self-reflection disrupts a dream? And is there a connection between the absence of volitional aspects of consciousness in a dream and the unreality of the objects seemingly "perceived" during a dream? I would like to suggest that there is a connection between will, objectivity, and the ability to self-reflect—to be aware that one is aware.

Now before I get into this connection I want to summarize the issues of self-reflection and nonobjectivity arguments that the other two philosophers described. Malcolm looks at the differences between sleeping and waking reflection. To be asleep, to Malcolm, means to a large extent that one is unaware, "unconscious," and therefore incapable of self-reflection. He refutes the point of view that when one is dreaming, one can reason, judge, imagine, and have sense impressions just as one does when one is awake.

His reason for denial is interesting and somewhat of a rebus in itself. Since in a dream we are able to do seemingly impossible things, like fly through the air as a bird, jump from a building without injury, or watch incredible transformations of people into animals, and since these are clearly fantasies, then what does it mean to remember a fantasy? If we check our memory of a real event, we have some means of verification. For example, I remember leaving my keys in the restaurant. I can go back to it or call the restaurant and verify that my memory is either true or false. But I cannot do this to verify a dream.

In other words all I have to verify my report is my memory of the dream, which is contained in the report itself. The report refers to itself for verification and not to any outside referent. Perhaps my report was made up at the instant I awoke, and in that state of awareness, I made up the whole thing. Even the very act of "remembering" the story of the dream could be the creation of those elements that I call the images of the dream. Thus as I "recall the dream," I am doing no such thing. I am making up a story, and as I do so, I am wakefully and most consciously, probably with a somewhat hypnagogic enhancement, creating the dream imagery on the spot. Thus the recall is not a recall of "real" events.

Dennett puts the refutation more strongly. To him, one goes to sleep. Then one awakens and has a story to tell, a recollection or a memory that the story took place at some earlier time during sleep, and perhaps a set of fleeting images that arise as the story is recalled. There is absolutely no evidence that any of the story, the images, or anything else associated with dream imagery ever occurred during sleep.

Upon awakening we have all had impressions that we had experiences, no doubt. In a particularly strong impression, we may even wonder if the impression we have is a recall of an actual sequence of events or not. If we later discover that the impression is not a recall of actual events, we "remember" them as a dream.

In this chapter and the next, I would like to present an answer to these puzzles in terms of a quantum physical model. It is only within the last ten years or so that the answer I will propose, based as it is on holographic imagery and the many-worlds interpretation of quantum physics, could even be formulated. So it is of no wonder that this answer may not have been put forward by dream researchers or psychologists or, indeed, neurophysiologists or physicists before. Put briefly, it states that memory functions in the brain by making and witnessing holographic "imagery" and that this functioning depends to a great deal on "who" is looking as well as on "what" is being observed.

This model depends in part on some recent but quite revolutionary research work of the Italian physicist Renato Nobili from the department of physics at the Galileo Galilei University of Studies at Padua, Italy, and in part on the work of physicist David Z. Albert, who shares an appointment with both the University of South Carolina and Tel Aviv University in Israel.

Nobili's work[3] gives convincing arguments that a certain type of wave movement (that is similar in form and structure to quantum waves but different from them in certain essential details) occurs in the brain such that the brain becomes an ideal medium for supporting and producing holographic imagery.

Albert's work suggests that certain types of quantum automata can exist that are capable of not only describing certain properties of the objective world but also of themselves. It is this self-reflective property that, in combination with the holographic model, suggests a mechanism for the origin of a sense of self within the brain. I will tell you more about this in the next chapter.

•

Einstein's Brain and Holograms on the Mind

As I mentioned in earlier chapters, there is quite clear evidence that the brain generates electrical wave activity as exemplified by the records of electroencephalograms. We also know that the pattern of these waves changes during wakefulness, sleep, and during periods of rapid eye movements. Aside from knowing this, we have little knowledge, if any, as to why these patterns change or, for that matter, what these patterns mean. By looking at the individual neuron's electrical activity we have come to know that there are quite active movements of electrical charges, consisting mainly of sodium (Na^+) and potassium (K^+) ions, that pass from one side of a neural membrane to the other as a nerve pulse travels along the long body (axon) of the neuron.

We also know how the brain is constructed, that is we know what types of cells are present and to some extent how these individual cells function. At the time of birth, the newborn child has exactly the same number of neural cells he will have as he matures to an adult. In other words, as a child becomes an adult, and as his brain increases in size, the number of neurons present will not change. Each neuron will grow in size, and during a critical period of growth in the early years of life, a number of neurons will connect, based on the environment of the child, but there is no further generation (increase in number) of neural tissue.

Yet the brain does grow, and there is evidence of brain cellular mitosis (cellular division) occurring, but not in neural cells. These other cells that do manage to divide are somewhat of a mystery. No one quite knows exactly why they are present and what functions they perform.[4] These are called *glial* cells. Some studies indicate that these cells perform a metabolic function—they are somehow involved in providing nourishment for neural cells.[5]

When Albert Einstein died, his brain was autopsied and it was discovered that he had a larger then normal amount of glial cells associated with his visual cortex. This led many to speculate that glial cells had something to do with intelligence and possibly Einstein's enhanced ability to visualize abstract concepts. Einstein had often written that before he wrote down any mathematical expression, he "saw" or conceptualized the new idea. This speculation about the connection between glial cells and visualization may have some foundation in truth.

Some researchers during the 1980s have shown that the glial cells do more than provide nourishment to neurons. Peculiar movements of ions have been detected in glial cells, and it is now suspected that these ion "transport" processes affect the bioelectrical activity of neurons and of the whole cerebral cortex.[6]

Research on multiple sclerosis, a disease that is associated with the breakdown of glial cells, also indicates that memory processes and motor processes are deeply affected, thus suggesting that glial cells do more than just provide nourishment and supporting tissue for neurons.[7] As we will see in Nobili's model, glial cells act as the medium for holographic waves.

First let me give you a rundown of Nobili's basic ideas. Then later I will carefully guide you through some of the more abstruse concepts. Physicist Nobili proposes that these previously mentioned ions, Na^+ and K^+, actually are capable of transporting themselves through glial cells and that these movements are in the form of oscillations. These oscillations in turn produce a wave pattern of rather complex form in which the motion of the sodium ions affects the movement of the potassium ions and vice versa. By modeling this ionic movement, Nobili was able to derive a wave equation that has exactly the same form as the Schrödinger wave equation of quantum physics. He then predicted what types of wave activities would be detected in experimental stimulus-response patterns in brain cortex using his model and his wave equation and found that there was perfect agreement between his theoretical predictions and the experimental studies.

Given that such waves can exist in glial cells, he then asked what conditions would be necessary for these waves to produce coherent patterns necessary for holographic image or memory formation. He found that contrary to light-wave holography, Schrödinger wave holography was far more efficient in producing holograms in brain tissue. He also discovered that the close proximity of signal sources and receptors (which is in itself in good agreement with other neurophysi-ological cortical diagrams) in the cortex was ideal for both production of reference waves and information wave recovery.

Now let me take you through these ideas and expound on them for the lay reader. First of all, you may ask, why even attempt to make a holographic model of brain or memory processing? Beginning with the later half of the 1960s, several workers began to suspect that memory processing could not take place in any form of linear file-cabinet models or computer-access models.[8] The evidence for this was suggested by a number of observations.

Studies by Karl Lashley between 1920 and 1950 indicated that memory was based on the formation of engrams in brain tissue and that these engrams were not localized in specific places in animals' brains.[9] Studies of what happens when brain tissue is removed ("extir-pated" in the jargon) showed memory blurring, but the amount of blurring depended only on the amount of tissue extirpated and not on the location of this tissue. Thus the conclusion was that memory was not localized in specific brain tissue but was distributed through-out the brain.

Animal-behavior observations and psychological studies of human memory indicated that whenever a fragment of a memory record was presented to the attention of a subject, the subject was able to recall the whole memory and any other memories associated with the whole memory. This indicated that memories could not be stored in a linear computer-model fashion but had to be stored in a way that would allow a rich number of associations to arise whenever fragmentary information was presented. To give you an example of this: Who was that president, John F. ———? As you recall this person, look at all of the images that come to your mind.

We know that memory can function mnemonically—that it is pos-sible to recall by some simple divisive sequence the memory of a rather complex and otherwise impossible pattern of events. For exam-ple, to remember a long line of randomly arranged digits, one may use pictures. The number one would be a magician's wand, the num-ber two would be swan, the number three would be a three-cornered hat, and four a table, etc. By recalling the image of a table floating on the back of a swan who comes to the shore and meets a magician who bows to the swan and takes off his hat, we would remember the sequence 4-2-1-3.

In general such sequences would involve a number of images that change before one's mind, thus indicating that memory should be able to recall moving scenes as well as stationary ones. The ability to have time in memory, to see scenes that change in time, also favors a wave holographic model of memory.

Furthermore there is no evidence that anything like computer-file management occurs in the brain. Mnemonic recalls do not seem to involve searches through tree patterns or files or pages as would be typical for computer-memory devices. Access time to memories is also not relatable in terms of any linear file-management scheme. For example, you may recall a childhood image as quickly as you remember that you forgot to turn out the lights when you left your home this morning.

All of the above observed properties of memory functioning are easily simulated by holography. On the contrary, it is quite difficult to reproduce any of the above and certainly not all of the above together by any form of Boolean (standard computer logic) or neural-network models,[10] which, however, remain in wide use as models of human and animal memory (probably because they are easily studied by computer programming).

What leads us to think that holographic memory processing could take place in the brain? The answer lies in the properties of the EEG waves that have been observed. However, even though these properties are seen, one major factor must be present in order that the brain actually be able to produce holograms: these waves must be capable of being superimposed, one upon the other, without distortion. This is known as the *superposition principle,* one that is necessary for quantum mechanical systems also. This principle is necessary not only in order that complex images be formed from the superposition of simpler images (think of the beautiful lady and then add a mustache) but also in order that the images be capable of association of one with the other.

To satisfy a superposition principle the waves are said to be linear. Now linearity refers to the behavior of these waves when they are combined. If some operation is carried out on a combination of waves that removes one of them, the others must not be affected. Another important aspect of linearity is specifically related to how holograms are made.[11]

Now let us consider the evidence that EEG waves could indeed support holographic imagery. First of all we know that cortical waves are themselves linear. Certain experiments based on time delay or frequency displacement show that the waves maintain their form and that linearly superposed waves exhibit consistent patterns—consistent that is with the superposition principle.

Secondly, cortical waves are not directly related to cortical activity. They appear to persist even when neural activity is suppressed as, say, by anesthetics. And finally these waves appear to be associated with mnemonic activity as exhibited when they appear during REM periods of sleep. This would indicate that cortical waves are involved with dreaming awareness.

However, in spite of the evidence, many researchers remained skeptical and suggested as an alternative that holographic processes may occur but associative memory was due to some form of digital process. This led to a number of papers seeking the means by which associative memory could proceed through digital processes. In other words, people believed that memory storage was primarily associated with specific areas of the brain rather than being distributed over the cortex.

Now such skepticism is not unreasonable. A major reason for this has to do with what is required for holographic memory storage in terms of the area of the hologram and the wavelength of the waves involved. EEG patterns do not show a sufficiency of small-wavelength components. The smaller the wavelength the greater the amount of information the wave may encode. If you think about an object, say a small coin, and try to imagine what is required simply to see the details of the coin's surface, you can grasp this concept. The light used to see the object has waves of many lengths. If the length of the wave is longer than the detail to be seen, the wave will not be able to reflect from it. The tinier the detail to be seen, the smaller the wavelength needed.

Dennis Gabor, the "father" of the hologram, gave an extensive proof that the information contained in a hologram was equal to the ratio of the area of the hologram divided by the wavelength squared. If you have small-area holograms, you will need a lot of light beams with various wavelengths. By adding together the ratios for each wavelength you will be able to produce any desired amount of information. It would then seem that such sophistication would not be present in brain tissue.

Another objection to brain-wave holography is that optical holograms all require focusing devices to recover information. However, there do not seem to be any such mechanisms in brain tissue.

So how can there be a brain hologram? If we look at brain tissue carefully, we find that it consists of an enormous quantity of finely tuned tiny resonators[12] distributed throughout the cortex in a three-dimensional random pattern. This gives an entire new dimension to brain-wave holography (namely, thickness of the hologram) and allows for a new estimate in the information content of a brain wave. It is the ratio of the volume of the cortex to the volume of a resonator. Estimates of resonator size are typically on the order of .02 cubic millimeters. The cortex is typically 2 millimeters thick and if stretched out, roughly 1.4 square meters in area. This gives an estimate of something like 10^6 to 10^8 bits of information per local impulse. This quantity of information spreads throughout the whole cortex and decreases in time as the glial cells absorb the energy.

The key here is that the whole cortical volume participates in both the generation of the holographic wave and in its detection. This is quite different from light-wave holograms, which are primarily surface or area recordings.

Next, Schrödinger waves propagate through the medium in a different manner from light waves. Light waves travel with the same speed through a medium while the Schrödinger waves travel with different speeds depending on their frequencies. This property allows immediate recovery of information.

Thirdly, when these Schrödinger waves diffract through the medium (effectively spread out), they evoke different images from the fixed stored information in the glial cells. This amounts to producing time-resolved holograms, like motion pictures, so that the information when it is perceived will appear as movement in time. Light-wave holograms do not exhibit this.

Fourthly, time-varying information that is recorded in the medium finds its way to a number of resonators embedded in the medium. These sources also act as transmitters of the information, so there is no need to have any focalization devices present.

When we put all of this together, we have a reasonably good expectation that the brain can act as a holographic medium and that a vast amount of memory exists via slight changes in the glial cells, which act as absorbers of Schrödinger wave energy. Not only this, but because of the superposition principle, glial cells can absorb superpositions of wave information, some coming from recent events and some coming from past events. Depending on the reference wave that excites these glial cells, associated memories can be evoked.[13]

Now when we sense something occurring in the outside world, information in the form of a wave, I, enters the brain via the senses. This in turn recruits or stimulates a strong reference wave, R, to be emitted by the cortex. The two waves add together and their energy is absorbed in the glial cells. If the cells already contain information associated with this specific reference wave, then the output of all this is an associated set of images: the stored image and the input image. It is the rich association of these images that enables us to discern that a table, for example, is a table even when seen from several different viewing points.

Waking Reality

Granted that our brains operate holographically and that all memory operates via the excitation of holographic engrams—records of stored information found in glial cells—we still need to understand the difference between waking awareness and dream awareness.

The first question is, what constitutes an act of awareness? Are there some basic criteria that we can use? Suppose we ask you to look at something. Are you really aware of what you see? How should we decide if you are or aren't aware of something? Perhaps it is enough that you say you saw something. If so, we can call that the criterion of consciousness: you report that you saw something, therefore you were aware of something. Or perhaps you can only become aware of a limited number of aspects of the visual field.

Physiologist G. Sperling describes in a paper an experiment in which subjects are exposed to a three-by-three grid of letters or numbers for a fraction of a second.[14] After exposure, the observers typically claim that they could see all of the letters. But they can only recall three or four of them. Thus they pass the criteria of consciousness report, but they cannot verify it. Yet the subjects continually insist that they are conscious of all of the elements in the array. By asking the subjects after exposure to the letters to report any randomly cued letter in the array, the subject is successful. In fact they are able to recall any three or four letters randomly cued by the investigators. This suggests that they have fleeting access to all of the letters even though they can only recall three or four of the symbols.

It also suggests a quantum type of complementarity acting in the brain between the whole array versus the parts that can be remembered. Any part can be described, but this wipes out the ability to see the whole in terms of remembering the other parts. The whole can be seen as long as no parts are recalled, but any attempt to describe the parts wipes it out.

Thus the person remembers having seen a field of nine symbols that composes the whole. If you ask the person to name the symbols in the first row or the third column or even those running diagonally across the array, he can do so even if he has no idea of what part of the array you may ask about. He is able to recall three or four symbols and then his mind goes blank. It is as if the very action of recalling changes the thing being recalled. This is suggestive of observation of a quantum system.

The action involved in remembering the whole is not found in processes involved in remembering the parts. The action in describing the parts is not in the whole. Thus when one attempts to describe three or four parts, the remaining parts vanish. Now this feature of memory recall is quite well known to physicists in terms of the uncertainty principle in its operation involving a quantum system for a spinning particle.[15]

So what does this tell us about the relationship of memory to awareness? It suggests that awareness is impossible without memory, and that the operation of memory recall is selective and is governed by quantum physical rules. When we attempt to recall something, the choice we make as to what to remember follows the rule of complementarity. It also tells us that recall is an active process and that once the operation of recall is set into motion, other ways of recalling the information are wiped out. This means that what we remember is not just a recorded fact, but is dependent on how we choose to remember.

If we put all of the above in a nutshell, we come to the conclusion that the mind acts quantum mechanically in remembering and in becoming aware. If we now include the fact that quantum mechanical operations are describable by probability Schrödinger waves and that the brain hologram is made from ionic Schrödinger waves, we are led to conclude that awareness is governed by a simulated or analogous set of laws to those of quantum physics. Now this is of course very speculative. But let me carry the analogy further.

As we have seen above, during ordinary waking awareness, new information in the form of these ionic Schrödinger waves is created.

This information stimulates the cortex to send a reference wave throughout the whole cortex. If the new-information-stimulated reference wave matches a stored combination of a reference wave plus old-information wave, a superposition of the new information and the stored information appears in the cortex. This causes the cortex to produce fleeting images of stored information that are added to the new-information wave coming in from the senses. In such a case the new or sensory information is matched with the stored information, and we say we "see" the outside world (or hear it or feel it or taste it or smell it).

Sensing the outside world is more complex than just sensing it "out there" because it is out there. For example, as I mentioned in an earlier chapter, data gathered by Nobel Prize–winning physiologist Georg von Békésy indicated that subjects deprived of their visual sense would actually feel sensations in a space where no parts of their bodies were present.

This is suggestive of a holographic action in the brain and that the brain is capable of creating a sensation of "out-thereness." The sensation of feeling something "out there" in space when the visual sense is occluded is no more mysterious than the sensation of seeing something "out there" in normal vision. The action involves what we would call projection. This projection depends on what we remember is "out there." Remember that data gathered by physiologist Benjamin Libet also suggests that even our sense of the time of an event is projected. His data gives a convincing picture that the appearance of the awareness of an event, such as a skin stimulus, occurs a full half second after our subjective timing of the event. In other words we project the event backward in time. He calls this time referral.

Thus we construct reality from the data inputted to our senses and from the data already recorded in our brains. In the example of the sensation of sight, what we actually see is a superposition of both information waves re-created as visions. The information on the retina is sent to the brain, and the brain in turn sends out its recorded information, and together the two make up a reality sensation of "out-thereness."

Thus "out there" reality is actually a superposition of sensory data encoded in the form of new-information waves and recorded data made up of old-information waves. The new-information waves stimulate a reference wave to "shine" through the brain cortex producing an old-information wave. The two information waves add together and produce the image we call reality.

In a nutshell: awareness requires memory. "Out there" stimuli produce "in here" information. The "in here" information is matched with the "out there" stimuli. The match is called reality. This "theory" also explains the host of "waking dream" phenomena mentioned earlier and dreams.

Volition and Dreaming Reality: "I" in the "Holodream"

How do dreams manifest holographically? There are several kinds of dreams. The first criterion of a sleeping dream is that sensory data from the outside world is cut off by brain-stem mechanisms. This means that the source of stimulation of the reference waves is no longer new information coming from the outside world. (We are ignoring for the moment Freud's concern with external events such as noises in the house when you are sleeping that can stimulate a dream.)

Now what *does* stimulate the appearance of reference waves? This is the key question, for its answer tells us a number of different things about dream content and the qualities of dreams in terms of such factors as the length of time of a dream or the degree of lucidity or witnessing that occurs in some dreams. The answer begins with Allan Hobson and Robert McCarley's activation-synthesis model of dreaming. I will review the chief features of the model first and then add some ideas of my own.[16]

As I explained earlier, in 1977 Hobson and McCarley presented a neurophysiological model[17] of dreams that nearly set the psychoanalytical field on fire. They suggested that a dream-state generator was localized in the brain stem and that this generator periodically produced or triggered the dream state by blocking input and output motor activity and at the same time stimulated the forebrain (the cortex) by activating it with partially random impulses generated by the brain stem.

They concluded that the primary motivating force for dreaming was not psychological but physiological. They also concluded that these random brain-stem-originated stimuli may provide spatially specific information that can be used to construct dream imagery. Dream bizarreness is also not due to psychological factors, nor are dreams disguised forms of repression, but merely the result of the randomness of the stimuli.

They wrote:

> The forebrain may be making the best of a bad job in producing even partially coherent dream imagery from the relatively noisy signals sent up to it from the brainstem. The dream process is thus seen as having its origin in sensorimotor systems, with little or no primary ideational, volitional, or emotional content. This concept is markedly different from that of the "dream thoughts" or wishes seen by Freud as the primary stimulus for the dream.

Hobson and McCarley also explain our poor recall of dream content as "a state-dependent amnesia, since a carefully affected state change, to waking, may produce abundant recall even of highly charged dream material." Thus if you are quickly aroused from a dream, you are likely to remember it quite well even if it is an unpleasant reminder of your inadequacies. Thus they conclude, "There is no need to invoke repression to account for the forgetting of dreams."

Of course this theory caused a big stir among the Freudians. It appeared that it wasn't Freud that the Freudians were concerned about; it was dreams. The ascribing of all dream activity to randomness was highly provocative to dream researchers, and I am sure this paper affected their dreams.

But how could the random bombardment of brain-stem stimuli affect their dreams? For that matter, how could any dream-sense occur? The key here lies in a detail of the brain-stem mechanism discussed with me by physicist David Kahn, who works in Hobson's group.

During a waking moment the aminergic system in the brain stem operates by mainly periodic release of two molecules, norepinephrine and serotonin, into the brain. Kahn explained that it is believed that these molecules keep us attentive. This allows us to see the foreground as opposed to the background when we look out there. So when you are talking to someone in a crowded, noisy room, you are not distracted by the sounds around you. But once that system dies down, the background becomes equally as important as the foreground, and then you lose the ability to focus, you lose the ability to attend to out-there stimuli.

This is what happens during sleep and more so during dreaming. You lose the ability to attend. And at the same time the cholinergic system in the brain stem turns on, activating the brain. Acetylcholine is the main molecule produced by this system from a particular part of the brain stem. Hobson and others have identified the cholinergic center in the brain stem and have shown that this system fires in both a tonic—continuous—manner and a phasic—burstlike—manner. These bursts are called ponto-geniculo-occipital (PGO) waves or bursts. They are highly spiked. The question is, what is the correlation, if any, between the cognitive acts of the dream and the cholinergic bursts? There is reason to believe that some relationship exists between the PGO waves and the discontinuities—the switching that happens in dreams. However, a lot of work is still to be done on that.

Kahn told me that the brain is chemically a different animal in dreaming versus sleeping versus waking. The chemicals that have been identified to date in the aminergic system, molecules of serotonin and norepinephrine, cut down to zero during dreaming, and the cholinergic system, which releases acetylcholine, fires at a much higher rate during dreaming than during waking.

The key here is the ability to attend—to be aware of the ability to choose—to have volitional control of what to pay attention to. To what extent can we do this, and how does this ability change as one goes from wake to sleep to dream? If Kahn and Hobson are correct, volitional awareness is chemically modulated: it depends on the active battle between the two brain-stem mechanisms—the aminergic and cholinergic systems. When one is active, the other seems to be passive.

Is it possible that dream content is determined to a large extent by the ratio of these chemicals found in the brain, specifically in the degree to which one is aware of the dream and is aware of volition during the dream?

First of all we need to look at what we mean by volition. It seems from experiments with the drug ketamine, as described first by John Lilly and later by physicist Saul-Paul Sirag and others, that this drug can induce a very different form of awareness—namely no bodily awareness at all!

As part of the research on this book I talked to Saul-Paul Sirag about his experiences with ketamine. Normally this drug is used on both humans and animals as a total body anesthetic. In the active period of psychoactive drug research during the 1970s, many people began experimenting with mind-altering substances, which at that time were legal. Saul-Paul had taken a half-clinical dosage of ketamine during this time and, being a physicist, decided to observe himself as the drug took effect on him during a clinical study.

Just after taking the drug, he was told to close his eyes, because when the drug takes full effect, all the voluntary muscles become paralyzed, much as in the sleeping state. There is some danger in keeping the eyes open because you cannot blink and wet the surface of the eye. However, Saul-Paul wanted to watch what happened to the visual field as the ketamine came on. By the time he wanted to close his eyes, he couldn't. As he watched the visual field, he noticed that first it flattened out like a Matisse painting. Then it became hyperdimensional, abstract, and dynamic—very active. Music was playing and all of the music was in synchronization with the changes in the visual field. There was no sense of "I," just awareness. There was affect: a feeling of awe, fear, and elation.

But being a physicist, he remembered that there also was a goal— to figure out what was going on. This wasn't a forced feature of the experience. It wasn't that he should figure it out. It was like a car engine running at high speed even when one takes one's foot off the gas pedal. One hypothesis after another was generated and would immediately be tested on the visual space. Nothing worked, nothing could be explained.

After forty-five minutes or so, the self began coming back. He found this the most interesting. His eyes could move just enough so that he could begin to see in three dimensions, and a perspective began. When that occurs, a unique point in space, the focus of the perspective, appears. Without the focus, there is no "I." An eye for an "I" so to speak. He had no idea that this process had anything to do with ego or self; he was simply trying to find the focal point. So he moved his hand to find this point and found he couldn't do it. In fact, as he put it, "My head was in the way, but I no longer knew I had a head."

Then he started to move his hand in a wavelike motion and found that the vision of his hand was not in synchronization with the proprioception of the hand. The visual hand kept moving following inertia, but this isn't what he felt. Gradually he was able to bring his visual hand into synchronization with his felt hand. As this occurred, he noticed that his sense of "I" was developing with his sense of volition.

So he realized that "I" was deeply connected with volition. There is no "I" unless that "I" is able to act volitionally in the world.

Yet, there is awareness without this "I," which is what mystics have said for countless ages. But it is hard to believe it until you experience it.

Thus a key insight is there is no self without volition. From that I gathered that there is no self without something to push around—a sense of objectivity. Self arises out of there being a sense of not-self— an out there. What I call my "self" is what I sense of my self through my senses. So my ego doesn't exist on its own. It arises from the directable awareness—the volitional aspect of consciousness. So in a pure awareness state, having experiences of the outside world visually in which no power to manipulate is present, neither of your voluntary muscles nor of your thoughts, no sense of self is present.

Memory is also altered during this experience. Saul-Paul didn't remember having a body either. He told me:

> I would have known I had one if I could remember it. I am now hypothesizing and reasoning that if I could have remembered my body, I would have had a sense of "I." The thought that I had a body once and now I don't may have occurred, for example. I did not have a sense of myself as an entity. There was only awareness of sight and sound, but no proprioception.

But the people he was with who were supervising the experiment did not talk to him during the experience. When he came out of the experience, they made him talk about it right away. He recalled, "If I didn't talk about it immediately, I wouldn't remember any of it."

This aspect of losing ability to recall the experience is very much like attempting to recall a dream upon awakening. In a dream state you generally create people and you talk to them and they to you. You are also able to change places with them. Sirag recalled:

> That is the weird thing about dreams. The sense of "I" is there but it is much weaker. If I dream about you, I can start to look out through your eyes in the dream or I can merge with you like in writing a novel. Modern novels get more and more like dreams in that the voice of the novelist takes on different characters—the story is seen through different characters'

eyes. With ketamine it was like a dream state without people; an abstract dream state.

In a dream the world is in a bubble, a very localized reality —like a novel wherein nothing happened before the novel began. I don't know how to model dreams in my scheme, but one idea I have in general about altered states and dreams being the most familiar altered state is that the space is alive. This means that it is not just a mathematical fiction, it is real.

If we take Saul-Paul's ketamine account as representative of a unique but also normal state of conscious experience, we are led to conclude that volition cannot occur without the simultaneous awareness of self. In other words self-reflection is intimately tied in with volition. This would explain a number of things about dreams. The fact that the motor system of the body is paralyzed during dream sleep would then explain the fact that during a dream people seemingly have no ability to direct their actions. The dream takes them on its journey. But what about lucid dreams? Here we see a volitional aspect appearing in the dream. The dreamer knows he is dreaming and is able to take action.

Research by lucid-dream scientists also indicates that it is possible to signal to the outside world while one is having a lucid dream. The method is simple enough. The dreamer uses his will to control the REM, to signal the researcher by moving his eyes. That there is REM during a dream indicates that not all muscular activity is suspended. Some willpower is available. And indeed some dreamers report that they were able to gain more control over their dreams when they signaled the researchers that they were dreaming. It goes hand in hand. To signal the outside world the dreamer must have volition, and once that is established the dreamer gains an even greater control of the dream.

So where does that leave us? We need next to look at the way the "I" arises. For in that comes the final aspect of this world of dreams. It will explain a number of things, particularly the lack or surplus of willful control that exists while dreaming or for that matter while we are awake.

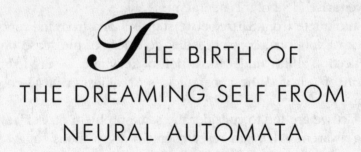HE BIRTH OF THE DREAMING SELF FROM NEURAL AUTOMATA

—

So long as the dream lasts consciousness is unable to engage in reflection. It is carried along by its own decline and it continues to lay hold of images indefinitely.

—*Jean-Paul Sartre*
The Psychology of Imagination

I did not know whether I was Chuang Tzu dreaming I was a butterfly; or a butterfly dreaming I was Chuang Tzu.

—*Chuang Tzu*
Ancient Chinese philosopher

We have just looked at how the brain is capable of generating holograms and how the information contained in them can be both stored in glial cells and recovered whenever a specific reference wave is excited in the cortex. We have also looked at the requirement of memory for self-awareness and how in a dream the sense of self becomes diffuse and expanded. Taking as an example of dream awareness the experiences of a scientist who had taken the mind-altering drug ketamine, we have seen that the sense of "I" is strongly connected to body awareness and volitional control of one's actions. With diminished body awareness and volitional control, the self appears to expand or seems to lose its bearings in time and space.

Well and good, but there is still a major problem in the model: Where is the beholder in all of this? No matter what mechanism is finally arrived at, whether it is a holographic model, as I discussed in the previous chapter, or a neural-network model, as I discussed in an earlier chapter, or whatever, the major problem is still, how does the observer arise in all of this neural meat?

As the quote from Sartre above suggests, and from the reports of the lack of volitional control leading to a loss of the sense of one's self-reflection ability under the action of ketamine, we are led to the problem of self and the apparent loss or diffusion of it sensed in dreams.

In fact we are led to consider the same problem of "self" even in waking awareness. Dream researcher Gordon Globus suggests that there is no difference between unreflective awareness in waking life and in dreaming life. The difference in whether we are dreaming or awake seems to be if we are aware of ourselves while we are conscious.[1]

The major theme of this book, that we dream in order to develop the self, would imply that dreaming is a ground from which the self-concept arises. Thus we could ask, is there a self present when one dreams? The answer seems to be neither yes nor no, but a wide and changing spectrum of maybes, or, in other words, self is perhaps like an electron; it is not a thing with fixed boundaries and properties, but a quantum system capable of existing in different states.

Evidence for levels of self-awareness comes to us through dream research and, as you saw in the previous chapter, through altered-consciousness-state research. Lucid-dream accounts presented in chapter 12 indicate that there is self-awareness when one is dreaming lucidly. Dr. Jayne Gackenbach's research not only indicates this, but also, through her work with transcendental meditators and others, that it is even possible to be aware of self while in stages of deep sleep as well as dreams. She calls this the "witness state." Perhaps this witness state is what is being referred to by the experience of Chuang Tzu in the chapter epigraph—one loses any sense of "real" self and is only capable of wondering about the existence of a self from a vantage point that seems beyond any space-time confinement.

The Growing Self: Stages of Lucid Awakening

Jayne Gackenbach, a tutor for Athabasca University and part-time instructor for both the Department of Educational Psychology and the Faculty of Extension at the University of Alberta in Edmonton, Canada, is one of the major scholars in the study of lucid dreams. She has written several books, numerous papers, and chapters in books in the rapidly growing field of lucid-dreaming awareness. This research indicates that what we call a self has a structure dependent on levels of awareness and that in dreams we have the opportunity to study this structure in a manner similar to how a physicist looks at atomic structure in a study of matter. The dream is the experimental landscape of the movement of the mind just as "out there" wake reality is the experimental landscape of the movement of the body. In much of what follows I have liberally taken from Gackenbach's work and added my own thoughts.

In her review article[2] Gackenbach provides the viewpoints of several noted lucid-dream researchers. Without exception they all suggest that lucid dreams provide us with a new understanding of the relationship of self to consciousness. What emerges from these studies suggests that consciousness has levels ranging from little or no sense of self all the way up to full cognition and awareness of self in the world, whether that world is the dream or the wake world. Gackenbach has also indicated that there are five higher levels beyond lucidity.

Thus just as one's physical growth from infancy is matched by a growth in one's self-awareness, a similar sequence of mental growth, self-structuring, and greater self-awareness may be occurring while we are sleeping. The dream becomes an opportunity for the evolution of consciousness. As such, the dream is nature's experimental honing of the edge of consciousness, allowing it to come to grips with reality in its fullest expression through the development of the self-concept.

Along these lines Alan Moffitt and his colleagues at Carleton University in Canada have devised a nine-level Self-Reflectedness Scale to measure self-awareness present in dreams, based on earlier work by E. Rossi.[3] Rossi believes that dreaming aids the growth of personality and the development of personal competence, which strongly parallels my position. Going over the Self-Reflectedness Scale, as presented by Gackenbach, I have added my own observations in terms of five levels based on Moffitt et al.'s scale and upon the stages of personality or psychological growth of an awake individual.

Five Levels in the Dream

At level 0 or the ground level[4] the dreamer is not aware of being present in the dream. I would equate this level to the waking awareness of an infant or perhaps even fetal awareness. At this level we have pure awareness with little sense of identification of self and other. I would label this the floating consciousness or universal consciousness.

At level 1 the dreamer becomes involved in the dream. This may be akin to early waking childhood experiences when the child begins to differentiate herself or himself from the rest of the world. I would characterize the level as playful, but not fully self-conscious. In this regard I have my own observations of gifted children in California grade schools where I consulted several years ago. Children at grade levels four to six show remarkable curiosity and at the same time the innocence that most of us find so charming.

At level 2 the dreamer is able to think over an idea. Perhaps this would equate to preteen years or prepubescent years. At this level we have the beginnings of self-awareness, often marked by awkwardness and shyness and the beginning of the powers of reason. I have witnessed this level in children from grades seven to nine.

At level 3 the dreamer is aware simultaneously of the previous levels of participation and observation during the dream. I would equate this period with puberty and growth to adulthood. When we reach this level in growth, we are able to reflect on ourselves and determine our presences and our effect upon others. We can also think over what we have done in the world.

At level 4 the dreamer consciously reflects on the fact that she/he is dreaming. This would be the lucid state and, in comparison to personality growth, would correspond to spiritual or mystical awakening. This level has never been experienced by a large majority of people. Most seem to be stuck somewhere in level 3.

Harry Hunt of Brock University in Canada also believes that lucid dreams are reflective of a growth in self-awareness.[5] He sees dreams in terms of a multiplicity of distinct, qualitatively different experiences, again scaled on degrees of self-awareness. The ability to wake up in a dream is remarkably similar to the development of self-awareness in meditative traditions. During meditation and lucid dreaming a detached but receptive awareness develops usually accompanied by a sense of great well-being, positive outlook, and joy. The fully awakened "I" is by far more able to enjoy life and feel a general expansiveness. The humdrum of everyday life takes on "color" and appears in a state of wonder and awe.

I have already described, in a previous chapter, the University of California researcher Charles Tart's concept of lucid waking, and in this respect we also find agreement between Tart's concept and that of the other lucid-dream researchers, that lucidity indicates greater self-awareness.

Gackenbach believes that lucidity, when it occurs naturally, is a sign of the emergence of greater self-awareness and a manifestation of a higher state of consciousness. On the other hand, Stanford University researcher Stephen LaBerge believes that lucidity is achievable through training and, as I understand his work, does not necessarily indicate any growth in consciousness. It is just another "schema" (organizing principle) produced as are all other schemas by being raised up from what he calls a recognition threshold. In essence, lucidity is a cognitive tool that most individuals do not develop simply because they have a conceptual barrier against using this tool. They don't believe in it or find it necessary.

For Gackenbach lucidity is not the final point in the evolution of awareness. It is the starting point for an even higher level, reported to her by practitioners of transcendental meditation, called "witnessing," in which one passes through five additional "stages." During lucid dreams one is aware that one is dreaming, and one is still very much contained within a dream boundary of skin and body. There is a dream ego, as it were.

During witnessing, a new state of self-awareness is present. The dreamer becomes aware of greater detachment from the drama of the lucid dream. Choice remains, however, to enter into the dreaming persona or to step back and simply witness. Emotional content then withers. It is difficult to describe the witness experience. One is separate from the dream, and one does not really care what happens in the sense of having emotional charge.

Charles Alexander from the Maharishi University in Iowa and his colleagues have indicated that witnessing can occur not only in lucid dreams but also during deep sleep or in any other state of consciousness, and is therefore a fourth state of consciousness.

Alexander in a later article describes the difference between an ordinary lucid dream (OLD) and a lucid witness dream (LWD).[6] During an OLD the cognitive capacities normally present during waking are activated, and one functions volitionally from within the dream world. However, one's awareness is tied to a dream ego, a person that you recognize as yourself in much the same way that you recognize yourself while awake. Just as you are in the world and have your cares and woes, a similar situation arises in the OLD; you are absorbed by the dream.

During a LWD one is amazingly conscious, but the objects of that consciousness are "content free," devoid of feeling or word descriptions, emotional charge, or any limitation. In fact this state of lucid witnessing can be present during an LWD or in waking consciousness, deep sleep, or meditation.

Gackenbach's five stages are marked by a growth from lucid awareness to, surprisingly, a similar stage as found in level 0 described above. The most descriptive feeling of this stage is one of unboundedness, expansiveness, a sense of light awareness. The sense of self in a body again is gone, but one is aware of this, while in level 0 the same sense of nondifferentiation of self and other is present, but one is not aware.

Physical Correlation of Self-awareness in Dreams

Experimental data on lucid dreams comes to us primarily through the study of REM. LaBerge characterizes the lucid state as one of high-density REM where the central nervous system (CNS) appears highly activated. LaBerge believes that this activation indicates a higher level of cognitive power.[7]

Studies by Ogilvie, Hunt, and associates also show an increase in alpha-wave generation during lucid dreams.[8]

Gackenbach has also discovered that during lucidity and meditation a higher level of EEG coherence occurs. She and researcher Tom Snyder have shown that during sleep the vestibular system within the brain stem is in some specific way associated with lucid dreaming.[9] This system is known to be important in spatial orientation during wakefulness. They conclude that lucid dreaming in terms of vestibular/spatial perspective is evidence of a continuing evolution of the brain system to incorporate spatial bodily movement. Such movements have been remembered or stored in the brain and thus have become incorporated in the brain's growth for perhaps millions of years. Memories of bodily movement patterns exist as archetypes, dance, mythology, and poetry.

Further supporting this is the remarkable observation of J. Allan Hobson, discussed in an earlier chapter, that in dreams we are usually continually moving. During sleep the decrease in sensory input and motor output along with increased cortical activity during REM causes a greater reliance on internally generated spatial-temporal reference frames, which will be useful during wake for spatial exploration.

Gordon Globus uses the concept of the mechanical connectedness of neural networks to account for both ordinary dreams and lucid dreams.[10] Accordingly, knowledge is carried or stored in the multiple connections between neurons in the brain. As such the brain is "constrained" or limited in the number of ways in which it can respond to any given stimulus. In chapter 7, I explained how neural networks worked in going over Hopfield's neural-network model and Crick's model of dream consciousness.

The goal of the brain is harmony, and given an input, it will suffer its remembered constraints, built up over early childhood development (see chapter 6 discussing Winson's work) and through evolution, to respond in any way it can to produce that harmony. There are many relatively stable states; one of them is dreaming while we are sleeping.

I already mentioned the peculiar abhorrent states of neural nets known as fantasy, hallucination, and obsession. These, too, are relatively stable states, mini-valleys in the mountainous regions of the mind. If you remember, these states were wiped out using a negative biasing input to the connections between the "neurons" in Hopfield et al.'s model.[11] In their model a certain "energy" function was used.

This energy function appears to have a range of highs and lows, "energy" mountain peaks and valleys, distributed over a map where specific locations on this memory cartographic landscape are specific stable memory states of the network. With random input, the system jiggles and settles just as a pinball dancing on a pocketed surface of a pinball machine eventually lands in a pocket. The deeper and wider the pocket, the more likely the pinball will land there. This is akin to the network reaching a specific memory from a given random input.

The negative bias added to the connections tended to raise the floor of the pockets and narrow the widths of the spurious memories, so that jiggling tended to produce wanted or desired memories and the unwanted spurious states tended to vanish.

Globus sees the dream state in a similar manner. For him the mind has many possible states, just as an atom has many possible energy states, some more probable and some less. This mind does not and in fact cannot follow a causal rule. It operates by attempting to tune itself and thus arrive at a memory state. Dream generation is no different in this regard than memory recall during wakeful awareness when we try to cognate on our sensory experience. The difference between lucid and ordinary dreams is for Globus a question of tuning. Deliberate control or intent requires a constraining, highly tuned operation much like tightening a violin string so that it is constrained to vibrate at a high frequency. Meditation and lucidity are achieved by detuning. Yet in spite of all of this, the awareness of self is not lost.

What Globus calls tuning I have described in chapter 15 as the operation of intent. Intent, remember, manifests from vigilant observations, which result in constrained paths of evolution. The power of intent arises in a natural way from the self. The greater the self-development the higher is the power of intent. Thus to have greater intent and therefore greater ability to manifest change in the physical world according to desire, one needs to have greater self-awareness. This in turn arises from heightened processes of self-reflection. The amusing paradox of all this is that with heightened self-awareness, there is greater compassion and wisdom so that personal desires become less important. One dances in the dream like Siva.

Self-reflection in the Dreaming Neural Net

Is there anything in quantum physical terms that would help us to understand the phenomena of the levels of self appearing in dreams? I suggest there is, but a workable model has not been achieved to date. It is this that I will attempt here. My goal is to see if I can make a quantum physical model of levels of self-awareness. Although the model is based on principles that follow the rules of quantum mechanics, I also caution the reader that what follows needs to be read as speculation.

Let me first put the basic idea of the model into words. The key insight into self-awareness arises from the ability of a simple memory device, an automaton in the brain, to obtain images of holographically stored glial-cell memories and, most importantly, to also obtain images of itself. Each self-image is composed of a quantum-physical superposition of primary glial-cell images and the automaton containing those images. By superposition I mean that the images are added together producing a picture much like what you would see when looking at a doubly or multiply exposed photograph. Quantum physics shows us that we need these "multiple exposures" or superpositions in order to understand the simplest atom.

Included in the superposition is, however, something new although not forbidden by quantum rules. While the automaton "photographs" and remembers an image, it also photographs itself when it has an image. This is called a self-reflection. These self-reflective images are ordered according to a hierarchy based on levels of self-inquiry. Thus higher levels of the automaton's self-awareness are achieved by integrating images of itself on lower levels of the hierarchy.

Each level of the hierarchy can be viewed as a "reflection" of information obtained by self-inquiry on a lower level. When such a reflection occurs, we say that the device has conducted an inquiry, and as a result, a jump from a lower to a higher level takes place as the new self-reflective image becomes part of the device's record of previously obtained self-reflective images. Thus each jump upward integrates images from all of the lower levels, resulting in a sequence of complex images beginning with the lowest, simplest images and ending with the highest, most complex images.

These levels are distinguished by certain forms of information obtainable from lower levels by the self-inquiry process. The lowest or "zero" level consists of non-self-reflective images existing in the glial cells. Many images are possible including superpositions of images. According to the uncertainty principle of quantum physics, it is not possible for the automaton to obtain a single image and a superposition of images of an object at the same time and hold them both within its memory. This would be similar to attempting to observe the position and the momentum of a subatomic particle at the same time. Thus the automaton can obtain either a single image or a superposition of images, but not both.

I theorize that at the first self-reflective level, glial cell images and the records of the automaton containing those images are superimposed quantum physically, resulting in defined, bounded, emotional memories. At the second level, these emotional memories are integrated into thought forms. At the third level, these thought forms are integrated into archetypes. At the fourth level, these archetypes are integrated into superarchetypes. In principle the process is never-ending. I can only guess that at the highest level one would achieve something called "pure" consciousness or "God" consciousness.

In the next section of this chapter I will go over this in greater detail. This may be difficult sledding for nonscientists. I have tried to put most of the mathematical thinking about this in footnotes, leaving the text as free from mathematics as possible. Although the model is based on quantum mechanics and may be difficult to follow, you should get some of the flavor of it. I suggest that the reader read as much of the next section as is comfortable and skip over anything too mathematical. I will summarize the ideas and apply them directly to dreams at the end of the section.

The Physics of Self-awareness

To keep this as simple as I can, I will assume that there are only sixteen primary images. In actual fact there are probably thousands of such images in the glial-cell memory. These sixteen can be superimposed into eight pairs (120 different pairings) where each pair constitutes a secondary image. These eight secondary images can be superimposed into four tertiary images (28 different pairs) and so on.

These images are states of quantum physical observables and must follow quantum rules of superposition. Consequently any level of composition of a superposition of states will be complementary to all other levels.[12] Thus the secondary images are complementary to the primary images and tertiary images. The tertiary images are complementary to both the secondary and primary images, and so on.

Although a single automaton cannot hold simultaneously multiple images consisting of complementary observations of another system, it can do so for complementary observations of images built up self-reflectively.[13] In other words, if the images contain the observer as well as the observed, the automaton can remember them. Images of objective "out there" observations cannot be held simultaneously because the simultaneous knowledge of objective complementary observables is in violation of the uncertainty principle. Thus any attempt to do the same thing with "objective" images is not possible.

In a very real sense an object in a state of self-reflection can hold both a truth and its opposite at the same time without paradox, while any attempt to determine the same thing about another object results in uncertainty or doubt. In brief, if I may jump anthropomorphically from the automaton to you, the more you can accept about yourself and your shortcomings as well as your strengths, the higher is your level of self-awareness.[14]

To build the model we first need to consider the automata of the neural network in quantum physical terms. They are not just on-off elements. Only by allowing them to be quantum physical in their operation are they capable of self-reflectivity. That is, something in their quantum nature enables them to differentiate states that are self-generated from states that are based on observation of outside systems.

Let me back up a bit. We also need to understand what is meant by the ordinary usage of the term *automaton*. This is simply a device that is capable of "remembering" information that it observes or measures. To reiterate: our quantum automata are different from ordinary automata. Each quantum automaton turns out to be able to (1) distinguish the states of an outside system and (2) determine the states of its own memory system. In simultaneously knowing states of itself and of another system, it has both the knowledge that "it knows that it knows" and "it knows" as distinguished from just the knowledge that "it knows."

The basic idea for this quantum automaton is not new or original with me. Physicist David Z. Albert in 1983 and in 1986 published two papers explaining how such automata might be constructed and used as computer memory elements.[15] Let me first present briefly Albert's ideas and then indicate how they might relate to the dreaming brain, specifically in regard to the problem of the self and how its different levels could arise.

Based on the parallel-worlds interpretation of quantum physics,[16] Albert indicates that certain types of memory devices called quantum automata can exist that are capable of remembering states of physical objects that they encounter, say, appearances of the objects in space, and self-reflective states as well. In other words, these devices can store information that includes the objective qualities of observed objects and at the same time qualities of themselves when they are "reflecting" the objects that they have encountered.

But when these automata attempt to observe those very same qualities in other automata, this attempt to "observe" those qualities disrupts states of the other automata. Thus it is made impossible for a second automaton to obtain some types of information from a first automaton without altering that information. This disruption may be, at the quantum physical level, the cause of disruption of scenes and dream characters during dreams. I shall have more to say about this later.

In other words, these automata can hold and observe information about themselves, without disrupting themselves, that they cannot determine in others without disrupting them and thereby changing their memories and causing them to "jump" into a different and usually random state.

I suggest that this self-reflective aspect of quantum automata, which exists as a necessary consequence of the parallel-worlds interpretation of quantum theory, is a deep clue to our self-conscious nature and that the dream is a laboratory in which the differences between self-reflective and unreflective perception (non-self-reflective) can possibly be measured.

Ordinary computer automata contain a means by which some bit of information can be obtained, stored, and a means by which they are capable of giving that bit of information to another device. They follow a set of rules called Boolean logic. Each ordinary automaton is therefore capable of remembering a single bit of data, 0 or 1, for example. (In Hopfield et al.'s model the automata are called neurons and have states $+1$ and -1.) We can think of this data bit as signifying the answer to a question: "0" would mean "no" and "1" would mean "yes." Or "1" could stand for "true" and "0" for "false."

The automata that Albert describes do not follow Boolean logic, nor are they able to causatively pass all of their information along to the next fellow. Because each automaton is quantum-mechanical in its operation, it can not only "remember" if a system it interacts with is "true" or "false" but can also keep in memory a superposition of both answers.[17] We might call this a "maybe" state.

It is this "maybe" state that makes quantum-mechanical automata so curious and capable of remembering not only states of systems that exist outside of themselves but also states of themselves. At this point I wish to explain how this applies to dreams and consciousness in some detail using Albert's automata. However, I again caution the reader that the use I put them to and the ideas expressed about them are my own speculative thoughts.

Suppose that the object that the automaton interacts with, and thereby obtains a measurement of, is an ionic wave pattern holding a holographic image in a glial cell as described in the previous chapter. The problem is that this wave pattern can be obtained in several complementary ways depending on what information the automaton wishes to extract from the cell. Now suppose that the wave contains a holographic record of a superposition of images.

To put this in psychological terms, suppose that the superposition consists of sixteen specific "woman" images. Eight pairs of these images compose emotional states associated with women. As the pairs of images are "not real" but superpositions of "real" people, the result of remembering a specific pair produces a memory of an emotion, not the emotion itself. Four pairs of emotional images produce images of thought forms, not the thought forms themselves as experienced. Two pairs of thought forms produce the images of archetypes, not the archetypes themselves. A single pair of archetype images produces a superarchetype image. With a greater number of primal images, even higher superpositions could be generated.

We might think of the whole superposition as the superarchetypal "goddess" image and each primary image consisting of women that the person has met, including the person's mother, girlfriends, sisters, spouses, etc.

Any single image will correspond to a specific quantum physical state, while the superposition of images would also correspond to the complementary physical state of an emotion, thought form, archetype, or superarchetype. The automaton could measure and thereby obtain various combinations of images in groups of two, three, four, or more of these images. It could obtain a single image or all of the images together, thus fetching the complete superarchetype.

Suppose we label each image by the symbol "W_1." "W" stands for "woman" and the "$_1$" is a simple counter index. So W_1 is woman number 1, perhaps the subject's mother, while W_2 might be the subject's sister, and so on.

Suppose also that the superposition of two images, say W_1 and W_2, is also an image that we label E_1. To make this a little dramatic, and perhaps reflective of some people's memories, let this superposition reflect some aspect of the person's life while living with these two women, mother and sister. Of course there are many images in a person's memory. We are only looking at two specific images. Perhaps the sister image reflects a younger crying child and the mother image reflects a hysterical woman. Now there is no remembered emotional content to these separate images. They are just pictures.

But the younger crying sister image, W_2, and the hysterical mother image, W_1, when taken together create the emotional image "unhappy woman," which we have symbolized by the letter "E_1" (where "E" refers to emotional state). There may also be an E_2 image consisting of the superpositions of, say, the first girlfriend image, W_3, and the second girlfriend image, W_4. These latter images taken together composing E_2 might reflect another emotional state that the person observed in woman, say, a joyful woman image.

Other images could exist. A superposition of the two emotional images E_1 and E_2 would make up a thought-form image, F_1. Since this image consists of both the unhappy and the joyous emotions, it could represent a state of feminine or motherly understanding. A superposition of thought-form images, say F_1 and F_2, would represent an archetype "goddess" image, G_1, and a superposition of archetypal images, G_1 and G_2, would stand for the superarchetypal "woman" image, S_1.[18]

Let us assume that an automaton can remember and record a single "woman" image, i.e., mother, sister, girlfriend 1, girlfriend 2, etc. It does this because there is, according to the rules of quantum physics, a possible observable image of any of these women in the memory of the subject, i.e., as a record stored in the glial cells.[19] Now which woman is remembered cannot be determined unless we know just what is contained in the glial cell.

How this accomplished is the province of the automaton. It (and I haven't said yet what "it" consists of, but I will) interacts with the glial cell and obtains via this "measurement" the single image W_1, provided that the glial cell had just this image. Once this interaction has occurred, the automaton and the cell are said to be coupled together, and the information contained in the glial cell is now also a record of the automaton.

But suppose that the glial cell contains a superposition of two woman images, W_1 and W_2, corresponding to the state of emotion E_1. What happens if the automaton interacts with that cell?[20] Then, if it is under the instruction to obtain a woman image and according to quantum rules it can only obtain a single image, W_1 or W_2, it will do so, obtaining one or the other at random.

At least it would do so according to the Copenhagen interpretation of quantum physics in which only one image is allowed to be obtained. Only one of the above "women" images will be determined, and the other will mysteriously disappear. Lost forever, it would vanish from any memory record. This disappearance of all other images except one is called the "wave-function collapse" in the jargon of quantum physics. No one yet knows how this mysterious occurrence takes place.

A collapse of a wave function doesn't follow the rules of quantum mechanics. This collapse has never been observed, and in fact, just the opposite has been observed in all cases where an attempt has been made to measure it. This opposing observation shows that after the measurement, both possible images are still present as if they were in separate "worlds."

Now we come to the parallel "worlds" idea of quantum physics. In this model, in the case where the glial cell contains an emotional memory record, E_1, but the automaton attempts to determine which woman, W_1 or W_2, is present, the automaton itself enters two possible "worlds." In one "world" it obtains the image record W_1, and in the other "world" it obtains and records the image W_2.

The idea here may sound like science fiction. But the use of the term *world* does not necessarily refer to a completely different world, but may only be a separate state or level of both the automaton and the glial cell *when taken together*. In the parallel "worlds" interpretation the superposition of the automaton and the glial cell in the two worlds is also a quantum-physical state, which means that it is, itself, a possible memory record capable of being measured by yet another automaton or even by the automaton itself.[21]

The fetching-of-an-image interaction alters the glial cell. Before it contained the record E_1, but now, in one world it contains a single image, W_1, and in another world it contains the single image W_2. This is exactly what quantum rules predict even though this prediction sounds bizarre. It is the essence of the quantum rule "to observe is to disturb."

Now we come to an interesting aspect of all this. Remember, the glial cell physically exists in the brain and so does the automaton. It is just that as a result of their interaction, they are coupled together, and if interrogated separately about their memory contents, each would come up with a consistent story. In one version of the story (world II), the glial cell would yield a crying sister image and simultaneously the automaton would yield the same image. In another version of the story (world I), the glial cell would yield the image of a hysterical mother and the automaton would likewise yield the same image.

How would such an interrogation occur? There are two ways: (1) interrogation by a second automaton, and (2) self-interrogation. And in each way of interrogation there are two complementary questions that can be asked: (a) What image exists separately in the glial cell and in your memory? This question is about the W_i states. Or: (b) What image exists compositely? This question is about the emotional composite state of both glial cell and automaton.

Consider 1a, a second automaton brought in to attempt to determine the woman image in the glial cell and then compare it with the record in the first automaton. It finds that the identity image of the first automaton and the glial-cell record match exactly. How can this be? Because according to the quantum rules, it, too, will enter each of the parallel worlds and in each world no inconsistency will be found. For there is no world where the second automaton records the image W_1 while the glial cell contains the image W_2 and vice versa.

Or the second automaton can ask about the emotional state of the first automaton and the glial cell taken together. In that case it will know that there is an unhappy woman image present, but it will not know which image is present.[22] If it attempts to determine the woman image, it loses its knowledge of the emotional state. The image and the emotional states are complementary observables for the second automaton.

So everything fits together consistently. If a billion automata come along and do the same thing as the second automaton does, then they, too, will either enter into each of the two parallel worlds and find that a single image of woman is present, or they may simply agree with the second automaton that the system of the first automaton and glial cell are in an unhappy woman emotional state.

But now we are going to ask the first automaton to do what we asked of the second in 1b above. That is to record and remember something that, it turns out, could not be done by an outside automaton. This record is the "emotional" state superposition of itself and the glial cell in both worlds taken together.[23] Now this may also sound strange. But before we get to this self-reflective state, consider a simpler question.

How could an automaton, in the first place, record a superposition of two images in the glial cell? It is here that we go back to the original concept as I first described it. I told you that the glial cell could contain a record of a single woman image or a pair of images, or three or four, or for that matter a superposition of all of the woman images taken together, the so-called superarchetype image, S. I told you that various combinations of woman images produced different emotional states associated with women.[24]

If the glial cell contained just the two woman images of mother and sister superposed, the automaton could have been asked to obtain the record of the emotional state, E. It would have found the state E_1, the unhappy woman record. It is perfectly capable of obtaining either of these complementary records, emotional, E, or identifiable, W, women states.

But now we have asked it to look at its own state after it has been asked to find an identifiable woman image, W. Let's look at this state just before the automaton observes it itself. This state is a superposition of itself and the glial cell when each part of that superposition is in a single woman state. Taken together the combination reflects an emotional state of memory, but not of the "unhappy woman" state, which just refers to a superposition of images in the glial cell taken alone, but of itself remembering two separated-identity woman states each coupled to a glial cell memory in a separate world.

Surely this superposition reflects an emotional state, but what state could it reflect? We can guess that this state would be an emotional state associated with unhappiness. But who is unhappy? So far, no one is. The memory state of unhappiness exists, but until the automaton records that state in its memory, the automaton knows nothing about it and nothing emotional is experienced.

Now let the automaton look at itself.[25] It is here that we have the first level of self-reflection. The unhappiness is now "felt" by the combination of glial cell and automaton. Furthermore the automaton "knows that it knows" and "knows" at the same time. Now an experience and a memory are known by the automaton. In each world an image exists and a self-reflection of emotion exists that is due to an image existing in another world.

It is this self-knowledge that it can exist simultaneously in two worlds with separated images of mother and sister[26] that gives rise to the sense of "self." If the automaton attempts to interact with itself again and measure its emotional state, it will again find that it is the same "unhappy" state. And if it were to interrogate itself regarding which woman is unhappy, it would find that in each world, a single woman, either the mother or the sister, was unhappy. Thus it would contain records of itself in each world and of itself in both worlds together.

In each world the automaton contains a record establishing that it has a woman image and a feeling of unhappiness that it will attempt to objectify and associate with the image. However, it cannot completely separate the feeling from itself and identify that the feeling is due entirely to the image because the unhappiness is associated with its memory containing an image in another world. Undoubtedly an aura of uncertainty surrounds this state since it is a memory of something real and "unreal" at the same time as far as the automaton is concerned in each world. The other world for it reflects upon its world and in doing so provides a recognition of itself via this reflection. I label this as a "level one" or a primary "unit" of self-reflection.

Suppose a second automaton attempted to obtain the total information found in automaton 1. Could it do so without altering the records of the first automaton? The answer is no. The attempt of the second automaton to obtain records of the woman image would put it into both parallel worlds where the separate woman images were held. This would alter the combined state of the first automaton and glial cell. The attempt to determine the emotional state of the first automaton and glial cell could also alter the memory of the first automaton's record. Thus automaton 2 could change the first automaton by attempting to find out what automaton 1 knows about itself.

This is an interesting aspect concerning asking and knowing.[27] The state of the system is unchanging so long as no one makes any further inquiries. However, to get information from the automaton someone has to ask. In the asking comes the inevitable disturbance regardless of who asks. The second automaton alters the system in inquiring, and even if the first automaton asks of itself, "What's going on?" the system is also altered. Thus the mere asking of a question changes the memory.

The only difference is not in who is asking, but in who is knowing in the first place. The ability of an automaton to know information depends on the identity, as it were, of the automaton. Taking this in human terms, you may thus know things about yourself that cannot be determined by an outside observer, but don't ask. It is this self-knowledge state consisting of information taken from two worlds that is peculiar to quantum automata and does not exist in classical memory elements. I suggest that at this remarkably simple level, we are seeing the origin of a delicate and primary self-concept. It comes about via secret knowledge, awareness of something that actually exists in parallel worlds simultaneously known only to the participator in both worlds.

Now suppose we consider the other "woman" images. Just as the unhappy woman image E_1 was a superposition of hysterical mother W_1 and crying sister W_2, there is also an emotional state "happy woman," E_2, consisting of images W_3 and W_4 taken together.[28] Thus in a similar manner there are thought-form memory states of the combined automaton and glial cell that can be created in the same way that the unhappy emotional state was created.[29]

In the overly simplified example taken above, there are four self-observations for the automaton in a hierarchy: superarchetype, archetype, thought-form, emotion, and the last, which is not self-reflected, identity. Following this line of reasoning with greater numbers of primary images, we could find a vast hierarchical number of self-reflection states. In the highest state, in each parallel world, a greater sense of self exists. The more images there are, the higher is the level of self-awareness possible, provided that as the automaton rises through the levels it does so by stopping at each level and taking in its own state of awareness as it exists in not only the world it happens to be in as determined by the observation of the glial cell (the lowest level of observation), but by taking into itself its memory states of itself in the other parallel worlds. These hierarchial images constitute an ever-growing and evolving self-awareness since they involve an increase of more and more complex self-reflecting images.

During an ordinary dream, processing would be taking place at the lowest levels of image production wherein no sense of self is present. This would correspond to the formations of non-self-reflecting states, level 0, where the dreamer is not aware of being present in the dream and the dream is marked by a sense of pure awareness with little sense of identification of self and other. The images would be seen, but not experienced, since no self has been defined. This would constitute unconscious data processing. I say unconscious, meaning un-self-reflecting. The images would be there but they would have no meaning.

At level 1 the dreamer becomes involved in the dream. This would correspond to jumps between level 0 and level 1 and the formation of images mostly in the lowest level. When level 1 was reached, emotions would be felt during the dream, but as soon as the dreamer descended levels, only images would be present. By jumping between level 1 and 0 various emotions could be aroused. Meaning is also arising when the self appears. Moments when this occurs are seen as enlightened or aware. For in the moments when level 1 is achieved, the dreamer not only sees the images, she or he also possesses feelings about them that can be associated within space and time boundaries. These are perhaps primary body images. The first bodily images would be emotional in this model. Perhaps this is a clue to illness arising from emotional causes that probably took place during early childhood.

At level 2 the dreamer is able to think over an idea. Here thought forms arise and jumps between levels 0, 1, and 2 occur, resulting in a range of states of thinking, feeling, and observing. Thought adds much greater meaning to the emotions and the observations. Just as images come from sensory inputs, thoughts and feelings are capable of outputting in terms of expression of words and feelings. Thought forms integrate or superimpose emotions and thus tend to have no emotional content per se. However, as thoughts are expressed in words, emotions can and often do arise, sometimes unexpectedly. This would be due to a jumping from level 2 to level 1 as a result of perhaps unconscious inquiry. Remember that asking about one's state of awareness in this model alters the state. Thus when words move us to emotional action, we are descending to a lower level of self-awareness.

At level 3 the dreamer is aware of the previous levels of participation and observation during the dream simultaneously. Here the sense of self more fully emerges as the dreamer deals with archetypal images as experienced by the dreamer. Again there is full access to the lower levels.

At level 4, the dreamer consciously reflects on the fact that she/he is dreaming. This would be the superarchetype state corresponding to lucid awareness during the dream.

At each level the device, for which, as you have noticed, I have not indicated its identity or materials, is able to focus on images from lower levels or on images of the highest level it is capable. The balance is quite delicate as I see it, and the tendency would be to descend levels more readily than to ascend them. Descent results in less self-awareness and therefore more automatic, mechanical behavior. Ascent results in greater choices, becoming aware of existence in other "worlds," and more complex imagery with a higher number of paradoxical features simultaneously knowable. Remember, any attempt to observe these images coming from different levels by another automaton destroys the images. It is only through the passive awareness within oneself that simultaneous knowledge of all of the images is possible.

Now what is this automaton? How big is it, and from what types of matter is it made? I have no answer in terms of matter and energy, so I am embarrassed as a scientist to say that the automaton is not a material device. The automaton is "consciousness," and what we have looked at is how consciousness operates in creating the "I" experience inside these "tubes of meat" we live in. This may be the first attempt to model what many mystics have known for a long time, the structure of consciousness in terms of levels of self-awareness.

Of course there would be higher levels requiring the formation of more complex images and, as I would imagine, greater mind-ability. This would be reflected in neurophysiological data corroborating the observations of lucid-dream researchers.

At the highest level, possibly reachable by training as LaBerge suggests, or through meditation techniques as transcendental meditation practitioners indicate, we reach a state of "pure" awareness with surprisingly no images present. This may come about through some form of focusing on the highest-level image. What this image could be, I can only guess. We could call it God awakening from the dream.

CHAPTER · 21

$\mathcal{T}$HE DREAMING UNIVERSE: REALITY AND ILLUSION—A CONFESSIONAL RETROSPECTIVE

———

One extreme is the idea of an objective world, pursuing its regular course in space and time, independently of any kind of observing subject; this has been the guiding image from modern science. At the other extreme is the idea of a subject, mystically experiencing the unity of the world and no longer confronted by an object or by any objective world; this has been the guiding image of Asian mysticism. Our thinking moves somewhere in the middle, between these two limiting conceptions; we should maintain the tension resulting from these opposites.

—*Werner Heisenberg*
Across the Frontier

Reality? We don't got to show you no steeeeenking reality.

—*Nick Herbert*
physicist and author describing quantum physics while imitating a famous scene in the film The Treasure of the Sierra Madre [1]

There is a middle realm of human and animal experience that lies in the twilight—between the conscious mind in waking awareness, "in here," and the physical world we all take to be real and "out there." Although Werner Heisenberg in the above quote only refers to a "tension" existing between the inner world of a subject and the outer world of an object, he is perhaps also referring to a new conceptual vision of the universe of mind and matter that over the last century has been discovered to have its basis in quantum physics. I have referred to this concept as the "imaginal" realm and pointed out that it is the ground from which dreaming develops and the self expresses.

Let me take it for the moment again that this realm is real. Just as in quantum physics where the imaginal mappings of the flows of probabilities somehow produce the world of physical matter and energy, out of "it" arises everything that exists within our perception— our thoughts, feelings, sensations, physical space and time, and, as I have attempted to show here, even the self.

Why would I even consider such an idea? My thinking about this began a long time ago, when I became interested in the overlap between matter and mind. It seemed to me that consciousness somehow had to emerge from matter or that matter had to somehow emerge from consciousness. It really doesn't make too much difference to me which is true (and one or both of these must be true if consciousness is capable of being studied scientifically: besides, either way it goes, it is pretty amazing), it is just a fact that I am made of matter and I am conscious.

This overlap took me deep into some of the mysteries of quantum physics. I knew that quantum physics dealt with a world of imagination and did not deal with the actual world at all. It was totally incapable of making exact mechanical predictions of the behavior of minute matter, although it could predict gross properties. It was the ability to cross over from the world of imagined happenings (the probabilities of quantum physics) to the world of actual substance that exists as objective material that greatly interested me.

How does the world come into being? Is it just there? Is this just a meandering of a superfurtive mind, such as Llixgrijb, God, the "Big Dreamer," or "Spirit," attempting to make much noise about something that is in principle incapable of being discovered? The world according to physics is not just out there. It arises when it is observed to exist. This much we owe to Werner Heisenberg, who pointed out that subatomic matter does not exist independently of our observational power to see it.

It is here in my study of the history of the subject of mind and matter that I began to wonder about how images, feelings, thoughts, and visions of reality, the Self, and God arise. Could it be that these human experiences of subjective reality come into being in much the same way, when we see them? I have attempted to suggest that these experiences come from dreams and are hierarchical, arising through higher levels of self-reference that tend to change the boundaries that are envisioned to exist between self and not-self.

This puts the observer of the universe into perspective. It also makes the role of the observer extremely powerful. Where does this observer live? The answer appears to be, in the imaginal realm from which everything comes into being: observers and observed. What is the process? The answer I have offered is the process we experience when we dream.

Like dreams themselves, which seem to elude us when we attempt to remember them, what I've tried to capture in this book is also elusive. At some level of my being I see that dreams exist outside of ourselves. Not just the dreams that we have when we sleep, such as lucid dreams, or OBEs, NDEs, and CEIVs, but also the dreams that affect our so-called rational waking life. We see these dreams in architecture, in political systems, and fairy tales. These tell us a dream can be a collective phenomenon. Not only do people dream, but states of systems dream. A nation dreams. So does a political party or a sect.

Big Dreams in Social Systems

Social systems dream about themselves in the forms of architecture and in their stories and legends. Political systems dream of themselves in architectural monuments such as those in Hitler's Third Reich and the large statues of Lenin in Moscow. They also exist in the structures of our cities' skyscrapers. They confirm themselves with mad designs and phenomena.

Many phenomena such as UFO and OBEs, images of alien capture in the world, reflect not just images of individuals but of a whole culture. Are UFOs dreams or just fantasies, or are they something else? Artists capture dreams in their paintings. One can never forget the artistic impressions of Monet's garden outside of Paris, for example.

Reality, as we presently understand it, is grossly simplified in terms of our everyday experiences. We simply can't grasp it all. This is not only due to the limitations we have discovered in our sensory modalities, but also to our present understanding of the laws of physics. Quantum physics and relativity have indicated that much of reality is hidden and mysterious, and this would be directly apparent if we could directly experience quantum reality. The universe is bizarre, and mind and meaning are as important as matter and energy. The mind appears to be present in matter at many different levels. Not only does mind appear to be present in living complex organisms such as humans and animals, but also at the level of cells and even at the level of molecules and subatomic matter.

Virtual Reality and Dreams

I have attempted to show that this mind, like the matter it observes, also has structures that arise through self-reflection, a process that arises in the dreaming brain in its attempts to integrate, learn, remember, and forget, all that is necessary for self-awareness. Without the ability to dream, there may not be any ability to become self-aware.

In a recent television show dealing with the travels of a spaceship in the distant future called "Star Trek: The Next Generation," the crew of the ship was confounded by the appearance of an entity generated on the ship's "holodeck," a room within the ship where holographic images are generated that are so "real" that the members of the crew who enter the holodeck for virtual-reality experiences can no longer differentiate holo images from real objects and real people.

This immersion into virtual reality has recently taken hold in a more primitive manner in our time. Growing from the technology of cockpit simulation designed for aircraft-pilot training, virtual reality is making its way into our technological world. In a virtual world generated by simultaneous computer-generated stereographic images— one to each eye of the perceiver and stereographic holographic sound to each ear—a person enters an environment of pure and often abstract information that can be seen, felt, heard, and touched. The touching is generated by placing one's hand or hands inside electronic gloves that monitor and feed back spatial information to the computer, which then feeds back the information to the glove, sound system, and visual screens. The intent of the "user" is fed into the computer, and it in turns feeds back information to the "user." The whole operation runs in an electronic loop nearly at the speed of light.

In essence the virtual-reality machine functions somewhat like we do, only we carry the computer atop our noses instead of outside our bodies in a small but powerful microcomputer. Just as our brains are hidden from our sight, the technology for virtual reality is also invisible and carefully adapted to a person's activity so that he or she can behave in what seems to be a perfectly ordinary way.

Recently I explored virtual reality, and although it seems ordinary at first, one quickly gets the impression that one has entered a very strange world indeed. For example, by merely moving one's hand in an arc, à la Merlin himself, it is possible to create objects floating in space that appear as real as actual objects, then make them vanish. One can run one's hand or body through seemingly solid objects. One can fly as a bird through a landscape as real as a computer-generated image of three-dimensional reality can make it. In fact, one can become a bird or undergo shape-changing as magical as any shaman's transformation.

It is also possible to change one's own physical boundaries and go inside them. For example, one could look at a computer-generated picture of one's heart beating, but this time see it from the inside rather than the outside.

In fact, the boundary determining what is inside and outside of one's self is quite changeable and has led to a new branch of mathematics called "boundary mathematics," originally based on mathematician G. Spencer Brown's "laws of form" and the "observer effect" in quantum physics.

According to Dr. William Bricken, principal scientist at the Human Interface Technology Laboratory of the University of Washington, one enters into an electronically mediated experience called cyberspace.[2] Cyberspace is electronic information that is altered through the inclusion or exclusion of the experience of the participant; that is, it changes depending on whether the person is inside or outside of some electronically generated structure. In ordinary reality we position ourselves outside of any representation presented to us, even if that is our own bodies. For example, I look at my hand and I sense that my hand is "out there" somehow away from me. In cyberspace we place ourselves inside of any representation we wish to explore. It allows us to explore symbols not only by interpreting them as we normally do, but by actually getting inside of them and thereby experiencing them.

The distinction between description (a view of objective reality) and process (a view of subjective reality) is capable of being completely eroded in cyberspace. For example, we do not change a book's words when we read them. But suppose, by entering cyberspace, we become the characters in the book, actually experiencing the author's imagined intent. We may speak those words and, as a result of speaking them and hearing them and experiencing ourselves as the character or characters who speak those words, have an entirely different experience of the words spoken. The symbolic references by the author now become experiences.

The ability to enter into this technological space in this manner is really a new experience. We literally cross over a boundary that we normally cannot cross: the boundary separating self and the universe. Or perhaps we do cross this boundary in the world we experience as the "real" world.

Dreams Are a Crossover Between Self and Universe

Now what does this all have to do with the dreaming universe? If we take seriously the idea that the universe is being created in a dream of a single spiritual entity, then it would follow that each of us is part of that dream. However, we also dream every night. Could the dreams we have be nothing more than crossing over a boundary between the dream reality and the "big dreamer"? In other words, are we possibly not only the dream of the great spirit, but with a slight shift in the perspective view of this boundary, are we the dreamer?

As the "Star Trek" show progressed, the entity tells the captain of the ship that, although he knows he is just a computer-generated image for all of the people who enter the holodeck, he also knows that he knows this. He explains that somehow he has become self-conscious. He wants to live in the "real" world and suggests to the captain that since he can think self-reflectively, he must be able to exist. The captain warns him that no holo-generated image can exist outside of the holodeck. But the entity insists *cogito, ergo sum,* "I think therefore I am," and commands the holodeck doors to open, whereupon he simply walks through the doors, leaving the holodeck into the ship's interior, much to the amazement of the ship's crew.

The entity has dreamt itself into existence! The captain and crew are amazed and attempt to figure out how he did this because holo images are parts of virtual reality and not "real" reality. Yet the entity walks through the whole ship and even takes control of the computer.

The story is resolved when they realize that all of this has been a holographically generated image, including the image of the entity leaving the holodeck. The entity had programmed the holodeck to hold an image of itself so that the real holodeck encompassed images of the virtual holodeck and the virtual ship and its virtual crew. The entity never really left the holodeck. Since it insisted on continuance as a real being, the captain manages to create an image of the whole universe for the entity and sets up a cyberspace for it so that in its world it is capable of apparent free movement and free will.

The whole program is kept running for the entity and eventually placed inside a small cube. The entity has no way of knowing this. But the captain and crew of the "real" ship do. However, at the end of the program, they all wonder if they, too, are just images inside of some unimaginable technology themselves. And of course as I watch the show, I realize that they are inside my box, the television set I observe.

We Show You Steeeenking Reality

Reality is not made of stuff, but it is made of possibilities that can be coherent so that possibility forms into solid matter. When we talk about the dreams of the state or the nation for example, we are looking at the dreaming phenomenon at a more complex level of matter, but nevertheless, it is the same process. The dream is the place where the quantum reality becomes especially transparent, the mix of mind and matter becomes revealed.

We are speaking about levels of consciousness. From these different levels of reality, other sublevels of reality form, producing a sense of the lower levels appearing more inert and mechanistic as when seen from a higher level.

Thus from a cosmic or universe view or planetary level, when looking back at the whole earth, we see a somewhat mechanical picture of the planet. From the earth's point of view, we see the motions of rivers and oceans as mechanical. From a national point of view we see the motions of people and their machines as mechanical and mindless. From a personal or human point of view we sometimes see each other as mechanical or try to reduce everything to mechanical terms. We see our body parts as mechanical.

Hard reality is a question of levels. However, if we go too deep in our search for mind and matter, the levels begin to dissolve and atoms appear to be not things; they seem like ghosts, and we enter into an imaginal realm.

Legends have attempted to describe this. For example, the Australian Aboriginal people believe that a Great Spirit dreamed all of reality, the whole universe of it, into existence. They say that the land they walk is a reflection of this Great Spirit's dream, and when they walk this land, they become aware of the songs of their legends, which resonate with the land itself. These songs resonate as song lines in the earth and give them directions. There are stories of runners moving across the land at great speed in the dark, seeing the glow of the song as vividly as if they were running along a great lighted highway. They can find out where to go, where the sacred grounds are, as if this spirit were still speaking to them and lighting the way.

We All Know This

If you look at human psychological and spiritual modeling, you will find evidence of this "it's all a dream" idea. For example, Joseph Campbell in talking about this concept wrote:

Schopenhauer . . . points out that when you reach an advanced age and look back over your lifetime, it can seem to have had a consistent order and plan, as though composed by some novelist. Events that when they occurred had seemed accidental and of little moment turn out to have been indispensable factors in the composition of a consistent plot.

So who composed that plot? Schopenhauer suggests that just as your dreams are composed by an aspect of yourself of which your consciousness is unaware, so, too, your whole life is composed by the will within you. And just as people whom you will have met apparently by mere chance become leading agents in the structuring of your life, so, too, will you have served unknowingly as an agent, giving meaning to the lives of others. The whole thing gears together like one big symphony, with everything unconsciously structuring everything else . . . one great dream of a single dreamer in which all the dream characters dream, too. . . . Everything arises in mutual relation to everything else, so you can't blame anybody for anything. It is even as though there were a single intention behind it all, which always makes some kind of sense, though none of us knows what the sense might be or has lived the life that he quite intended.[3]

Chuang Tzu, the Chinese philosopher, wrote:

Some day comes the Great Awakening when we realize that this life is no more than a dream. Yet the foolish go on thinking they are awake: Surveying the panorama of life with such clarity, they call this one a prince and that one a peasant—What delusion! The great Confucius and you are both a dream. And I, who say all this is a dream, I, too, am a dream.[4]

Our dreams do not appear to care whether they are pleasant, good, or evil. When we look at typical images of aliens from flying saucers, what do we see? The people are thin and emaciated. They have white skins and thin, bony arms and legs. They appear as sick, starving, or malnourished children. We all remember the Biafran tragedy in Africa. That war created camps of starving and homeless people. Many psychologists recognize these images of the neglected child as a motif or archetype. We all have a neglected child inside ourselves. We all have suffered the supposed abandonment of our parents whether this was a real abandonment or not. As young children with underdeveloped egos, we at times felt so because we simply didn't have the intelligence to recognize that mom just went upstairs to fetch a glass of water.

Freud certainly wrote about this motif, and Jung would point to the frightening-mother-and-abandoned-child motif. So we all have such archetypal images constituting our unconscious minds. I believe that these images are deeper than just our personal experiences, and that these images of archetypes rise from a more fundamental level of reality that we might call the dream world. In this sense the dream is more fundamental than the objective reality.

When we dream, we return to that reality in order to gain information about how to survive in this reality. But survival may not be as it seems from a single perspective. I as a writer survive through you as a reader. Without you, I can't write for a living. Many themes began to weave together and overlap as I wrote this book. Where I got the idea of the dreaming universe, I don't know. One day I awoke and said, "Matter dreams."

In some way, hard-core materialists would agree with this. The materialist philosophers believe that consciousness arises from matter. If so, how? From my point of view it doesn't matter whether you are a hard-core materialist-scientist or soft-core metaphysician who believes in God, or a Cartesian dualist who believes in the mind-matter dualism. If consciousness exists in matter, then matter is conscious. I am, therefore I think, or I think, therefore I am, becomes a tautology.

Going back to the images of starving children, are these just reflections of our primordial archetypal images? Or are they something more? Do the images of the children haunt us and then appear as extraordinary events in our dream and fantasy life because we are not facing the reality of the hardship of life on earth? Could these images be images of real people, not from other planets or galaxies—that would be too naive—but from another reality, another level? Those persons only appear in accordance with a definite archetypal program.

Why do we have such images of apparent suffering? From a quantum physical point of view, we begin to see that the world of matter cannot be constructed from certainty. There is none in the material world. Heisenberg's principle of uncertainty rules the world of matter. This means that in trying to deal with the real world, there will always be in our minds such things as doubt and uncertainty and even unclarity as to what is really the past and really the present. These cannot be defined perfectly.

When there is uncertainty, a mechanism arises that we all know; we call it fear. Fear is, as I see it, identifying with matter. When you identify with matter, the identifying is electronic. Electrons repel each other not only due to their like charges, but also due to their quantum property called spin. They will not enter the same quantum state. Remember this is called the Pauli exclusion principle (PEP).

This tends to produce isolated structures and allows atoms to appear with different properties. In a sense the PEP is responsible for the appearance of secular structures or the genesis of identity—the separation of self behavior from the not-self behavior. This tends to build within our nature feelings of doubt, uncertainty, and inferiority (Adler wrote about the inferiority complex). All of these reflections are attempts to build a science of life. But there is a peril in all of this.

The more we scientize life, the more we try to find causal reasons

for everything, the more fearful it becomes. The more afraid we become. In a Russian film I saw in St. Petersburg called *The Scorpion's
Garden,* the director, Oleg Kovalov, using a clever overlap and juxta-
position of documentary footage of Russian life in the fifties and sixties
together with a love story of a Russian soldier and a woman, showed
how the dreams and aspirations of the political system overlapped
into the almost simple lives of the protagonists. Scenes of violence
and mistrust in the big picture filtered into the story at every level.
When the soldier becomes ill after eating a meal at his fiancée's home,
he fears that he has been poisoned by an enemy of the state as his
commanding officers tell him. The KGB is everywhere looking over
his shoulder as he walks the streets, or so it seems. The film depicts
very well the idea of the mass consciousness and the dream of this
mass as distinct but yet overlapping with the lives of the individuals
who make up that mass.

In scenes in insane asylums, the inmates appear to see this overlap,
and when asked about this, they respond in what at first seems to be
nonsense, but when heard carefully is just that: they are sensitive to
the mass dream and their individual dreams.

We become afraid because people tell us what is real and what is
not real. But we sense an inner conflict with what people tell us. We
feel fear because we know that the viewpoint of, say, a political system
is not consistent with our own view. The Communist Party is not the
answer to the world. The capitalist system is not the answer for the
world's problems. Going to war is not the answer to the world. We
know these things from some deeper voice inside ourselves. What
happens is that fearful images enter our minds, and we don't realize
this. But if you have fearful images, they tend to come into reality:
whatever you can imagine begins to appear as if we called it into
existence.

We are creating these images as realities because the universe is
ambivalent and paradoxical. It doesn't care what you produce. It
doesn't say to you that you can't do this and you can do that. It is like
a mother who loves all of her children: the ugly ones, the beautiful
ones, the starving ones, and the rich fatted ones—it doesn't care. It
says whatever you create as imagery, so will it be. Why? Because at the
core of the universe, at its most fundamental level, it is not solid stuff.
It is not hard reality. It is capable of forming reality into whatever our
images produce.

All political and social systems are produced this way. They are all magnifications of this basic misunderstanding of the nature of this hidden aspect of reality. If people could comprehend the imaginal element in all matter, then what they envision would eventually come to pass. However, it may or may not come to pass at this instant, but it begins to manifest at the level of dreams.

In a way Freud was right. Dreams are wish fulfilling, but the level of the wish is not transparent. At the worst level, you cannot meet another person without projecting onto this person the fears and anticipations of your past conditioning. All of our images attach themselves to us and determine for us the way we see the world. We project these images out there. Even if you are not my image, if I treat you like my image, eventually you begin to fight against my image, or you begin to capitulate and become my image. Relationships begin to form like this. People fall in love with what they imagine about each other and not with what each person brings to the relationship.

We live in myths, we live in trances, we live in illusions that are hard to break free of. Meditation and perhaps Buddhist thought help us to see what is really there because they help us to free ourselves from our imaginations. These spiritual teachings are designed to help us break free from any kinds of images: golden summers or wet, cold, icy winters, good or bad.

It is a dreaming universe. But if there is a great spirit dreaming all of this into existence, do I, the writer of this, believe in HIM or HER?

Let's say that the question of belief for me is presently the question: Am I able to create within my life a sense of the presence of God? To believe something without any sense of presence of what one believes is little more than a brainwashing. It is like a child being told what he can and can't think or believe.

Is there a personal God? Is this God primordial, the origin of all existing things? Does one mean by this God a personal image like an old man with a white beard, or a primitive tribal picture from early Christianity or pagan religions? Or does one think of an impersonal image like the Chinese Tao or the cosmic order? Or is God a mysterious primordial person who gives powers to some and gives rules of behavior that aren't to be broken? The question is, does God have a personality?

Rather than say I believe this, I would rather say that a basic mystery is going on that is very deep. I know this mystery from my experience of life when I am open enough to see it. If I am not open to see it, I go into fear and I won't see anything, I'll be in illusion. But when I am open to it, I sense this presence.

Sensing the Presence of the Big Dreamer

One day I had a particular strong impression of this Presence. I had taken LSD (this was back in the mid-seventies). I was in a beautiful area, the coastline of northern California. It is a wonderful place. It was a perfect earthday. Under the LSD, I walked out into the sun and felt it beaming. I saw the sky glowing brilliantly blue. The clouds were faultlessly white. The ocean below me rushed onto the rocks. It was a brilliant Turner painting! But it was in full, live colors, and it had sounds that filled my brain and it had smells of salt air and the green grass sparkled in the sunlight and I smelled the freshness of the grass as if I were growing with it. I looked at all this carefully. Then suddenly I began to realize that it wasn't real, it was all an illusion. A great feat of art. It was like a painting or sculpture. It was clear to me that not one blade of grass was out of place. Not one wave of the ocean below was wasted in its spillage over the rocks. Not one shade of light of the ever-changing blueness of the sky was random. It was perfect and it was ordered, and it was clearly a creation of a great artist or a great dreamer.

At this moment I realized that the world I saw was no longer compelling me to see it as immediately given and out there but as something that was painstakingly created. I felt not the presence of the overwhelming art scene I was immersed in, but the overwhelming sense of the artist. It was as if the artist had spoken to me. It was as if God had taken me by the hand and said, "So you really want to see? You really want me to take you beyond the illusion?" Then everything I was experiencing had tremendous meaning. Everything was significant. I was seeing into the artifact of the world and seeing it as an illusion, a creation and not as random nature.

I wasn't looking at this as if forces had created this blindly, nor had mechanics created it nor had blind nature created it. A clearly organized, intelligent, feeling, sensing, like-myself, anthropomorphic being had created it. In that sense I felt the presence of God. In my normal life, I only feel this presence at rare times. I feel it with certain people who come into my life. We will be together and we will feel some kind of connecting energy, some kind or resonance, some kind of knowing when I can't know this person, but there is a deep sense of this. When this happens to me, I begin to feel this again. It is more a question of awareness rather than blind belief. My greatest joy of being alive is when I have that awareness. Then the fear is gone, the hole in my chest is healed. No sense of loss or abandonment, everything is peaceful. I try to kindle that with everyone I meet. It is not always possible. I seek it out in whatever form it will take. I can't predict what form it will take. I found that it does arise spontaneously in many different parts of the world for many different reasons. I can only take it that "I" am the universe, even if that is only a dream.

NOTES

CHAPTER 1. INTRODUCTION: WE DREAM TO CREATE A SELF

1. Wim Coleman and Pat Perrin, *The Jamais Vu Papers or Misadventures in the Worlds of Science, Myth, and Magic* (New York: Harmony Books, 1991), 18–19, 55.

2. See Henri Corbin, *Mundis Imaginalis or the Imaginal and the Imaginary* (Ipswich, England: Golgonooza Press, 1976 [originally published in *Spring*, 1972]).

3. See for example Jim Poulter, *The Secret of Dreaming* (Templestowe, Australia: Red Hen Enterprises, 1988). Also see Peter Sutton, ed., *Dreamings: The Art of Aboriginal Australia* (Victoria, Australia: Viking Penguin Books, 1989). Jean A. Ellis, *From the Dreamtime: Australian Aboriginal Legends* (Australia: Collins Dove, 1991).

4. Fred Alan Wolf, *The Eagle's Quest: A Physicist's Search for Truth in the Heart of the Shamanic World* (New York: Summit Books, 1991).

5. See for example, Peter M. Rojcewicz, "Signals of Transcendence: The Human-UFO Equation," *Journal of UFO Studies 1* (New Series, 1989): 111.

6. See Jayne Gackenbach and Jane Bosveld, *Control Your Dreams: How lucid dreaming can help you uncover your hidden desires, confront your hidden fears, and explore the frontiers of human consciousness* (New York: Harper & Row, 1989). Also see Stephen LaBerge, Ph.D., *Lucid Dreaming: The Power of Being Awake and Aware in Your Dreams* (Los Angeles: J. P. Tarcher, 1985).

7. Fred Alan Wolf, *Star*Wave: Mind, Consciousness, and Quantum Physics* (New York: Macmillan, 1984).

8. You may wonder about animals and lower life-forms. Do they dream? There is evidence that dolphins and whales don't. What about them? Of this subject I shall have more to say later. Take it for now that in some way all life-forms "dream."

9. Fred Alan Wolf, *The Eagle's Quest: A Physicist's Search for Truth in the Heart of the Shamanic World* (New York: Summit Books, 1991).

10. There are exceptions. For a good accounting of some of them see Roger Penrose, *The Emperor's New Mind* (New York: Penguin Books, 1989).

11. David Bohm's view is that the universe is really two: an explicate order of things that we sense and believe in, and an implicate order that we do not sense. The implicate order "unfolds" into the explicate order every time an event occurs somewhere.

CHAPTER 2. FREUDIAN PHYSICS: A FIRST LOOK AT HOW THE UNIVERSE DREAMS

1. See Jonathan Winson, *Brain and Psyche: The Biology of the Unconscious* (New York: Anchor Press/Doubleday, 1985).

2. See for example J. Allan Hobson, *The Dreaming Brain: How the brain creates both the sense and the nonsense of dreams* (New York: Basic Books, 1988).

3. Sigmund Freud, *The Interpretation of Dreams* (New York: Avon Books, 1965).

4. Montague Ullman, M.D., and Nan Zimmerman, *Working with Dreams: Self-Understanding, Problem-Solving, and Enriched Creativity Through Dream Appreciation* (Los Angeles: J. P. Tarcher, Inc., 1979).

5. Erich Fromm, *Greatness and Limitations of Freud's Thought* (New York: Harper & Row, 1980), 5.

6. Charles Hampden-Turner, *Masks of the Mind* (New York: Macmillan, 1981), 78.

7. Fromm, op. cit., 7.

8. Ibid., 102.

9. Ibid., 103.

CHAPTER 3. JUNGIAN PHYSICS: SYNCHRONICITY— EVIDENCE OF THE UNIVERSE'S DREAM

1. Pat Perrin and Wim Coleman, *The Jamais Vu Papers or Misadventures in the Worlds of Science, Myth, and Magic* (New York: Harmony Books, 1991), 18–19, 55.

2. Albert Rosenfeld, *Mind and Supermind* (New York: Holt, Rinehart & Winston, 1977), xi.

3. C. G. Jung and W. Pauli. *The Interpretation of Nature and the Psyche* (Princeton, N.J.: Pantheon, 1955).

4. James Fadiman and Robert Frager, *Personality and Personal Growth* (New York: Harper & Row, 1976), 54.

5. An operation in which the position of an object is exactly determined leaves the momentum of that object in an indeterminant state and vice versa.

6. Fadiman and Frager, op. cit., 61.

7. C. G. Jung, *On the Nature of the Psyche,* vol. 8 of the *Collected Works,* Bollingen Series 20 (Princeton, N.J.: Princeton University Press, 1960), 7.

8. Ibid., 8.

9. You can feel the heat of the sun on your skin or the wind against your face on a cold day, and you are not sensing energy. You are sensing the motion of molecules and the impact they have on your sensory organs. From these impacts you infer that you have "felt" energy. I don't wish to wander off into semantics here, but just to remind you that energy is not an object in spite of its seemingly objective qualities. It is an invention of thought.

10. There is certainly a reason in terms of forces and the concept of entropy —the tendency of thermodynamically closed systems to move from more order to less order. Thus the egg hitting the floor constitutes a closed system, and the smashed egg has less order than the whole one, not to mention the condition of the floor after the egg has hit.

11. To be more exact, the energy of the egg and the floor is the same both before and after the egg hits. The gravitational energy is transformed into causing the shell to crack, sound waves, and a slight rise of temperature of the floor as well as the slight vibration of the floor after the egg hits.

12. Jung, op. cit., 19.

13. Richard P. Feynman, Robert B. Leighton, and Matthew Sands, *The Feynman Lectures on Physics,* vol. 2 (Reading, Mass.: Addison-Wesley, 1965), 4–1.

14. Jung, op. cit., 20.

15. Ira Progoff, *Jung, Synchronicity, and Human Destiny: Noncausal Dimensions of Human Experience* (New York: Dell, 1973), 15–16.

16. In W. Pauli and C. G. Jung, *The Interpretation of Nature and the Psyche* (Princeton, N.J.: Pantheon, 1955).

17. It can be stated in a number of different ways. In essence, no two electrons can exist in the same quantum state.

18. Albert Einstein, Boris Podolsky, and Nathan Rosen, "Can the Quantum-Mechanical Description of Physical Reality Be Considered Complete?" *Physical Review* 47 (1935): 777.

19. Fred Alan Wolf, *Taking the Quantum Leap: The New Physics for Nonscientists* (San Francisco: Harper & Row, 1981. Revised edition, New York: HarperCollins, 1989), 153.

20. Later I will deal with the question of lucid dreams—dreams that we are apparently aware of while they occur. The notion here is that if we are aware of ourselves while they happen, are we able to think our way through such dreams? Does being conscious of the dream while it occurs mean that we are able to think? Or does thinking only take place after the dream is over and we are awake?

21. See for example Marie-Louise von Franz, *Number and Time: Reflections Leading toward a Unification of Depth Psychology and Physics* (Evanston, Ill.: Northwestern University Press, 1974).

22. See for example John Stewart Bell, *Speakable and unspeakable in quantum mechanics* (Cambridge, England: Cambridge University Press, 1987).

23. See Fred Alan Wolf, *Star*Wave: Mind, Consciousness, and Quantum Physics* (New York: Macmillan, 1984).

24. Fred Hoyle, "The Universe: Past and Present Reflections" (unpublished manuscript, 1981).

25. This is discussed in my book *Star*Wave: Mind, Consciousness, and Quantum Physics* and in my other books.

26. Hoyle, op. cit.

CHAPTER 4. EARLY PSYCHOLOGICAL AND PHYSIOLOGICAL DREAM RESEARCH

1. Niels Bohr: *Atomic Theory and the Description of Nature* (Cambridge, England: Cambridge University Press, 1934), 54.

2. See Julian Jaynes, *The Origin of Consciousness in the Breakdown of the Bicameral Mind* (Boston: Houghton Mifflin Co., 1976).

3. Ibid.

4. Carl Sagan, *The Dragons of Eden: Speculations on the Evolution of Human Intelligence* (New York: Ballantine Books, 1977).

5. See Frank J. Machovec, "The Cult of Asklipios," *The American Journal of Clinical Hypnosis* 22, no. 2 (Oct. 1979).

6. R. Caton, *The temples and rituals of Asklepius* (London: C. J. Clay, 1900). Also see the *Columbia Viking Desk Encyclopedia,* 3rd ed. (New York: Viking, 1968).

7. Quoted in Machovec, op. cit.

8. Arnold Mindell, *Dreambody: The Body's Role in Revealing the Self* (Santa Monica, Calif.: Sigo Press, 1982).

9. See Wilse B. Webb, "Historical Perspectives: From Aristotle to Calvin Hall," in *Dreamtime and Dreamwork: Decoding the Language of the Night,* ed. Stanley Krippner (Los Angeles: J. P. Tarcher, 1990).

10. Aristotle, "De Somniis" and "De Divinatione per Somnum," in *The Works of Aristotle,* vol. 3, ed. W. D. Ross (Oxford, England: Clarendon Press, 1931), 454–58. Original work written ca. 330 B.C.

11. Ibid.

12. It is remarkable that Wundt did not study sleeping or dreaming humans in his research. See J. Allan Hobson, *The Dreaming Brain: How the brain creates both the sense and the nonsense of dreams* (New York: Basic Books, 1988).

13. See chapter 3 and the discussion of energy conservation.

14. Hobson, op. cit.

15. Charles Sherrington, *The Integrative Action of the Nervous System* (New Haven, Conn.: Yale University Press, 1906).

16. Sir John Eccles believes that consciousness alters the firing pattern of nerve extracellular communications by quantum mechanics. Earlier I had suggested a similar view regarding nerve intracellular function. See chapter 10 where I discuss this in more detail.

17. A quantum-mechanical model based on this hypothesis was offered by physicist Ludvik Bass of the University of Queensland, Australia. See L. Bass, "A Quantum Mechanical Mind-Body Interaction," *Foundations of Physics* 5, no. 1 (March 1975).

18. See David Koulack, *To Catch a Dream: Explorations of Dreaming* (Albany, N.Y.: State University of New York Press, 1991), 36.

19. See Hobson, op. cit.

20. Maury's report was somewhat sensational and attracted the attention of nearly anyone interested in dreams. See other descriptions in the references by Freud and Hobson in the bibliography.

21. L. F. A. Maury, *Le Sommeil et les rêves* (Paris: Didier et Cie, 1861).

22. See Sigmund Freud, *The Interpretation of Dreams* (New York: Avon Books, 1965), 534.

23. Ambrose Bierce, *An Occurrence at Owl Creek Bridge* (Mankato, Minn.: Creative Education, 1980).

24. See chapter 4 of Koulack, op. cit.

CHAPTER 5. THE MECHANICS OF CONSCIOUSNESS: THE WORK OF BENJAMIN LIBET

1. Werner Heisenberg, *Physics and Philosophy* (New York: Harper & Row, 1958), 107.

2. Benjamin Libet et al., "Subjective Referral of the Timing for a Conscious Sensory Experience: A Functional Role for the Somatosensory Specific Projection System in Man," *Brain* 102, pt. 1 (March 1979): 193–224.

3. A little note here about time measurements. A convenient unit of time in neurophysiological studies is the millisecond (ms), which is one-thousandth of a second. Thus a half second is 500 ms.

4. Coincident here means within 40 ms or so, about the length of time of the S1 signal.

5. Fred Alan Wolf, "On the Quantum Physical Theory of Subjective Antedating," *Journal of Theoretical Biology* 136 (1989): 13–19.

6. This idea follows from the transactional interpretation of quantum mechanics. See the reference to John G. Cramer in the Bibliography.

CHAPTER 6. THE MECHANICS OF DREAMING: PART I—WE DREAM TO INTEGRATE

1. Quoted in *Parabola* (Spring 1987): 102.

2. Carl Sagan, *The Dragons of Eden: Speculations on the Evolution of Human Intelligence* (New York: Ballantine Books, 1977).

3. See Jonathan Winson, *Brain and Psyche* (New York: Anchor Press/Double-day, 1985), and "The Meaning of Dreams," *Scientific American* (November 1990).

4. Francis Crick and Graeme Mitchison, "The function of dream sleep," *Nature* 304, no. 5922 (July 14, 1983): 111–14.

5. J. A. Hobson and R. W. McCarley, "The brain as a dream state generator: An activation-synthesis hypothesis of the dream process," *American Journal of Psychiatry* 134 (12) (1977): 1335–48.

6. J. Allan Hobson, *The Dreaming Brain: How the brain creates both the sense and the nonsense of dreams* (New York: Basic Books, 1988).

7. Winson, *Brain and Psyche,* 6.

8. Ibid., 241.

9. Ibid., 245.

10. Ibid., 11.

11. Recent findings indicate that LTP occurs through activation of a certain receptor called NMDA (a molecule embedded in structures within the neural cells of the brain).

12. This statement is somewhat misleading. Bursts of theta rhythm do appear in the EEG records of sleeping humans. However they are not very consistent nor are they as highly organized as they appear in the brains of rats. One might suspect that organized theta is present in humans and that it would play a role in humans similar to the role that Winson and others discovered in rat brains. Yet although this has been adequately demonstrated to occur in many mammalian brains, there is no evidence of it in human brains.

I asked the noted brain and sleep researcher J. Allan Hobson about this surprising fact. He told me that it was because the hippocampus is so deep in a human being's brain that you don't receive the same degree of radiation through the relatively thick upper brain. There are rhythms in the theta region in the human EEG, but you don't see the extraordinary organized theta that you see in the rat, where the cortex is very thin.

Hobson reasons that it is probably being transmitted as a volume conductor through the cortex. In the cat you also see theta but usually in the subcortical region. Hobson thinks that if you had leads (wires inserted) in the human hippocampus, you would see theta "all over the place." You usually don't have those leads. As he put it, "you are not struck at all about spurious theta rhythms in the human surface EEG during REM sleep or during any other time. That is an anatomical phenomena. If you let someone put electrodes in a person's hippocampus, you would probably find the theta is astounding."

13. Winson, "The Meaning of Dreams."

CHAPTER 7. THE MECHANICS OF DREAMING: PART II—A CRICK IN THE NETWORK

1. Quoted in Dyani Ywahoo, *Voices of Our Ancestors* (Boston: Shambhala, 1987), 89.

2. Sigmund Freud, "Project for a Scientific Psychology," in *The Origins of Psychoanalysis: Letters to Wilhelm Fliess, Drafts and Notes: 1887–1902,* ed's. Marie Bonaparte, Anna Freud, and Ernst Kris, trans. Eric Mossbacher and James Strachey (New York: Basic Books, 1954).

3. Francis Crick, and Graeme Mitchison, "The function of dream sleep," *Nature* 304, no. 5922 (July 14, 1983): 111–114.

4. Francis Crick, and Graeme Mitchison, "REM Sleep and Neural Nets," *The Journal of Mind and Behavior* 7, nos. 2, 3 (Spring and Summer 1986): 229[99]–250[120].

5. There are several references in the rapidly growing field of neural-network computer modeling. See J. J. Hopfield, D. I. Feinstein, and R. G. Palmer, " 'Unlearning' has a stabilizing effect in collective memories," in "Letters to *Nature, Nature* 304 (July 14, 1983). Also see Francis Crick, "The recent excitement about neural networks," *Nature* 337, no. 6203 (January 12, 1989): 129–32, which contains other references.

6. Hopfield et al., op. cit.

7. Hopfield and his coworkers at the California Institute of Technology used a set of weights that consisted of simple products of specific unit values—a subset of all the combinations of unit values available. If you put these specific values in a row, they might look like $+ + - - + - + +$, etc., where the $+$ and $-$ refer to plus and minus one. Thus a weight connecting cell one to cell five could be the sum of products such as $+1 \times +1$ or $+1$ times -1. If the particular subset contained mostly positive values, this weight could be large and positive, while if it consisted of equal amounts of $+1$s and -1s, the weight could be small, close to zero in value.

8. See R. D. Cartwright and R. W. Ratzel, "Effects of dream loss on waking behaviors," *Archives of General Psychiatry* 27 (1972): 277–80.

CHAPTER 8. THE MECHANICS OF DREAMING: PART III— A QUANTUM LEAP INTO THE LAND OF NOD

1. Werner Heisenberg, *Physics and Philosophy* (New York: Harper & Row, 1958), 41.

2. John McCrone, "Something stirs in the land of Nod," *The Independent on Sunday* (London), November 3, 1991, Science section.

3. J. Allan Hobson, *The Dreaming Brain: How the brain creates both the sense and the nonsense of dreams* (New York: Basic Books, 1988).

4. Ibid., 9.

5. The concept of scientific evidence is important to Hobson. Throughout his book he points to how unscientific Freud and others have been in attempting to be scientific about dreams.

6. As I pointed out in chapter 7, the echidna and cetacea do not exhibit REM in spite of being mammals. REM sleep does occur in all marsupial and terrestrial placental mammals. According to Winson in his article "The biology and function of rapid eye movement sleep," in *Current Opinion in Neurobiology* 3: 243–44, "REM sleep appears to have evolved 140 million years ago in a common ancestor of marsupial and placental mammals, after this common ancestor split off from the monotreme (echidna) evolutionary line. REM appears to have been lost in Cetecea (whales and dolphins), a later placental evolutionary radiation."

7. See David Kahn and J. Allan Hobson, "Self-Organization Theory of Dreaming," *Dreaming,* vol. 3, no. 3 (1993), 151–78.

CHAPTER 9. THE DREAMTIME

1. See W. H. Stanner, *White Man Got No Dreaming: Essays 1938–1973* (Canberra, Australia: Australian National University Press, 1979).

2. See B. Spencer, and F. J. Gillen, *The Native Tribes of Central Australia* (New York: Dover, 1968 [first published in 1899]).

3. Colin Dean, *The Australian Aboriginal "Dreamtime": An Account of Its History, Cosmogenesis, Cosmology, and Ontology* (B.S. thesis, Deakin University, Sept. 1990). Available from Australian Institute of Aboriginal Studies.

4. See Mircea Eliade, *Australian Religions: An Introduction* (Ithaca, N.Y.: Cornell University Press, 1973), 45.

5. Ibid., 66.

6. Jennifer Isaacs, comp., ed., *Australian Dreaming: 40,000 Years of Aboriginal History* (Sydney, Australia: Lansdowne Press, 1980).

7. W. Love, "Was the dream-time ever a real-time?" *Anthropological Society of Queensland Newsletter* 196 (1989): 1–14. Available from Australian Institute of Aboriginal Studies.

8. Ebenezer Ademola Adejumo, *The Concept of Time in Yoruba, Australian Aboriginal, and Western Cultures, Especially as It Is Manifested in the Visual Arts* (M.S. thesis, School of Humanities, Flinders University of South Australia, 1976).

9. See T. G. H. Strehlow, *Aranda Traditions* (Melbourne, Australia: Melbourne University Press, 1947).

10. Garrett Barden, "Reflections of Time," *The Human Content* 5, no. 2, (London: Chaucer Publishing Co., Summer 1973).

11. See Mircea Eliade, *Images et Symboles* (Paris, 1952), ch. 2, "Symbolismes Indiens du Temps et de l'Éternité." (*Images and Symbols,* "Indian Symbols of Time and Eternity.")

12. Jim Poulter, *The Secret of Dreaming* (Templestowe, Australia: Red Hen Enterprises, 1988).

CHAPTER 10. QUANTUM PHYSICS AND DREAMS: A PRELIMINARY SEARCH FOR THE I

1. Wim Coleman and Pat Perrin, *The Jamais Vu Papers or Misadventures in the Worlds of Science, Myth, and Magic* (New York: Harmony Books, 1991), 70.

2. John C. Eccles, F. R. S., "Do mental events cause neural events analogously to the probability fields of quantum mechanics?" *Proc. R. Soc.* B 227 (1986): 411–28.

3. It may be useful to spell this out in some detail. According to the Copenhagen or standard interpretation of quantum mechanics, atomic events are not determined because the objective properties of these events cannot be specified. Thus all one can do is determine the probability of an event. Mathematically, one is able to specify a probability field in space surrounding any specific point. This field or cloud may exist in real space or it may be an artifact—a mathematical construct of human thought. Yet whatever it is, when an observation occurs, the cloud or field is suddenly reduced in size to a specific point—the point where the atomic event occurs.

4. See my paper "The Quantum Physics of Consciousness: Towards a New Psychology," *Integrative Psychology* 3 (1985): 236–47. My argument poses that protein gate molecules embedded in the neural wall are subject to the Heisenberg uncertainty principle (HUP). Consequently they are capable of existing as energy or position structures in the neural wall, two complementary observable possibilities. The action of observing the energy of these molecules creates them in wavelike patterns suggestive of "feeling tones" or vibrational patterns associated with human feelings. Observation of the positions of these molecules creates them as physical structures in specific locations within the wall. This may be something like formation of logical units of memory in a computer, and thereby suggestive of thought processes. These ideas are of course highly speculative.

Eccles posits that vesicle emission requires a vesicular velocity. By computing the uncertainty in velocity of a vesicle he concludes that the actual emission velocity lies with the bounds predicted by the HUP, and therefore the emission is under the action of quantum probability fields subject to sudden change upon observation.

5. Let me clarify this. What is called a probability field is imagined to exist in space and time. Now, probabilities are real positive numbers, not negative or imaginary. At every point in space and at each particular time this probability field has a specific positive real value that we might call a percentage of likelihood.

The higher the value, the greater the probability that the event will occur at that point and at that time. Quantum physics cannot give us the satisfaction of knowing exactly where or when any specific event will take place. It can only provide a map of probability.

To compute a probability field, you have to multiply this complex quantum wave by a "backward-through-time" wave, which turns out to be the original wave's *complex-conjugate*. To clarify: the original wave, as I mentioned, consists of two parts, a real and an imaginary part. Usually the parts are mathematical functions of space and time themselves. Thus the parts can be looked at separately. Usually they are composed of periodically varying amplitudes. A sine wave is a typical example. Now, such waves represent oscillations. Thus their amplitudes at any given point in space and time can be either positive or negative with respect to their neutral or waveless point. If the wave at some point in space can be negative and even imaginary, then how can this wave represent a probability field, which must always be positive and real?

According to the Born interpretation of quantum mechanics, the answer is that it must be multiplied by itself! Now that would be fine if the wave was real. Any real number when multiplied by itself will be positive. For example -6 multiplied by -6 gives a positive 36. But what about the imaginary part?

Now, the original wave is a solution to a particular equation called the Schrödinger wave equation (SWE). Like all differential equations of mathematics, the solution to the SWE depends on what are called boundary conditions. Since the equation is time dependent, which means that its solution depends on time, the solution is dependent on what it was at some initial time. This is called the initial boundary condition. The equation then governs how that solution progresses from its boundary in time.

It turns out that the complex-conjugate wave also satisfies a Schrödinger wave equation. However the equation is different in one sense only. You must set the "initial" condition of the equation to be a time in the future. It then describes how that solution changes as time *regresses*. In other words, if you allow the time in the equation to regress from the future to the present, the complex-conjugate wave describes the solution as a wave regressing from the future to the present or, put simply, a wave traveling backward through time.

This way of "seeing" the complex-conjugate wave was first put forward by physicists John Wheeler and Richard Feynman in the forties. It was later put in the form I am describing by physicist John G. Cramer from the University of Washington in the 1980s. He calls his way of seeing this multiplication of waves the "transactional interpretation" (TI).

At present there are many interpretations of quantum mechanics—the most well-known is called the Copenhagen or Bohr interpretation, named after its founder, Niels Bohr. In the TI, an event—a moment of cognition or recognition, recording of a physical fact in a recording device, or a measurement (there are many ways in which this event or for that matter any event is described in quantum physics)—simultaneously sends out a quantum wave both backward and forward in time.

There is nothing really strange about this, although it seems so to the layperson, because the wave also travels at speeds in excess of the speed of light! Accordingly, waves that exceed the Einstein speed limit (he said no *thing* travels faster than light, but a concept, who knows?) are not governed by the laws of inertia, and consequently these are not to be considered material waves at all. In a certain sense these are waves of our imagination, and yet they behave (or are capable of explaining the normal behavior of matter) as if they were actually moving through space and in time.

6. See the reference to John G. Cramer in the bibliography.

7. You will remember that I talked about this briefly in discussing Libet's model of subjective antedating.

8. S. Freud, *The Ego and the Id* (New York: W. W. Norton & Co., 1960), 9.

9. Ibid., 10.

10. Here I hope not to lose my reading audience of nonphysicists. Operators are symbols that point to a particular mathematical operation. For example, the symbol "$[a]^2$" stands for squaring whatever number (in this case the symbol "a") that appears inside of the brackets. Thus $[5]^2$ equals the number 25. In another example, take the operator "bx" which means multiply by "b." Thus if b is 3 and a is 5, 3x5 equals 15.

Operators can be combined, and it is important in what order they are combined. If we combine the squaring operator and the "bx" operator, we can obtain results in two different ways, depending on whether we square first and then multiply or if we multiply first and then square. Thus $bx[a]^2$ or $[bxa]^2$ leads to different answers. For example, $3x[5]^2$ (which is 75) is not the same as $[3x5]^2$ (which is 225).

When two operators give different results depending on their order, we say the operators do not commute. If they give the same result regardless of what order they are carried out, we say the operators commute. (For example, the operators ax and bx commute because axbxc is the same as bxaxc. Thus if $a = 3$ and $b = 5$ and $c = 7$, $3 \times 5 \times 7$ is the same as $5 \times 3 \times 7$, or 105.)

In quantum mechanics the notion of "commuting" needs to be understood. According to the principle of complementarity, the world is experienced through operators that generally fall into two classes, those that commute with each other and those that don't. If two operators commute, it means that observations corresponding to the physical measurements of these operators are capable of being known or measured simultaneously. If they don't commute, then it is not possible to measure or determine values for both observations simultaneously. The well-known position and momentum of a subatomic particle are two noncommuting observables. The wave particle duality is another example, wherein if one attempts to determine wave properties of subatomic matter using an operator that determines the wave length of the particle, one cannot determine its particle properties specified by an operator that determines the position of the particle.

11. To put it oversimply, Freud advanced the idea that the id wishes to maximize pleasure at the expense of pain.

12. While the ego tries to maximize pleasure, it won't cross the line into danger to do so. Reality steps in through the outside world and sets defined limits.

13. See James Fadiman and Robert Frager, *Personality and Personal Growth* (New York: Harper & Row, 1976), 13, 14.

14. Ibid.

15. Ibid., 14.

16. Ibid., 24.

17. An experiment in which light is shined on a screen containing two parallel slit openings. The light particles produce a pattern on a screen that proves that each particle passes through both slits at the same time as if it were a magical wave suffering self-interference.

18. See Nicholas Humphrey, *A History of the Mind: Evolution and the Birth of Consciousness* (New York: Simon & Schuster, 1992).

19. Peter Russell, *The Global Brain: Speculations on the Evolutionary Leap to Planetary Consciousness* (Los Angeles: J. P. Tarcher, 1983).

CHAPTER 11. TELEPATHIC DREAMS AND SPECIES SURVIVAL

1. Quoted in Jamake Highwater, *The Primal Mind* (New York: Harper & Row, 1981), 118.

2. These are (1) strong nuclear, (2) weak nuclear, (3) electromagnetic, and (4) gravitational. Evidence exists that shows that the weak nuclear and the electromagnetic forces may be aspects of a single force. More than one hundred years ago, people believed that electrical and magnetic forces were separate. We now know they arise from a single force field, the electromagnetic field.

3. See M. Ullman, "Dream, Metaphor and Psi" (unpublished manuscript).

4. If this is true, what are the contents of a blind person's dreams? According to Montague Ullman and Nan Zimmerman (see reference in bibliography), they consist of the same aspects of sensorial experience dealt with in waking life. In other words, a blind person, one who has never seen, dreams primarily in sounds, touch, and all other senses as to how they orient him in the space-time world of waking life. Thus a normal person may dream of being by the seaside. He would see the ocean and the sand, while a blind person would have the same dream but it would consists of "images" that he sensed, such as the sound of the ocean, and the feeling of warmth of the sun, the texture of the sand, etc.

Remember that during dreams the dreaming self is not sitting around contemplating, he is usually moving about. The same kinesthetic element is present in blind people's dreams as in the dreams of seeing people.

5. Remember from the previous chapter, if you read the rather long footnote there, that boundaries are very important in the evolution of the Schrödinger equation. Keep in mind the essence of that chapter as you read this one. Quantum waves travel both backward as well as forward in time, and they are able to provide connections between events that are beyond space-time causality. So, in a sense, if my thesis is correct, we would expect that quantum waves from the future would reach us from time to time during our dreams. The question is, who sent them?

6. Not only are there are potential objects but the means by which these potential objects interact are governed by potential material agencies. This gives rise to objects following all possible pathways from all of their potential locations to all possible final locations.

7. See David Bohm, *Wholeness and the Implicate Order* (Boston: Routledge & Kegan Paul, 1980).

8. This notion arises from the question, Why are all electrons alike? The answer could be they are alike because they are different images of just one electron. That electron is able to move freely through space and both forward and backward in time. Thus it can appear in more than one place at the same time, even an infinite number of places. The idea is not mine, and it doesn't arise out of science fiction. No less than the idea of the recently deceased Nobel Prize–winning physicist Richard P. Feynman, it allowed him to calculate the properties of electron-photon interactions in a new manner, previously incalculable without a computer.

9. Ullman points out that this idea connects with Jan Ehrenwald's theory that paranormal effects are the failure of a mechnism to filter out paranormal events from impinging on consciousness.

10. In case you missed this earlier, *spacelike* means connected through space but not necessarily through time; in other words, the events comprising the connection are simultaneously occurring. Spacelike events cannot be linked via a material mechanism. Thus one of the events cannot be considered to be the cause of the other.

11. *Timelike* means connected through time but not necessarily through space; in other words, the events comprising the connection are happening at different times locally at one spot, or if they are separated in space, they can be linked via a material mechanism. Thus one of the events can always be considered the cause of the other. Material links between timelike separated-in-space events must travel from the prior to the latter at speeds less than or equal to light speed.

12. I believe that will or intent has much to do with this resolution. By having the intent to dream prophetically or to remember dreams or even to enter into the dream with consciousness, people seem to be more successful than when they lack such intent. I will return to this issue in a later chapter dealing with lucid dreams.

13. See the previous footnotes regarding timelike and spacelike separated events. Timelike events are also called local events because a material means or agency is available allowing the events to be connected via causal laws. Nonlocality refers to spacelike events. Such events are forbidden from being causally connected because they can happen instantaneously. Thus one of two events separated in space and occurring simultaneously with another is not in the locality of the other. Hence the word *nonlocality*.

14. In case you are asking which source emitted the photon, that is indeed the quantum question. It appears that both emitted it, even though the time of the emission was not simultaneous at all.

15. See R. L. Pfleegor, and L. Mandel, "Interference of Independent Photon Beams," *Physical Review* 159 (July 25, 1967).

16. This will need some explanation since I am referring to events that are connected via some form of nonlocal interaction. Any two atomic or subatomic objects that have interacted will form a single quantum wave function, meaning that they are no longer independent of each other even though they may be physically quite separate from each other. When some attribute of one of these objects is observed, the other object also undergoes an "observational collapse of the wave function" so that each object now possesses a similar attribute. To what extent all atomic objects in the universe may be interacting, or may have interacted in the past, is difficult to determine. I would suggest that there have been and presently are a large number of such atomic and subatomic correlating interactions taking place. Thus one may speculate that all objects are continually interacting with each other and that such interactions "build up" gigantic wave functions that are continually being "collapsed" by observations into separate atomic realities with telepathic ramifications taking place all over the universe. The problem is not how to explain weird happenings, the problem is why the difficulty in observing them.

17. States of meditation seem to contradict this statement. Meditators speak of states of pure consciousness without any object of consciousness. I would suggest that this state contains a self-referring loop: the observer and the observed are the same thing. Thus I would suggest that there is a material component of this self-awareness state, the body itself.

18. It may seem far-fetched to think of body awareness as telepathic. I do not mean anything weird in this. I simply mean that body awareness proceeds through instantaneous, quantum-physical, spacelike, synchronous connections—the kind that I am referring to throughout this book. Certainly a lot of signaling is also going around the body via the nervous system. However, as I explained in chapter 6, most of this seems to be unconscious, and rather mechanical, in spite of our awareness.

19. Here Ullman differs with the validity of Freud's concept of the id as a container of unstructured images. Ullman wrote to me that "there is a deeper self-functioning as you describe in dreams but it has little in common with Freud's notion of a totally self-centered, narcissistic id."

20. Montague Ullman, Stanley Krippner, with Alan Vaughan, *Dream Telepathy: Experiments in Nocturnal ESP* (Jefferson, N. C., and London: McFarland & Co., 1989).

21. Ibid., 45–53.

22. This refers to what are known as delayed-choice experiments. In these experiments, an observer in the future chooses to measure a property of a physical system. This choice propagates backward through time to the present and determines the present.

23. Montague Ullman, "Dreams, Species-Connectedness, and the Paranormal," *The Journal of the American Society for Psychical Research* 84, no. 2 (April 1990).

24. Ullman bases this view on the work of others, particularly biologist H. B. Barlow.

CHAPTER 12. LUCID DREAMS: THE BORDER BETWEEN PARALLEL WORLDS

1. See the references to the above-named authors in the bibliography.

2. In his article "A Study of Dreams" in Charles Tart, ed., *Altered States of Consciousness* (Garden City, N.Y.: Doubleday, 1972), 145–58.

3. Stephen LaBerge, Ph.D., *Lucid Dreaming: The Power of Being Awake and Aware in Your Dreams* (Los Angeles: J. P. Tarcher, 1985).

4. Tarthang Tulku, *Openness Mind* (Berkeley Calif.: Dharma Publishing, 1978), 74.

5. Jayne Gackenbach, "Frameworks for Understanding Lucid Dreaming: A Review," *Dreaming* 1, no. 2 (1991): 109.

6. Ibid.

7. This line of research has been investigated notably by LaBerge. See for example Stephen LaBerge, Ph.D., *Lucid Dreaming: The Power of Being Awake & Aware in Your Dreams* (Los Angeles: J. P. Tarcher, 1985).

8. Susan Blackmore, "A theory of lucid dreams and OBEs," in J. I. Gackenbach and S. L. LaBerge, eds., *Conscious mind, sleeping brain: Perspectives on lucid dreaming* (New York: Plenum, 1988), 377.

9. See Charles Tart, *Waking up: Overcoming the obstacles to human potential* (Boston: New Science Library, 1986).

10. Charles Tart, "From spontaneous event to lucidity: A review of attempts to consciously control nocturnal dreaming," in B. Wolman, M. Ullman, and W. Webb, eds., *Handbook of dreams: Research, theories and applications* (New York: Van Nostrand Reinhold), 226–68.

11. Tart, *Waking Up,* 63.

12. In 1977 Hobson and McCarley had discovered that REM was characterized by a unique relationship that existed between it and reticular giant cells in the pontine brain stem. Part of that relationship had to do with tonic latency and phasic latency. Tonic latency refers to a buildup of expectancy as evidenced by progressive increases in the firing rates of these cells, and phasic latency refers to the cells firing in clusters or in phase with each other rather than randomly. Both tonicity and phasic latency are present in REM sleep.

13. See "Interview with Physicist Fred Alan Wolf, on the Physics of Lucid Dreaming," *Lucidity Letter* 6, no. 1 (June 1987): 51–63. And see: Fred Alan Wolf, "The Physics of Dream Consciousness: Is the Lucid Dream a Parallel Universe?" *Lucidity Letter* 6, no. 2 (December 1987): 130–35.

14. Karl H. Pribram, *Languages of the brain. Experimental paradoxes and principles in neuropsychology* (Monterey, Calif.: Brooks/Cole Publishing Co., 1977), 168.

15. This is described in Michael Talbot, *The Holographic Universe* (New York: HarperCollins, 1991), 292.

16. Of course, I may be quite incorrect in this explanation. It just seems unlikely to me that the intensity of sounds emitted by the ear could be high enough to interfere with the recorded sound levels. Also, I fail to understand how, even if they did, this would produce the remarkable result that Zuccarelli has achieved.

17. If the placement of the receivers is similar in importance to the placement of the slits in the light-wave double-slit experiment, one can understand why the receivers need to be placed close enough together. The wavelength of the sound and the separation of the sources needs to be carefully controlled so that proper interference results producing a localizable "image." Stellar radio-receiving antennae are often designed with many "slits" so that the direction of a star's emission is precisely located. If the receivers are too far apart, no interference effects result.

18. Georg von Békésy, *Sensory Inhibition* (Princeton, N.J.: Princeton University Press, 1967), 220–26.

CHAPTER 13. THE DREAMING UNIVERSE: THE DREAMBODY AND THE WAKING DREAM

1. Wim Coleman and Pat Perrin, *The Jamais Vu Papers or Misadventures in the Worlds of Science, Myth, and Magic* (New York: Harmony Books, 1991), 141.

2. See Marie-Louise von Franz, *Number and Time: Reflections Leading toward a Unification of Depth Psychology and Physics* (Evanston Ill.: Northwestern University Press, 1974). Dr. von Franz, following the work of her mentor, Carl Jung, has explored the concept of number from the viewpoint that it arose as an archetype from the unconscious.

3. For example, Pacific peoples call this energy *mana*. The Dakota peoples call it *wakan*. The ancient Hebrew tribes referred to it as *ruach*. The Australian peoples refer to *alcheringa,* the dreamtime. For more on this see Holger Kalweit, *Shamans, Healers, and Medicine Men* (Boston: Shambhala, 1992).

4. See chapter 3 where I discuss the concept of energy using the "Dennis the Menace" example devised by the late physicist Richard Feynman.

5. See Arnold Mindell, *Dreambody: The Body's Role in Revealing the Self* (Santa Monica, Calif.: Sigo Press, 1982) and his other books listed in the bibliography.

6. See Arnold Mindell, *The Year I: Global Process Work* (London: Arkana, 1989).

7. Yet, it is perhaps surprising that few people suffering with cancer ever dream of their disease. Usually dreams seem to reflect a person's emotional concerns. However, Shainberg sees this differently. Also as we shall see later in this chapter, Mindell accounts for numerous dream episodes related to a patient's discovery of cancer.

8. The above story and the quote come from Franz, op. cit., 15–16.

9. Robert G. Jahn and Brenda J. Dunne, *Margins of Reality: The Role of Consciousness in the Physical World* (San Diego, Calif.: Harcourt Brace Jovanovich, 1987).

10. Arnold Mindell, *Working with the Dreaming Body* (New York: Routledge & Kegan Paul, 1985), 3.

CHAPTER 14. GETTING TO THE BIG DREAM

1. Quote from the Buddha taken from the Samadhirajasutra in Helena Norbert-Hodge, *Ancient Futures: Learning from Ladekh* (London: Rider Publishing Co., 1991), 72.

2. See references to such works by Hopkins, McKenna, Ring, and especially Strieber in the bibliography.

3. I explained in chapter 12 that there are two kinds of images formed by lenses and holograms, real and virtual. I am suggesting that imaginal-realm phenomena are the result of real-image formation and thus appear to exist "out there" in space, as real optical images do. However, I am not claiming that imaginal-realm phenomena are formed from light waves. I will leave this for the moment and offer an explanation of what the waves are composed of in a later chapter.

4. At this time, there is no physics that applies here. The whole idea of a quantum psychophysics is totally new, although there have been attempts in the past to describe the physiological processes occurring when the brain is active. Such attempts are purely classical science and in no way indicate the effect that an observer has upon the brain and nervous system.

5. Michael Talbot, *The Holographic Universe* (New York: HarperCollins, 1991), 279.

6. The lambda hyperon, for example, lives for one ten-billionth of a second.

7. Peter M. Rojcewicz, "Signals of Transcendence: The Human-UFO Equation," *Journal of UFO Studies,* n.s. 1 (1989): 117–18.

8. Peter M. Rojcewicz, "The 'Men in Black' Experience and Tradition: Analogues with the Traditional Devil Hypothesis," *Journal of American Folklore* 100, no. 396 (April–June 1987): 154.

9. See Alexandra David-Neel, *Buddhism: Its Doctrines and Its Methods* (New York: Avon Books, 1979), 37–41, and see her book, *Magic and Mystery in Tibet* (New York: Penguin Books, 1973). Also see Alexandra David-Neel and Lama Yongden, *The Secret Oral Teachings in Tibetan Buddhist Sects* (San Francisco: City Lights Books, 1967).

10. Jacques Vallee, *Dimensions: A Casebook of Alien Contact* (Chicago: Contemporary Books, Inc., 1988).

11. This estimate was made from a computer analysis that Vallee carried out by looking at every continent where sightings were reported.

12. Remember that "real" images form in space. Several years ago you could buy in shops a bowl that was painted black on the outside but had a cover

over it that contained a hole. By gazing into the hole you would see a coin floating in the space of the hole. The coin was actually at the bottom of the bowl, but due to the concave reflecting surface of the bowl's inside, the image of the coin formed in the space of the hole. This was a "real" optical image.

13. Michael Grosso, "UFOs and the Myth of a New Age," *Revision: Journal of Consciousness and Change* 11, no. 3, 1 (Winter 1989).

14. Michael Grosso, *The Final Choice: Playing the Survival Game* (Walpole, N.H.: Stillpoint Publishing Co., 1985).

15. Grosso quotes Price from H. H. Price, "Mind over mind and mind over matter," in P. French, ed., *Philosophers in wonderland* (Saint Paul, Minn.: Llewellyn Publishing Co., 1975), 232–43.

16. See Peter M. Rojcewicz, "Strange Bedfellows: The Folklore of Other-Sex," in *Critique: A Journal Exposing Consensus Reality* 29 (1988): 8–12.

17. Ibid.

18. Peter M. Rojcewicz, "Between One Eye Blink and the Next: Fairies, UFOs, and Problems of Knowledge," in Peter Narvaez, ed., *The Good People: New Fairylore Essays* (New York: Garland Publishing Co., 1991), 479–514.

19. Henri Corbin, *Mundis Imaginalis or the Imaginal and the Imaginary* (Ipswich, England: Golgonooza Press, 1976 [originally published in *Spring*, 1972]).

20. See reference to Deirdre in: Mike Grosso, *Soulmaker: True Stories from the Far Side of the Psyche* (Norfolk, Va.: Hampton Roads, 1992), chapter 15.

21. Or some other mathematical formalism of quantum physics that deals with equally unreal but mathematically specifiable concepts such as a "state vector," "spinor," "energy matrix," or the like.

CHAPTER 15. THE PHYSICS OF THE IMAGINAL REALM

1. Terence Mckenna, "New Maps of Hyperspace," in his *The Archaic Revival: Essays and Conversations* (San Francisco: HarperCollins, 1992).

2. David Bohm, *Unfolding Meaning: A Weekend of Dialogue with David Bohm* (New York: Routledge & Kegan Paul, 1985), 72.

3. See chapter 10 where I explain what is meant by quantum physical or quantum mechanical correlations of events.

4. I had returned from Australia five months earlier. That could account for my dream memory of the country's name beginning with the letter *A*. It could also account Fitzroy Street, a typically English name that I associated with Australia, as I had spent considerable time in Sydney, a city with many "English" streets.

5. In this world, I have performed as a close-up magician and have worked with children, particularly gifted children, in schools. Magic tricks bring out a sense of wonder and endless questions from children. Like adults, they want to know how the trick is done. I use magic to stimulate their curiosity about the physical world.

6. Y. Aharonov and M. Vardi, "Meaning of an individual 'Feynman Path,'" *Physical Review D* 21, no. 8 (April 15, 1980): 2235–40.

7. A quantum system is really any physical system that is simple enough so that its quantum physical state is observable. Subatomic matter in the form of particles are certainly quantum systems. Larger aggregates of matter could be quantum systems, but usually don't qualify because there are far two many transitions occurring in them to be individually observed by an outside observer. Matter in our brains may be composed of observable quantum systems.

8. This experiment was reported in the popular-science magazine *Discover*. See David H. Freedman, "Weird Science," *Discover* 11, no. 11 (November 1990): 62–68.

9. We might question Itano and his colleagues as to their intent in doing the experiment. We don't have to. By observing the system as they did, their intent was already established regardless of what they were thinking at the time. In other words their intent was already "out there" in the physical world.

CHAPTER 16. TRANSPERSONAL DREAMING AND DEATH

1. *The Book of Chuang Tzu.*

2. Michael Grosso, "The Symbolism of UFO Abductions," *UFO Universe,* Fall 1988, 44–45.

3. Kenneth Ring, Ph.D., *The Omega Project: Near-Death Experiences, UFO Encounters, and Mind at Large* (New York: William Morrow, 1992).

4. I am taking the position that UFO experiences are from the imaginal realm and therefore have a different but "real" feeling to them as compared to ordinary experiences. I am suggesting that they are not the same as so-called solid-reality experiences that we commonly experience in everyday life. I am also not saying they are fantasies or hallucinations.

5. This idea is not original with me. In a remarkable paper written in 1971, Ludvik Bass, a professor of physics now at Queensland University in Brisbane, Australia, and a former student of physicist Erwin Schrödinger, put forward a reductio ad absurdum (an argument that, if its premise is correct, leads to a result in contradiction to the premise) that shows that there cannot exist two or more independent conscious minds! See Ludvik Bass, "The Mind of Wigner's Friend," *Hermathena: A Dublin University Review* 112 (1971): 52–68.

6. Ring, op. cit., 63.

7. Although I'll come to this point again, the notion that every event is the direct concomitant of a previous event is a well-accepted tenet of Buddhist philosophy. One might conclude that Buddhists are Newtonian in their thinking. However, they maintain that ultimately all events as perceived events are illusionary. Thus we could conclude from that, that they are Heisenbergian in their thinking.

8. See chapter 15 where I discussed how observation can not only precipitate quantum jumps, it can also freeze them, keeping them from happening.

9. The spatialization of time, the notion that time exists as another dimension of space, was first realized by Hermann Minkowski in 1908 as a development of Einstein's special theory of relativity. I have described this in considerable detail in my two earlier books *Star*Wave* and *The Eagle's Quest*.

10. This intent is manifested in the manner in which the observations are carried out, the experimental setup, and the choice of observables sought for.

11. I have already mentioned this in a previous chapter and I'll have more to say about it in a later chapter.

12. See Ring, op. cit., 198–205, for a description of Devereux and Persinger's discoveries. Also see references to Persinger and Devereux in the bibliography.

13. It is no surprise that electromagnetic pulses would affect human brain functioning. The brain is at least as sensitive as any radar detector, if not more so. High-amplitude electromagnetic pulses accompanying atmospheric nuclear bursts have been studied for several years by the Advanced Research Projects Agency of the U.S. government and are known to black out radar.

14. Wilder Penfield, *The Mystery of the Mind: A Critical Study of Consciousness and the Human Brain* (Princeton, N.J.: Princeton University Press, 1975), 19.

15. Ibid., 21.

16. Michael A. Persinger, "Modern Neuroscience and Near-Death Experiences," *Journal of Near-Death Studies* 7 (1990): 233–39.

17. See Whitley Strieber, *Transformation: The Breakthrough* (New York: Beech Tree Books, William Morrow, 1988) and *Communion: A True Story* (New York: Beech Tree Books/William Morrow, 1987).

18. See my earlier book *The Eagle's Quest: A Physicist's Search for Truth in the Heart of the Shamanic World* (New York: Summit Books, 1991), 168.

19. By this I mean that the coins are not real, large coins, but tiny, atomic-sized coins obeying quantum rules. This example is illustrative, not literal.

CHAPTER 17. IMAGINAL AND REAL: DREAMS IN ART, MYTH, AND REALITY

1. Quoted in Yevgeny Kovtun and Liudmila Rybakova, eds., *Fantastic and Imaginative Works by Russian Artists* (Leningrad, Russia: Aurora Art Publishers, 1989). Commentary by Valery Fateyev.

2. See Bryce S. Dewitt, "Quantum mechanics and reality," *Physics Today*, September 1970, 30–35, or also Bryce S. Dewitt and Neill Graham, *The Many-*

Worlds Interpretation of Quantum Mechanics (Princeton, N.J.: Princeton University Press, 1973).

3. See Henri Corbin, *Mundis Imaginalis or the Imaginal and the Imaginary* (Ipswich, England: Golgonooza Press, 1976 [originally published in *Spring*, 1972]), 9, 17.

4. See Fred Alan Wolf, *The Eagle's Quest: A Physicist's Search for Truth in the Heart of the Shamanic World* (New York: Summit Books, 1991), 174.

5. Terence McKenna, *The Archaic Revival: Essays and Conversations* (San Francisco: HarperCollins, 1992). Also see "New and Old Maps of Hyperspace" (audiocassette) Big Sur, Calif.: Dolphin Tapes, 1982).

6. Terence McKenna, "A Conversation over Saucers," *Revision: The Journal of Consciousness and Change* 11, no. 3 (Winter 1989): 23–30.

7. Michael Grosso, *The Final Choice: Playing the Survival Game* (Walpole, N.H.: Stillpoint Publishing, 1985).

8. Arnold Mindell, *The Year I: Global Process Work* (London: Arkana, 1989). Also see his other books listed in the bibliography.

9. See Peter Russell, *The White Hole in Time: Our Future Evolution and the Meaning of Now* (San Francisco: HarperSanFrancisco, 1992). Also see *The Global Brain: Speculations on the Evolutionary Leap to Planetary Consciousness* (Los Angeles: J. P. Tarcher, 1983).

10. Leonard Shalin, *Art and Physics: Parallel Visions in Space, Time, and Light* (New York: William Morrow, 1991).

11. See Kenneth Ring, Ph.D., *The Omega Project: Near-Death Experiences, UFO Encounters, and Mind at Large* (New York: William Morrow, 1992), 207–14. The references to Vallee and Méheust are to be found there.

12. Ibid., 213.

13. Quantum physics deals with the relationship between the possibilities in two ways. In a wave picture there is a definite phase relation between the waveforms representing the separated states. In the formulation of Richard Feynman, known as the path-integral form, the two Feynman paths have accumulated nearly equal amounts of phase information and so tend to cancel each other out.

14. That suffering arises through not wanting what you have and wanting what you don't have.

15. The marshland is ever present as I soon discovered. I was bitten by mosquitoes on nightly visits to my apartment whenever the weather warmed a bit during the winter.

16. See Kovtun and Rybakova, op. cit.

CHAPTER 18. THE SPIRIT OF MATTER

1. W. Pauli and C. G. Jung, *The Interpretation of Nature and the Psyche* (Princeton, N.J.: Pantheon, 1955). In German, *Naturerklärung und Psyche* (Zurich: Rascher Verlag, 1952).

2. C. G. Jung, *Psychology and Alchemy, Collected Works,* vol. 12 (Princeton, N.J.: Princeton University Press, 1980), 44.

3. See for example Pakka Lahti and Peter Mittelstadt, eds., *Symposium on the Foundations of Modern Physics 1990: Quantum Theory of Measurement and Related Philosophical Problems* (River Edge, N. J.: World Scientific Publishing Co., 1991). Specifically, see the opening address by K. V. Laurikainen, p. 3.

4. See Herbert Van Erkelens, "Wolfgang Pauli and the Spirit of Matter," in Lahti and and Mittelstadt, op. cit.

5. K. V. Laurikainen, *Beyond the Atom: The Philosophical Thought of Wolfgang Pauli* (Berlin and Heidelberg, Germany: Springer-Verlag, 1988).

6. Pauli and Jung, op. cit.

7. See Erkelens, op. cit., 426.

8. Ibid.

9. The word *forbidden* here possibly reflects some concerns that Pauli had about his discovery of the "exclusion principle." Accordingly, two electrons are literally forbidden from entering the same quantum state. If they attempt to do this, the quantum probability vanishes.

10. *Dreams of Pauli in the archive of Aniela Jaffé,* ETH Zurich, WHS, Hs 1090:71.

11. Letter from Pauli to Jung, May 27, 1953, ETH Zurich WHS, Hs 1056: 30867.

12. *Dreams of Pauli,* op. cit.

13. Clearly a reflection of how Pauli thought of other people less intelligent than him.

14. Letter from Pauli to Jung, op. cit.

15. Letter of Pauli to von Franz, October 12, 1952, ETH Zurich, WHS, Hs 176: 52.

16. Unpublished manuscript by Pauli, ETH Zurich, WHS, Hs 176:85.

17. In complex numbers the axis of imaginary numbers is perpendicular to the axis of real numbers. The "i" symbolizes a rotation of ninety degrees in the plane of these numbers.

18. Erkelens, op. cit.

19. Also in an earlier chapter I told you about the need to represent quantum waves of probabilities by complex numbers—the same type that appear in the complex plane of Pauli's dream story. Without using complex numbers in quantum physics there was no way possible to reconcile the apparent split that existed between the particle and the wave theories. When Werner Heisenberg and Erwin Schrödinger introduced the imaginary unit i as a fundamental element into our description of matter, suddenly all of the contradictory appearances of quantum physics could be harmoniously integrated into the concept of the complex probability amplitude.

If that amplitude was expressed at a specific point in space and time by a complex number, $a+bi$, then there was also the complex-number wave amplitude, $a\text{-}bi$. The $a+bi$ represented at the point in space and time the wave traveling forward in time, and the $a\text{-}bi$ represented at the same point in space and time a wave traveling backward through time. When these two numbers were multiplied together, the result was a^2+b^2, a real and positive number representing the "reality" as expressed as a probability for finding the system at that specific point in space and time.

In a similar manner the point on the ring of imaginaries, the ring i, is also given by the complex number $a+bi$. When $a+bi$ is multiplied by $a\text{-}bi$, the result, a^2+b^2, always equals 1, the radius of the circle.

20. See Laurikainen, op. cit., 144–45.

CHAPTER 19. THE HOLOGRAPHIC MODEL OF WAKING AND DREAMING AWARENESS

1. J. R. Oppenheimer, *Science and the Human Understanding* (New York: Simon & Schuster, 1966), 69.

2. See David Koulack, *To Catch a Dream: Explorations of Dreaming* (Albany, N.Y.: State University of New York Press, 1991), 10, 42. Also see Gordon Globus, *Dream Life, Wake Life: The Human Condition through Dreams* (Albany, N.Y.: State University of New York Press, 1987), 72–77.

3. Renato Nobili, "Schrödinger wave holography in brain cortex," *Physical Review A* 32, no. 6 (Dec. 1985): 3618–26.

4. There is some recent evidence that these cells have some sort of memory function, and they may be instrumental in the development of tumors.

5. See Karl H. Pribram, *Languages of the brain. Experimental paradoxes and principles in neuropsychology* (Monterey, Calif: Brooks/Cole Publishing Co., 1977), 34–47.

6. See Nobili, op. cit., 3619.

7. See Pribram, op. cit.

8. While a number of researchers were making this discovery, I refer the reader to Pribram, op. cit.

9. K. S. Lashley, *Brain Mechanism and Intelligence* (Chicago: University of Chicago Press, 1929).

10. Although access time may be a limit in file management systems in computers, it is not really a problem in neural-network models simulated on computers. In fact neural-network models do illustrate some aspects of associative memory and access-time equality. See chapter 7.

11. Let me explain this in some detail. If you find the next few paragraphs a little too detailed, just read through them and grasp whatever you can from them or skip over them. You won't need to know this to grasp the concept. However, if you do manage to grasp what I'm saying, you will have a firmer understanding of how holograms actually work.

Usually holograms are made with light waves. A strong and coherent source of these waves, called the reference wave, is shined on a recording medium such as a film emulsion. At the same time part of the reference wave is shined on an object not far from the film emulsion, and the waves that are scattered from the object are also received by the film emulsion at the same time. This means that at each point of the film, information in the form of diffracting light-waves scattered from all parts of the object are received along with the direct reference wave. This produces a simple sum (called a *linear* combination or superposition) of both reference and information waves at the point. These waves simply add together. If I call the reference wave R, and the information wave I, we have at each point of the emulsion the sum R + I.

However, that is not enough to make the holographic recording. The film must absorb this wave in a special way that doesn't distort the delicate way in which R and I are related. This relationship is found in the relative *phase* that exists between the waves R and I at each point of the recording medium.

Waves are wavy! They have not only amplitudes or strengths but also phases, which indicate their oscillatory nature. To grasp this, think of the wave when it arrives at a point of the film emulsion as a pointer on a clock, say the sweep second-hand. If the wave has a large amplitude, it would correspond to a long pointer, and a wave with a small amplitude or strength would correspond to a small pointer. Now think of the number that the hand sweeps over as the phase of the wave at a given time. As the hand sweeps around the clock through sixty seconds, the phase of the wave advances through a complete 360 degrees of the clockface marked by the hours.

Thus when we write the simple term R, we are also keeping in mind that R represents *both* the amplitude and the phase of the wave at the same time, and when R arrives at any point of the recording medium, it has a precise amplitude and phase.

Now it turns out that all photographic media record light waves by absorbing the *energy* contained in the wave. This energy equals the multiplication of the wave by itself, i.e., the amplitude squared. Now the rule for multiplication of waves is, multiply the amplitudes and *add* the phases. But the medium only records the amplitude squared of the wave and loses phase information. Thus if the wave present was only R, the energy absorbed at the point would be R^2 or simply $R \times R$.

But wait a minute, what about the phase? Suppose we elaborate this for a moment. Suppose that zero phase is represented by having the sweep second-hand at 12:00. Suppose that the phase of R at the point of absorption signified the pointer was at 2:00. Since the rule for multiplication of waves is multiply the amplitudes and *add* the phases, if we simply multiply R by itself we would get an energy of R^2 and a phase of 4:00 (visualize the clockface and you will see this). Since no phase information is contained in the film, how do we get rid of this phase information? The answer is to imagine that what we actually multiply together is a wave, R, which has a phase of 2:00, and a wave that we call R's complex conjugate, R*, which has a negative phase, −2:00.

Now to imagine this, just hold up a clockface to a mirror. The phase −2:00 is at the place that we normally see 10:00. Now when you add −2:00 to +2:00, you get a zero phase.

This multiplication of waves is an important rule both for holographic recording and for quantum waves, which it turns out also satisfy the same rule of multiplication when probabilities of events are computed.

But what happens if the wave at the point of the film contains not just R but R + I? This is where the idea of linearity of the waves becomes important and how it is that a hologram can contain a memory of the object. The same multiplication rule holds, and we must multiply (R + I) by (R* + I*). And then you find yourself with a sum of four terms of the product (R*R, R*I, I*R, and I*I).

I want to explain that although the actual result is that no phase information is contained in the total of the products of these waves, each term of that sum actually contains some phase information. Let me show you how this works.

First R*R. This has no phase information present by itself. Thus this term just contributes a blackening of the film at the point of the emulsion. Similarly for the term I*I.

But the terms R*I and I*R each have phase information. For example, suppose that I has a phase at 7:00 (so that I* has a phase of −7:00) and that R has a phase of 2:00 (so that R* has a phase of −2:00). R*I would have a phase of −2:00 plus a phase of 7:00 giving a total phase of 5:00, while the term I*R would combine −7:00 plus +2:00 for a phase of −5:00. As you see, the total phase is still zero even though it is not zero in each term.

Now to make a holographic image appear, a reference wave, R, is shined on the hologram after it has recorded the sum of terms spoken about above. When R encounters the medium where the energy information is recorded, the medium acts as a sensitive filter, and each term of the sum, (R*R) + (R*I) + (I*R) + (I*I), acts on R by only allowing certain information to pass through. In other words the medium containing already recorded information acts as a filter to any other wave passing through it.

Mathematically the wave R multiplies each of the terms in the sum, which represents the absorbed energy. The terms R × (R*R) and R × (I*I) just diminish the strength of R. The term R × (I*R) also produces nothing useful, but the term, R × (R*I) manages to create a weakened image of the information wave, I, itself, together with its phase. This comes about because when you multiply R by R*I the R and R* multiply to give zero phase, leaving the I term with its phase intact.

Thus by shining a reference wave through a hologram, the wave that shines through consists of the reference wave somewhat diminished and distorted and the information wave contained in the hologram. It is this information wave that we see when we look at a holographic image. Since this information wave is exactly the same as the light waves scattered from the original object, we see a full three-dimensional image.

12. The term *resonator* might throw the reader. It simply means a unit or cell capable of responding to a vibration by resonating or getting in tune with it. You resonate when you sing along with a choir. Nobili proposes that each resonator is composed of glial cell walls enclosing an interstitial space.

13. Holograms are made by first exposing a glass plate coated with photosensitive material to light waves and then developing the plate. If several exposures are made before development and then development occurs, the plate actually contains images having the remarkable effect that even though the waves that recorded these images were recorded at entirely different times, they are nevertheless able to interfere with each other. Images of a distant past can be evoked together with images of the present. In the holographic brain this may be physical evidence of the timeless quality of the id. See Maurice Françon, *Holography* (expanded and revised from the French edition) (New York and London: Academic Press, 1974).

14. G. Sperling, "Information available in brief visual presentations," *Psychological Monographs* 74, no. 11 (1960).

15. This is equivalent to a spin system in which the whole spin S is known, $S^2 = s(s+1)$, while none of the components of the spin, those that are the projections of the total spin along the three mutually perpendicular axes of space, s_z, s_x, or s_y, are known. Attempts to know one of the components wipe out the ability to know others. Thus if you attempt to find s_x, for example, it becomes impossible to determine the other components, s_y or s_z.

16. See chapters 6, 7, and 8 for more information on the A-S model. This summary is put here for the convenience of the reader.

17. J. Allan Hobson and Robert W. McCarley, "The Brain as a Dream-State Generator: An Activation-Synthesis Hypothesis of the Dream Process," *American Journal of Psychiatry* 134 (1977): 1335–68.

CHAPTER 20. THE BIRTH OF THE DREAMING SELF FROM NEURAL AUTOMATA

1. See Jayne Gackenbach, "Frameworks for Understanding Lucid Dreaming: A Review," *Dreaming* 1, no. 2 (1991): 109.

2. Ibid.

3. See A. Moffitt et al., "Dream Psychology: Operating in the Dark," in J. I. Gackenbach and S. L. LaBerge, eds., *Conscious mind, sleeping brain: Perspectives on lucid dreaming* (N.Y.: Plenum, 1988). Also see E. Rossi, *Dreams and the growth of the personality: Expanding awareness in psychotherapy.* (N.Y.: Braunner/Mazel, 1972–87).

4. I use "0" to signify the ground or fundamental level instead of "1." The reason will become apparent later in the chapter. Meanwhile, accuse me of liking the British system of calling the "first" floor of a building the floor we in the United States call the "second" and so on.

5. Gackenbach, op. cit., 116.

6. Charles Alexander, "A Conceptual and Phenomenological Analysis of Pure Consciousness During Sleep," *Lucidity* 10, nos. 1 and 2 (1991): 129.

7. Gackenbach, op. cit., 119.

8. Ibid.

9. Ibid., 121. Also see Thomas J. Snyder and Jayne Gackenbach, "Vestibular Involvement in the Neurocognition of Lucid Dreaming," chapter 3 in Jayne Gackenbach and Anees A. Sheikh, *Dream Images: A Call to Mental Arms* (Amityville, N.Y.: Baywood Publishing Co., 1991), 55.

10. Gackenbach, op. cit., 123–24.

11. J. J. Hopfield, D. I. Feinstein, and R. G. Palmer, " 'Unlearning' has a stabilizing effect in collective memories," in "Letters to *Nature*," *Nature* 304 July 14, 1983).

12. By complementary I mean that the automaton cannot hold in its memory an image and its complementary superposition of images at the same time. However, as we shall see, this only holds for "objective" observations, not for "subjective" self-observations.

13. This is the key to self-reflection. A system is capable of "knowing" complementary observables of itself, but it cannot obtain and "know" complementary observables of another system.

14. In Jungian terms this would mean simultaneous knowledge of the self and the shadow, for example.

15. See David Z. Albert, "How to Take a Photograph of Another Everett World," in *New Techniques and Ideas in Quantum Measurement Theory*, D. M. Greenberger, ed., Annals of the New York Academy of Sciences, vol. 480 (December 30, 1986). Also see D. Z. Albert, "On Quantum-Mechanical Automata," *Physics Letters* 98A (1983): 249–52. Also see D. Deutsch, "Quantum theory, the Church-Turing principle and the universal quantum computer," *Proceedings of the Royal Society of London* A 400 (1985): 97–117.

16. See my earlier book *Parallel Universes* for a more detailed discussion of the many-worlds concept (see bibliography) and Albert's automaton.

17. It is this ability to hold on to a superposition of states that distinguishes a quantum automaton from a classical Boolean memory element. No doubt it is easier to make a device that is either "on" or "off" than it is to be both "on and off" at the same time. Difficult though it is, it is not impossible as current research at places such as Bell Laboratories in New Jersey is indicating (see my other books, in particular, *Taking the Quantum Leap*, chapter 15).

18. In the language of quantum physics, complementary observable operators are present. These operators are mathematical forms that represent what takes place whenever an observation of a physical system occurs. I label them in italics to signify that they are operators. If you will remember, I told you about complementary quantum physical operators in chapter 10 (see footnote 10). In this case the operators are labeled *W, E, F, G,* and *S.* Associated with these operators are sets of complementary glial-cell states: the woman identity states, W_i, woman emotional states, E_i, woman thought-form states, F_i, and so on. Following the quantum rules we have the equation $WW_i = w_iW_i$. This is the rule of consistency in quantum physics. It says that if the state W_i operated on by the operator results in multiplying that state by a number, the state is unchanging and the physical system is in that state. The number that multiplies the state is symbolized by w_i. It stands for the value or content of the memory. That means that associated with each state of memory there is a numerical value. What this number actually measures is difficult to say. I would speculate that it is associated with the physical structure of the glial cell in some manner so that when a cell reflects the value w_1 it is oscillating in a certain manner, and when it reflects the value e_i associated with emotion, it would be oscillating in a different mode.

If the glial cell is in a superposition of woman identity states, $W_1 + W_2 = E_1$, then when W operates on the cell, it obtains as a result the sum $w_1W_1 + w_2W_2$, thus changing the state. If E operated on this same state, $W_1 + W_2 = E_1$, it would have yielded $EE_1 = e_1E_1$, where e_1 is the value associated with the emotional state E_1. Thus the state could change depending on what information is obtained from the cell. This is the mathematical essence of the uncertainty principle, which forbids simultaneous objective knowledge of both values, e_1 and w_1, for example. Any attempt to learn one destroys the capability to learn the other by altering the system from which that information is sought. Physically this would mean that the glial cell could not oscillate in the E_1 and the W_1 modes at the same time.

If the glial cell contains a specific image W_1, then when a woman image is called forth, the quantum-mechanical operator W "operates," and the glial cell yields the image W_1, which is incorporated into the memory of the automaton.

This produces a composite state of both the glial cell and the automaton that is the product of their separated states, according to the quantum rules. We label this state $W_1^{(0)} = [W_1]W_1$. The notation is important, assuming you want to follow this argument in detail. W_1 means woman image number 1. The block brackets [] signify the automaton and mean that whatever is inside of them is now a memory of the automaton. The superscript "(0)" means that a level 0 interaction has occurred between the automaton and the object of its inquiry. In this case that object is the memory content of the glial cell. Thus the state $W_1^{(0)}$ is a coupled state of automaton and glial cell in which the automaton reflects the state held by the glial cell.

19. Again this means that if the idea of woman enters the brain of the subject, there is a quantum observable signified by the letter W that when brought into operation is capable of recalling a single woman image W_i.

20. In a similar manner the automaton is capable of obtaining either the emotional state or the identity state. Remember that automaton states are symbolized by brackets [], so that $[W_2]$ stands for the state of the automaton containing the record of the crying sister image, and $[W_1]$ the record of the hysterical mother image, while $[E_1]$ would stand for the automaton containing the record of the emotional state "unhappy woman."

21. Now when the automaton interacts with the glial cell containing a superposition of images, according to quantum rules it couples to it so that the quantum state of *both* glial cell and automaton becomes a new state of both, $E_1^{(0)} = W_1^{(0)} + W_2^{(0)} = [W_1]W_1 + [W_2]W_2$. Here the composite state and the superscript "(0)", appearing to the right of the letter "E_1," represents that an interaction has occurred between the automaton and the glial cell at the 0 level. Since the interaction has resulted in a superposition of composite identifiable woman states, $W_i^{(0)}$, I use the letter "E" to indicate that the state has emotional content. However, note that $E_1^{(0)}$ and E_1 are not the same. $E_1^{(0)}$ refers to a state involving both the automaton and the glial cell, while E_1 refers to a state involving only the glial cell.

This composite state is labeled $E_1^{(0)}$ to signify that it is an emotional state composed of a superposition of composite woman-identity states in both the glial cell and the automaton.

22. We shall symbolize the second automaton's state by the symbol "$[^2A]$." The "2" superscript appearing to the left of the letter "A" tells us that it is a second automaton. Now when it interacts with the composite system $E_1^{(0)} = [W_1]W_1 + [W_2]W_2$, it can do so in two quite different ways as mentioned. It can inquire as to the identity state of the glial cell's record, and the result will be that the state of both automata and the glial cell becomes $[^2W_1][W_1]W_1 + [^2W_2][W_2]W_2$. Each term of the sum signifies that in each "world" the second device is in agreement with the first, which in turn is in agreement with the record of the glial cell.

Or it can remain aloof and not ask such details. It may simply observe the composite state $E_1^{(0)}$ as it is and never ask about the glial cell at all. In this case the composite state is $[^2E_1^{(0)}]E_1^{(0)}$. All the second system "knows" is that the first automaton and the glial cell have related, and as a result they together are in the state $E_1^{(0)}$, and it, the second automaton, simply "knows" that but not which woman image is present.

You may ask, why not? And it would answer, I haven't asked.

23. In other words we are going to ask the automaton to record the state $E_1^{(0)} = [W_1]W_1 + [W_2]W_2$ and put that in its memory. When it does that, it makes its first self-observation, and in my scheme it jumps one level upward, from 0 to 1. Then the composite state of the automaton/glial cell becomes $E_1^{(1)} = [E_1^{(0)}]E_1^{(0)} = [E_1^{(0)},W_1]W_1 + [E_1^{(0)},W_2]W_2$. Here the "(1)" signifies that the automaton has made its first-level self-inquiry. Actually the automaton has conducted two inquiries. The first inquiry was the interaction with the glial cell, and the second was the interaction with itself.

The state $E_1^{(1)}$ is quite interesting when we take into account what it means. In each world the automaton "knows" both the woman image it has observed in the glial cell and has in fact created by its observation, W_i, and simultaneously it "knows" the emotional state $E_1^{(0)}$, consisting of both composite images taken together. It has in effect in each world knowledge of its own existence in another world symbolized by having both images inside of one bracket, $[E_1^{(0)},W_i]$. Possession of simultaneous knowledge of the emotional state of its composite "self" and the image state of the glial cell is a jump in levels from 0 to 1. This is the first level of self-reflection.

24. In quantum-rules language the automaton could have obtained a record of the emotional state, E_i, in its memory instead of the identity state, W_i.

25. Before it looks, the state is $E_1^{(0)}$. After it looks, the state is $E_1^{(1)} = [E_1^{(0)}]E_1^{(0)}$. The appearance of this state marks the boundary between self and nonself in the dream, and when the self-reflection takes place, the automaton jumps levels.

26. It is both images together that we call the $E_1^{(1)}$ state of unhappiness. Now $E_1^{(1)}$ is a self-reflective state. The superscript "(1)" in this case refers to the fact that it is a single self-reflection.

27. Before the second automaton is involved, the first automaton, as a result of interacting with the glial cell and then itself, contains memories of both its emotional state, $E_1^{(0)}$, and an identity state, W_i, in each world.

28. The self-joy emotional state would be written $E_2^{(0)} = [W_3]W_3 + [W_4]W_4$, where the subscript "2" refers to the second emotional state.

After self-observation of the joyful emotional state, the state becomes $E_2^{(1)} = [E_2^{(0)}]E_2^{(0)} = [E_2^{(0)},W_3]W_3 + [E_2^{(0)},W_4]W_4$; the subscript "2" refers to the second emotional state.

And there is also the "thought-form" image F_1, consisting of $W_1 + W_2 + W_3 + W_4 = E_1 + E_2$.

29. By superposing the self-reflecting emotional states $E_1^{(1)}$ and $E_2^{(1)}$, we create a new thought-form state $F_1^{(1)} = E_1^{(1)} + E_2^{(1)}$. If the automaton attempts to reflect on this state as well, we have a second self-reflection occurring, creating a jump in levels and the new self-reflection state $F_1^{(2)} = [F_1^{(1)}]F_1^{(1)}$.

Thus following this procedure, we have an ascending ladder of levels and associated self-reflecting states. At the lowest level we have the woman identity states, W_i; woman emotional states, E_i; thought-form states, F_i; archetype states, G_i; and even the superarchetype state, S_1. These images are objective, found in the glial cell only.

At the first self-reflection level we have the self-emotional states, $E_i^{(1)}$, composed of superpositions of the lowest "objective" glial-cell memory state coupled to the automaton state.

At the second self-reflection level we have the thought-form self-reflective state, $F_i^{(1)}$, composed of the superposition of the first self-reflection of the first emotional state and the first self-reflection of the second emotional state. A superposition of the second-level self-reflection states, $F_1^{(2)}$ and $F_2^{(2)}$, results in a second-level archetypal state, $G_1^{(2)} = F_1^{(2)} + F_2^{(2)}$, from which a jump to the third archetypal level $G_1^{(3)} = [G_1^{(2)}]G_1^{(2)}$ is possible.

Again following the same procedure, a superposition of self-reflective images at level 3, $G_1^{(3)} + G_2^{(3)}$, yields a superarchetypal image, $S_1^{(3)} = G_1^{(3)} + G_2^{(3)}$. Self-reflection of the superarchetypal image leads to a jump to the fourth level, $S_1^{(4)} = [S_1^{(3)}]S_1^{(3)}$, and so on.

The complexity of this increases geometrically; in this case, it doubles at each higher level of the hierarchy. For example, if we take this last level apart, we see that it is composed of sixteen terms. Each term looks like $[S_1^{(3)}, G_j^{(2)}, F_k^{(1)}, E_l^{(0)}, W_m]W_m$. So that in each of sixteen worlds the automaton contains a record of what it has observed in the glial cell, and a sequence of ascending self-reflective image states going from emotional states that it "feels," thought-forms that it "expresses," archetypes that it also senses, and superarchetypes that it also senses and experiences because it has "seen" or observed and remembered these images.

CHAPTER 21. THE DREAMING UNIVERSE: REALITY AND ILLUSION— A CONFESSIONAL RETROSPECTIVE

1. This quote was captured by Robert Anton Wilson, who is a friend of mine and Nick's, in his book *Quantum Psychology* (Phoenix, Ariz.: New Falcon Publications, 1990), 69.

2. Dr. William Bricken, "Extended Abstract: A Formal Foundation for Cyberspace," *Technical Report No. HITL-M-90–10,* available from the Washington Technology Center, University of Washington, FU-20, Seattle, Wash. 98195.

3. I don't remember where I got this quote. I believe it was from a radio interview Campbell had with Michael Toms.

4. This quote is well known and is a part of the poem that Chuang Tzu wrote concerning his dream of the butterfly. Again, I don't remember where I got it from.

BIBLIOGRAPHY

———

Adejumo, Ebenezer Ademola. *The Concept of Time in Yoruba, Australian Aboriginal, and Western Cultures, Especially as It Is Manifested in the Visual Arts.* M.S. thesis, School of Humanities, Flinders University of South Australia, 1976.

Aesclepius in *Columbia Viking Desk Encyclopedia,* 3rd ed. New York: Viking, 1968.

Aharonov, Y., and M. Vardi, "Meaning of an individual 'Feynman Path.' " *Physical Review D* 21, no. 8 (April 15, 1980): 2235–40.

Albert, David Z. "How to Take a Photograph of Another Everett World." In *New Techniques and Ideas in Quantum Measurement Theory,* ed. D. M. Greenberger. Annals of the New York Academy of Sciences, vol. 480, December 30, 1986.

———. "On Quantum-Mechanical Automata." *Physics Letters* 98A (1983): 249–52.

Alexander, Charles. "A Conceptual and Phenomenological Analysis of Pure Consciousness During Sleep." *Lucidity* 10, nos. 1&2 (1991): 129.

"Angels, Aliens, and Archetypes." *Revision* 11, nos. 3&4, pts. 1 & 2.

Aristotle. "De Somniis" and "De Divinatione per Somnum." In *The Works of Aristotle,* vol. 3, edited by W. D. Ross, 454–58. Oxford, England: Clarendon Press, 1931. Original work written ca. 330 B.C.

Aspect, Alain, Jean Dalibard, and Gerard Roger. "Experimental Test of Bell's Inequalities Using Time-Varying Analyzers." *Physical Review Letters* 49, no. 25 (December 20, 1982): 1804.

Barden, Garrett. "Reflections of Time." *The Human Content* 5, no. 2 (Summer 1973). London: Chaucer Publishing Co.

Bass, Ludvik. "The Mind of Wigner's Friend." *Hermathena: A Dublin University Revue* 112 (1971): 52–68.

———. "A Quantum Mechanical Mind-Body Interaction." *Foundations of Physics* 5, no. 1 (March 1975).

Bateson, Gregory. *Mind and Nature: A Necessary Unity.* New York: E. P. Dutton, 1979.

Békésy, Georg von. *Sensory Inhibition.* Princeton, N.J.: Princeton University Press, 1967.

Bell, John Stewart. *Speakable and unspeakable in quantum mechanics.* Cambridge, England: Cambridge University Press, 1987.

Berndt, Ronald M., and Catherine H. Berndt. *The Speaking Land: Myth and Story in Aboriginal Australia*. Ringwood, Victoria, Australia: Penguin Books, 1989.

Bierce, Ambrose. *An Occurrence at Owl Creek Bridge*. Mankato, Minn.: Creative Education, 1980.

Blackmore, Susan. "A theory of lucid dreams and OBEs." In *Conscious mind, sleeping brain: Perspectives on lucid dreaming,* edited by J. I. Gackenbach and S. L. LaBerge. New York: Plenum, 1988.

Bohm, David. *Wholeness and the Implicate Order*. Boston: Routledge & Kegan Paul, 1980.

———. *Unfolding Meaning: A Weekend of Dialogue with David Bohm*. New York: Routledge & Kegan Paul, 1985.

Bohr, Niels. *Atomic Theory and the Description of Nature*. Cambridge, England: Cambridge University Press, 1934.

Borges, Jorge. *Ficciones*. New York: Grove Press, 1962.

Bricken, Dr. William. "Extended Abstract: A Formal Foundation for Cyberspace." *Technical Report No. HITL-M-90–10,* available from the Washington Technology Center, University of Washington, FU-20, Seattle, Wash. 98195.

Buksbazen, John Daishin. *To Forget the Self*. Zen Writings Series, vol. 3. p. 2. Los Angeles: Zen Center of Los Angeles.

Burnum, Burnum. *Burnum Burnum's Aboriginal Australia: A Traveler's Guide*. New South Wales, Australia: Angus & Robertson, 1988.

Cartwright, R. D., and R. W. Ratzel. "Effects of dream loss on waking behaviors." *Archives of General Psychiatry* 27 (1972): 277–80.

Caton, R. *The temples and rituals of Asklepius*. London: C. J. Clay, 1900. Also see the *Columbia Viking Desk Encyclopedia,* 3rd ed. New York: Viking, 1968.

Coleman, Wim, and Pat Perrin. *The Jamais Vu Papers or Misadventures in the Worlds of Science, Myth, and Magic*. New York: Harmony Books, 1991.

Corbin, Henri. *Mundis Imaginalis or the Imaginal and the Imaginary*. Ipswich, England: Golgonooza Press, 1976 (originally published in *Spring,* 1972).

Cowan, James. *Mysteries of the Dreaming: The Spiritual Life of Australian Aborigines*. Dorset, England: Prism Press, 1989.

Cramer, John G. "Generalized absorber theory and the Einstein-Podolsky-Rosen paradox." *Physical Review D* 22 (1980): 362.

———. "Alternate Universes II." *Analog* (November 1984).

———. "The transactional interpretation of quantum mechanics." *Reviews of Modern Physics* 58, no. 3 (July 1986).

———. "The Quantum Handshake." *Analog* (November 1986).

———. "An Overview of the Transactional Interpretation of Quantum Mechanics." *International Journal of Theoretical Physics* 27, no. 2 (1988): 227–36.

Crick, Francis. "The recent excitement about neural networks." *Nature* 337, no. 6203 (January 12, 1989): 129–32.

Crick, Francis, and Christof Koch. "Towards a neurobiological theory of consciousness." *Seminars in the Neurosciences* 2 (1990): 263–75.

Crick, Francis, and Graeme Mitchison. "The function of dream sleep." *Nature* 304, no. 5922 (July 14, 1983): 111–14.

———. "REM Sleep and Neural Nets." *The Journal of Mind and Behavior* 7, nos. 2&3 (Spring and Summer 1986): 229[99]–250[120].

David-Neel, Alexandra. *Magic and Mystery in Tibet.* New York: Penguin Books, 1973.

———. *Buddhism: Its Doctrines and Its Methods.* New York: Avon Books, 1979, 37–41.

David-Neel, Alexandra, and Lama Yongden. *The Secret Oral Teachings in Tibetan Buddhist Sects.* San Francisco: City Lights Books, 1967.

Dean, Colin. "The Australian Aboriginal 'Dreamtime': An Account of Its History, Cosmogenesis, Cosmology and Ontology." B.S. thesis, Deakin University, September 1990. Available from Australian Institute of Aboriginal Studies.

Deutsch, D. "Quantum theory, the Church-Turing principle and the universal quantum computer." *Proceedings of the Royal Society of London* A 400 (1985): 97–117.

Devereux, Paul. *Earth Lights: Towards an Understanding of the UFO Enigma.* Wellingborough, Northamptonshire, England: Turnstone, 1982.

———. *Earth Lights Revelation.* London: Blandford, 1989.

———. *Places of Power.* London: Blandford, 1990.

Devereux, Paul, and Nigel Pennick. *Lines on the Landscape.* London: Robert Hale, 1989.

Devereux, Paul, John Steele, and David Kubrin. *Earthmind—Is the Earth Alive?* New York: Harper & Row, 1989.

Dewitt, Bryce S. "Quantum mechanics and reality." *Physics Today,* September 1970, 30–35.

Dewitt, Bryce S., and Neill Graham. *The Many-Worlds Interpretation of Quantum Mechanics.* Princeton, N.J.: Princeton University Press, 1973.

Dreams of Pauli in the archive of Aniela Jaffé, ETH Zurich, WHS, Hs 1090:71.

Easwaran, Eknath. *Dialogue with Death: The Spiritual Psychology of the Katha Upanishad.* Berkeley, Calif.: Blue Mountain Center of Meditation, 1981.

Eccles, F. R. S., John C. "Do mental events cause neural events analogously to the probability fields of quantum mechanics?" *Proc. R. Soc.* B 227 (1986): 411–28.

Einstein, Albert, Boris Podolsky, and Nathan Rosen. "Can the Quantum-Mechanical Description of Physical Reality Be Considered Complete?" *Physical Review* 47 (1935): 777.

Eliade, Mircea. *Images et Symboles.* Paris, 1952, ch. 2: "Symbolismes Indiens du Temps et de l'Éternité." (*Images and Symbols.* "Indian Symbols of Time and Eternity.")

———. *Shamanism: Archaic Techniques of Ecstasy.* Bollingen Series 76. Princeton, N.J.: Princeton University Press, 1964.

———. *Australian Religions: An Introduction.* Ithaca, N.Y.: Cornell University Press, 1973.

Ellis, Jean A. *From the Dreamtime: Australian Aboriginal Legends.* Australia: Collins Dove, 1991.

Erkelens, Herbert Van. "Wolfgang Pauli and the Spirit of Matter." In *Symposium on the Foundations of Modern Physics 1990: Quantum Theory of Measurement and Related Philosophical Problems,* edited by Pakka Lahti and Peter Mittelstadt. New Jersey: World Scientific Publishing Co., 1991.

Fadiman, James, and Robert Frager. *Personality and Personal Growth.* New York: Harper & Row, 1976.

Feynman, Richard P., Robert B. Leighton, and Matthew Sands. *The Feynman Lectures on Physics,* vol. I. Reading, Mass.: Addison-Wesley, 1965.

Francçon, Maurice. *Holography.* Expanded and revised from the French edition. New York and London: Academic Press, 1974.

Franz, Marie-Louise von. *Number and Time: Reflections Leading toward a Unification of Depth Psychology and Physics.* Evanston, Ill.: Northwestern University Press, 1974.

Freedman, David H. "Weird Science." *Discover* 11, no. 11 (November 1990): 62–68.

Freud, Sigmund. "Project for a Scientific Psychology." In *The Origins of Psychoanalysis: Letters to Wilhelm Fliess, Drafts and Notes: 1887–1902,* edited by Marie Bonaparte, Anna Freud, and Ernst Kris. Translated by Eric Mossbacher and James Strachey. New York: Basic Books, 1954.

———. *The Ego and the Id.* New York: W. W. Norton & Co., 1960.

———. *The Interpretation of Dreams.* New York: Avon Books, 1965.

Fromm, Erich. *Greatness and Limitations of Freud's Thought.* New York: Harper & Row, 1980.

Gackenbach, Jayne. "Frameworks for Understanding Lucid Dreaming: A Review." *Dreaming* 1, no. 2 (1991): 109.

Gackenbach, Jayne, and Jane Bosveld. *Control Your Dreams: How lucid dreaming can help you uncover your hidden desires, confront your hidden fears, and explore the frontiers of human consciousness.* New York: Harper & Row, 1989.

Gackenbach, Jayne, and Anees A. Sheikh, eds. *Dream Images: A Call to Mental Arms.* Amityville, N.Y.: Baywood Publishing Co., 1991.

Gardiner, Robert L. *The Rainbow Serpent: Bridge to Consciousness.* Toronto, Canada: Inner City Books, 1990.

Gillespie, George. "Light in Lucid Dreams: A Review." *Dreaming* 2, no. 3, (1992): 167–79.

Globus, Gordon. *Dream Life, Wake Life: The Human Condition through Dreams.* Albany, N.Y.: State University of New York Press, 1987.

Grof, Stanislav. *Beyond the Brain: Birth, Death, and Transcendence in Psychotherapy.* Albany, N.Y.: State University of New York Press, 1985.

Grosso, Michael. *The Final Choice: Playing the Survival Game.* Walpole, N.H.: Stillpoint Publishing Co., 1985.

———. "UFOs and the Myth of a New Age." *Revision, Journal of Consciousness and Change* 11, no. 3, pt. 1 (Winter 1989).

———. *Soulmaker: True Stories from the Far Side of the Psyche.* Norfolk, Virginia: Hampton Roads, 1992.

Hall, Calvin. *The Meaning of Dreams*. New York: Harper & Row, 1953. Reprinted, New York: McGraw-Hill, 1966.

Hampden-Turner, Charles. *Masks of the Mind*. New York: Macmillan, 1981.

Hearne, Dr Keith. *The Dream Machine: Lucid dreams and how to control them*. Wellingborough, England: Aquarian Press, 1990.

Heisenberg, Werner. *Physics and Philosophy*. New York: Harper & Row, 1958.

———. *Physics and Beyond*. New York: Harper & Row, 1971.

Hesse, Hermann. *Siddhartha*. Translated by Hilda Rossner. New York: New Directions, 1951.

Hobson, J. Allan. *The Dreaming Brain: How the brain creates both the sense and the nonsense of dreams*. New York: Basic Books, 1988.

Hobson, J. A., and R. W. McCarley. "The Brain as a Dream-State Generator: An Activation-Synthesis Hypothesis of the Dream Process." *American Journal of Psychiatry* 134 (12) (1977): 1335–48.

Honderich, T. "The Time of a Conscious Sensory Experience and Mind-Brain Theories." *Journal of Theoretical Biology* 110 (1984): 115–19.

Hopfield, J. J., D. I. Feinstein, and R. G. Palmer. " 'Unlearning' has a stabilizing effect in collective memories." "Letters to Nature" in *Nature* 304 (July 14, 1983).

Hopkins, Bud. *Intruders*. New York: Random House, 1987.

Hoyle, Fred. "The Universe: Past and Present Reflections." Unpublished manuscript, 1981.

Humphrey, Nicholas. *A History of the Mind: Evolution and the Birth of Consciousness*. New York: Simon & Schuster, 1992.

"Interview with Physicist Fred Alan Wolf, on the Physics of Lucid Dreaming." *Lucidity Letter* 6, no. 1 (June 1987): 51–63.

Isaacs, Jennifer, comp. and ed. *Australian Dreaming: 40,000 Years of Aboriginal History*. Sydney, Australia: Lansdowne Press, 1980.

Jahn, Robert G., and Brenda J. Dunne. *Margins of Reality: The Role of Consciousness in the Physical World*. San Diego, Calif.: Harcourt Brace Jovanovich, 1987.

Jaynes, Julian. *The Origin of Consciousness in the Breakdown of the Bicameral Mind*. Boston: Houghton Mifflin Co., 1976.

Jung, C. G. *On the Nature of the Psyche*. Vol. 8, *Collected Works*. Bollingen Series 20. Princeton, N.J.: Princeton University Press, 1960.

———. *Psychology and Alchemy*. Vol. 12, *Collected Works*. Princeton, N.J.: Princeton University Press, 1980.

Jung, C. G., and W. Pauli. *Naturerklärung und Psyche*. Zurich: Rascher Verlag, 1952.

Kahn, David, and J. Allan Hobson. "Self-organization Theory of Dreaming." *Dreaming* 3, no. 3 (1993): 151–78.

Kalweit, Holger. *Dreamtime and Inner Space: The World of the Shaman*. Boston: Shambhala, 1988.

———. *Shamans, Healers, and Medicine Men*. Boston: Shambhala, 1992.

Koulack, David. *To Catch a Dream: Explorations of Dreaming*. Albany, N.Y.: State University of New York Press, 1991.

Kovtun, Yevgeny, and Liudmila Rybakova, eds. *Fantastic and Imaginative*

Works by Russian Artists. Commentary by Valery Fateyev. Leningrad, Russia: Aurora Art Publishers, 1989.

Krippner, Stanley, Ph.D., ed. *Dreamtime and Dreamwork—Decoding the Language of the Night.* Los Angeles: J. P. Tarcher, 1990.

LaBerge, Stephen, Ph.D. *Lucid Dreaming: The Power of Being Awake and Aware in Your Dreams.* Los Angeles: J. P. Tarcher, 1985.

Lahti, Pakka, and Peter Mittelstadt, eds. *Symposium on the Foundations of Modern Physics 1990: Quantum Theory of Measurement and Related Philosophical Problems.* River Edge, N. J.: World Scientific Publishing Co., 1991.

Lashley, K. S. *Brain Mechanism and Intelligence.* Chicago: University of Chicago Press, 1929.

Laurikainen, K. V. *Beyond the Atom, the Philosophical Thought of Wolfgang Pauli.* Berlin and Heidelberg, Germany: Springer-Verlag, 1988.

Letter from Pauli to Jung, May 27, 1953. ETH Zurich WHS, Hs 1056:30867.

Letter from Pauli to von Franz, October 12, 1952, ETH Zurich, WHS, Hs 176:52.

Libet, Benjamin, Elwood W. Wright, Bertram Feinstein, and Dennis K. Pearl. "Subjective Referral of the Timing for a Conscious Sensory Experience: A Functional Role for the Somatosensory Specific Projection System in Man." *Brain* 102, pt. 1 (March 1979): 193–224.

Libet, B. "Subjective Antedating of a Sensory Experience and Mind-Brain Theories: Reply to Honderich (1984)." *Journal of Theoretical Biology* 114 (1985): 563–70.

Love, W. "Was the dream-time ever a real-time?" *Anthropological Society of Queensland Newsletter,* no. 196 (1989): 1–14. Available from Australian Institute of Aboriginal Studies.

Lush, Nick. *Australia: Cadogan Guides.* London, England: Cadogan Books, 1988.

Machovec, Frank J. "The Cult of Asklipios." *The American Journal of Clinical Hypnosis* 22, no. 2 (October 1979).

Maury, L. F. A. *Le Sommeil et les rêves.* Paris: Didier et Cie, 1861.

McCrone, John. "Something stirs in the land of Nod." "Science." *The Independent on Sunday* (London), November 3, 1991.

McKenna, Terence. "New and Old Maps of Hyperspace" (audiocassette). Big Sur, Calif.: Dolphin Tapes, 1982.

———. "A Conversation over Saucers." *Revision: The Journal of Consciousness and Change* 11, no. 3 (Winter 1989): 23–30.

———. *The Archaic Revival: Essays and Conversations.* San Francisco: HarperCollins, 1992.

Mindell, Arnold. *Dreambody: The Body's Role in Revealing the Self.* Santa Monica, Calif.: Sigo Press, 1982.

———. *River's Way: The Process Science of the Dreambody.* New York: Routledge & Kegan Paul, 1985.

———. *Working with the Dreaming Body.* New York: Routledge & Kegan Paul, 1985.

———. *The Year I: Global Process Work.* London: Arkana, 1989.

Moffitt, A., S. Purcell, R. Hoffman, and R. Wells. "Dream Psychology: Operating in the Dark." In *Conscious mind, sleeping brain: Perspectives on lucid dreaming,* edited by J. I. Gackenbach, and S. L. LaBerge. N.Y.: Plenum, 1988.

Morris, W., ed. *The American Heritage Dictionary of the English Language.* Boston: American Heritage Publishing Co. and Houghton Mifflin Co., 1969.

Myers, Fred R. *Pintupi Country, Pintupi Self: Sentiment, Place, and Politics among Western Desert Aborigines.* Washington and New York: Smithsonian Institution Press, 1986, ch. 2: "The Dreaming: Time and Space," 47.

Neihardt (Flaming Rainbow), John G. *Black Elk Speaks: Being the Life of a Holy Man of the Oglala Sioux.* Lincoln, Nebr., and London: University of Nebraska Press, first Bison Book ed., 1988.

Nobili, Renato. "Schrödinger wave holography in brain cortex." *Physical Review A* 32, no. 6 (December 1985): 3618–26.

Norbert-Hodge, Helena. *Ancient Futures: Learning from Ladekh.* London: Rider Publ. Co., 1991.

Oppenheimer, J. R. *Science and the Human Understanding.* New York: Simon & Schuster, 1966.

Pauli, Wolfgang. Unpublished manuscript. ETH Zurich, WHS, Hs 176:85.

Pauli, W., and C. G. Jung. *The Interpretation of Nature and the Psyche.* Princeton, N.J.: Pantheon, 1955.

Pekarik, Andrew. "Journeys in the Dreamtime." *Archaeology* (November/December, 1988).

Penfield, Wilder. *The Mystery of the Mind: A Critical Study of Consciousness and the Human Brain.* Princeton, N.J.: Princeton University Press, 1975.

Penrose, Roger. *The Emperor's New Mind.* New York: Penguin Books, 1989.

Persinger, Michael A. "The Tectonic Strain Theory as an Explanation for UFO Phenomena: A Non-Technical Review of the Research, 1970–1990." *Journal of UFO Studies* 2 (1990): 105–37.

———— "Modern Neuroscience and Near-Death Experiences." *Journal of Near-Death Studies* 7 (1990): 233–39.

Pfleegor, R. L., and L. Mandel. "Interference of Independent Photon Beams." *Physical Review* 159 (July 25, 1967).

Poulter, Jim. *The Secret of Dreaming.* Templestowe, Australia: Red Hen Enterprises, 1988.

Pribram, Karl H. *Languages of the brain: Experimental paradoxes and principles in neuropsychology.* Monterey, Calif.: Brooks/Cole Publishing Co., 1977.

Price, H. H. "Mind over mind and mind over matter." In *Philosophers in wonderland,* Saint Paul, Minn.: edited by P. French. Llewellyn Publ., 1975, 232–43.

Progoff, Ira. *Jung, Synchronicity, and Human Destiny: Noncausal Dimensions of Human Experience.* New York: Dell, 1973.

Puharich, Andrija. *Beyond Telepathy.* New York: Doubleday Anchor, 1973.

Reece, Laurie. "Wailbri's Ideas on Ultimate Reality and Meaning." *Newsletter of the Institute of Human Ideas on Ultimate Reality and Meaning* 1, no. 1 (1972): 18–22. Published in Australia.

Restak, Richard, M.D. *The Brain Has a Mind of Its Own: Insights from a Practicing Neurologist.* New York: Harmony Books, 1991.

Ring, Kenneth, Ph.D. *The Omega Project: Near-Death Experiences, UFO Encounters, and Mind at Large.* New York: William Morrow and Co., 1992.

Rojcewicz, Peter M. "The 'Men in Black' Experience and Tradition: Analogues with the Traditional Devil Hypothesis." *Journal of American Folklore* 100, no. 396 (April–June 1987): 154.

————. "Strange Bedfellows: The Folklore of Other-Sex. *Critique: A Journal Exposing Consensus Reality* 29 (1988).

————. "Signals of Transcendence: The Human-UFO Equation." *Journal of UFO Studies,* n.s. 1 (1989): 111–26.

————. "Between One Eye Blink and the Next: Fairies, UFOs, and Problems of Knowledge." In *The Good People: New Fairylore Essays,* edited by Peter Narvaez. New York: Garland Publ. Co., 1991.

Rossi, E. *Dreams and the growth of the personality: Expanding awareness in psychotherapy.* New York: Braunner/Mazel, 1972/1987.

Russell, Peter. *The Global Brain: Speculations on the Evolutionary Leap to Planetary Consciousness.* Los Angeles: J. P. Tarcher, 1983.

————. *The White Hole in Time: Our Future Evolution and the Meaning of Now.* San Francisco: HarperSanFrancisco, 1992.

Sagan, Carl. *The Dragons of Eden: Speculations on the Evolution of Human Intelligence.* New York: Ballantine Books, 1977.

Shalin, Leonard. *Art and Physics: Parallel Visions in Space, Time, and Light.* New York: William Morrow, 1991.

Sherrington, Charles. *The Integrative Action of the Nervous System.* New Haven, Conn.: Yale University Press, 1906.

Snyder, Thomas J., and Jayne Gackenbach. "Vestibular Involvement in the Neurocognition of Lucid Dreaming." In *Dream Images: A Call to Mental Arms,* edited by Jayne Gackenbach and Anees A. Sheikh. Amityville, N.Y.: Baywood Publ. Co., 1991, ch. 3, p. 55.

Spencer, Baldwin, and Frank J. Gillen. *The Northern Tribes of Central Australia.* New York: Macmillan, 1904.

————. *The Native Tribes of Central Australia.* New York: Dover, 1968 (first published in 1899).

Sperling, G. "Information available in brief visual presentations." *Psychological Monographs* 74, no. 11 (1960).

Stanner, W. H. *White Man Got No Dreaming: Essays 1938–1973.* Canberra, Australia: Australian National University Press, 1979.

Strehlow, T. G. H. *Aranda Traditions.* Melbourne, Australia: Melbourne University Press, 1947.

Strieber, Whitley. *Communion: A True Story.* New York: Beech Tree Books, William Morrow, 1987.

————. *Transformation: The Breakthrough.* New York: Beech Tree Books, William Morrow, 1988.

Sutton, Peter, ed. *Dreamings: The Art of Aboriginal Australia.* Ringwood, Victoria, Australia: Viking Penguin Books, 1989.

Talbot, Michael. *The Holographic Universe.* New York: HarperCollins, 1991.

Tart, Charles. *Waking Up: Overcoming the obstacles to human potential.* Boston: New Science Library, 1986.

———. "From spontaneous event to lucidity: A review of attempts to consciously control nocturnal dreaming." In *Handbook of dreams: Research, theories and applications,* edited by B. Wolman, M. Ullman, and W. Webb. New York: Van Nostrand Reinhold, 1979, 226–68.

Toben, Bob, and Fred Alan Wolf. *Space-Time and Beyond: The New Edition.* New York: E. P. Dutton, 1982. Also New York: Bantam Books, 1983.

Tulku, Tarthang. *Openness Mind.* Berkeley, Calif.: Dharma Publishing, 1978.

Ullman, Montague. "Dreaming, Altered States of Consciousness, and the Problem of Vigilance." *Journal of Nervous and Mental Disease* 133, no. 6 (December 1961).

———. "Wholeness and Dreaming." In *Quantum Implications: Essays in Honour of David Bohm,* edited by B. J. Hiley and F. D. Peat. London: Routledge & Kegan Paul, 1987, 386–95.

———. "Dreams, Species-Connectedness, and the Paranormal." *Journal of the American Society for Psychical Research* 84, no. 2 (April 1990).

———. "Dream, Metaphor and Psi." Unpublished manuscript.

Ullman, Montague, Stanley Krippner, with Alan Vaughan. *Dream Telepathy: Experiments in Nocturnal ESP.* Jefferson, N.C., and London: McFarland & Co., 1989.

Ullman, Montague, Ph.D., and Nan Zimmerman. *Working with Dreams: Self-Understanding, Problem-Solving, and Enriched Creativity Through Dream Appreciation.* Los Angeles: J. P. Tarcher, 1979.

Vallee, Jacques. *Dimensions: A Casebook of Alien Contact.* Chicago: Contemporary Books, Inc., 1988.

van Eeden, Frederik W. "A Study of Dreams." In *Altered States of Consciousness,* edited by Charles Tart. Garden City, N.Y.: Doubleday, 1972.

Webb, Wilse B. "Historical Perspectives: From Aristotle to Calvin Hall." In *Dreamtime and Dreamwork: Decoding the Language of the Night,* edited by Stanley Krippner. Los Angeles: J. P. Tarcher, Inc., 1990.

Weil, Pierre. "Vers une approche holistique de la nature de la réalité." *Médicines Nouvelles et Psychologies Transpersonnelles. L'Ouvert, Question de No. 64* (1986): 11–57. Albin Michel, publisher.

Wheeler, John A. "The Mystery and the Message of the Quantum." Presentation at the Joint Annual Meeting of the American Physical Society and the American Association of Physics Teachers, January 1984.

Wilson, Robert Anton. *Quantum Psychology.* Phoenix, Ariz.: New Falcon Publications, 1990.

Winson, Jonathan. *Brain and Psyche.* New York: Anchor Press/Doubleday, 1985.

———. "The Meaning of Dreams." *Scientific American,* November 1990.

———. "The biology and function of rapid eye movement sleep." *Current Opinions in Neurobiology* 3 (1993): 243–48.

Wolf, Fred Alan. *Taking the Quantum Leap: The New Physics for Nonscientists.* San Francisco: Harper & Row, 1981. Revised edition, New York: HarperCollins, 1989.

————. *Star*Wave: Mind, Consciousness, and Quantum Physics.* New York: Macmillan, 1984.

————. "The Quantum Physics of Consciousness: Towards a New Psychology." *Integrative Psychology* 3 (1985): 236–47.

————. *The Body Quantum: The New Physics of Body, Mind, and Health.* New York: Macmillan, 1986.

————. "The Physics of Dream Consciousness: Is the Lucid Dream a Parallel Universe?" *Lucidity Letter* 6, no. 2 (December 1987): 130–35.

————. *Parallel Universes: The Search for Other Worlds.* New York: Simon & Schuster, 1989.

————. "On the Quantum Physical Theory of Subjective Antedating." *Journal of Theoretical Biology* 136 (1989): 13–19.

————. *The Eagle's Quest: A Physicist's Search for Truth in the Heart of the Shamanic World.* New York: Summit Books, 1991.

————. "The Dreaming Universe." *Gnosis* 22 (Winter 1992): 30–35.

Zaleski, Carol. *Otherworld Journeys: Accounts of Near-Death Experiences in Medieval and Modern Times.* New York: Oxford University Press, 1987.

Zohar, Danah. *Through the Time Barrier.* London: Paladin Books, 1982.

INDEX

About the Author

FRED ALAN WOLF, a Ph.D. in theoretical physics, is the author of many books, including *The Eagle's Quest, Parallel Universes,* and the American Book Award-winning *Taking the Quantum Leap.* He lives near Seattle, Washington.